Strategic Operations Management

Second edition

Steve Brown, Richard Lamming, John Bessant and Peter Jones

ELSEVIER
BUTTERWORTH
HEINEMANN

AMSTERDAM • BOSTON • HEIDELBERG • LONDON • NEW YORK • OXFORD
PARIS • SAN DIEGO • SAN FRANCISCO • SINGAPORE • SYDNEY • TOKYO

Elsevier Butterworth-Heinemann
Linacre House, Jordan Hill, Oxford OX2 8DP
30 Corporate Drive, Burlington, MA 01803

First published 2000
Second edition 2005

British Library Cataloguing in Publication Data
A catalogue record for this book is available from the British Library

Library of Congress Cataloguing in Publication Data
A catalogue record for this book is available from the Library of Congress

ISBN 0 7506 6319 7

For information on all Butterworth-Heinemann publications
visit our website at www.bh.com

Typeset by Charon Tec Pvt Ltd. Chennai, India
www.charontec.com
Printed and bound in Italy

Working together to grow
libraries in developing countries

www.elsevier.com | www.bookaid.org | www.sabre.org

ELSEVIER   BOOK AID International   Sabre Foundation

Contents

Introduction to operations management

Introduction

The strategic importance of operations

If you were to speak to a senior-level manager within an organization, the likelihood is that, within a short period of time, you would be a having a conversation that included a number of management terms – *core competences*, *key performance indicators* and *critical success factors*, among others. Ask the same manager about how operations and operations management line up within these terms and the likelihood is that he or she might be mystified or perplexed by the question. We'll explore the key reasons for this in Chapter 2, but we begin our text by stating:

Operations and operations management are of strategic importance to an organization.

This is because all of the aspirations that modern day organizations have to excel in any of the following – *mass customization, lean production, agile manufacturing, customer-centric provision* and so on – depend on the ability of the organization to actually *do* these things and such capabilities reside within operations. For example, when, in the late 1990s, Toyota announced their strategic intention to expand capacity and produce even more automobiles – in what was already an over-saturated industry – they did so knowing that they had exceptional operations capabilities that would outperform other competitors. By the beginning of 2004, Toyota had indeed fulfilled their promise and had become the number two car producer in the USA. Similarly, Dell Computers have in-house capabilities that others have found difficult to emulate

(Brown, 2000). This has led to the demise of some firms as well as mergers of others within the PC industry (in particular, Hewlett Packard and Compaq) who simply could not compete against Dell's ability to customize personal computers.

However, in contrast to Toyota and Dell, the problem with some organizations is that they simply do not have senior-level personnel in place who fully understand the potential that operations can have and, as a consequence, capabilities are often either not developed or, worse still, given up by firms by divesting plants and services within the organzation.

The central aim of this book is to deal with issues of operations management within a strategic context. So, in the next chapter we will look at how operations strategies can be devised and implemented. In the subsequent chapters we look at key strategic issues of the transformation process, innovation, inventory, supply, capacity, human resources, and development and growth.

The purpose of this chapter is to introduce the basic framework, scope and management of activities involved in operations management, to understand some of the complexities in operations and appreciate the strategic importance of operations management.

In this chapter, we will discuss some of the previous misconceptions that need to be corrected if an organization is to be able to compete by using its operations' capabilities, and we look at the importance of linking both manufacturing and services together in order to provide the *total provision* or *offer* of goods and services to the end customer.

In the next chapter, we develop some of these basics into the *strategic* role and importance of operations management. One of the problems that organizations often have is in *not* seeing the *strategic* importance of their operations management capabilities and so, in the next chapter, we develop some of these basics into the *strategic* role and importance of operations management.

Let's start with a brief, real-life case, which is provided to indicate the enormous responsibilities facing the operations manager.

Case: Sunnyside Up

'If you were going to design a new fast-food concept for the UK, where would you start?' This is the question Chris Cowls, a former Franchise Director of Burger King, and his colleagues asked themselves. It is a tough market to get into and depends on operating very efficiently on tight margins in order to make any profit. What is more it is dominated by major international brands, such as McDonald's and KFC, that have high public recognition and a national network of outlets, usually in prime high street locations. So any new concept would have to overcome the barriers to entry, provide competitive advantage and appeal strongly to customers. Cowls' team believes that 'Sunnyside Up' did just that.

The fast-food market in the UK has an annual turnover of £7.2 bn, serving 1.5 bn meals a year. This represents over a quarter of all the meals eaten away from home and the sector is continuing to grow at 5 per cent per annum. There are nearly 20 000 outlets employing nearly 200 000 staff. Many of these are owner-operated small businesses, including sandwich bars and ethnic take-away restaurants. But the sector is dominated by major international brands offering products based around burgers, pizza or chicken. Between them, McDonald's, Burger King and Wimpy have nearly 1000 outlets; Pizza Hut, Perfect Pizza and Pizzaland 650 restaurants; and KFC and Southern Fried Chicken 450 units. Many of these brands are managed in the UK as corporate franchises – for instance, Whitbread have the Pizza Hut franchise.

Success in the fast-food business depends on a number of key factors. High volume business is essential, so outlets need to be located where pedestrian and/or motor traffic is high. The majority of brands are on the high street in prime retail areas. To increase sales opportunities in these high-rent locations, take-out as well as eat-in sales are essential. The meal product therefore needs to be designed to enable this, hence the success of the hamburger. To sustain high volume, meal prices have to be competitive, which requires low levels of waste and tight control over production. Fast-food operators achieve this by keeping to a minimum the product range, i.e. menu items, so that stock control is simplified. Each commodity may be used in a variety of ways. For instance, the bun can be used for the hamburger, the cheeseburger, the jumbo burger and so on. In some operations, food items are cooked to order, also avoiding waste, but in burger restaurants at peak times, burgers are pre-cooked and ready-wrapped for immediate sale (hence 'fast' food). To avoid waste here, operators depend on accurate forecasting of demand to ensure they produce the right quantity of each item. They also forecast demand to ensure they staff their operations as efficiently as possible, by rostering staff to work flexible shift patterns.

Chris Cowls knew all this, having worked for a major burger chain and roadside dining chain. The question was how could he and his colleagues capture a share of this growing and lucrative market?

They began with the product. Every major product segment had at least two major brands competing for business. What was needed was a menu concept for which there was high demand but no major competition. They selected 'all-day breakfast in a bun' as their core product – hence the brand name 'Sunnyside Up'.

Most of the big burger chains were offering fast-food breakfasts, i.e. in a bun, but all of them stopped serving it by 11.00 a.m. in order to switch production to their own core product. But experience showed, especially from roadside sales, that breakfast was popular all day, not just the morning. Market research also showed that breakfast was an expanding segment of the market. The menu would therefore be based around combinations of egg, bacon and sausage served in a bun, along with pancakes served either savoury or sweet. This led to another feature, namely serving freshly ground coffee. Most fast-food chains did not serve this kind of coffee, although new speciality chains such as Costa Coffee were doing so.

The next issue was location. All the best locations were occupied by existing fast-food outlets. Sunnyside Up needed different locational criteria to the typical restaurant. Cowls and the team decided that the concept should be aimed at 'host environments'. Rather than locate on the high street, their outlets would be located inside existing service businesses, such as supermarkets, offices, retail areas, sports arenas, and so on.

This had a number of advantages. First, such locations had the high level of passing traffic this operation required. Second, franchise contracts could be signed with major companies, thereby facilitating access to the finance needed to build each outlet. Third, the concept could be rolled out very quickly, thereby achieving the economies of scale needed to sustain marketing, IT and systems expenditures.

But location in a host environment creates one major problem – outlet size. While the supermarkets or cinemas want a fast-food service, they did not want to allocate too much space to it. So Sunnyside Up is designed to have a micro-footprint. That is, it maximizes sales in the smallest space available. The total space required is $32\,m^2$. This is the smallest footprint of any UK fast-food concept. To achieve this, the team researched the latest fast-food equipment to find deep-fat fryers, griddles, hot cupboards and coffee machines that were small, easy-to-use and efficient. This equipment also had to fit together to create the system the team had designed. The micro-footprint also means that Sunnyside Up can easily go into a 'food court' – branded counters serving food with shared seating.

One consequence of the small scale was that staffing levels are low. One person can operate the food production area and one or two the service counter. The use of disposables means that wash-up is almost non-existent. Equipment maintenance and cleaning is carried out by these staff during slack periods. There is limited provision for eat-in customers, on stools at eating shelves. Most customers are expected to take-away (which makes sense in filling stations, sports arenas and cinemas).

While sales volumes in such small operations will not match those achieved by fast-food restaurants on the high street, Cowls and his team have rewritten the 'rules of the game'. Their concept can be built into a host environment for less than £50 000 and their operating costs are also low. The average projected sales volume of £3000–5000 per week is more than enough to give a good return on capital invested. Indeed, one major food-service contractor has become a corporate franchisee, in order to include Sunnyside Up in its portfolio of brands. This has led to 14 restaurants being opened across the UK in offices, factories and colleges, often as part of a food court.

This case is important because it brings together a number of key issues that need to be in place if we are to understand the profound importance of, and the contribution made by, operations management. The ability to enter and compete in both new and existing markets is very dependent on operations capabilities. Of course, other areas are also vitally important – marketing, finance and other major functions – and we are not seeking to play operations against these other areas. However, we argue that operations management is about uniting these other areas and functions into a central core of capabilities for the organization. This is true in both manufacturing and service settings. For example, we noted Toyota's success earlier and it is well documented how other Japanese organizations have been both aggressive and remarkably successful in their pursuit of targeted markets. We should be careful not to dismiss Japanese capabilities in operations simply because of the downturn in the Japanese economy at the end of the 1990s. This downturn had more to do with a range of financial factors rather than diminishing capabilities in operations. We should bear in mind that, in the new millennium, it is still Honda and, particularly, Toyota whose operations capabilities remain the criteria by which the rest of the car industry is judged.

The key means of doing so was described by Hayes and Pisano (1994, pp. 80–81):

Japanese companies began in the late 1970s to assault world markets in a number of industries with increasing ferocity. Their secret weapon turned out to be sheer manufacturing virtuosity. Most were producing products similar to those offered by Western companies and marketing them in similar ways. What made these products attractive was not only their cost but also their low incidence of defects, their reliability, and their durability.

That is not to say that Japanese and other world-class organizations are internally myopic and operations-driven and ignore customer requirements. We are certainly not advocating that a firm's strategy should be limited by its current operations capabilities. What we are saying is that world-class firms are able to outperform other organizations and satisfy customer requirements by virtue of their remarkable operations capabilities, which are aligned to market requirements. So it is with Sunnyside Up. In this case there was a need to align concerns of operations with the provision of customer service. Specifically, in our case, the major issues raised for the company intent on entering the very competitive fast-food market include a number of important areas that fall under the responsibility of operations managers:

- Management of value.
- Capacity management.
- Location decisions.
- Process management.
- Managing technology.
- Human resources management.
- Integration and affiliation.

We shall deal with each of these in turn.

Management of value

Traditionally, operations management has been very concerned with managing costs, but this important element of responsibility has changed recently to the management of value. Back in 1980, Harvard Professor Michael Porter suggested that organizations needed, ideally, to compete *either* on low cost *or* to provide differentiated products in order to be profitable and to avoid being 'stuck in the middle'. However, this is now seen as overly simplistic, because an organization competing in today's volatile market requirements may have to offer both low cost and differentiated features, together with ongoing innovation and rapid response and delivery times simultaneously, merely to be able to compete at all in markets!

The implications for the operations manager are clear. In value-conscious markets, where margins are usually very slim – for example, in fast-food and other high-volume sectors – costs and prices must be carefully controlled. The ability to do so does not necessarily mean an automatic reduction in workforce numbers and other drastic measures. Instead, accumulated know-how, experience, appropriate use of technology and better process quality through continuous improvement or *kaizen* will enable the organization to reduce costs (*kaizen* is discussed in Chapter 8). Such capabilities need to be developed and guarded over time (Barney, 1991; Teece *et al.*, 1997). Alternatively, where the organization is offering differentiated products, then, according to Porter (1980), it may charge premium prices. This, though, does not mean that costs are ignored. In premium-price market segments, the task for the operations manager is, amongst other things, to enable large margins to be obtained between premium price and actual costs. Such margins can be achieved by eliminating waste in all forms – the essence of lean thinking (Womack and Jones, 2003).

Capacity management

Capacity was another major factor in our case. High volume was an issue here, and managing capacity is common to both manufacturing and service elements in ensuring the total provision to end customers. The operations manager needs to know about both the overall, company-wide capacity as well as department-specific capacity inputs and outputs. This will enable the operations manager to schedule without creating overload or 'bottlenecks' in certain areas (capacity is discussed in Chapter 7).

Location decisions

Location was an important consideration in our case and is linked to strategic capacity decisions – as well as supply management, which is explored in Chapter 6. Organizations will face important choices concerning location, and this applies where there is a wish to expand in outlets both within the country of origin and also where expansion via international/global efforts are concerned. The Japanese car transplants, especially in the UK and North America, are an important example of such capacity expansion via strategic location decisions. As we saw in our case study, a number of American service giants – including McDonald's – have been very aggressive in their growth strategies. These strategies have been realized by determining strategic locations for the business.

Process management

Managing processes that result in products or services is a major concern of operations managers. The operations manager has to understand the nature, specification and assembly/delivery of the product or service. Over-design can cause major problems of organizations intending to innovate new products and services, and will take up unnecessary time and capacity. As we shall see in Chapter 4, there has been an increased awareness of organizations to include operations managers in the early stages of new product development in both manufacturing and service sectors. For the operations manager, the range of products or services on offer has to be managed in order to satisfy the mix of volume and variety for customers. This is achieved by having appropriate process technology in place, which can deal with customer requirements of volume and variety.

Managing technology

Included in the task facing the Sunnyside Up team was searching for and purchasing appropriate equipment. Investing in the appropriate equipment or technology, maintaining it and reinvesting are crucial decisions for operations managers. The temptation for some managers is *not* to invest, believing that such a risk is not necessary since the current machinery 'can cope' and 'has done well for us in the past'. In fact, this may be the correct decision if the useful life of the technology is shorter than the period over which the organization would need to recoup the investment – a situation that would hardly have seemed likely a decade ago. With product lives shortening in many product markets, the period between purchasing equipment and that equipment being made obsolete by newer technology is never certain. However, the approach of not investing could hardly be called strategic and may actually be shortsighted – often quickly depriving the organization of being able to compete in the long term against other organizations that have made more appropriate decisions. It is a question of maintaining secure access to the necessary technology. Being left with out-of-date technology, which has yet to be paid for, however, is a major liability for an organization and may even cause insolvency.

Human resources management

The management of human resources was a relatively small factor in our case study, but is often a major concern for operations managers. As the need for adherence to narrowly defined functional arrangements declines, managing human resources is no longer the prerogative of one department (personnel, human resources, management development and so on) but is, rather, an integral feature of any would-be world-class operations company.

Developing human resources is clearly evident in the following (*Business Week*, 5 May 2003):

> Survival isn't just a matter of smart machines. Workers have to get smarter as well, and show a willingness to learn new technologies, says John A. McFarland, CEO of Baldor Electric Co., the largest maker of industrial electric motors in the US. A versatile corps of workers has helped Baldor ride out the manufacturing recession without a layoff.

It is important to note how Baldor's approach to managing human resources has had strategic benefits, allowing them to compete successfully in spite of the recession in which the industry found itself. Human resources impact a number of areas of interest to the operations manager, including ideas for innovation (Chapter 4), quality improvements (Chapter 8) and process developments (Chapter 3) – all of which are dependent upon human resource know-how and inventiveness. Indeed, management of the supply chain (Chapter 6) is also very dependent upon the ability to form strategic partnerships throughout the supply chain, and this comes from human resource capability and not from technology or equipment.

Integration and affiliation

This brings us to the questions of the extent to which an organization owns and controls all the resources needed to make the product or deliver the service. In the Sunnyside Up case, affiliation through corporate franchise agreements with large-scale operators was a key element of their operational strategy. Affiliations such as franchising, sub-franchising and contracting are common in service organizations and are becoming more common in manufacturing. Firms in both sectors have tended to extend control over resources through forward, backward or horizontal integration (merger and acquisition). For example, for many years, firms in the brewing industry have forward integrated into distribution and retailing through licensed premises or pubs.

It becomes clear from discussion of the above case, therefore, that operations management is very wide in scope of responsibilities and will draw upon a range of functions within the organization and not be limited to a specific department. Understanding operations management really is vital if the organization is to compete effectively.

Definitions of operations management

Part of the problem for would-be operations managers is that definitions of operations management are, themselves, sometimes confusing; we need to clarify its role. In their text, Muhlemann *et al.* (1992, p. 8) indicate the reason for the problem:

> Of all managerial tasks the production/operations management function is the hardest to define since it incorporates so many diverse tasks that are interdependent. To divide it up, therefore, is to destroy it.

As we saw in the Sunnyside Up case, there were indeed a number of interdependent activities and concerns for the operations manager; these had to be dealt with simultaneously in order for market entry to take place. However, the above quote from Muhlemann *et al.* speaks of operations management as a 'function' and it is here that one of the issues arises. We argue that operations is not so much a function as a company-wide and inter-firm activity embracing a number of different areas and utilizing them in order to satisfy customers.

Another issue that needs to be addressed is distinguishing between manufacturing/production and operations. We concur with Samson's (1991, p. 2) view when he states:

> ... manufacturing management and strategy (are) subsets of Operations Management and strategy ....

This is important because, often, the terms *operations* and *manufacturing* strategy are used interchangeably in the literature, and we must be careful to distinguish between the two. In the next chapter we examine the importance of developing a specific operations strategy as part of the wider business strategy for the organization. At this point, though, we need to be clear that operations strategy is concerned with all activities from basic inputs into completed goods and services for the end customer. As Hill (2000, p. 5) explains:

> The operations task ... concerns the transformation process that involves taking inputs and converting them into outputs together with the various support functions closely associated with this basic task.

Such transformation processes can be applied to three main categories – materials, customers and information. Material processing operations are typically associated with manufacturing, customer processing operations with some sectors of the service industry, and information processing operations with other service sectors. In practice, most businesses rely on a combination of materials, customer and information processing. In a factory, processing materials is obvious and easily observed. These trans-formations (i.e. of parts into finished products) are not so obvious in many service operations. For example, banks, hospitals, social services and universities transform inputs into outputs, and thus all carry out operations management. There may well be differing views as to what the outputs are – and there may be several that are provided at the same time. For example, a university has a number of inputs (including staff expert-ise and experience, funding from the government, funding from stu-dents themselves or their sponsors, allocation of time) and these are then transformed by a number of operations (time spent in the classroom, scheduling students for particular courses, etc.) in order to provide out-puts. The immediate output would be 'successful students' – those who have gained their intended qualifications. However, there would be a number of, perhaps harder to identify, beneficiaries or recipients of these outputs – including potential employers and society in general.

Hill's (2000) definition of the task of operations management, which we cited above, is useful because it indicates the important link that operational activities have with a wider organization base. As we indi-cated earlier, it is important to view operations as a core activity rather than the prerogative of one department only. It also demonstrates that operations management can be applied to a very wide range of human economic activity. There are significant sectors of an economy, both in terms of numbers employed and their contribution to gross national product, which engage in transformational processes that are more or less completely ignored in many operations management texts. These include tourism (tour operating, visitor attractions and so on), the con-struction industry, medicine, the arts (theatres, cinemas, galleries), util-ities (gas, water, electricity, sewerage) and the armed services. We shall therefore strive in this text to include as many sectors of the economy as possible to illustrate operations management principles and practice.

Developing a definition of operations management

We offer the following as the basic definition of operations management:

Operations management is concerned with those activities that enable an organization (and not just one part of it) to transform a range of basic inputs (materials, energy, customers' requirements, information, skills, finance, etc.) into outputs for the end customer.

This is important because we must always bear in mind that operations do not take place in one confined area of the organization. Rather, various forms of operations will take place simultaneously across the organization. For example, in a manufacturing plant we might assume that operations take place merely at the point of production, but this limits what is actually taking place. In reality, a range of operations will be undertaken in addition to the manufacture of the product, such as inventory handling, logistics, information processing and office administration. Similarly, in services, the obvious point where we may think operations takes place is in the direct contact between the service provider and the recipient of the service. This contact is sometimes called the 'moment of truth'. However, behind the scenes (in services, this is often called 'back-office' operations) there will be a number of operations that would have needed to be in place. In services, the difference between the point of contact and all of the support activities has been likened to an 'iceberg' (Normann, 2000), as shown in Figure 1.1.

The organization uses different kind of inputs (the transformational inputs, such as plant, buildings, machinery and equipment) as well as less tangible but important inputs (such as learning, tacit knowledge and experience) and transforms these into outputs. A basic, organization-specific model of operations is shown in Figure 1.2.

This basic model, which appears in many management texts, can be expanded to identify main activities within operations, as shown in Figure 1.3.

Although models like these are often used, we argue that operations management in the modern era is more complex than this. The major

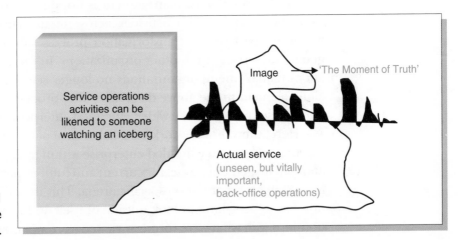

Figure 1.1
The iceberg principle in service operations.

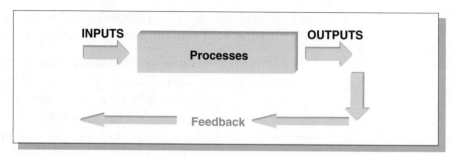

Figure 1.2
The basic
operations system.

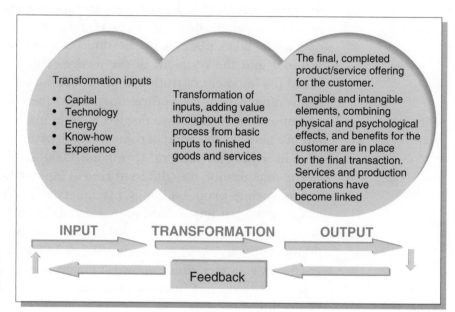

Figure 1.3
Factors within the
input/output model
of operations.

issue is that operations management is not only an organizational-wide issue, but also includes activities across organizations. Obviously, an important part of the transformation process will include purchasing goods and services from other organizations. In the modern era of operations management, organizations no longer see themselves as a stand-alone element in the above diagrams – the 'processes' – but will instead see themselves as part of a wider, extended enterprise, as shown in Figure 1.4. Here, there is a network of collaborative partners, all of whom link together to form an extended enterprise within an industry. So the operations management model for current and future operations is no longer limited to an organization-specific arena. This means that the organization has to be willing to look outside of itself and to form strategic relationships with what were formerly viewed as competitive organizations.

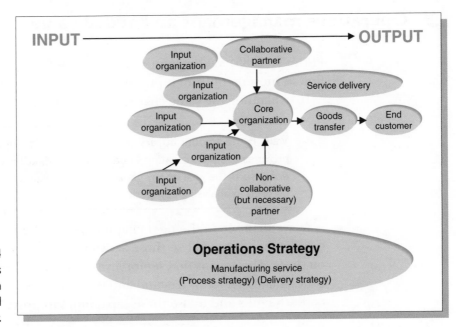

Figure 1.4
The operations infrastructure from basic inputs to end customer.

The application of this model is further developed in both Chapters 4 on innovation – where collaboration has become increasingly important – and Chapter 6 on supply management, where the organization has to deal with collaborative (and not so collaborative) relationships with other organizations. In the past, organizations tended to favour owning all activities within the supply chain from basic materials and inputs through to end customer. In the relatively 'cash-rich' days of the 1970s, for example, there was a great deal of vertical integration taking place within large US and European corporations, whereby large manufacturing organizations sought to gain control and drive down costs by owning the supply chain. In service organizations too, there was a tendency to own the supply chain. This was evident in the UK, for example, when banks decided to buy forward into estate agencies in the housing market. As we shall see in Chapter 5, the problem with this is that organizations in both manufacturing and service operations will often be pulled in too many different and conflicting directions. The chief difficulty for organizations that are intent on pursuing a vertical integration strategy is that the organization moves into areas in which it may have little or no expertise. Once we realize that operations is no longer an organization-specific affair, but is instead part of an extended supply chain involving collaboration with both vertical and horizontal partnerships, the strategic importance of operations begins to come into focus.

Operations management and added value

Porter's (1985) value chain model is a useful means of tracking the flow of movement from inputs to outputs, as shown in Figure 1.5.

In explaining the value chain model, Porter (1985, p. 38) states that:

> Value is the amount buyers are willing to pay for what an organization provides them … creating value for buyers that exceeds the cost of doing so is the goal of any generic strategy. Value, instead of cost, must be used in analysing competitive position ….

As we shall see in the next chapter, part of the strategic task for the organization is to analyse those activities that it does best and to focus on these. This means that senior-level managers, dealing with strategic issues, need first to understand and then to focus on the organization's core strengths and to use these capabilities to provide added value for

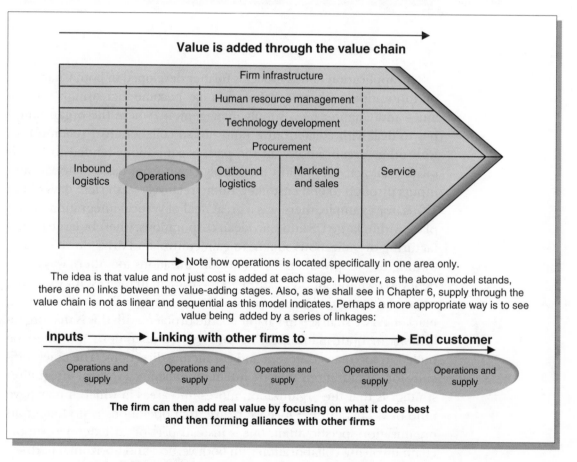

Figure 1.5
Porter's value chain (adapted from Brown, 1996).

the organization's customers. In doing so, the organization must then become dependent upon strategic partnerships with other organizations in order to provide value in those areas and activities that it has now subcontracted.

The extent to which the organization will decide to be involved in all areas of this transformation process is a critical issue for organizations. As we shall see in the next chapter, operations management is very much linked to key strategic business decisions, such as:

- What business is the firm really in?
- What does the firm do best?
- Should it outsource some of its activities, and if so why, where and how?
- How can opportunities become quickly exploited and how can the firm's capabilities help to ward off external threats from new and existing players?

We need to view operations management as part of a fluid, interactive, mutually beneficial series of relationships between raw materials and end customer.

Many organizations encapsulate what business they are in through a mission statement. This usually states where a firm expects to be at some time in the future. However, from an operations perspective, it may be more useful to adopt what has been called the 'service concept' statement. This articulates both customers' perceptions of what the firm has to offer and the firm's own view of its business proposition. It therefore incorporates more than a typical mission statement, providing all stakeholders in the business – notably customers, shareholders and employees – with a mental map of what the firm offers, stated in terms of benefits and outcomes. Although called a 'service concept', it can apply equally to manufacturing. For instance, Daewoo adopted an integrated approach to making and selling cars in the UK, through its own chain of salesrooms, with a salesforce paid salaries rather than on commission. Likewise, IBM no longer thinks of itself as a computer manufacturer but as a firm providing 'business solutions'.

At the heart of every service concept is value, which we have discussed already. In addition to value, Johnston and Clark (2001) argue that the service concept must also include and explain:

- the operation – how the product will behave or the service will be delivered;
- the experience – the processes with which the customer will engage;
- the outcome – the result for the customer.

So, for example, Sunnyside Up's service concept could be 'to provide customers with a hot, easy-to-eat meal product quickly and cheaply over the counter, throughout the day and in locations where normally such products and services were not provided'.

Part of the problem facing the operations manager, therefore, has been determining where operations management really lines up in the wider aspects of the organization in which they are operating. This is where strategy comes into play. Strategy is about 'how' the organization will conduct business.

Thus, not only is the organization concerned with transferring goods and services to end customers, it has to do so in a value-adding way. Value added, in most simplistic terms, means that the income or benefit derived from performing a particular operation is greater than the cost of doing so. All organizations, whether they are in private or public sector, or in manufacturing or services, have operations within them. Increasingly, value-adding operations are important to both private and public sectors. In private sectors, many industries and markets are so competitive that the organization cannot afford to be involved in non-value-adding activities. This is not simply down to costs, but is also concerned with problems which non-value-adding activities might incur, such as slow delivery speed, poor delivery reliability and (lack of) flexibility.

The scope of responsibility for operations managers

As we have noted, operations take place throughout the entire supply network in order to transform and complete the provision of goods and services to end customers. This means that operations managers have responsibilities both within their own organizations and in the relationship with suppliers and distributors within the supply chain. The extent to which operations managers become involved in activities in the entire supply chain depends on a number of factors, including:

- *The nature of the industry.* In some industries (for example, automobiles and market sectors within high-tech), two-way collaboration involving operations managers between two or more organizations is now commonplace. This is seen as a means to develop best practice and is often a central feature of innovation.
- *The reputation of the organization.* For example, because of its immense expertise, Toyota has often been involved in working with suppliers in developing skills and know-how within

the supplier's plant. This enables know-how and expertise to become shared.

- *The size of the organization.* As we shall see in Chapter 5, in spite of the trend toward collaboration, some organizations will exercise their 'muscle' and influence on the supplying or distribution organization. The sheer size enables them to do so – this was a tactic used by General Motors in the early 1990s and, as we shall discover, this approach does not necessarily achieve long-term rewards for the larger organization.

The range of responsibilities that operations managers have within the plant or service itself is both profoundly important and wide in scope; this range was illustrated by the Sunnyside Up case. These responsibilities include the management of:

- *Human resources.* Our case had a small employment base but their input was critical.
- *Assets.* These include fixed assets – machinery, equipment and plant, and current assets. An important concern for operations managers is inventory.
- *Costs.* We noted earlier how managing costs is a central area of responsibility for operations managers and played an important part in Sunnyside Up's desire to enter the fast-food market.

Human resource management in operations has come to the fore in recent years due to the flattening of the organizational hierarchy in many organizations. Where the hierarchy is very 'flat', employees take responsibility in major areas and 'operators' become 'managers'. As we shall see in Chapter 7, such responsibility may give rise to better performance in quality and encourages ideas for innovation in all its forms. In recent years, front-line operators have been increasingly involved in such areas as recruitment and training.

Managing assets is an integral part of the operations manager's role. Hill (2000) observes that up to 70 per cent of assets may fall under the responsibility of operations management. The greatest single cost in the transformation process within a manufacturing environment is usually in materials management. However, as we shall see in Chapters 5 and 6, this still remains a problem for many organizations for two reasons. First, materials management becomes relegated to a tactical-clerical buying function, and is not seen in the strategic framework that it needs. Second, the organization will need to form excellent relationships with suppliers and such relationships are still difficult for organizations that are unable to form these strategic links.

The critical link with marketing

In the next chapter we discuss how operations management needs to be linked with customer requirements, and how the aims of operations management include supporting the business in the market-place and enabling the organization to compete successfully against other players. The task facing operations is perfectly summarized by Ridderstrale and Nordstrom (2000, p. 157):

> Let us tell you what all customers want. Any customer, in any industry, in any market wants stuff that is both cheaper and better, and they want it yesterday.

This is wonderful for us as customers but the downside is that it presents a massive challenge to operations managers. In order for operations managers to achieve these customer requirements, operations needs to be closely allied to marketing and must have a good knowledge of customer requirements. By doing so, operations can help to shape future sales in existing markets as well as helping to determine the viability of entering new markets. One of the most critical areas of responsibility, therefore, is in working closely with marketing. Capacity, quality, delivery capabilities and costs are all within the realm of operations management. Discussing these traits becomes part of the overall information for marketing, as shown in Figure 1.6.

In service industries, the link between operations and marketing has always been close. This is because service firms have always recognized that having the customer in the business itself provided them with ideal opportunities for sales and marketing efforts, such as upselling and promotions. Heskett (1986) developed a model showing the interaction between marketing, the service concept and operations strategy. These are linked by market positioning and value/cost leverage, as illustrated in Figure 1.7.

The manufacturing/service divide

As we shall see in the next section, we are not advocating that managing service and manufacturing operations are identical. Clearly, there are differences. But both manufacturing and services are vital and, in contrast to the old-fashioned view of manufacturing versus services, it is clear that both depend on each other in modern economies.

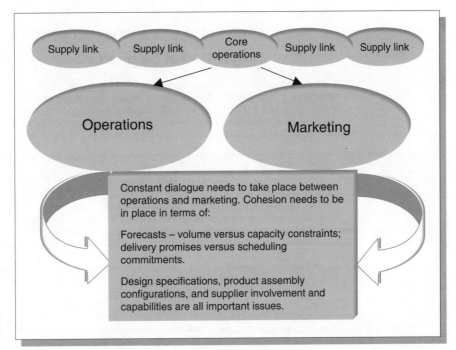

Figure 1.6
The critical link between marketing and operations.

If we look at the *Fortune* 500 (US firms) and the *Fortune* Global 500, it is important to bear in mind that the massive retail outlets (a service setting) are very dependent upon manufactured goods. We shall provide telling examples of the dependency in Chapter 5. But manufactured goods in turn depend on excellent service in retail outlets. This may seem obvious, but often people will classify retail as a service industry, as if, somehow, it is an entity that is entirely independent from manufacturing. The 35 largest global companies listed in the *Fortune* 500 in terms of revenues are listed in Table 1.1.

However, although we are not suggesting that manufacturing is 'better' than services, we must say that service exports have not managed to plug the gap between manufactured imports and exports in many countries, and this is especially evident in the UK and US. Table 1.2 shows how the gap between imports and exports has influenced the recent trade deficit.

In the UK, a report in *The Guardian* (16 February 2004, p. 23) on the UK economy provided some useful insights:

> ... 1997 was the last year in which Britain had a trade surplus. It was only £1 bn but it was the culmination of a steady improvement. ... In 1998, that small surplus was turned into a deficit of £8.5 bn, followed by £15.9 bn in 1999, £19.6 bn in 2000, £27.6 bn in 2001 and £31.4 bn in 2002. ... There are two ways of coping with a situation where supply is

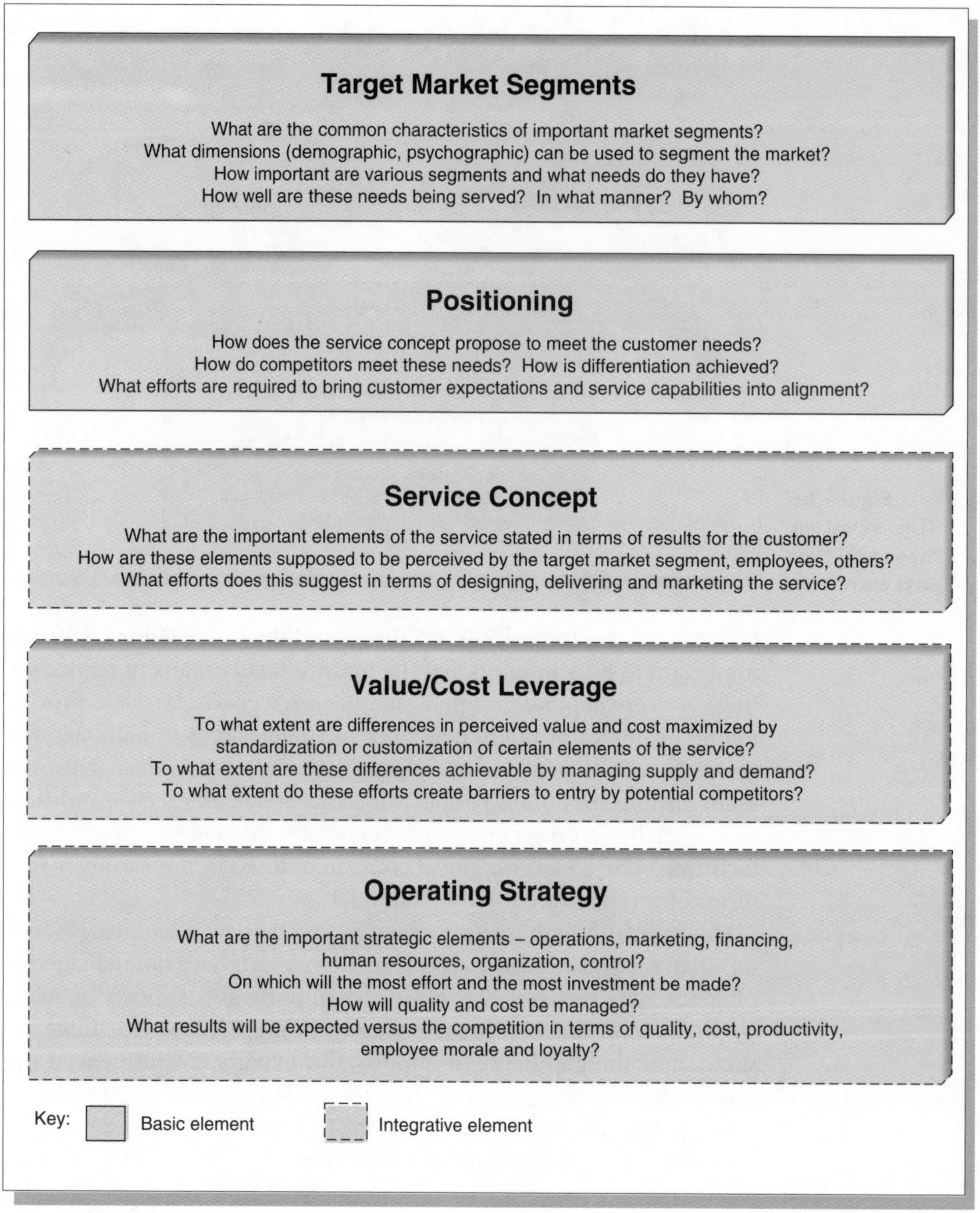

Target Market Segments

What are the common characteristics of important market segments?
What dimensions (demographic, psychographic) can be used to segment the market?
How important are various segments and what needs do they have?
How well are these needs being served? In what manner? By whom?

Positioning

How does the service concept propose to meet the customer needs?
How do competitors meet these needs? How is differentiation achieved?
What efforts are required to bring customer expectations and service capabilities into alignment?

Service Concept

What are the important elements of the service stated in terms of results for the customer?
How are these elements supposed to be perceived by the target market segment, employees, others?
What efforts does this suggest in terms of designing, delivering and marketing the service?

Value/Cost Leverage

To what extent are differences in perceived value and cost maximized by
standardization or customization of certain elements of the service?
To what extent are these differences achievable by managing supply and demand?
To what extent do these efforts create barriers to entry by potential competitors?

Operating Strategy

What are the important strategic elements – operations, marketing, financing,
human resources, organization, control?
On which will the most effort and the most investment be made?
How will quality and cost be managed?
What results will be expected versus the competition in terms of quality, cost, productivity,
employee morale and loyalty?

Key: ☐ Basic element   ⬚ Integrative element

Figure 1.7
Heskett's service operations model (adapted from Heskett, 1986, p. 30).

Table 1.1
The Global 500 in 2003

Global rank 2003	Global rank 2002	Company	Country	Sector	Turnover ($ million)
1	2	Microsoft	USA	Software and computer services	28 365.0
2	1	General Electric	USA	Diversified industrials	130 685.0
3	3	Exxon Mobil	USA	Oil and gas	204 506.0
4	4	Wal-Mart Stores	USA	General retailers	244 524.0
5	6	Pfizer	USA	Pharmaceuticals and biotechnology	32 373.0
6	5	Citigroup	USA	Banks	
7	9	Johnson & Johnson	USA	Pharmaceuticals and biotechnology	36 298.0
8	10	Royal Dutch/Shell PLCINV	Netherlands/ UK	Oil and gas	179 431.0
9	8	BP	UK	Oil and gas	178 721.0
10	12	IBM, International Business Machines	USA	Software and computer services	81 186.0
11	11	American International Group	USA	Insurance	
12	15	Merck	USA	Pharmaceuticals and biotechnology	51 790.3
13	17	Vodafone	UK	Telecommunication services	35 818.7
14	21	Procter & Gamble	USA	Personal care and household products	40 238.0
15	7	Intel	USA	Information technology hardware	26 764.0
16	13	GlaxoSmithKline	UK	Pharmaceuticals and biotechnology	33 258.3
17	22	Novartis	Switzerland	Pharmaceuticals and biotechnology	23 606.5
18	29	Bank of America	USA	Banks	
19	14	NTT DoCoMo	Japan	Telecommunication services	43 055.0
20	16	Coca-Cola	USA	Beverages	19 564.0
21	26	Berkshire Hathaway	USA	Insurance	
22	19	Verizon Communications	USA	Telecommunication services	67 625.0
23	27	I-ISI3C Holdings	UK	Banks	

Table 1.1 (*contd*)

24	20	Cisco Systems	US	Information technology hardware	18 915.0
25	25	Total Fina Elf	France	Oil and gas	110 261.6
26	28	Toyota Motor	Japan	Automobiles and parts	125 765.3
27	34	Nestlé	Switzerland	Food producers and processors	64 937.4
28	39	Wells Fargo	USA	Banks	
29	54	Amgen	USA	Pharmaceuticals and biotechnology	5523.0
30	48	Dell Computer	USA	Information technology hardware	35 404.0
31	30	Nokia	Finland	Information technology hardware	32 276.3
32	32	ChevronTexaco	USA	Oil and gas	98 691.0
33	43	Royal Bank of Scotland	UK	Banks	
34	33	PepsiCo	USA	Beverages	25 112.0
35	18	SBC Communications	USA	Telecommunication services	43 138.0

Source: Fortune, 21 July 2003.

> inadequate to meet demand: put up prices or import more. ... At this point, some of you will be thinking that this only relates to goods. Isn't the service sector the saviour of the balance of payments? Aren't we rather good at what the experts call 'invisible exports', even though nobody knows for sure what they are? To which the answer is yes, but only up to a point. Services have performed well in recent years, helping to offset the growing deficit in goods. Note, however, that the record £15.2 bn surplus in 2002 was only a third as big as the £46.4 bn deficit in goods. ... In the longer term, however, the question is whether services and investment can continue to mask the deterioration in trade in goods. There has to be doubt as to whether they can.

Thus, the perceived wisdom that a loss in manufacturing output is compensated by services is not valid. Both sectors depend upon each other, of course, and they are not mutually exclusive, but weaknesses in the manufacturing base can have profound repercussions for the economic wealth of nations.

Although the US managed to improve its manufacturing base dramatically during the 1990s and now has many plants that can be termed *world-class*, the damage to the economy is ongoing because the

Table 1.2
US international trade 1998–2002

Year	BALANCE ($ million)		
	Exports	**Imports**	**Total**
1998	682 138	911 896	−229 758
1999	695 797	1 024 618	−328 821
2000	781 918	1 218 022	−436 104
2001	729 100	1 140 999	−411 899
2002	693 103	1 161 366	−468 263

Source: U.S. Commerce department.

US still imports more manufactured products than it exports, as we see in Table 1.2. The difference is not met by the export of services.

Warnings about the problems of neglecting manufacturing operations had been offered by a number of academics over a number of years, and Garvin (1992, p. xiv) describes how:

> All too often, top managers regard manufacturing as a necessary evil. In their eyes, it adds little to a company's competitive advantage. Manufacturing, after all, merely 'makes stuff'; its primary role is the transformation of parts and materials into finished products. To do so it follows the dictates of other departments.

Garvin (1992, p. xiv) argued that the definition of manufacturing has to be seen in a wider context and he quotes the Manufacturing Studies Board publication, *Toward a New Era in US Manufacturing*, in which it is stated:

> Part of the problem of US manufacturing is that a common definition of it has been too narrow. Manufacturing is not limited to the material transformation performed in the factory. It is a system encompassing design, engineering, purchasing, quality control, marketing, and customer service as well.

Harvard Professor, Wickham Skinner, whose contribution to our understanding of the role of operations within a strategic context has been seminal, perfectly captured the problem for US and many European nations when he stated (Skinner, 1985, p. 55):

> Manufacturing is generally perceived in the wrong way at the top, managed in the wrong way at plant level, and taught in the wrong way in the business schools.

The dire consequence of this has been manifested in the massive decline of the manufacturing bases in many countries, notably in the USA. This trade deficit – typically brought about by inadequate performance in a range of operations – has had some profound consequences, as *Industry Week* (30 May 2003) noted:

> 'We are losing jobs to low-wage nations like China, and when Congress finally wakes up, our manufacturing base will be eroded,' warns Zawacki, who also is chairman of the Precision Metal Association, a trade group of about 1300 North American companies. Even as what he terms the 'Big Guys' take off for China and other low-wage countries, 'small and medium manufacturers, mostly suppliers, are trying to hang on without any support,' he claims. 'I am scared for my kids and future generations.' As a result of outsourcing production both in the US and overseas, IBM Corp. is 'just a shadow of [its] former self in terms of manufacturing operations,' asserts Edward W. Davis, a Professor at the University of Virginia's Darden Graduate School of Business Administration in Charlottesville. And a rule-of-thumb calculation suggests that the movement of manufacturing operations to China in 2002 cost the US about 234 000 jobs.

The problem was made even clearer in the following (*Industry Week*, 30 May 2003):

> US manufacturing executives, in addition to their understandable concerns about a US economic recovery from recession that has been agonizingly slow, are worried, among other things, about innovation, outsourcing, protecting proprietary technologies, and perceived imbalances between the US dollar and other currencies. ... Manufacturing is at a crossroads. ... We face fundamental changes, which if left unaddressed, could result in huge economic losses and the erosion of our industrial leadership.

In addition, *Business Week* (5 May 2003) provided further insights into job losses due to the decline in manufacturing:

> Since the manufacturing sector tipped into recession in mid-2000, it has shed 2.1 million jobs, leaving fewer industrial workers in the US than at any time since the early 1960s.

We are not suggesting that there is an easy solution to these problems. What we shall see in Chapter 2, though, is that often decisions to outsource, downsize and abandon manufacturing activities within the firm are made by those who may know very little about operations. The strategic implication is clear: getting rid of manufacturing is relatively easy to do; getting it back is almost an impossibility for firms.

Looking back ...

Before we discuss the major points of strategy in the next chapter, it is important to note that the reason why strategy is vital is that the nature of most operations has undergone major changes over time, as shown in Figure 1.8.

We will discuss each of the key periods in operations and then in Chapter 2 we will develop this further by explaining how these changes had profound importance to the way that strategy is both formulated and implemented within firms.

The craft era

The first major era is now referred to as 'craft' manufacturing and service 'shop' delivery. This system was European in origin and linked to the way in which skills were developed: the apprentice–journeyman–master progression, which led to the creation of guilds of skilled people who sought to control the supply of their speciality, and the consolidation of skill within a subsector of society (as, for example, skills were passed on from father to son). This was noted for low-volume, high-variety products, where workers tended to be highly skilled and quality was built into the very process of operations. It was also appropriate for largely national markets, supplied internally with minimal imports and exports. Some craft manufacturing still remains today, in markets where exotic products and services can control demands through some unique feature or high level of desirability. For instance, some house building, furniture making, clock and watch making are

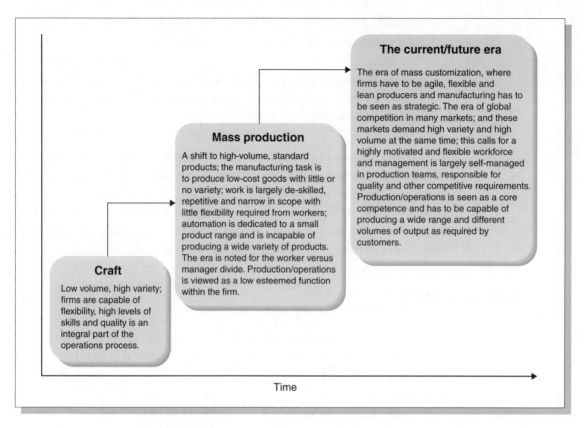

Figure 1.8
The transition from craft to strategic operations.

still carried out by skilled craftsmen/women working on a single or few items of output at a time. While the processes and techniques used by these craftsmen/women are highly inefficient, the unique quality of their products commands a premium price, as illustrated by the second-hand value of products such as a Daniels pocket watch or a Morgan car. In the case of Morgan, however, it is a mistake to conclude that the passenger car industry might still be able to employ craft production. Morgan is unashamedly part of a sector that is closer to specialist toys than that concerned with personal transportation. It is also the end of a very thin tail, other parts of which (AC, Aston Martin, Rolls Royce, etc.) have already been absorbed by volume producers, keen to operate in exotic niches for purposes that are closer to corporate advertising than to income generation. In the clothing industry, one significant sector of the industry – *haute couture* – is based on the craft production approach. In services, the craft era has also continued – perhaps even more so than in manufacturing. The slower pace of change within services derives from the extent to which customer processing operations can adopt new technologies and new systems. Only services that require little skill at the operating level (such as FMCG or petrol retailing) or processing large amounts of information (such as financial services) are significantly different now from what they were like even 30 years ago. Many services such as hotels, schools, hospitals, hairdressers, vehicle repair and transportation have changed very little, despite new technologies.

The mass production era

The second major era is known as mass production, although once again its principles were by no means restricted to manufacturing. This system grew in North America to accommodate three principal requirements of the developing giant: the need to export, the need to provide employment for a massive, largely unskilled workforce, and the need to establish itself as a world player, which meant infiltrating other regions with ideas clearly associated with the USA. In short, the Americans could not play by the European rules, so they reinvented the game: innovating by destroying the competitive position of craft production. The system was massively successful and changed the working and buying practices of the world in the first three decades of the twentieth century. In order to sell the standardized products made by standardized operations practices, mass production had to standardize the market requirements too. Fortunately, the market was immature and would do what it was told to do. Thus, mass production reversed the paradigm of craft production: volume was high with little variety. The marketing ploy (and the resultant manufacturing strategy) was exemplified by Henry Ford's famous declaration, from now on, 'a customer can have a car painted any colour he likes, as long as it is black!' In mass production, workers were typically unskilled. This was the era owing much to the contribution of F.W. Taylor's *Scientific Management*, whereby workers had very narrowly defined jobs, involving repetitive tasks, and quality was left to 'quality experts' at the final stage of the overall process rather than being an integral part of operations at each step (Taylor, 1912).

Taylor enabled firms, for the first time, to control costs, times and resources, rather than rely on skilled craftsmen and women to decide what was appropriate. Coupled with the developments made in mechanization and employee co-ordination during the European industrial revolutions, Taylor's ideas provided an entirely different way of operating.

In 1926, *Encyclopaedia Britannica* asked Henry Ford to christen his system and he called it mass production. He meant 'mass' in the sense of large volume production. Perhaps he did not see the other meaning of mass as 'heavy and cumbersome', which is what the system turned out to be (in terms of management systems and superstructure), once the market no longer bought what it was told.

These principles originating in the 1920s were slow to be adopted in services, but by the 1970s, Ted Levitt, from Harvard Business School, was able to identify the 'production-lining' (Levitt, 1972) of service and the 'industrialization' (Levitt, 1976) of service. He cited fast food, the automatic teller machine (ATM) outside banks and supermarket retailing as examples of this. Schmenner (1986) coined the phrase 'mass service' to exemplify this type of service operation. More recently, the aspects of working life that are typical in this mass production context have been extended to life in general by Ritzer (1993), who refers to it as the McDonaldization of society. The shift from 'craft' marketing to marketing in the mass production age is clearly demarcated by the publication of Levitt's (1960) article in the *Harvard Business Review* entitled 'Marketing myopia'. In mass production, customers bought what was supplied; producers concentrated on keeping costs, and hence prices, down, and focused on selling to customers through aggressive advertising and sales forces. As organizations were product-led, operations management was relatively straightforward. Mass producing goods at the lowest cost meant minimizing component and product variety, large production runs and scientific management. The success of Ford made this view highly persuasive. In 1909, the Model T automobiles were sold for $950, but by 1916, following the introduction of the assembly line, it had fallen to $345, and three-quarters of the cars on American roads were built by Ford (Bryson, 1994).

However, as Levitt (1960) pointed out, Ford was eventually outstripped by General Motors, who were not product-led but market-led. They gave customers what they wanted – choice, model updates, a range of colours (not just black!).

The symbol of this age is the brand. Originally (in the craft era) the brand was a mark on the product, often a signature – for example, on a painting – or symbol, signifying its ownership or origin. But in mass production the brand took on far more significance. It became the means by which one product (or service) could differentiate itself from a competitor's product (or service). Procter & Gamble set up brand managers in 1931 to sell their different soap products. Later the brand also became a guarantee of product/service quality. Kemmons Wilson's motivation in 1952 to open the first Holiday Inn hotel was his own disappointment with the variable standards and sleaziness of the motels he stayed in whilst on a family holiday. The success of delivering a consistently standard level of service resulted in Wilson opening one hotel every two and half days in the mid-1950s.

But by the 1990s, brands had come under threat. Markets are highly fragmented, the proliferation of niches makes target marketing more difficult, product and service life cycles are shortening, and product/service innovation is quicker than ever before; increasing customer sophistication has reduced the power of advertising. As a result, a more holistic view of operations management is required, as Crainer (1998) suggests:

Companies must add value throughout every single process they are involved in and then translate this into better value for customers.

This is because the modern era has brought profound changes in operations management and operations has to be at the heart of successful strategic thinking.

The modern era

The third era (the current and, for the foreseeable future at least, the likely scenario) is more difficult to name and has been called various things. The terms used to describe the current era include:

- *Mass customization* (Pine *et al.*, 1993) – reflecting the need for volume combined with recognition of customers' (or consumers') wishes.
- *Flexible specialization* (Piore and Sabel, 1984) – related to the manufacturing strategy of firms (especially small firms) to focus on parts of the value-adding process and collaborate within networks to produce whole products.
- *Lean production* (Womack *et al.*, 1990) – developed from the massively successful Toyota Production System, focusing on the removal of all forms of waste from a system (some of them difficult to see).
- *Agile* (Kidd, 1994) – emphasizing the need for an organization to be able to switch frequently from one market-driven objective to another.
- *Strategic* (Hill, 2000; Brown, 1996) – in which the need for the operations to be framed in a strategy is brought to the fore.

Whatever it is called, the paradigm for the current era addresses the need to combine high volume and variety together with high levels of quality as the norm, and rapid, ongoing innovation in many markets.

It is, as mass production was a hundred years ago, an innovation that makes the system it replaces largely redundant.

As each era appeared, however, it did not entirely replace the former era. As we have seen, a few pockets of craft manufacture still exist. Mass production is still apparent in chemical plants and refineries and other high-volume/low-variety environments. However, many are changing fundamentally as existing economies of scale are questioned: thus, steel manufacture faces variety requirements and has to develop 'mini-mills' to lower economic batch sizes; the same is true for brewers and pharmaceutical companies.

Forces that drive change in operations management

We know that operations management has gone through three periods of change from craft, through mass production, to the present era. We know that different sectors of many economies have gone through these periods at different rates. In some, the transition has been incremental, in others spasmodic, usually in response to some new invention. We also know that in some industries there has been an almost complete transition from the old approach to the newest, whereas in others there remains a high proportion of craft manufacture or old style service delivery. Why is this so? If we can understand these forces then we may be able to predict what changes are likely to occur in the future.

We would argue that the three key forces to date have been economic, social and technological, or to put it more simply wealth, fashion and invention. Wealth influences economic activity and hence operations management in two main ways. The aspiration to become wealthy provides a highly proactive workforce, while the attainment of wealth creates a growing market for all kinds of goods and services. When a significant proportion of a population is relatively poor, goods and services have to be provided at the lowest possible cost and consumers are prepared to accept standardization. The wealthy can afford customized products and indeed demonstrate their wealth by doing so. Furthermore, social and economic status is not demonstrated simply by ownership but by style, fashion or 'quality'. For what the American economist, Thorstein Veblen, called 'conspicuous consumption' it is not just enough to have a television, but to have a digital television; not enough to have a mobile phone but the latest hi-tech version with a personalized key pad; not enough to own a car but important to have a 'special edition'. Fundamentally, goods and services can be categorized as necessities or luxuries. Necessities are those goods and services that are *perceived* by people to be essential. These are normally food, drink, health products/services, housing and so on. Making a product or delivering a service that is perceived as essential clearly has advantages, as even during periods of shortage or economic downturn consumers will continue to purchase these items. What is deemed essential by the population of one country or by one group of people, however, may not be desired by another population or group. But not only does 'fashion' vary between groups, it also varies over time within groups. Luxury products and services that were once fashionable become unfashionable. Up until the 1960s, nearly everyone wore a hat (as evidenced by any black and white movie made and set in the 1940s or 1950s). This is no longer the case. It is claimed that the hat-making industry was sent into decline by President Kennedy – the first US president to walk to his inauguration in Washington in January without a hat, hence making hat wearing unfashionable. Many industries operate in a context of uncertainty derived from the impact of changes in fashion – toys, clothing, shoe manufacture, entertainment, the media, fabric manufacturers and so on.

Wealth and fashion are the powers that drive the forces of demand for goods and services, while invention enables or constrains supply. If costs are to be driven down then new ways of doing things are required. The mass assembly solution to lower costs created by Ford does not work for all industries. It may be highly effective in those industries that rely on the assembly of parts to produce finished goods, but there are many sectors, even in materials processing, that do not function in this way. It also does not work well in customer processing operations (although in Russia, some eye operations are carried out on patients who are placed on a conveyor belt that moves them from one specialist surgeon to another!). As well as process redesign, invention can also create new machinery or equipment for use within the transformation process. The single most important recent invention in this respect is undoubtedly the microprocessor (1975), which has been integrated into machinery and control systems throughout the manufacturing and service sector, in order to increase speeds and accuracy, reduce labour input and so on. Finally, invention also creates new types of product and services that have not existed before. This means that being the best at producing any product or delivering any service is not sufficient, if the market for that output is replaced by demand for something different. This questions the wisdom of such phrases as 'best practice' and 'world-class': expertise may only be temporary. There are many companies that were the world-class or best practitioners who no longer exist because people stopped wanting their products or services and the associated skills became redundant.

The era of volatile markets and industries

This analysis of the forces that drive change helps to explain the current situation. The current era has been called one of 'chaos' (Peters, 1987; Stacey, 1993). Creating and sustaining competitive advantage in either manufacturing or service firms is both complex and difficult, and a number of giant organizations have been humbled in recent times, apparently unable to do just that. Examples of giants in manufacturing and service sectors suffering declines by the mid-1990s include Boeing, Caterpillar, Dayton-Hudson, Du Pont, Texas Instruments, Westinghouse and Xerox. In the early 1990s, huge financial losses were incurred by giants such as Citicorp, America's biggest international bank (a loss of $457 million in 1991); General Motors suffered losses of $23.5 billion in 1992 and IBM had losses of $8.1 billion in 1993, having enjoyed profits of $6 billion in 1986. By the end of the 1990s, IBM was again reaping profits of around $8 billion per annum.

Such erratic performances have led to a number of observers doubting the validity and worth of being in the *Fortune* 500. This was exemplified by the management guru, Peter Drucker, declaring 'The *Fortune* 500 is over.' Volatility seems common to many firms who have appeared in the *Fortune* 500 and, during the 1980s, nearly 50 per cent (230 firms) disappeared from the *Fortune* 500. Such volatility has impacted on senior personnel within firms (who are the supposed chief strategists), and boardroom casualties in the 1990s included Robert Stempel at General Motors, Michael Spindler at Apple, Eckhard Pfeiffer at Compaq and John Akers at IBM.

The reasons for such 'turbulence' are complex, but fundamentally go back to the three forces identified above – wealth, fashion and invention. Whereas, in the past, wealth was confined to a relatively small proportion of countries, it is now more widespread. This means that wealth creation, in the form of significant economic activity, and market demand are global. Such globalization creates complexity. Second, fashion becomes global through the worldwide media of the cinema and television. When movie or sports stars are seen to frequent certain types of establishment, wear identified types of clothing or use certain types of product, consumers are influenced in their views and values. Paid product placement in films is now a significant proportion of profit for some types of movie and most sports stars earn more from their affiliation with goods manufacturers than they do from their salaries or winnings. Third, the pace of invention is increasing, as we shall see in Chapter 4.

Manufacturing versus services in operations management?

In Chapter 2 we shall discuss the vital importance of an operations strategy. We argue that operations strategy includes both manufacturing and services activities, and that these need to be integrated into a combined, holistic manner. However, we have identified that these sectors may well process different things, which we have categorized as materials, customers and information. This may have implications for the specific implementation of strategy, but not for operations management principles or issues *per se*. Comparing manufacturing and service industries can be useful, but in an operations management context we suggest that some of the divisions between them are overstated.

For example, in its review of 75 years of management thinking, the *Harvard Business Review*, in 1997, traced the operations management thread from 'production' in 1922, with such functions as 'inventory control' mechanization, etc. to 'growing attention of service management' in the mid-1970s, 'lean manufacturing' in the late 1980s and 'supply chain management' in the mid-1990s. By the end of their story, the generic term for the area of business upon which we are focusing is 'adding value' (*Harvard Business Review* supplement, September–October 1997).

Similarly, Gilmore and Pine (1997) traced the developments of operations over time and concluded that the consumer will increasingly think in terms of 'experiences' rather than a manufacturing or service offering, as shown in Figure 1.9.

Similarly, the renowned management academic, C.K. Prahalad, stated in 2002 (*Financial Times*, 2002):

> People talk about the convergence of technologies. I think the most fundamental convergence is between the role of producer and the role of consumer. ... The consumer goes from being a very passive person to being a very active co-creator of products, services and value. ... Companies spent the 20th century managing efficiencies. They must spend the 21st century managing experiences.

We believe that this is an important contribution, but we add that instead of seeing manufacturing versus services we need to see manufacturing

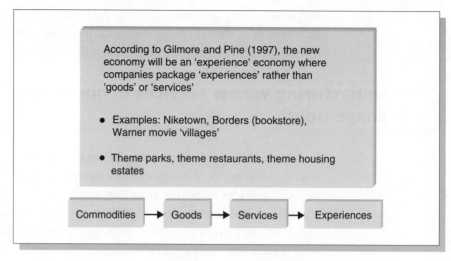

Figure 1.9
Changes from 'commodities' to 'experiences'.

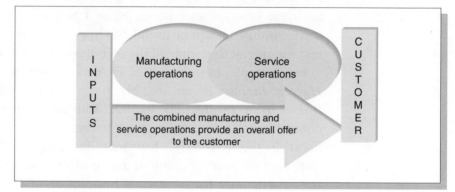

Figure 1.10
The manufacturing/ service interface in the offer to the customer.

alongside services in terms of understanding the range of interlinking activities from basic inputs to end customer delivery. We illustrate this in Figure 1.10.

We argue that the distinction between manufacturing and services is not quite as profound as often stated, for a number of reasons.

First, manufacturing and service operations often link together in providing a *total customer offering* within the supply chain. For example, the automobile industry is often seen as a purely manufacturing concern and much research has been undertaken on Japanese versus Western approaches to manufacturing (for example, see Womack *et al.*, 1990; Lamming, 1993). For the automotive customer, however, the service end of the overall supply chain may be, at key points of the transaction, equally important in the decision to purchase. Activities such as arranging finance, offering warranties and guarantees, together with general after-sales service, are often critical. In many cases, it does appear that the automobile manufacturers have made great strides in assembling cars, but have yet to master leanness in their distribution chains; indeed, this is now the subject of important research and development, as the vehicle assemblers pursue the holy grail of the 'three-day car' (i.e. a situation in which the customer can specify any car they want and have it within 3 days). In the computer industry, the customer is paying not only for the 'tangibles' (hardware and software), after-sales service is an important part of the overall offering and the assurance of help-lines for troubleshooting problems is a key feature in the complete transaction. In that sense, therefore, we should not see operations in terms of manufacturing versus services but, rather, as a combination of joint efforts throughout the entire supply chain as a means to providing customer satisfaction. Consequently, the issue of quality will depend not only on the performance of a car, but also on the service quality provided at the point of sale to the customer.

Second, some of the distinctions are not quite as pronounced as may first appear. For example, the following are typical statements concerning service industries and their contrast to manufacturing operations:

- The product is intangible.
- Services cannot be kept in stock.
- Services vary and cannot be mass-produced.
- There is high customer contact.
- Customers participate in the service.
- Facilities are located near to customers.
- Services are labour intensive.
- Quality is difficult to measure.
- Quality depends largely on the server.

We shall now take each of these in turn and explore them.

The product is intangible

Is this necessarily the case? Increasingly, service organizations speak in terms of 'products' for their customers. This is very clear across a range of financial services where the term, *product*, is used and where the 'intangible' becomes 'tangible'. For example, customers choosing a mortgage can think in terms of a range of products: fixed versus variable rates; the duration of the loan; comparisons between various interest rates tied to a particular offer. Vacations or holiday packages are within the realms of services, yet holiday organizations speak in terms of 'packages'. Similarly, time-share organizations will make the intangible more identifiably tangible. They will speak in terms of purchasing and accumulating a number of points to obtain a particular holiday or time away. Airline organizations that offer 'air miles' for their customers offer the same approach. In education, universities are able to offer a range of 'products', or different modes of attendance for a particular degree. An MBA, for example, may be offered by distance learning, or by a 1-year intensive programme, or a 2- to 3-year part-time mode, or in a sporadically attended, weekly intensive, modular design. Being able to offer a range of products means that, although a professional service is being provided, the potential students on the course can choose a particular offer over another because certain, identifiable, tangibles have been put in place – duration of course, modes of attendance, etc.

Services cannot be kept in stock

In 'tangible' services (such as restaurants, fast-food chains and car repair outlets) the supporting element of the service – supplies – is clear and will be kept in stock. In service retail outlets, the goods have to be available for the customer. In professional services – a solicitor, a doctor or a consultant, for example – it becomes clear that delivery of the services depends on the intellectual capital, experience and 'know-how'. That being the case, we can speak in terms of a body of knowledge or know-how being accumulated over time and 'stored' in readiness. This may be by a particular individual specializing in one area or by a group of professionals who can offer a variety of professional services. Likewise, there are some products that cannot be kept in stock for long – most obviously perishable food products. But other markets which are subject to rapid, short-term changes in demand, such as the pop music industry, also make it inadvisable to hold stock for too long. Whilst the physical shelf-life of a CD may be many years, the sellable shelf-life will only be as long as the music is popular.

Services vary and cannot be mass-produced

Again, such an assertion depends on where and how we view the service. As a generic term, fast-food restaurants would come under a 'service' as opposed to 'manufacturing'. Clearly, where there is a considerably high tangible feature or input as part of the service provision, we can say that the product can be produced in volume and is not a truly unique event at the point of service delivery. All fast food is mass-produced to some degree. In Russia, eye surgery on cataracts has been 'production-lined'. In the field of education, the provision of distance learning has highly standardized the student experience. The issue of volume and variety is an important one for manufacturing and services, and this is discussed in Chapter 3.

There is high customer contact

Technology has made a great deal of difference in tempering this statement. Clearly, in many financial transactions there may be little or no customer/client contact. Also, if you take a long-distance flight you will discover that even in a 'customer care' service, the actual amount of contact between customer and provider may be minimal. One of the authors estimated that, in an 8-hour flight from the USA to the UK, no more than 2 minutes was spent in contact with staff. That is not a criticism of the service – in fact, when a passenger wants to use the flight to sleep, the very last thing that he or she wants is to be disturbed by a service offering that the passenger does not want!

In manufacturing environments, while it may be true to say that within the manufacturing end of the supply chain it is unlikely that the customer comes into contact with the manufacturing plant itself, this is not always the case. In a job shop environment, for example (see Chapter 3), there may be joint design and strong customer links with the supplier. Conversely, in services, there will not always be high customer contact. Financial services are a point in case. Often customers do not engage in contact with other persons during the provision of the service. Indeed, there may be occasions when the customer does not need or require such contact – obtaining funds from a cash machine involves little contact and it is wholly appropriate for this to be so. Even in professional services, there may not be a great deal of customer involvement (although the client will be billed for hours spent by the professional).

Customers participate in the service

As we have noticed, this is not necessarily the case, or if there is 'participation' it may be to a very small degree. This is noticeable where automation helps to speed up the process and, by implication, to reduce the amount of time required by the customer in the service transaction.

Facilities are located near to customers

This used to be a critical distinction between manufacturing and services. In the past we could have said, with high levels of confidence, that manufacturing plants are located close to suppliers for ease of transportation; in contrast, services are located near to customers. We saw this as part of the decision-making process for Sunnyside Up. This distinction between manufacturing and services is still valid in some cases. Large retail organizations will, typically, be located close to a large town or be close enough to a city to attract customers. Here, a key factor is capacity for customers, especially in determining the size and ease for customers in car-parking facilities. However, the increase in technology in many service operations has often reduced the need for facilities to be physically close because much of the transaction can be automated via computer, telephone, fax or other types of technology, as is the case with insurance, hotel reservations or banking services. The Internet will play a central role in such decoupling, as the success of Amazon.com demonstrates in book retailing.

Services are labour intensive

We need to focus on specific service sectors in order to evaluate the application of the statement. Sure, in high-volume manufacturing it is true to say that direct labour costs are relatively small – typically less than 10 per cent in industries such as automobiles and markets within 'high tech'. In manufacturing, the largest cost will tend to centre on materials or inventory management. In services, though, if there is a large tangible element to the overall provision of the service (for example, fast foods), then labour will similarly form a small part of the overall costs. Increasingly, technology in services has helped to reduce the extent of labour involvement in the transaction process and therefore labour costs are reduced to suit.

Quality is difficult to measure and depends on the server

One of the myths surrounding service provision is that quality is impossible to measure. For sure, measuring quality within manufacturing plants might be seen as easier in that the product can be measured in terms of weight, height, overall dimensions and so on. But such measurement is only part of the overall evaluation of quality (we discuss this further in Chapter 8) and it is sufficient to say here that there has been a major shift in recent years concerning quality, particularly in professional services. In services, time is an important dimension in measuring quality – speed and reliability of response are measurable and quantifiable. Such measures are used in the fire service – the frequency of timely responses within specified standards to fire alarms, for example. The same type of measure is used in responses from ambulance crews to emergencies. In health care, measurements such as patient waiting lists for operations, or the time spent waiting in Accident and Emergency units, or patient throughput times and other time-related measures are used as part of the quality assurance procedures. However, speed of response times may not be sufficient, as we can see in the following example (Arussi, 2002):

> A large US auto insurance company had a long-standing rule that when a customer called to cancel a policy, it would honor the request immediately in order to heighten efficiency. Recently, though, the company launched a pilot program to gather information from departing customers. Skillful, gentle questioning let the company not only identify the reasons for cancellation, which is very valuable marketing information, but also retain 17% of those customers who had called to cancel. Of course, the average discussion time increased, but the agents generated a significant amount of additional revenue. The company has since abandoned its speed-at-any-cost policy.

In professional services, quality has become an important issue. For example, the Law Society in the UK takes a much more involved role than it used to regarding the provision of the service quality by solicitors. This is due, in part at least, to the fact that clients are far more likely to take action against their solicitors than used to be the case, and their ability to do so is due to a far greater understanding and awareness of critical issues surrounding service quality in professional services.

In consumer services, within retail outlets or various types of franchises, firms will utilize 'mystery shoppers' to gain feedback and thus measure the performance of the server. Sometimes such feedback can be quite negative, as exemplified in the following (*Fortune*, 30 September 2002):

> A McDonald's memo accusing franchisees of service shortcomings has McDonaldland grimacing. In the three-page document obtained by *Fortune*, which was recently sent to McDonald's franchisees in the Raleigh region, vice president Marty Ranft cites 'alarming research' showing how bad service has gotten. 'Mystery shoppers' hired by the company to make unannounced visits found that restaurants were meeting speed-of-service standards only 46% of the time, with three of every ten customers waiting more than 4 minutes for their meals – an eternity in the fast-food business. It also cited complaints of 'rude service, slow service, unprofessional employees, and inaccurate service'.

The letter is a stunning admission. For years, CEO Jack Greenberg insisted that his pricey 'Made for you' food-preparation system would spur lacklustre sales. 'They're finally admitting that service is a big problem,' says Dick Adams, a franchisee consultant based in San Diego. Perhaps a bigger problem is the stock: it just hit a 7-year low.

Understanding services in the offer to customers

One of the most important areas is the design and execution of the processes through which the service is delivered to the customer. This is illustrated in Figure 1.11.

The service management system

Normann (2000) provides a useful model that identifies five important aspects of the service management system, which is shown in Figure 1.11. We'll discuss the five aspects in turn.

Market segment

The market segment is important because it describes the particular types of clients for whom the service management system is targeted. It defines where the organization chooses to be – as well as where it chooses *not* to be.

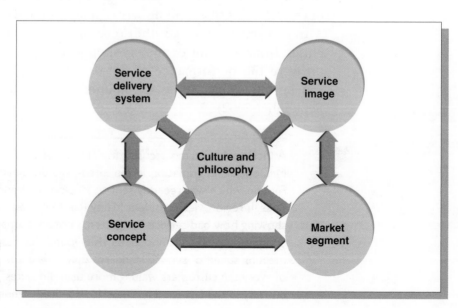

Figure 1.11
The service management system (based on Normann, 2000).

Culture and philosophy

Normann suggests that the core of the service management system is the company's culture and philosophy. This describes the overall values and principles guiding the organization, including values about human dignity and worth. This is of paramount importance for some companies (The Body Shop being a prime example) and forms part of their mission statements.

Service image

The image is vitally important because, within services, customers typically participate in the production of a service as well as its consumption. As a result, the physical environment in which the service is produced has important effects:

- the *external environment*, including location, premises, ease of access, ambience;
- the *internal environment*, including atmosphere and structure, within which the service personnel operate.

Thus, the service image becomes part of the information system for influencing clients and customers alike.

The service concept

The *service concept* is the specification that describes the benefits offered by the service. This becomes a key element in the customer's perception of the 'moment of truth', when the service provider and customer actually meet. The service concept can include a complex set of values – physical, psychological and emotional – and these affect both what the company does and how it is perceived by its customers and clients. The service concept also describes the way in which the organization would like its employees and stakeholders to perceive its service offering.

The service concept includes the *service package* within the offer, and includes both the physical and tangible elements of the service offering and its intellectual/intangible elements. The total service package – the bundle of goods and services (Heskett *et al.*, 1990) – includes:

- *physical items* – the physical good that is changing hands, if any (often called facilitating goods in services);
- *sensual benefits* – aspects that can be experienced through the sensory system (explicit intangibles);
- *psychological benefits* – emotional or other aspects (implicit intangibles).

The service delivery system

The service delivery system is the way in which the service concept and service package are actually delivered to the consumer. This process may include customer participation in the manner in which the offer is designed and delivered to customers, including personnel, clients, technology and physical support. The service delivery system is dictated by and defined by the service concept.

Manufacturing and services – the key point

Many articles and texts make sweeping distinctions between manufacturing and services. We argue that this is not always helpful when trying to manage operations. What provides better insight is in viewing manufacturing and service operations as collaborative activities in providing goods and services to customers. A more relevant distinction is to differentiate between those operations that process materials and those that process customers. It needs to be remembered that materials do not think or act for themselves, whereas customers can and do. Service companies that forget this and start to treat their customers as if they were materials will not survive in the long term, even if they provide excellent value.

Summary

- The range of responsibilities that operations managers have within the plant or service itself is both profound, important and wide in scope.
- Operations management is concerned with those activities that enable an *organization* (and not one part of it only) to transform a range of basic inputs into outputs for the end customer.
- Operations management is very wide in scope of responsibilities and will draw upon a range of functions within the organization, not be limited to a specific department.
- Operations management is concerned with uniting these other areas and functions into a central core of capabilities for the organization.
- Operations management is no longer limited to a narrow focus on organization-specific activity. In the modern era of operations management, organizations no longer see themselves as a stand-alone element in the overall 'process' but will, instead, see themselves as part of a wider, extended enterprise.
- Not only is the organization concerned with transferring goods and services to end customers, it has to do so in a value-added way. Value added, in most simplistic terms, means that the income or benefit derived from performing a particular operation is greater than the cost of doing so. All organizations, whether they are in the private or public sector, or in manufacturing or services, have operations within them. Increasingly, value-added operations are important to both private and public sectors.
- The link between operations and marketing is a critical one. Constant dialogue needs to take place in order to satisfy customer requirements. Expertise in one may be negated by failure in the other.

- Instead of seeing manufacturing versus services, we need to see manufacturing alongside services in terms of understanding the range of interlinking activities from basic inputs to end customer delivery.
- The distinction between manufacturing and services is not quite as profound as often stated for a number of reasons; the key issue is more likely to be differences between materials, customer or information processing operations.

Key questions

1   What are the major areas of responsibility for operations managers?
2   Why is it important to go beyond the organization-specific, input/processes/output model in modern-day operations management?

References and further reading

Arussy, L. (2002) Don't take calls, make contact. *Harvard Business Review*, **80**(1), 16–18.

Barney, J.B. (1991) Firm resources and sustained competitive advantage. *Journal of Management*, **17**, 99–120.

Brown, S. (1996) *Strategic Manufacturing for Competitive Advantage*. Hemel Hempstead: Prentice Hall.

Brown, S. (2000) *Manufacturing the Future – Strategic Resonance for Enlightened Manufacturing*. London: Financial Times Books.

Bryson, W. (1994) *Made in America*. London: Minerva.

Business Week, The flexible factory, 5 May 2003.

Crainer, S. (1998) *Thinkers that Changed the Management World*. London: Pitman.

Financial Times (2002) 13 December, p. 14.

Fortune, Fast food, slow service, 30 September 2002.

Fortune, The Global 500, 21 July 2003.

Garvin, D. (1992) *Operations Strategy, Text and Cases*. Englewood Cliffs, NJ: Prentice Hall.

Gilmore, J.H. and Pine, J. (1997) Beyond goods and services. *Strategy and Leadership*, May/June, **25**(3), 10–18.

The Guardian, 16 February 2004, p. 23.

Hayes, R. and Pisano, G. (1994) Beyond world-class: the new manufacturing strategy. *Harvard Business Review*, January–February, 77–86.

Heskett, J.L. (1986) *Managing in the Service Economy*. Cambridge, MA: Harvard Business School Press.

Heskett, J., Sasser, E. and Hart, C.W. (1990) *Service Breakthroughs*. New York: Free Press.

Hill, T. (2000) *Production/Operations Management.* Hemel Hempstead: Prentice Hall.

Industry Week, Manufacturing's global future, 30 May 2003.

Johnston, R. and Clark, G. (2001) *Service Operations Management.* Hemel Hempstead: Prentice Hall.

Kidd, P. (1994) *Agile Manufacturing – Forging New Frontiers.* Reading, MA: Addison Wesley.

Lamming, R. (1993) *Beyond Partnership.* Hemel Hempstead: Prentice Hall.

Levitt, T. (1960) Marketing myopia. *Harvard Business Review,* July–August, 35–56.

Levitt, T. (1972) The production-line approach to service. *Harvard Business Review,* **50**(5), 20–31.

Levitt, T. (1976) The industrialisation of service. *Harvard Business Review,* **54**(5), 32–43.

Muhlemann, A., Oakland, J. and Lockyer, K. (1992) *Production and Operations Management.* London: Pitman.

Normann, R. (2000) *Service Management,* 3rd Edition. New York: Wiley.

Peters, T. (1987) *Thriving on Chaos.* London: Pan Books/Macmillan.

Pine, B., Bart, V. and Boynton, A. (1993) Making mass customization work. *Harvard Business Review,* September–October, 108–119.

Piore, M. and Sabel, C. (1984) *The Second Industrial Divide: Possibilities for Prosperity.* New York: Basic Books.

Porter, M. (1980) *Competitive Strategy.* New York: Free Press.

Porter, M. (1985) *Competitive Advantage.* New York: Free Press.

Ridderstrale and Nordstrom (2000) *Funky Business.* London: FT Books.

Ritzer, G. (1993) *The McDonaldization of Society.* California: Pine Forge.

Samson, D. (1991) *Manufacturing and Operations Strategy.* Sydney: Prentice Hall.

Schmenner, R.W. (1986) How can services business survive and prosper? *Sloan Management Review,* **27**(3), 21–32.

Skinner, W. (1985) *Manufacturing, the Formidable Competitive Weapon.* New York: Wiley.

Stacey, R. (1993) *Strategic Management and Organizational Dynamics.* London: Pitman.

Taylor, F. (1912) *Scientific Management.* Hanover, NH: Dartmouth College.

Teece, D., Pisano, G. and Shuen, A. (1997) Dynamic capabilities and strategic management. *Strategic Management Journal,* **18**(7), 509–533.

Womack, J. and Jones, D. (2003) *Lean Thinking,* 2nd Edition. New York: Simon & Schuster.

Womack, J., Jones, D. and Roos, D. (1990) *The Machine that Changed the World.* New York: Rawson Associates.

CHAPTER 2

Strategic operations management

In this chapter we will expand upon a number of key issues faced by operations managers in both manufacturing and service environments that we discussed in Chapter 1. We will develop the theme of how operations management must be seen in terms of *strategic* importance and how strategies have to be in place if the organization wants to be able to compete in the modern business world.

In Chapter 1 we looked at the major responsibilities that face operations managers. As we saw, these responsibilities are wide in scope and extremely important by themselves. It is important to bear in mind that operations managers have responsibilities that go beyond management of assets, costs and human resources in the transformation process (as important as these managerial responsibilities are!). In the current business environment, operations must be managed in a way that will enable the firm to compete against extensive and increasing competition from around the world. This means that managing operations takes on wholly different requirements to how it was performed in the past. In short, operations management becomes *strategic* operations management.

The modern business world requires rapid and continuous innovation, and there is global competition in many industries and markets. This chapter addresses key areas, including:

■ Understanding the nature of strategy.
■ The vital role of operations strategy.

- Manufacturing and operations strategy.
- Why many firms struggle with forming operations strategies.
- Service operations strategies.
- Strategic resonance.
- The need for flexibility and agility.
- The nature and importance of strategy in dealing with competitive conditions.
- Competitive analysis and profiling.
- Operations management as part of developing core competences.

The purpose of this chapter is for the reader to:

- understand why there is a need for all organizations to develop operations strategies;
- gain insights into how operations strategy has developed over time;
- provide indications of the process and content of strategy;
- appreciate why some organizations struggle with devising and implementing operations strategies.

Understanding strategy

We do not pretend that strategy is easy or straightforward. Strategy is clearly a complex issue (Whittington, 2001; Mintzberg *et al.*, 2000), but we can say that a number of recurring factors are integral to the strategy process. For us, strategy is:

- concerned with meeting existing market needs as well as exploiting opportunities for potential market segments (Kim and Mauborgne, 2002; Nunes and Cespedes, 2003);
- about making the best use of resources, and to leverage these resources either alone or with partners (Wernerfelt, 1984; Barney, 1991; Dierickx and Cool, 1989; Lamming, 1993; Hines, 1994; Stump *et al.*, 2002; Ireland *et al.*, 2002);
- the ultimate responsibility of senior-level managers within the firm – of course, we recognize the vital of importance of a range of stakeholders in the process, both within the firm and with external linkages to the enterprise (Frambach *et al.*, 2003; Hax and Majluf, 1991; Dougherty and Corse, 1995);

■ about devising and implementing processes that will enable the enterprise to compete and, ideally, to create competitive advantage (Whittington, 2001; Hamilton *et al.*, 1998);

■ concerned with developing capabilities within the firm's operations that are superior to other competitors and that other competitors either cannot copy or will find it extremely difficult to copy (Teece *et al.*, 1997; Eisenhardt and Martin, 2000).

These indications of what strategy is about are important because they are all linked to operations management in various ways. That is not necessarily a problem in itself: the problem is that firms often do not organize themselves in a way that will allow them to make the best possible use of their operational capabilities. This is true of both manufacturing and service organizations. If anything, the situation has been even worse in service organizations, which have lagged considerably behind the revolution in manufacturing practices that has taken place over the last 30 years. While there is now a well-established service management academic discipline in some business schools and an emerging research agenda, this is a very recent phenomenon. Service operations thinking may be said to have originated with the publication of Sasser *et al.*'s book on the subject in 1976.

To begin with, the very idea that operations should be seen as a 'strategic' factor is still a problem for some firms, whose overall strategy may be governed by a few people at the top of the hierarchy of the firm who might know very little about production and operations management. As a result of this, the rationale behind, and the measurement of the success of, business decisions may be driven almost entirely by short-term financial criteria. As we noted in Chapter 1, such an approach may often rob the firm of vital investment to support and sustain key operations areas, such as technology, plant modernization and ongoing training. In 1997, Lord Simon, UK Minister for Competitiveness, in HM Treasury (himself an ex-industrialist) blamed the parlous state of the British manufacturing sector on three factors: uncertainty in currency exchange rates, poor labour productivity and prolonged lack of investment over two decades.

The use of management accounting tools and 'justification by numbers', although important, is not enough. For example, there simply is no formula to determine financial ratios or outcomes if the firm *doesn't* invest in these key areas. Ultimately, if the firm fails to invest – and, as we shall see in Chapter 3, the opposite extreme of 'throwing money at the problem' is not the answer either – then the net result is that the firm will fail to compete and will face decline.

The distortion brought about by lack of investment was perfectly captured by an American academic lamenting the situation in his country (Professor Edward W. Davis, quoted in *Industry Week*, June 2003):

> 'This focus on quarterly profits among the large, publicly held companies is deathly. If there is any hope on the horizon for this country it is in the privately held, medium-size companies,' he says. 'I see them with a willingness to take greater risks in investments that benefit the competitiveness of the company and don't just make the ROI look better in the short run. I see them with a better balance of outsourcing.'
>
> 'If I could change one thing about this country that I think would help improve manufacturing in the long run, it would be to pass a law to forbid the reporting of company profits on a quarterly basis. I think that the short-term focus on profits has done more to hurt manufacturing than probably any other thing.'

Businesses face increasing levels of competition, which is becoming more global in nature in many industries. Coping with this competition demands that strategies are in place, because being prepared and poised to act rarely, if ever, comes about by accident or 'just happens' by chance.

The strategy mission

As we noted in Chapter 1, firms will often articulate a mission, linked to its strategy. This core mission does not have to be particularly lengthy, or wonderfully articulated when stated, but it does have to be meaningful. Examples include Komatsu's vision of 'Maru-C' – to encircle Caterpillar, Komatsu's major rival – and Coca-Cola's intention of being able to position a coke within 'arm's reach' of every consumer in the world are entirely appropriate for their firms. The mission is dependent upon what the firm does via its operations capabilities. On occasions, the core mission's intention may be a little more dramatic, as in Honda's case (Whittington, 2001, p. 69):

> ... when Honda was overtaken by Yamaha as Japan's number one motorbike manufacturer, the company responded by declaring '*Yamaha so tsubu su!*' (We will crush, squash and slaughter Yamaha!).

The ability to launch such a plethora of innovations in a short time came about by mobilizing a set of capabilities that had been developed over time by Honda. These operations capabilities were then able to be utilized in the market in order to ward off competitive advances. However, it is futile to assert a strategy if operations capabilities are not in place. One telling example of this problem was with Compaq. Compaq's problems began in 1994, when its former CEO, Eckhard Pfeiffer, announced that Compaq would make all its PCs on a 'build-to-order' basis by 1996. At the time of the 'build-to-order' statement from Pfeiffer, Compaq built less than 5 per cent of its machines to order. By the beginning of the new millennium, Compaq was way behind Dell in build-to-order capabilities and Dell had surpassed Compaq in desktop PC sales to US businesses for the first time. Perhaps more than any other single factor, it was the absence of customer-focused operations strategies that cost Pfeiffer his job.

The success of operations strategy has nothing to do with how long the planning process has taken, nor has it to do with how nicely or how wonderfully articulately the strategy is presented to the firm's employees – if indeed strategy is articulated to employees! Rather, the success of operations strategy will be determined by the extent to which it will focus operations' efforts into an integrated set of capabilities. These capabilities should, in turn, enable the firm to compete in the increasingly competitive environment common to many industries. It is not argued that manufacturing/operations managers should necessarily take the lead in business strategy, but that they should be an integral part of the strategic planning process. Without operations managers' capabilities, the best marketing and corporate plans have little chance of being achieved. The importance of being able to accomplish the strategic vision once it has been formed was highlighted by *Fortune* (8 March 2004):

Not only do the majority of the world's most admired companies have a winning strategy – they're also able to carry it out. That's the conclusion of a follow-up study conducted by the Hay Group in the last quarter of 2003. The study found that a key difference between the most admired companies and others surveyed lies in execution. 'It's not a secret what needs to be done,' says A.G. Lafley, CEO of Procter & Gamble, which ranked No. 1 in the household and personal products industry and had the highest overall score of any of the 346 companies on this year's list. 'The challenge is to put the strategy, systems, and capabilities in place, and then drive deployment and execution.'

What strategy is about

If the mission of the company is about stating *what* the firm is about, then strategy is about *how* the firm will achieve the mission. In Honda's case the mission (the 'what' element) was 'to crush, squash and slaughter Yamaha!', but the strategy (or the 'how' element) was by launching the dramatic rate and range of products in 18 months.

In essence, then, we can illustrate basic strategy in Figure 2.1.

However, in order to have a sense of what the organization can and cannot do, the senior-level strategists need to have a good understanding of operations capabilities. Of course, in a business world that is increasingly about forming networks it is important that strategists do not limit themselves to operations that reside within the firm only. But any firm wishing to be involved in supply chains/networks has to 'bring something to the party' in terms of a range of capabilities that other firms within the same network either do not possess or do not intend to acquire.

It is important that we do not think of operations as a limiting factor in strategic formulation. Indeed, many companies have senior-level strategists who do understand the capabilities within the firm and can think in terms of how these capabilities can be targeted to where the firm currently may not have a presence. For example, Sony is famous for exploiting its capabilities in miniaturization in a number of different markets. This 'reverse marketing' approach – using operations capabilities to target future markets – is part of the resource-based view of strategy, which we will discuss later. It is illustrated in Figure 2.2.

In order to understand strategy it is, perhaps, sensible to think of it in terms of both the process and content involved in the process. Figure 2.3 indicates the basic difference.

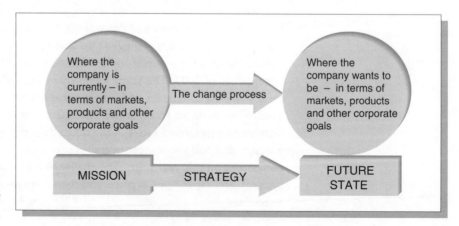

Figure 2.1
The basic strategy model.

In reality, the process (the 'who') defines to a large extent the content (or the 'what') of strategy. For example, if the strategy is made by senior-level managers the scope of the content, typically, will be wider and more 'business focused' than if the process were left to functionally focused managers. However, as we shall see, in order for strategy to be meaningful, the link between business and operations strategy is vital.

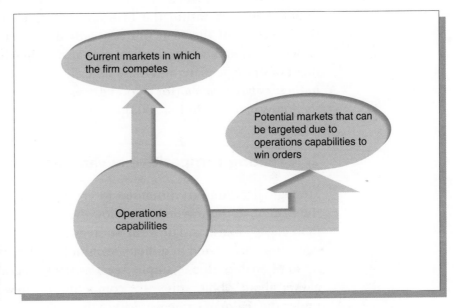

Figure 2.2
Using operations capabilities in strategy formulation.

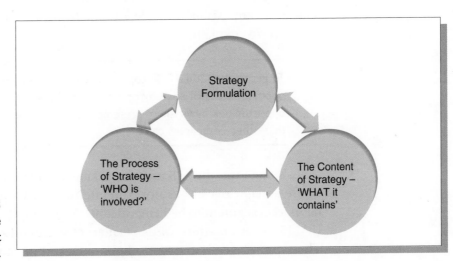

Figure 2.3
Understanding the process and content of strategy.

The vital role of strategy

Although there may not be absolute agreement on the definition of strategy, there are at least four characteristics that tend to distinguish *strategic* from *tactical* decisions.

1. The role of senior management

We can say that strategy *formulation* tends to be the prerogative of senior managers within the firm and the final decisions regarding the direction of the firm will rest with these senior-level managers. However, other levels of the firm may also be involved in the development of strategic plans and these other levels will certainly be involved in their *implementation* (for a good discussion on strategic formulation, see Johnson and Scholes, 2003).

2. Creating competitive advantage

Strategic decisions are intended to create competitive advantage for the firm or, at the very least, to allow the firm to continue to compete in its chosen markets. The term 'strategy', as used in the 'business strategy' sense, originated in military terminology. This analogy is not liked by some writers (for example, see Kay, 1993) because strategy is not always about obliterating the competition. However, it should fall under the realm of strategists within the firm to determine and exploit opportunities and, at the same time, to be aware of, and diffuse, potential threats from other players. So a feature of strategy is the need for awareness and vision outside of the firm, as Hamel and Prahalad (1994, p. 78) explain:

> To get to the future first, top management must either see opportunities not seen by other top teams or must be able to exploit opportunities, by virtue of pre-emptive and consistent capability-building, that other companies can't.

For some firms this will mean attacking and exploiting opportunities, where a major player has not paid attention or has believed a particular market segment to be insignificant. For example, in the early 1990s, IBM lost over one-third of its PC market share to Compaq and Apple. These two players (amongst others) attacked in key segments such as home use, education and small business users, all of which had been neglected by IBM in the pursuit of mainframe developments. Similarly, GM has lost vast amounts of market share (it went from a high in the domestic market of 61 per cent in 1979 down to 29 per cent by 2004) to the likes of Honda, Mazda, Toyota, Chrysler and Ford, who either attacked or, indeed, *created* market segments neglected by GM. These neglected or ignored segments included four-wheel drives, sub-compacts, turbos and minivans. On the other hand, ACCOR Hotels has come to dominate the hotel market in France by deliberately developing a strategy based on having a hotel brand for all market segments – Formula 1 and Urbis at the lower end of the market, Orbis and Novotel for the middle market, and Sofitel at the top end.

However, as we noted above, strategy does not necessarily concern itself with the destruction of other players but, if we expand the military application of strategy further, a firm may often develop alliances with other competitors rather than seek their destruction. These alliances may play a major factor in the success of the firm in specific areas, as we shall see in Chapter 4 on innovation and Chapter 6 on strategic partnerships in the supply chain. A key requirement for entry to these alliances, though, is in the operations capability that each firm can bring to a particular alliance.

3. The profound consequences of strategic decisions

A strategic decision can profoundly alter, and have major consequences for, the firm. Examples of such decisions might include: massive financial investment (for example, GM's $80 billion investment in technology in the 1980s); radical reconfigurations of entire business structures (as happened with many US 'giants', including IBM, in the 1990s); and radical downsizing within the enterprise (again exemplified in many US giants in the 1990s through to the present day). An operations strategy concerned with supply may lead to a reshaping of the organization, including outsourcing and insourcing operations, and configuring an internal supply chain, thus profoundly altering its nature.

4. Long-term horizons

Strategic decisions can have long-term implications for the firm and hence the factor of time is an important one for strategists (Das, 1991; Itami and Numagami, 1992). It is important to note that strategic

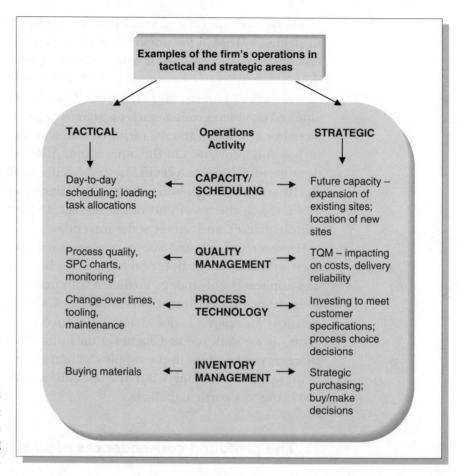

Figure 2.4
Tactical and strategic concerns in manufacturing operations.

planning is not simply crystal-ball gazing into the far future; for strategy to be effective, it also needs to have a sense of timing and urgency in its implementation.

There are a number of areas of operations that are simultaneously tactical and strategic in scope, and these are listed in Figure 2.4. The problem with many firms is that the perceived tactical concerns are seen to rest with production/operations staff, whereas the strategic concerns do not.

What is operations strategy?

There is no one best way to formulate strategy and the debate on whether strategy should be internal, resource-based or fully externally market-driven may be seen as of intellectual interest only. In practice, many organizations will combine both internal and external considerations in the same way that they tend to innovate as a result of both 'push technology' (from internal developments) and 'pull demand' (from market requirements). These capabilities are not limited to operations only but they must include operations capabilities, including quality, innovation, flexibility of volume and variety requirements, delivery speed and reliability. While excellent marketing skills need to be in place within an organization, they are of little use if there are not world-class operations management capabilities (internal and external) also in place to support the marketing intentions of the organization.

Every firm must be aware of external issues, including macro-economic factors, social and technological changes. The PEST model (Political, Economic, Social and Technical elements) is a convenient – but hardly exhaustive – approach to scanning external issues. However, the firm must also pay great attention to internal capabilities and to link these with opportunities and threats that may influence the firm. Brown *et al.* (2001) offer a simple model of managing the process (Figure 2.5).

In some firms, operations personnel will be involved from stage 2 onwards. However, some firms involve operations from stage 4 and, for others, stage 6 (design operations systems) is where production/operations come into the process – a role which is to react to plans and strategies *already in place*. However, by that stage, the original corporate aim could be 'out of line' with production/operations capability.

In the same way that there is no fixed way in the process of strategy, it is also best to see the *content* of strategy as a dynamic rather than fixed entity. However, we suggest that the content should include at least the following:

- process choice – the selection of the right approach to producing goods or delivering service;
- innovation – the adaptation or renewal of the organization's processes or outputs to ensure they adapt to changes in the external environment;
- supply chain management – the external management of relationships with suppliers to ensure the effective and efficient supply of inputs;
- control of resources – the internal management of inventories;
- production control – the effective and efficient management of processes;
- work organization – the management and organization of the workforce within the organization;
- customer satisfaction – the management of quality.

If any of these imperatives are mismanaged the future of the organization is placed in jeopardy. It is for this reason that each of these has a

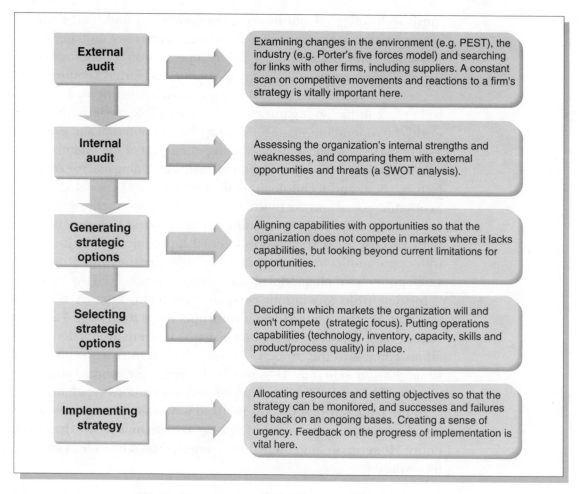

Figure 2.5
A simplified process of strategy (from Brown *et al.*, 2001).

chapter devoted to it and the key approaches to managing the imperative are identified. Specifically, an operations strategy must include
at least the following:

- amounts of capacity required by the organization to achieve
  its aims;
- the range and locations of facilities;
- technology investment to support process and product
  developments;
- formation of strategic buyer–supplier relationships as part of
  the organization's 'extended enterprise';
- the rate of new product or service introduction;
- organizational structure – to reflect what the firm 'does best',
  often entailing outsourcing of other activities.

Understanding manufacturing and operations strategy

Manufacturing strategy was the forerunner of the wider aspects of operations strategy. Manufacturing strategy was established as a core topic in operations management by the major contributions from US academics, including Skinner (1969, 1978, 1985), along with Hayes and Wheelwright (1984), as well as from the UK, particularly Terry Hill (1995). Skinner (1969) had pointed out that not only was the manufacturing function being neglected as a strategic element of the planning process, but also the linkage between manufacturing and strategic planning was elusive and ill-defined.

Over 35 years on since Skinner's seminal contribution, it has been estimated that over 250 conceptual and empirical papers on manufacturing strategy have been published in over 30 major journals (Dangayach and Deshmukh, 2001). The discussion on the role and purpose of manufacturing strategy has been broad and includes many frameworks for identifying key manufacturing decisions. Although there are no absolute agreements about the role of manufacturing strategy – and it has even been questioned by one of the field's leading scholars, Kim Clark, if manufacturing strategy is passé (Clark, 1996) – most writers agree that its potential role can be both central and pivotal. For manufacturing strategy to be useful, it needs to have consistency among decisions that affect business-level strategy, competitive priorities and manufacturing infrastructure (e.g. Skinner, 1969; Hayes and Wheelwright, 1984; Hill, 2000). Much of the degree to which manufacturing strategy will be effective relies on the internal consistency of manufacturing strategy, manufacturing capabilities, marketing – manufacturing congruence, and their effects on manufacturing performance (Bozarth and Edwards, 1997).

There is some confusion in terms of both where and when operations strategy might appear within the overall strategic planning process of the firm. For example, it has been questioned whether operations strategy has been replaced by specific approaches such as just-in-time (JIT; which we discuss in Chapter 5) and total quality management (TQM; see Chapter 8). Mills *et al.* (1995, p. 17) summarize the perceived confusion concerning operations strategy as applied to manufacturing when they ask:

What is a manufacturing strategy nowadays – is it world-class, lean production, JIT, cells or TQM? Is it none of them, some of them or all of them?

However, Hayes and Pisano (1994, p. 77) assert that manufacturing strategy is wider than this:

> Simply improving manufacturing – by, for example, adopting JIT, TQM or some other three-letter acronym – is not a strategy for using manufacturing to achieve competitive advantage.

The same could equally be true of services. However, there has been very little research into service strategy, so for a moment let us focus on manufacturing strategy. This perceived confusion with manufacturing strategy is discussed by Kim and Arnold (1996), who similarly conclude that managers often find it hard to distinguish between approaches such as JIT and other issues that might be included in manufacturing strategy. Some clarity of the process and content of strategy is provided by Hayes and Wheelwright (1984), who speak of four stages where manufacturing strategy (as part of operations strategy) can appear in, and contribute to, the firm's planning process. This is illustrated in Figure 2.6. Although the model relates, essentially, to the formulation of manufacturing strategy, we suggest that the same model could be used for services and, in any event, should be seen within the wider view of operations strategy.

Hayes and Wheelwright's (1984, p. 30) contribution is also important because it helps to explain what a manufacturing strategy should *contain*:

> … manufacturing strategy consists of a sequence of decisions that, over time, enables a business unit to achieve a desired manufacturing structure, infrastructure and set of specific capabilities.

Figure 2.6
Hayes and Wheelwright's four stages of strategy.

Stage 1: which they call *internally neutral* – the role here is to ensure that manufacturing will not disrupt the intention of the firm and manufacturing's role is purely reactive to an already devised strategy.

Stage 2: *Externally neutral* – the role here is for manufacturing to look externally and to ensure that it is able to achieve parity with competitors.

Stage 3: *Internally supportive* – here manufacturing exists to support business strategy. Manufacturing capabilities are audited and the impact of a proposed business strategy upon manufacturing is considered.

Stage 4: *Externally supportive* – here manufacturing is central in determining the nature of business strategy and the involvement is much more proactive.

The scope of structural/infrastructure areas that can form part of manufacturing strategy is wide-ranging and can include quality capabilities (including quality requirements that a plant might demand from its supplier base), manufacturing processes, investment requirements, skills audits, capacity requirements, inventory management throughout the supply chain and new product innovation. Manufacturing strategy is concerned with combining responsibility for resource management (internal factors) as well as achieving business (external) requirements (Swamidass and Newell, 1987):

> Manufacturing strategy is viewed as the effective use of manufacturing strengths as a competitive weapon for the achievement of business and corporate goals.

Although applied to manufacturing, the above analysis is equally relevant to services. Hence we can refer to an 'operations strategy' applicable to any business organization.

Why operations strategy is important

One of the key tasks for operations managers in developing strategy is that these managers are aware of competitive factors and as a result are able to put in place capabilities to deal with such competitive requirements. The link between these requirements and operations capabilities is shown in Table 2.1.

All capabilities depend, to a very large extent, on managing production/operations in a strategic manner. Forming an operations strategy that links into, and forms part of, the overall business strategy can also be a vital factor in uniting the organization. In spite of all of the chaos and turbulence in markets, a clear strategy can play an important part in the firm's success, as Hayes and Pisano (1994, p. 77) state:

> In today's turbulent competitive environment, a company more than ever needs a strategy that specifies the kind of competitive advantage that it is seeking in the market-place and articulates how that advantage is to be achieved.

The need for business and manufacturing strategies to be linked is as crucial today as in Skinner's day. Strategy matters because without

Table 2.1

The link between operations and competitive factors

Competitive factors	Operations task
Offer consistently low defect rates	Process quality
Offer dependable delivery	Delivery reliability
Provide high-performance products or amenities	Product quality
Offer fast deliveries	Delivery speed
Customize products and services to customer needs	Flexibility
Profit in price competitive markets	Low-cost production
Introduce new products quickly	Rapid innovation
Offer a broad product line	Flexibility
Make rapid volume changes	Flexibility
Make rapid product mix changes	Customization, flexibility
Make product easily available	Delivery speed/reliability (distribution)
Make rapid changes in design	Flexibility

Adapted from Brown (1996).

it firms' short-term decisions will conflict with their long-term goals (St John and Young, 1992). A firm must be poised and ready to meet future market opportunities, as illustrated in Table 2.1 (Brown, 1996). If not, strategic successes are as likely to be due to chance as to plan, and thus cannot be reliably sustained or repeated. Manufacturing plays an important role in the overall performance of the business unit, as measured by market share, growth and profits (e.g. Ramanujam and Venkatraman, 1987). Manufacturing capabilities – if properly utilized – can provide a 'competitive weapon' in the firm's strategic planning (Skinner, 1969). Manufacturing strategy contributes substantially to business strategy as well as operations management (Meredith and Vineyard, 1993), because the process, content and implementation of manufacturing strategy are the means by which manufacturing resources are deployed to complement the business strategy. Thus, manufacturing strategy influences areas as diverse as:

- selecting new process technologies (Honeycutt *et al.*, 1993; Beach *et al.*, 2000);
- developing new products (Spring and Dalrymple, 2000); and
- managing human resources (Youndt *et al.*, 1996).

Manufacturing strategy should be aligned to the business unit's competitive environment through business-level strategy (Ward and Duray, 1995), which requires linking business and manufacturing strategies.

Thus, the firm's external competitive environment affects the structure and infrastructure of operations and performance (Pagell and Krause, 1999). Manufacturing strategy should therefore be involved in strategy formulation and implementation at the business unit level.

A report published by the American Production and Inventory Control Society (APICS) (*Industry Week*, 7 December 1998, p. 35) corroborates this need to link the two levels of strategy:

> The first and largest implication delivered by the IW census is that there is a fundamental disagreement between the strategic level and execution of the business. This issue may have far-reaching effects for a company. ... Another large issue, that of management capability, also should be evaluated in the strategic deployment process. Senior managers should be assessing whether plant managers have the ability to absorb the strategic direction of the business and turn the vision into operating reality. ... Manufacturing executives need to look at themselves in the deployment process as well. They must question whether their expectations have been communicated effectively to plant managers. Conversely, they also need to evaluate whether the degree of support they provide in terms of involvement could alter their perception of operational execution.

Manufacturing strategy must match manufacturing capabilities with market requirements in three key areas (Brown and Blackmon, 2004):

1 Manufacturing strategy must support the goals of the strategic business unit (SBU) through being aligned with business-level competitive strategy (e.g. Skinner, 1969; Hayes and Wheelwright, 1984).
2 Manufacturing strategy must align with other functional-level strategies, particularly the marketing and human resources strategies of the SBU (e.g. Berry *et al.*, 1995; Deane *et al.*, 1991; Menda and Dilts, 1997).
3 Manufacturing strategy must lead to internal consistency within the manufacturing function (e.g. Hill, 1980, 1995).

Why many firms struggle with forming operations strategies

Companies are full of highly intelligent people, but often they struggle with the notion of operations strategy. We suggest the key for this is linked to the changes to operations management over time that we discussed in Chapter 1. Here we provide some insights into how the changes have had important impact on the formulation of operations strategy.

Looking back ...

The transition from craft, through mass production, to the current era, provides insight into the changing role of operations personnel within firms and at least three major factors emerge. First, we can say that operations personnel were often absent from the most senior levels of the firm as enterprises became larger and more functionally organized (Lazonick, 1990; Lazonick and West, 1995; Chandler, 1992). While there has been increasing importance placed on operations personnel in terms of their contribution to the firm's capabilities (see, for example, Womack *et al.*, 1990; Kenney and Florida, 1993), this has not necessarily included involvement in terms of their seniority within the hierarchy of the firm, which is a telling indication of the operations management role in many Western plants.

Second, the role of operations managers often became that of a technical specialism rather than an involvement in the business of the firm. Often, manufacturing's contribution, in terms of its capability, is ignored until *after strategic plans have been already formulated* by an elite planning group, whose understanding of the specifics of manufacturing or service delivery may be very limited (Hayes and Wheelwright, 1984). The relegation of manufacturing to a mere function, unrelated to the strategy process, is discussed by Lazonick (1990, 1991) and Prais (1981) in comparisons made between the UK and USA on the one hand and Japan and Germany on the other.

Third, strategy formulation and planning became the prerogative of senior managers and operations personnel were, typically, excluded from the process, because of their position within the firm, so that operations strategies, where they did exist, were merely the means by which an already existing business strategy became translated into plant operations. The need for a better, more integrated approach, involving all levels of the firm, was made by *The Economist* (24 June 1995):

> The trouble with many multinationals is that they are legacies of a very different era. Many grew up in the heyday of command-and-control management, when strategy was made by a tiny elite at the top, work was broken down into its simplest component parts and workers

were monitored by layer upon layer of managers. But today fashion is so fickle and markets so quicksilver that decisions are best taken by front-line workers rather than by lethargic middle managers.

The present-day problem

Many strategic decisions in firms are made by those who might know very little about manufacturing and service delivery, and whose approach to strategy is often dictated by purely financial and short-term applications. Thus, even a decision which might have long-term implications – investment in process technology or a cut in the training budget, for example – is sometimes made as a quick-fix, cost-cutting device rather than as a means to enhance capability in a number of competitive areas, other than low-cost production. In consequence, firms will often place too much of an emphasis on the wrong things. For example, 'productivity' and 'return on equity, or capital, employed (ROCE)' ratios – often touted by corporate officials within the firm – can be easily distorted to appear better than they really are, and it is vital to 'get behind the numbers' and calculations to know what the figures actually mean. For example, the productivity ratio is derived by dividing the firm's outputs/inputs. In Britain, whole areas of the manufacturing base declined between 1980 and 2000 but, during this period, Britain's productivity ratio was second only to Japan's – but for entirely different reasons. In Britain, inputs went down (sometimes in terms of whole industries) and the cost of this approach is best summarized by Hamel and Prahalad (1994, p. 9):

> Between 1969 and 1991, Britain's manufacturing output ... went up by a scant 10% in real terms. Yet over this same period, the number of people employed in British manufacturing ... declined by 37%. ... During the early and mid 1980s ... UK manufacturing productivity increased faster than any other major industrialized country except Japan ... British companies were, in fact, surrendering global market share.

And the same sort of 'improvement' through productivity was also apparent in the USA, where, as Dertouzos *et al.* (1989, p. 31) wrote:

> There is a dark side to these developments, however. A significant fraction of the productivity gains in manufacturing were achieved by shutting down inefficient plants and by permanently laying off workers

> at others. Employment in US manufacturing industry declined by
> 10 per cent between 1979 and 1986, and that loss of jobs accounted for
> about 36 per cent of the recorded improvements in labor productivity.

Similarly, the return on capital employed ratio (ROCE) by itself says very little. Of course, it is important to know how the firm's money is being used and to assess if it could be better used elsewhere (which is one of the reasons behind the ROCE ratio), but if a firm wants to appear to have sound ROCE it can achieve this quite easily – simply by not investing in the plant over a period of time. Of course, the plant will then be unable to compete against the world's best but, in terms of ROCE, the firm will look good. There have to be better ways of determining success for the firm, and one of the best ways for doing so lies in the role and contribution of operations strategy.

How operations strategy can contribute to the firm's overall strategy

Operations strategy can be vitally important to achieving business goals and gaining competitive advantage in at least two ways. First, it can be central to the *implementation* of an already devised business strategy, which, as we have already noted, operations personnel may or may not have helped to formulate. In this approach, operations' role is important in providing 'strategic fit' in focusing efforts and resources so that operations strategy is consistent with, and helps to support, the already devised business strategy (Hayes and Wheelwright, 1984; Miller and Roth, 1994).

Second, operations strategy can be used in a more proactive approach. Here, operational capabilities would be viewed as part of the core capabilities/competencies (Hamel and Prahalad, 1994), which can be exploited and used to create new opportunities and to target new areas. In this approach, operations' contribution would be central to the *planning* stages of business strategy and is not restricted to the implementation of an already devised strategy. This resource, competence-based approach to strategy has become an important feature in the literature on strategy (e.g. Hamel and Prahalad, 1989, 1990; Stalk *et al.*, 1992; Collis and Montgomery, 1995). This approach equates with stage 4 of Hayes and Wheelwright's (1984) model discussed earlier, whereby operations' role is central in *creating* strategies to gain competitive advantage. This approach places profound importance on the link between operational and business strategies in terms of consistency, and ongoing pursuit of the firm's objectives as indicated by Corsten and Will (1994, p. 111):

> Production is the key area for forming competitive advantage for a company. Therefore the aim of strategic production management is to provide competitive advantage by creating an optimal co-ordination between competitive strategy and production strategy.

More recently, the potential that such operations strategies can offer to mainstream strategy, particularly resource-based approaches, has emerged as an important contribution. For example, Corbett and Van Wassenhove (1994) and Gagnon (1999) view operations strategy as having a key role in the competence-based approaches to strategy and one that can nullify any notions of competitive trade-offs in strategy formulation. This is endorsed by Beach *et al.* (2000) and D'Souza and Williams (2000) in their respective discussions on the role of strategy in enhancing capabilities in flexibility. Similar claims for the importance of operations strategy have been made in relation to mass customization (Spring and Dalrymple, 2000). A key element of accruing capabilities in flexibility comes from the utilization of process technology where, again, the role of operations strategy can be pivotal (Kathuria and Partovi, 2000).

An important contribution on operations strategy came from Hill (1995, 2000). In this he talks about the need to have a fluid process that links corporate, marketing and operations strategies into a unified process, as illustrated in Figure 2.7.

As can be seen, the links between corporate, marketing and operations strategies are made very clear, and the need for dialogue between them is vital. There is no doubt that this model provides excellent insight into the process of strategy. However, as important as this model is, its focus is based on strategy within the firm. It is also important that the firm looks outside itself and sees how it lines up within what are, increasingly, complex networks. We will develop the process when we look at strategic resonance later in the chapter. For now, a note on order-winning and order-qualifying criteria is pertinent here.

Order-winning and order-qualifying criteria

A powerful means of linking operations capability with market requirements is presented by Hill (1995, 2000), where he discusses the need to understand order-winning and order-qualifying criteria. Order winners are those factors that win orders in the market-place over other

Figure 2.7
The Hill framework (from Hill, 2000).

competitors; order-qualifying criteria are those factors that the firm needs to be able to achieve in order to compete *at all* in the market-place. Without these capabilities the firm will lose orders – in fact, order qualifiers may become order losers for the firm. Order-qualifying criteria must not therefore be viewed as less important than order-winning criteria because failure to achieve these will cause the firm to decline. In the PC industry, an order qualifier must include up-to-date technology – without this the firm cannot hope to compete and will decline. Who in 2004 would boast of making Pentium 1 PCs at very low prices, for example? However, a range of order-winning criteria come into play: low cost is an obvious one, but delivery requirements are important too; in addition, the ability to configure to customer requirements (due to mass customization) is also important. Likewise, when John Martin transformed Taco Bell into a fast-food giant, he discovered that offering Mexican food was only an order-qualifying factor. Customers' order-winning criteria were found to be what was termed FACT (Fast, Accurate, Clean, Timely).

This approach – distinguishing between order-qualifying and order-winning criteria – provides a useful insight, but it is important to note the following caveats. First, order-qualifying and order-winning criteria may change over time; once a firm has undertaken an audit of these criteria it must be prepared to adapt as the criteria themselves change. In other words, the assessment of order-winning/qualifying criteria has to be an ongoing, dynamic process.

Second, the link between order-winning/qualifying criteria and process choice that Terry Hill makes has been questioned (and we highlight the problem with this in Chapter 3). The concern is that the firm may make similar products under one choice of process, but these might be targeted at more than one market segment and there may be conflicting and differing requirements in these segments for the same product made under the one type of process.

Third, consumers will not necessarily distinguish between order-qualifying and order-winning criteria and may, instead, look at the overall value or package being offered. For example, in buying a personal computer, the customer may have rough guides or indications of price and basic specifications, but will adjust both of these as the overall package offering becomes clearer.

Fourth, the organization must be prepared and able to improve all areas of operations management simultaneously. Again, this is very noticeable in the PC market, where up-to-date technology, rapid innovation of new products, high quality levels and low cost have to be achieved simultaneously.

Service operations – the service profit chain

One reason why strategic operations may be so important derives from a long-term research programme into successful businesses by a group of Harvard academics. In 1997, Heskett, Sasser and Schlesinger published their book on the 'service profit chain', which 'simply stated ... maintains that there are direct and strong relationships between profit, growth, customer loyalty, customer satisfaction, the value of goods and services delivered to customers, and employee capability, satisfaction loyalty and productivity'. Their model is illustrated in Figure 2.8. Although their work has focused on service firms, they themselves state they believe this may apply to goods as well as services.

Fundamental to the service profit chain is the idea that in order to achieve profits and growth for the firm, an operations strategy must be in place. In their terms, this strategy identifies where the most effort will be placed, how quality and cost will be controlled, and how performance will be measured against the competition. Derived from this is developed a so-called 'service delivery system', which is the specific

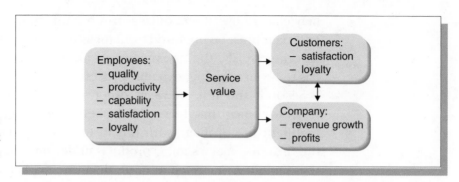

Figure 2.8
The service profit
chain (adapted from
Heskett *et al.*, 1997).

combination of facilities, layout, equipment, procedures, technology
and employees needed to achieve this strategy. Heskett *et al.* argue that
the highly successful firms they have studied, such as Southwest
Airlines and Wal-Mart, have achieved their success through the development and implementation of an operations strategy.

A key element of their research findings is evidence to suggest three
strong links in successful firms. First, there is a link between *employee
satisfaction* and *capability*. Put simply, happy employees are more productive and consistently deliver better quality. For instance, in Taco
Bell, the Mexican-style restaurant chain, it was found that the outlets
with the highest rates of staff retention (a major indicator of employee
satisfaction) consistently outperformed those with high staff turnover.
These differences were great – on average, high staff retention outlets
had double the sales and 55 per cent higher profits than the worst
ones. Similar links have also been reported in the financial services sector (Zornitsky, 1995). Not only did employee satisfaction lead to better
firm performance, related to this is a clear link between employee and
customer satisfaction. Heskett *et al.* have found this in Chick-Fil-A,
Bank of Ireland, MCI, Swedbank and AT&T Travel. Indeed, this view
has been adopted as a fundamental business philosophy in some firms.
For instance, J.W. Marriott Sr is often quoted as saying 'It takes happy
employees to make happy customers'. The third strong link is perhaps
not surprising – it is between customer satisfaction and growth/profits.
Heskett *et al.* report that Banc One found that, in all its operating divisions, there was a direct relationship between profitability and loyal
customers, whilst Waste Management reported 65 per cent more profitability in divisions with the highest levels of customer satisfaction.

The service profit chain concept therefore makes a strong argument
in support of strategic operations management. It also suggests that
how a firm measures its strategic performance may need to be considered. Heskett *et al.* are enthusiastic advocates of the balanced
scorecard approach.

Strategic resonance

Although much of the literature in both operations management and mainstream strategy has been useful, there are specific problems, which include the following:

- operations literature (and sometimes practice) sees the need to 'make the case' for strategy, but there is not a great deal of crossover to strategy mainstream;
- mainstream strategy will use terms like core competences, key success factors and so on without necessarily linking these with operations management;
- there is often a conflict between *resource-based* and *market-led* views of strategy.

As important as operations capabilities are, it is important that we do not excel in the wrong things! Verdin and Williamson (1994, p. 10) warn about this when they state:

> Basing strategy on existing resources, looking inwards, risks building a company that achieves excellence in providing products and services that nobody wants ... market-based strategy, with stretching visions and missions, can reinforce and complement competence or capability-based competition. And that successful strategy comes from matching competencies to the market.

A solution to the conundrum comes with the notion of *strategic resonance*. Brown (2000, p. 6) has previously defined strategic resonance as:

> ... an ongoing, dynamic, strategic process whereby customer requirements and organizational capabilities are in harmony and resonate. Strategic resonance is more than strategic fit – a term which has often been used (rightly in the past) to describe the 'fit' between the firm's capabilities and the market that it serves. Strategic resonance goes beyond that. Strategic fit may be likened to a jigsaw where all parts fit together. This is a useful view but it can have ... a very static feel to it. In strategic fit it is as if once the 'bits' are in place, the strategic planning is done.

By contrast, strategic resonance is a dynamic, organic process, which is about ensuring continuous linkages and harmonization between:

- the market and the firm's operations capabilities;

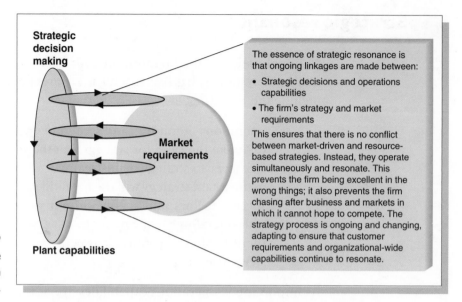

Strategic decision making

The essence of strategic resonance is that ongoing linkages are made between:

• Strategic decisions and operations capabilities

• The firm's strategy and market requirements

This ensures that there is no conflict between market-driven and resource-based strategies. Instead, they operate simultaneously and resonate. This prevents the firm being excellent in the wrong things; it also prevents the firm chasing after business and markets in which it cannot hope to compete. The strategy process is ongoing and changing, adapting to ensure that customer requirements and organizational-wide capabilities continue to resonate.

Market requirements

Plant capabilities

Figure 2.9
Strategic resonance
(adapted from
Brown, 2000, p. 6).

> ▪ the firm's strategy and its operations capabilities;
> ▪ all functions and all levels within the firm.

Firms need to find and exploit their strategic resonance: between markets and the firm; within the firm itself; and between senior-level strategists and plant-level operations capabilities.

The concept of strategic resonance is illustrated in Figure 2.9.

In essence, strategic resonance is concerned with managing two sets of capabilities that need to be in place simultaneously. These are:

> 1 within the firm's functions, so that there is cohesion and strategic alignment within them;
> 2 between the firm's capabilities and the market segments in which the firm wishes to compete.

Strategic resonance is also about ensuring that the firm will develop and protect those capabilities that can be used to exploit market opportunities. As we have indicated, such capabilities do not come about by chance.

A model of how strategic resonance ties in with resource-based and market-led views of strategy is illustrated in Figure 2.10.

The appreciation of the strategic resonance concept, and the recognition of it as a real issue that should concern firms, is important because the current competitive environment is increasingly characterized by rapid technological changes in new and existing products, brought about, in part at least, by enhanced levels of competition.

Strategic resonance could be seen perhaps as an element within the broader concept defined by Teece *et al.* (1997) of *dynamic capability.*

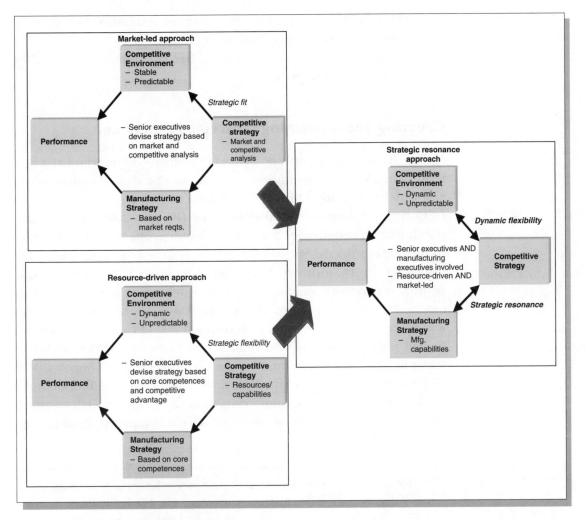

Figure 2.10
Strategic resonance versus resource-based and market-led strategies
(adapted from Brown and Blackmon, 2004).

However, the contribution of strategic resonance lies in understanding the current problems within the domain of strategic-level processes that need to be rectified so that capabilities can be developed over time and employed as needed in order to create, or respond to, market opportunities.

Strategic resonance addresses both the process and content of strategy in three ways:

1 It is a dynamic process whereby senior-level strategists communicate with operations personnel so that there is awareness about the capabilities (and incapabilities!) that reside within the firm's operations.

2 It is a dynamic process that ensures resonance between the firm and its existing customers.

3 It is a dynamic process that utilizes capabilities to search for new market segments.

Creating and sustaining strategic resonance

Michael Dell is an example of a Chief Executive Officer who has a profound knowledge of operations and may also be seen, simultaneously, as a Chief Operating Officer. There aren't too many cases where the CEO really does understand operations (Brown, 2000). Dell understands market requirements and how to utilize operations capabilities to meet these needs. Speed of response is now a critically important feature of the PC industry. Dell is more focused than any of its competitors on speedily manufacturing and delivering inexpensive, top-quality PCs. An example of Dell's remarkable operations capabilities was at the end of 1997 when Dell shipped 2000 PCs and 4000 servers loaded with proprietary and multimedia software to 2000 Wal-Mart stores in 6 weeks – just in time for the Christmas season (*Industry Week*, 16 November 1998). Clearly, Dell does not see any conflict between market demands and operations capabilities and, indeed, Dell measures success not only in financial terms but also in strategic operations performance (*Fortune*, 11 May 1998):

> He now wants to measure parts inventory in hours instead of days. '7 days doesn't sound like much inventory, but 168 hours does. ... In a business where inventory depreciates by 1 per cent per week, inventory is risk. A few years ago no one in this business realized what an incredible opportunity managing inventory was.'

On the global front, however, other results of Dell's policy – in its after-sales customer service – reveal that even best practitioners can misjudge the challenges and underestimate the complexities. In 2003, in a case that became a public embarrassment for the company, a blind customer obtained damages from Dell after the customer had called a helpline to ask for a service call to be made to fix a Dell computer. The company had placed its help desks in India, benefiting from the low costs (see Chapter 6 for further insights into this). The accompanying strategy to this globalization has been to create customer-replaceable units (CRUs) for components such as modems, which require the customer to dismantle parts of the computer, instructed over the phone by the help-desk person. This customer could not make the customer service engineer understand that they were blind, with the result that the useless instructions were simply repeated, as if by an automaton, until the customer hung up.

Becoming strategic, focused and holistic

As well as creating and sustaining strategic resonance, a firm has to ensure that it is strategic, focused and holistic in approach. Each of these three factors needs further explanation.

1. Strategic: first, strategy decisions really do need to be strategic

In recent times many firms seem to see cost-cutting and strategy as synonymous. For sure, downsizing and cost-cutting may well be necessary, particularly where management ranks are bloated and where strategy implementation becomes painfully protracted and damaging for the firm and its customers. But cost-cutting by itself will not be a sustainable strategy, and the full scope and possibilities of strategy must go beyond this. As we have indicated earlier in the chapter, there are at least four characteristics that tend to distinguish *strategic* from *tactical* decisions:

- The strategy must include, but not be limited to, senior-level management and it is these senior-level personnel who will, ultimately, have the 'final say' on the nature of the strategic direction for the organization.
- Strategy should create competitive advantage, or at the very least, enable the organization to survive within its chosen markets.
- Strategic decisions can have profound consequences in terms of resources and directions or options that the organization may have.
- Strategy has long-term horizons and cannot be limited to mere short-term financial results.

However, as we have commented on – there is often an inherent tension in the strategy process – those who make strategic (long-term) decisions are assessed by short-term criteria. In addition, the average life of a CEO in Europe and the USA is short, typically less than 3 years – hardly strategic!

2. Focused: the need to focus, Focus, FOCUS!!

Focus is essentially about deciding which businesses and markets the firm wants to be in and then ensuring that strategic resonance occurs between this intention and operations capabilities. In a sense, all firms have to focus to some degree because they do not have limitless resources and cannot therefore provide a limitless range or any volume of products or services in every market around the world. However, focus is much more specific than this and can have profound importance for the firm. In essence, focus is concerned with what the organization *will not do* as much as it is deciding what it will and this intention can become part of its core mission. For example, in 1991, Hewlett Packard intended to enter the PC market with great intensity and it succeeded in doing so, reaching a position in the top four PC manufacturers in the USA by 1997. Focus played a key part in Hewlett Packard's phenomenal rise in the PC market. Hewlett Packard decided that it would move away from being a manufacturer to being *an assembler* of products. This shift in focus places even greater emphasis on the need for excellent supplier relations throughout the supply chain, especially with those suppliers on whom Hewlett Packard greatly depends. However, since 2001 HP has decided not to assemble but to focus instead on service elements of the total provision to customers. This means that a range of capabilities have been lost – HP's assembly plants were well known for their expertise in assembly.

The organization can focus in a number of ways, including:

- Focusing on particular customer groups/market segments which it serves.
- Deliberately avoiding other market segments.
- Ensuring that strategic resonance occurs between customer requirements and plant capabilities and resources. Focusing the plant into a number of specified areas by customer, product or process is important to ensure that strategic resonance takes place between customer requirement and plant capabilities.
- Divesting non-core areas of the business, which in turn will impact on operations management. One of the easiest – and most dangerous – means of becoming unfocused is in acquiring other businesses.
- Concentrating on specific activities within the supply chain and forming strategic buyer–supplier relationships with other players in the supply network.

Focus also ties in with agility – by virtue of being freed up from areas in which it does not excel or have capability, the organization may concentrate on its core competencies and become agile by knitting these together with other operations required to satisfy simultaneous requirements of flexibility, delivery and cost. Very often, focus means concentrating on specific aspects of the supply chain to see where the organization really adds value and to subcontract whole areas in the supply process.

3. Holistic: the firm must become holistic in its vision and understanding of strategy

In a business sense, holistic means 'seeing the whole' in terms of where the business is positioned. Holistic includes – but is not limited to – integration of functions within the firm. Undoubtedly, the need to integrate various functions so that the firm moves in a unified fashion is vital if strategic plans are to be achieved. However, being holistic is wider than ensuring integration. Being holistic means that a firm is able to grasp the complete picture in its strategic vision. This includes understanding:

- the composition and changes within entire markets;
- complete configurations of supply networks and how the firm will feature in the configuration;
- the fit that a particular alliance will have with the firm;
- the impact of growth or divestment, including downsizing of staff.

Being holistic in approach means that strategic resonance is more likely to be achieved simply because a firm will not make a decision in isolation that might cause strategic dissonance to occur but will, instead, go in a particular strategic direction only once it has undertaken an holistic audit of strategy.

Strategic, focused and holistic in practice

Being strategic, focused and holistic is a powerful approach. It enables the firm to position itself in a truly strategic position rather than embarking on a knee-jerk, cost-cutting frenzy. In addition, it will ensure that the firm will not suffer from internal myopia, being pulled into different directions by the power of its internal functions. It will also prevent the firm from being pulled into different directions because, instead, it will be focused on businesses and markets and not functions and marketing! Being strategic, focused and holistic in approach will enable the firm to understand the likely repercussion that a particular strategic plan will have on the firm's numerous stakeholders in the business. Although the three factors – strategic, focused and holistic – are separate to some degree, the degree to which a strategy will succeed will depend to a large extent on how these factors themselves resonate. Consequently, the three entities should overlap to a large degree, as shown in Figure 2.11.

The problem for many firms is that strategic dissonance takes place between the firm and its customers. At the core of this is imbalance due to decisions being taken which are neither really strategic, nor focused, nor holistic. Compaq's involvement in NT workstations, the high-powered computers, is a case in point. In 1998, Compaq's market share declined from 22 to 14 per cent and part of the problem was that the supposed benefit from the purchase of Digital simply did not materialize (*Business Week*, 3 May 1999):

> Compaq thought Digital would help, but they found Digital didn't have a lot of expertise there, either. It used to, but lost it through years of downsizing.

Compaq's acquisition of Digital caused it to be become unfocused to some degree. Indeed, Compaq's overall acquisition strategy caused a

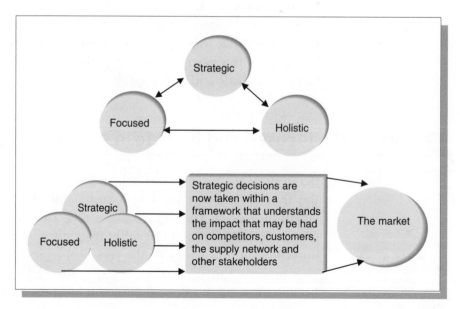

Figure 2.11
The strategic,
focused and holistic
approach.

number of problems and was one of a number of reasons why its merger with Hewlett Packard took place in 2002.

Competitive profiling in operations strategy

Part of the external audit that an organization undertakes is in benchmarking against 'best practice' of competitors in the same industry or by looking outside the industry to see if learning can be gained from other industries. For example, large computer firms will not always benchmark against each other in areas of services. Instead, they will often look to 'best service' companies as good criteria for service performance. For example, the NHS in the UK has used benchmarking with transport companies, including airlines. Of course, on the surface they are in entirely different businesses, but they do share a key process in common: moving people within the service.

However, it is important not only to benchmark against other organizations, but also to question if a particular capability that the organization might have provides any competitive advantage or value. In other words, the organization needs to avoid being good at the wrong things. For example, an organization may become obsessed with its own technology – the problem of technophilia (Bessant, 1993) – and forget that other key factors such as delivery speed and cost are paramount for its customers. The benchmarking process is illustrated in Figure 2.12.

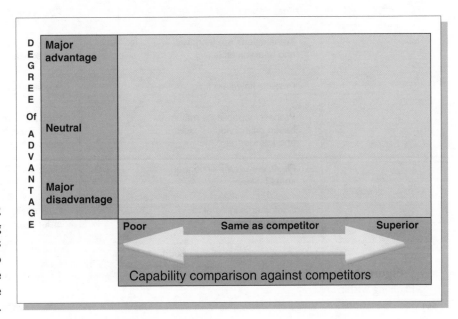

Figure 2.12 Using benchmarking of operations capabilities to determine competitive advantage.

When undertaking benchmarking as part of the company's strategic formulation, there are two key questions that need to be addressed:

1   Are the organization's capabilities superior to competitors?
2   Do the weaker areas cause major disadvantages?

This analysis is important because, without it, any firm can excel in the wrong things! An alternative approach from the service literature (Johnston and Clark, 2001) is to profile process based around the extent to which they are 'commodity' or 'capability' driven. 'Commodity processes' are essentially those that lead to high volume but limited variety outputs, whereas 'capability processes' lead to relatively low volume but a high variety of outputs. These two types of process have characteristics against which a specific process may be profiled, as in Figure 2.13.

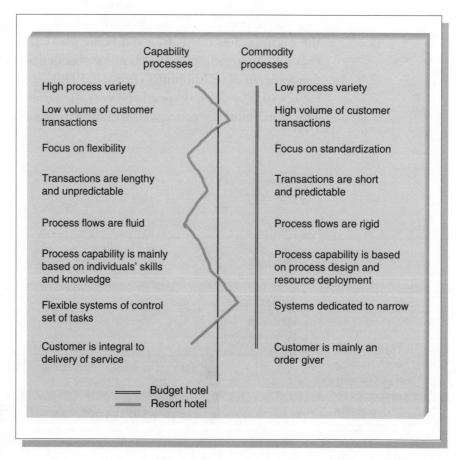

Figure 2.13
Profiling within service operations.

Operations as a 'core competence' and 'distinctive capability'

Some organizations view the abilities of their operations as a 'core competence' (Hamel and Prahalad, 1990, 1994) and a 'distinctive capability' (Kay, 1993). These two terms are quite similar because both emphasize the need to focus on, and build upon, those capabilities that the organization has which might provide competitive advantage. The firms need to have a bundle of skills in place that will enable them to create leverage or, at least, to be able to compete at all, against competitors. Such skills can have an important input in planning strategy. The role of internal resource-based strategies was developed in the 1990s (Hayes and Pisano, 1994; Hamel and Prahalad, 1994; Stalk *et al.*, 1992) and there has been considerable debate on the possible conflict between internal, resource-based strategies versus external, market-driven strategies.

Hamel and Prahalad (1994) define core competence as:

> ... a bundle of skills and technologies rather than a single discrete skill or technology. As an example, Motorola's competence in fast cycle time production ... rests on a broad range of underlying skills [p. 202] ... and a core competence is also a tapestry, woven from the threads of distinct skills and technologies. [p. 214]

Hamel and Prahalad's key points about the nature of core competencies are vital for any discussion on operations strategy. First, core competencies can provide a competitive advantage based around operations capability (Hamel and Prahalad, 1990, p. 80):

> ... a core competence should be difficult for competitors to imitate. And it *will* be difficult if it is a complex harmonization of individual technologies and production skills.

Second, the cultivation of these skills is a major challenge for, and increasingly a requirement of, CEOs, who will (Hamel and Prahalad, 1990, p. 91):

> ... be judged on their ability to identify, cultivate, and exploit core competencies.

If such CEOs know and appreciate little of operations capabilities, then clearly there will be problems.

Third, core competencies have to be part of the organizational learning of the firm and, again, this impacts on operations (Hamel and Prahalad, 1990, p. 90):

Core competencies are the collective learning in the organization, especially how to co-ordinate diverse production skills and integrate multiple streams of technologies.

Fourth, core competencies in operations capability enable the firm to be agile, able to exploit these capabilities in a number of different industry applications.

Exploiting internal capabilities does not mean that strategy is therefore fixed and rigid. Indeed, Hayes and Pisano (1994) talk of the need for strategic flexibility. Similarly, Corsten and Will (1994) warn against inflexibility brought about by a fixed adherence to a particular strategy and Beach *et al.* (1995) suggest that the ability of organizations to adapt to their changing environment is a corporate requirement. Such ideas are echoed by Gerwin (1993) and Gupta (1993).

The current era and its impact on the need for flexibility and agility

The need for some agility in operations was first highlighted by Skinner (cited in Wallace, 1989):

On Monday, they want low cost. On Tuesday, they want high quality. On Wednesday, they want no backorders. On Thursday, they want low inventories. On Friday, they want maximum overhead absorption, so we have to work the weekend.

We mentioned earlier how the current era in manufacturing and service demands that both high volume and high variety must be achieved. The problem for the modern operations manager, therefore, is that the requirements of cost, quality, no backorders or service queues, low inventories and so on, provided in the above quote by Skinner, are all needed simultaneously. This is good for customers who may demand such requirements but it poses major potential headaches for operations managers, who are charged with the responsibility of having to deliver all of these requirements simultaneously. This is a very different scenario from that of mass production or mass service to which we alluded earlier. Skinner's (1969, 1978) initial solution was to speak in terms of 'focused' factories – and he spoke of the need to have a trade-off between cost, quality, delivery and flexibility. This may have 'solved' the problem of the former, *mass production* era (1970s) and Skinner's suggestion was certainly a means of dealing with the perceived confusion in running a plant but, as Schonberger stated in 2001 (p. 21) – by which time the current era of mass customization was in place – the trade-off solution was not a solution after all:

> World class strategies require chucking the (trade-off) notion. The right strategy has no optimum, only continual improvement in all things.

The 1980s saw the apotheosis of strategic thinking, with the publication of Michael Porter's *Competitive Strategy* in 1980 and *Competitive Advantage* in 1985. In the former, Porter identified five competitive forces (suppliers, customers, substitutes, new entrants and rivalry), whilst in the latter he identified three generic strategies that could be applied to all industries (lowest cost production, differentiated production and focused production). The implications of this type of strategic thinking for operations management was to reinforce the scientific approach of shopfloor Taylorism and continue the emphasis on planning. Inherent in this thinking, especially Porter's generic strategies, is also the concept that cost and quality are a trade-off. In the current competitive arena, cost, speed, quality and other features are not trade-offs, but are, instead, combined in unique ways to meet strategic goals. Firms that are frequently cited as reinventing the rules of the game in their sectors are CNN, Federal Express, Body Shop, First Direct and Ikea.

We will discuss agility and mass customization in Chapter 3, but we mention them here because having an operations strategy is an important feature of agility. This is because such capabilities do not 'happen by chance' but have to be intentional and planned.

Agile or lean

We will discuss agility and leanness in other chapters, but a note is pertinent here. Modern managers are perhaps ill served by terminology, often shortened to just initials, and there is often contempt for those who seek to capture the essence of an idea in a 'buzzword'. The adjectives 'agile' and 'lean' were perhaps used by their progenitors to avoid this problem. However, some observers have felt that the two are in conflict, and thus devalued. Since we are using these and other terms in this book, it is perhaps necessary to discuss them briefly here. Simply put, leanness is taken as the state of an operation (in the extended sense: internal and external) when unnecessary resources have been eliminated, so that it may function as close to perfection as possible. Waste is identified in materials, time, labour, rework, poor design and so forth (some observers use the Japanese term '*muda*' for this, identifying seven different types). Agility, meanwhile, is seen as the nature of an operations system that enables it to change quickly, refocusing on new challenges. Clearly, to be agile a system needs to be lean – but not denuded of resources that enable the change to take place. The approach to operations strategy that results in leanness and agility is thus seen as common, for our purposes.

As we have mentioned before, the problems and requirements facing the firm include:

- rapid change and volatility in many markets;
- emergence of globalization in many firms;
- increased national as well as international competition;
- agility and flexibility.

Having operations strategies in place becomes an important feature in dealing with these requirements. The ability to deal with these requirements has to be planned and executed because these capabilities will not 'just happen'. The firm has to be equipped and strategies have to be in place to ensure that the firm can compete against other players. This is where strategy comes into play, and in the following sections we look at the nature and importance of strategy; how strategy is formulated; competitive profiling; and the debate on whether strategy is developed by exploiting the firm's capabilities or if it is down to reacting to requirements.

The need for agility and flexibility comes as a result of the operations capabilities of one or more players competing within particular industries. For example, in the computer industry, firms dealt in different ways with the shift to *mass customization* and *agility* in their operations.

The strategic challenge

The challenge for manufacturers, who predominantly process materials, is how to provide variety while producing high-volume outputs at low cost, whereas, for service firms, especially those processing customers, the challenge is how to provide individual customer service while lowering unit costs, possibly through higher volume output. For some firms, solving the problem of having differing competitive requirements was thought to be achievable by blanket investment – 'throwing money at technology'. In services, this has largely been through information technology and simple automation such as barcode readers in supermarkets and ATMs. In manufacturing, the technological 'solutions' have been more sophisticated, including manufacturing resources planning (MRP2), flexible manufacturing systems (FMS), computer-aided design and computer-aided engineering (CAD/CAM), computer-integrated manufacturing systems (CIM) and the all-encompassing 'enterprise resource planning' (ERP), of which perhaps the best known is the German software house SAP. Interestingly, ERP producers sell on the basis of capturing the entire operating systems within their software, unashamedly asking the customer to become completely dependent upon them. SAP have said publicly that their strategy is to become a 'healthy virus' within their customers' systems. There have also been attempts to redesign the system. Service firms have increasingly separated out the back-of-house or back-office operations from the front-of-house or front-office activities. This has been termed 'decoupling' (Lovelock, 1985). A second major system redesign has been to increase customer participation in their own service experience, which is a way of describing 'self-service'. System redesign in manufacturing has seen the introduction of cell and group technology configurations. All of these approaches are important and are discussed in Chapter 3. However, such approaches are not sufficient by themselves and, at best, form only part of wider strategic considerations. Operations strategy can be a driving force behind such continual improvements in all areas indicated by Schonberger, whereby the notion of trade-offs between various competitive requirements becomes redundant. Instead, accumulated operational capabilities, activated simultaneously, can equip and enable the firm to satisfy a wide variety of requirements.

The ability to be agile can be a powerful competitive weapon for the firm and, as Roth (1996, p. 30) states:

> The ability to rapidly alter the production of diverse products can provide manufacturers with a distinct competitive advantage. Companies adopting flexible manufacturing technology rather than conventional manufacturing technology can react more quickly to market changes, provide certain economies, enhance customer satisfaction and increase profitability. Research shows the adoption and

use of technological bases determines an organization's future level of competitiveness. Corporate strategy based on flexible manufacturing technology enables firms to be better positioned in the battles that lie ahead in the global arena.

In services, technology (especially computer technology) has radically altered many of the transformation processes associated with service provision. This applies especially to back-of-house activities – for example, cheque processing in banks, reservations in hotels and inventory management in retail stores.

The other 'revolution' in services might be seen as the opposite of 'high technology' – the significant growth of self-service. Many people have seen, and continue to see, this as a lowering of quality standards as a means of reducing costs. Significant savings in labour cost may be achieved if the customer does things previously done by a service worker. In effect, this is perceived as a trade-off, similar to that described by Skinner. But increasingly it is being understood that quality is enhanced if customers participate in their own service. For instance, diners who serve themselves from a restaurant salad bar enjoy a product individually customized to their personal tastes, appetite and value perception. From its humble origins in self-service cafeterias, this concept has developed to the notion of 'value constellations' as suggested by Normann and Ramirez (1993), in which the customer's role is explicitly adding value to an already high-quality product – for example, in self-assembly furniture as sold by Ikea.

Modern service firms, like their manufacturing counterparts, are now extending mass service into mass customization by adding value into low-cost services. In many respects this means allowing consumers to select from a range of service alternatives, each at a different price. It is now common in the USA for petrol filling stations to have two rows of pumps, one self-service and the other attended. Petrol is typically a few cents per gallon more expensive if it is served by the attendant. Supermarket consumers of the future will be faced with a range of alternatives, including compiling your own shopping list or letting the supermarket do it for you; emailing your list to the supermarket, dropping it off at the supermarket, or carrying it around the supermarket with you; filling your own trolley or paying someone to do it for you; putting your items through the check-out or billing yourself on a hand-held machine on the trolley.

The ability of some service firms to customize is based on the impact that computerizing their systems has had. Service firms know a great deal about the purchase behaviour of their customers. 'Data-mining', or the analysis of this customer information, enables service providers such as banks, retailers, hoteliers and restaurateurs to predict very accurately the needs of the customer, sometimes even before the customer is aware of these needs for themselves.

Industry Week's 2003 Best Plants winners: living the good life

Looking for the secrets to manufacturing longevity? *Industry Week's 2003 Best Plants* **winners offer their prescription for success.**

If you want to live to see your 100th birthday, or 90th at least, you have to stack the odds in your favour. Everyone knows that what we eat, whether we exercise or not, how much alcohol we drink and how safely we drive all play a role in how ripe an age we reach and how much we enjoy it when we get there.

The same assumption applies to managing a manufacturing operation. What it takes to run a world-class facility is no mystery. *Industry Week's 2003 Best Plants* winners and other pioneers have made incredible changes in the way they run their operations, aligning their production processes with customer needs and harnessing people's desire to make things better. As they'll be the first to say, all it takes is some skill and the resolve to do what most plant managers already know what needs to be done.

A standard longevity test – such as the one published online by the Alliance for Aging Research – asks about various risk factors and behaviour and then spits out an estimated life expectancy. Just as in business, where a technological innovation or foreign competitor can suddenly change the rules of the game, some of these factors are beyond our control. Women live longer than men, and family history is a key determinant of health. Such facts of life aren't worth worrying about. The behavioural factors we can influence are another story.

Like life-insurance agents consulting their actuarial tables, the judges for *Industry Week's 2003 Best Plants* competition weighed the management practices reported by the applicants, compared the raw performance metrics and improvement records and came up with their own life-expectancy ratings. This year's 10 winners:

- Exercise more. Where continuous improvement is ingrained in the work culture, there's no such thing as resting on laurels. Through lean initiatives at Boston Scientific Corp's Maple Grove operation, managers expect work teams to reduce total floorspace by 40 per cent, cut cycle times by 25 per cent and improve productivity by at least 20 per cent. Then, the following year, to do it again. The end result: the business stays limber and responsive to rapid market changes. Such hard work shows up in a number of areas, including customer lead times, which most of the *2003 Best Plants* cut by 37 per cent or more over the past 3 years.
- Monitor their health and watch what they eat. Most of us check our blood pressure and monitor our cholesterol levels to find out if we need to cut back on the high-fat foods and eat more fruits and vegetables (whether we act on our doctors' advice or not). Similarly, the *Best Plants* winners are obsessed by metrics. They track how they're doing on a weekly, monthly and annual basis to see where they need to improve their operations. Not only that, they do what they can to find out how they stack up against other manufacturers. Most of the winners conducted six or more major benchmarking studies last year.
- Are not overweight. Excess inventory hides problems, is a chore to manage and costs money. Although Dana Corp.'s facility in Owensboro, KY, which supplies truck frames to Toyota, was born lean not too many years ago, it's reduced total inventories by an additional 56 per cent over the past 3 years. Total inventory levels at the top 10 plants follow a similar downward trajectory, dropping an average of 50 per cent over the same span.
- Come from healthy stock. Any change initiative that isn't supported by upper management is doomed. Whether prodded or coddled by the corporate office, many of this year's *Best Plants* winners have earned recognition from headquarters as benchmark facilities within their organizations. Many of these companies have even devised their own formulas for becoming world-class. Under Kautex-Textron's operating system, followed by two of this year's winners, an eighth form of waste has been added to the standard list of seven: 'wasted talent'.

- Look forward to tomorrow. As people get older, staying engaged is one of the keys to living a long, happy life. In manufacturing this pursuit of lifelong learning manifests itself in non-stop training both in the classroom and on the shopfloor. At the Collins & Aikman plant in Guelph, Ontario, job instructions are communicated on personal computers at workstations that not only explain, but show how tasks should be performed. Most of *Industry Week's 2003 Best Plants* dedicated 2.8 per cent of their labour costs and over 70 hours of training per employee last year.

- Obey the rules of the road and buckle up. In business it's impossible to predict everything that the market will throw your way. It's best to be prepared. Operations with low levels of inventory and rapid cycle times inherently respond better to fluctuations in demand. On the journey to world-class, it's also a good idea to take care of your passengers. With the ultimate objective that all leave the factory at the end of their shift in the same condition in which they arrived, the winning plants achieved Occupational Safety and Health Administration incident rates about half of their industry averages.

- Drink in moderation. The *Best Plants* winners know how to celebrate. Walking through these facilities, you'll find people who smile and project an air of competent comradery. At every opportunity they recognize individual and team achievements. Autoliv's facility in Columbia City, IN, is home to local superhero Kaptain Kaizen, who congratulates team members on a job well done. Around the corner in Avilla, IN, increasing participation in Kautex-Textron's annual plant picnic itself has become an indicator of how much happier people are to work there.

One of the key factors of life expectancy calculators that doesn't necessarily hold true for manufacturing plants is age. With today's pace of innovation, younger plants can be outmoded almost as quickly as older ones. Survival depends on market success that in turn drives ongoing investments in new capital equipment and technology. Over half of this year's winners began life in the 1990s, but the Lockheed Martin facility in Syracuse has had several lives going back to the late 1940s, when it was part of General Electric Co.'s Electronics Park.

Yet in the final analysis, manufacturing success is about more than mere survival. It's about living the good life: serving customers well, making a healthy profit and having fun along the way.

Source: Living the good life. *Industry Week*, October 2003, Issue 10, p. 27.

Key question: What role do you think strategy had in subsequent performance of these plants?

Summary

- In addition to the huge managerial responsibility of managing key assets, costs and human resources, the contribution of production and operations management is vital because it can provide a number of competitive opportunities for the firm.

- Strategies must be in place if the organization is to compete in a business world which is now chaotic, requiring rapid and continuous innovation, and open to global competition in many industries and markets.

- In Japanese and other world-class companies, the contribution of operations management to business planning is central. This involvement helps to guide the firm by matching the firm's core capabilities with market requirements.

- There have been major transitions from craft to mass through to the current era of *mass customization*, *agility*, *leanness* and *strategic manufacturing*. Each of these has represented a major, worldwide innovation, with implications for strategy formulation and profoundly changing the way people work. In each case, the new paradigm has made the previous one largely, but not totally, redundant.

- Operations strategy is vital as part of the wider, business strategy, in integrating and combining major competitive requirements, including cost, delivery speed, delivery reliability, flexibility and customer-specific configurations.

- Having an operations strategy is important because the ability to be *agile*, *lean* and flexible does not come about by chance; such states are achieved by enabling the organization to be poised to achieve such requirements. Operations strategy becomes the means by which capabilities become realized.

Key questions

1 What are the links between operations strategy and business strategy?

2 What are the problems that might be faced in formulating an operations strategy?

3 Why have operations and business strategies become separated in some firms?

4 Why is operations strategy vitally important in modern-day operations management?

References and further reading

Barney, J.B. (1991) Firm resources and sustained competitive advantage. *Journal of Management*, **17**, 99–120.

Beach, R., Muhlemann, A., Paterson, A., Price, D. and Sharp, J. (1995) A process for developing manufacturing management information systems to support strategic change. In: *Advances in Manufacturing Technology*, Vol. IX, pp. 646–650. London: Taylor & Francis.

Beach, R., Muhlemann, A.P., Price, D.H.R., Paterson, A. and Sharp, J.A. (2000) Manufacturing operations and strategic flexibility: survey and cases. *International Journal of Operations and Production Management*, **20**(1), 13–27.

Berry, W.L., Hill, T.J. and Klompmaker, J.E. (1995) Customer-driven manufacturing. *International Journal of Operations and Production Management*, **15**(3), 4–16.

Bessant, J. (1993) The lessons of failure: learning to manage new manufacturing technology. *International Journal of Technology Management*, Special Issue on Manufacturing Technology, **8**(2–4), 197–215.

Bozarth, C. and Edwards, S. (1997) The impact of market requirements focus and manufacturing characteristics focus on plant. *Journal of Operations Management*, **15**(3), 162–180.

Brown, S. (1996) *Strategic Manufacturing for Competitive Advantage*. Hemel Hempstead: Prentice Hall.

Brown, S. (2000) *Manufacturing the Future – Strategic Resonance for Resonant Manufacturing*. London: Financial Times/Pearson Books.

Brown, S. and Blackmon, K. (2004) Aligning manufacturing strategy and business-level competitive strategy in new competitive environments: the case for strategic resonance. *Journal of Management Studies* (in press).

Brown, S., Blackmon, K., Cousins, P. and Maylor, H. (2001) *Operations Management – Policy, Practice and Performance Management.* Butterworth-Heinemann.

Business Week, 7 August 1995, p. 64.

Business Week, 3 May 1999.

Chandler, A. (1992) Corporate strategy, structure and control methods in the United States during the 20th century. *Industrial and Corporate Change,* **1**(2), 263–284.

Clark, K. (1996) Competing through manufacturing and the new manufacturing paradigm: is manufacturing strategy passé? *Production and Operations Management,* **5**(1), 42–58.

Collis, D. and Montgomery, C. (1995) Competing on resources: strategy in the 1990s. *Harvard Business Review,* **73**(4), 118–128.

Corbett, C. and Van Wassenhove, L. (1994) Trade-offs? What trade-offs? Competence and competitiveness in manufacturing strategy. *California Management Review,* **35**(4), 107–120.

Corsten, H. and Will, T. (1994) Simultaneously supporting generic competitive strategies by production management. *Technovation,* **14**(2), 111–120.

Dangayach, G.S. and Deshmukh, S.G. (2001) Manufacturing strategy: literature review and some issues. *International Journal of Operations and Production Management,* **21**(7), 884–932.

Das, T.K. (1991) Time: the hidden dimension in strategic planning. *Long Range Planning,* **24**(3), 49–57.

Deane, R.H., McDougall, P.P. and Gargeya, V.B. (1991) Manufacturing and marketing interdependence in the new venture firm: an empirical study. *Journal of Operations Management,* **10**(3), 329–343.

Dertouzos, M., Lester, R. and Solow, R. (1989) *Made in America.* Cambridge, MA: MIT Press.

Dierickx, I. and Cool, K. (1989) Asset stock accumulation and sustainability of competitive advantage. *Management Science,* **35**, 1504–1511.

Dougherty, D. and Corse, S.M. (1995) When it comes to product innovation, what is so bad about bureaucracy? *Journal of High Technology Management Research,* **6**, 55–76.

D'Souza, D.E. and Williams, F.P. (2000) Toward a taxonomy of manufacturing flexibility dimensions. *Journal of Operations Management,* **18**, 577–593.

The Economist, Survey of multinationals: who wants to be a giant?, 24 June 1995.

The Economist, 22 June 1996, p. S3:3.

Eisenhardt, K.M. and Martin, J.A. (2000) Dynamic capabilities: what are they? *Strategic Management Journal,* **21**(10/11), 1105–1122.

Fortune, 11 May 1998, **137**(9), p. 59.

Fortune, The secrets of execution, 8 March 2004.

Frambach, R.T., Prabhu, J. and Verhallen, T.M.M. (2003) The influence of business strategy on new product activity: the role of market orientation. *International Journal of Research in Marketing*, **20**(4), 377–397.

Gagnon, S. (1999) Resource based competition and the new operation strategy. *International Journal of Operations and Production Management*, **19**(2), 125–138.

Gerwin, D. (1993) Manufacturing flexibility: a strategic perspective. *Management Science*, **39**(4), 395–408.

Gupta, D. (1993) On measurement and valuation of manufacturing flexibility. *International Journal of Production Research*, **31**(12), 2947–2958.

Hamel, G. and Prahalad, C. (1989) Strategic intent. *Harvard Business Review*, **67**(3), 63–76.

Hamel, G. and Prahalad, C. (1990) Strategy as stretch and leverage. *Harvard Business Review*, **71**(2), 75–84.

Hamel, G. and Prahalad, C. (1994) *Competing for the Future*. Cambridge, MA: Harvard Business School Press.

Hamilton, R.D. III, Eskin, E. and Michaels, M.P. (1998) Assessing competitors: the gap between strategic intent and core capability. *Long Range Planning*, **31**(3), 406–417.

Hax, A. and Majluf, N. (1991) *The Strategy Concept and Process*. Englewood Cliffs, NJ: Prentice Hall.

Hayes, R. and Pisano, G. (1994) Beyond world-class: the new manufacturing strategy. *Harvard Business Review*, January–February, 77–86.

Hayes, R. and Wheelwright, S. (1984) *Restoring Our Competitive Edge*. New York: Wiley.

Heskett, J., Sasser, E. and Schlesinger, L. (1997) *Service Profit Chain*. New York: Free Press.

Hill, T. (1980) Manufacturing implications in determining corporate policy. *International Journal of Operations and Production Management*, **1**(1), 3–11.

Hill, T. (1995) *Manufacturing Strategy*, 1st Edition. Basingstoke: Macmillan.

Hill, T. (2000) *Manufacturing Strategy*, 2nd Edition. Basingstoke: Macmillan.

Hines, P. (1994) *Creating World Class Suppliers: Unlocking Mutual Competitive Advantage*. London: Pitman.

Honeycutt, E.D., Siguaw, J.A. and Harper, S.C. (1993) The impact of flexible manufacturing on competitive strategy. *Industrial Management*, **35**(6), 2–15.

Industry Week, 16 November 1998.

Industry Week, 7 December 1998.

Industry Week, Waking up to a new world, June 2003, **252**(6).

Ireland, R., Hitt, M.A. and Vaidyanath, D. (2002) Alliance management as a source of competitive advantage. *Journal of Management*, **28**(3), 413–446.

Itami, H. and Numagami, T. (1992) Dynamic interaction between strategy and technology. *Strategic Management Journal*, **13**, 119–135.

Johnson, G. and Scholes, K. (2003) *Exploring Corporate Strategy*. Hemel Hempstead: Prentice Hall.

Johnston, R. and Clark, G. (2001) *Service Operations Management*. London: Financial Times.

Kathuria, R. and Partovi, F.Y. (2000) Aligning workforce, management practices with competitive priorities and process technology: a conceptual examination. *Journal of High Technology Management Research*, **11**(2), 215–234.

Kay, J. (1993) *Foundations of Corporate Success*. Oxford: Oxford University Press.

Kenney, M. and Florida, R. (1993) *Beyond Mass Production*. New York: Oxford University Press.

Kim, J. and Arnold, P. (1996) Operationalizing manufacturing strategy – an exploratory study of constructs and linkages. *International Journal of Operations and Production Management*, **16**(12), 45–73.

Kim, W.C. and Mauborgne, R. (2002) Charting your company's future. *Harvard Business Review*, **80**(6), 76–83.

Lamming, R. (1993) *Beyond Partnership*. Hemel Hempstead: Prentice Hall.

Lazonick, W. (1990) *Competitive Advantage on the Shopfloor*. Cambridge, MA: Harvard University Press.

Lazonick, W. (1991) *Business Organization and the Myth of the Market Economy*. Cambridge, MA: Harvard University Press.

Lazonick, W. and West, J. (1995) Organizational integration and competitive advantage: explaining strategy and performance in American industry. *Industrial and Corporate Change*, **4**(1), 229–269.

Lovelock, C. (1985) Developing and managing the customer-service function in the service sector. In: Czepiel, J.A., Solomon, M.R. and Surprenant, C.F. (eds), *The Service Encounter*. Lexington, MA: Lexington Books.

Menda, R. and Dilts, D. (1997) The manufacturing strategy formulation process: linking multifunctional viewpoints. *Journal of Operations Management*, **15**, 223–241.

Meredith, J. and Vineyard, M. (1993) A longitudinal study of the role of manufacturing technology in business strategy. *International Journal of Operations and Production Management*, **13**(12), 4–25.

Miller, J. and Roth, A. (1994) Taxonomy of manufacturing strategies. *Management Science*, **40**(3), 285–304.

Mills, J.F., Neely, A., Platts, K. and Gregory, M. (1995) A framework for the design of manufacturing strategy processes: toward a contingency approach. *International Journal of Operations and Production Management*, **15**(4), 17–49.

Mintzberg, H., Ahlstrand, B. and Lamprel, J. (2000) *Strategy Safari: A Guided Tour Through the Wilds of Strategic Management.* London: Financial Times Books.

Normann, R. and Ramirez, R. (1993) From value chain to value constellation: designing interactive strategy. *Harvard Business Review*, **71**(4), 65–78.

Nunes, P.F. and Cespedes, F.V. (2003) The customer has escaped. *Harvard Business Review*, **81**(11), 96–105.

Pagell, M. and Krause, D.R. (1999) A multiple-method study of environmental uncertainty and manufacturing flexibility. *Journal of Operations Management*, **17**, 307–325.

Porter, M. (1980) *Competitive Strategy.* New York: Free Press.

Porter, M. (1985) *Competitive Advantage.* New York: Free Press.

Prais, S. (1981) *Productivity and Industrial Structure: A Statistical Study of Manufacturing in Britain, Germany and the U.S.* Cambridge, UK: Cambridge University Press.

Ramanujam, V. and Venkatraman, N. (1987) Planning system characteristics and planning effectiveness. *Strategic Management Journal*, **8**(5), 453–468.

Roth, A.V. (1996) Achieving strategic agility through economics of knowledge. *Strategy and Leadership*, **24**(2), 30–37.

St John, C.H. and Young, S.T. (1992) An exploratory study of patterns of priorities and trade-offs among operations managers. *Production and Operations Management*, **1**(2), 133–150.

Sasser, W.E., Olsen, R.P. and Wyckoff, D.D. (1976) *The Management of Service Operations.* Boston, MA: Allyn & Bacon.

Schmenner, R.W. (1986) How can services business survive and prosper? *Sloan Management Review*, **27**(3), 21–32.

Schonberger, R. (2001) *Building a Chain of Customers.* London: Hutchinson Business Books.

Skinner, W. (1969) Manufacturing – the missing link in corporate strategy. *Harvard Business Review*, May–June, 136–145.

Skinner, W. (1978) *Manufacturing in the Corporate Strategy.* New York: Wiley.

Skinner, W. (1985) *Manufacturing, the Formidable Competitive Weapon.* New York: Wiley.

Spring, M. and Dalrymple, J.F. (2000) Product customisation and manufacturing strategy. *International Journal of Operations and Production Management,* **20**(4), 23–36.

Stacey, R. (1993) *Strategic Management and Organizational Dynamics.* London: Pitman.

Stalk, G., Evans, P. and Shulman, L. (1992) Competing on capabilities: the new rules of corporate strategy. *Harvard Business Review,* **70**(2), 57–69.

Standard and Poor's Industry Survey, 3 June 1999.

Stump, R., Athaide, G. and Ashwin, W.J. (2002) Managing seller–buyer new product development relationships for customized products: a contingency model based on transaction cost analysis and empirical test. *Journal of Product Innovation Management,* **19**(6), 439–454.

Swamidass, P. and Newell, W. (1987) Manufacturing strategy, environmental uncertainty, and performance: a path analytical model. *Management Science,* **33**(3), 509–534.

Teece, D., Pisano, G. and Shuen, A. (1997) Dynamic capabilities and strategic management. *Strategic Management Journal,* **18**(7), 509–533.

Verdin, P. and Williamson, P. (1994) Successful strategy: stargazing or self-examination? *European Management Journal,* **12**(1), March, 10–19.

Wallace, T. (1989) *The Manufacturing Strategy Report,* No. 4, June. Cincinnati, OH: T.F. Wallace Inc.

Ward, P.T. and Duray, R. (1995) Business environment, operations strategy, and performance. *Journal of Operations Management,* **13**, 99–115.

Wernerfelt, B. (1984) A resource-based view of the firm. *Strategic Management Journal,* **5**(4), 171–180.

Whittington, R. (2001) *What Is Strategy – And Does It Matter?* London: Routledge.

Womack, J., Jones, D. and Roos, D. (1990) *The Machine that Changed the World.* New York: Rawson Associates.

Youndt, M.A., Snell, S.A., Dean, J.W. Jr and Lepak, D.P. (1996) Human resource management, manufacturing strategy, and firm performance. *Academy of Management Journal,* **39**(4), 836–865.

Zornitsky, J.J. (1995) 'Making Effective Human resource Management a Hard Business Issue' *Compensation & Benefits Management,* Winter, 16–24.

CHAPTER 3

Managing the transformation process

Introduction

The physical layout and the transformation process that an organization employs are critical factors for strategic operations management. This is because both the layout and, more specifically, the process transformation process (or *process choice* as it is sometimes called) provide massive clues about what the organization can do, as well as what it cannot do. This is important because sometimes an organization will be attracted to a market opportunity and the attempt will prove futile because the appropriate process choice is not in place. For example, a famous operations management case on this issue is the attempt by Babcock & Wilcox to enter the nuclear energy industry (Hill, 2000). This was a disaster because the required change of transformation – from line to job processes – was not undertaken by Babcock & Wilcox.

The purpose of this chapter is for the reader to:

■ understand the strategic significance of process choice;
■ realize that 'throwing money' at technology is not the answer, although appropriate investment in technology is a necessary requirement;
■ appreciate how process choice will help guide the organization, including how to avoid being pulled into market segments in which it cannot compete.

As we saw in Chapter 1, there have been three major eras in manufacturing: craft, mass production and the current era. This current era has been called a number of things, including *flexible specialization, mass customization, agile manufacturing* and *lean production*. These terms attempt to describe the simultaneous requirements of volume and variety that have placed enormous responsibility upon operations management. This is because the current era, with rapid change, fickle and dynamic global markets, constant innovation and immense demands of flexibility, requires processes that enable the firm to meet customer demands accurately (i.e. without relying on compromise). The key issue in addressing this situation is that, within the current turbulence in sales and supply markets, it is inappropriate to use methods and processes that were previously adopted under mass production (which enjoyed a totally different, acquiescent market). This is particularly relevant in the use of technology in process choice. The nature of the new market requirements demands operations management capabilities that deliver flexibility; this comes from an array of operating possibilities under the heading of 'flexible' manufacturing. This is discussed in this chapter.

Process technology is a key part of innovation, which we will discuss in Chapter 4. However, innovation is not restricted to the launch of new products (as vitally important as this is) – it includes acquiring and managing new process technology. Investment in process or product technology *per se* is not enough, however. An important part of the innovation process is in ensuring that there is sufficient and suitable *human* capacity – know-how and learning – in place to accompany and complement the investment in new process technology: this is the interface between technology management and operations management.

Process and product technology are often twin themes in the innovation process; this is because process technology must be in place to support new product innovations. Without this capability, new product developments will fail. New technology may also have important influence on the wider issue of the firm's overall capacity. Capacity should not be seen just in terms of volume, but also in the *variety* of products that the firm can provide. This capability – to produce a variety of products – is an important feature of the overall output of the firm.

Managing technology is a complex task because technology is uncertain and dynamic, and must be integrated with other areas, such as human skills and capabilities, cultural aspects (working practices), and financial protocols. Process choice – which is the means by which technology transforms inputs into products within the plant – is always a *major* strategic decision. This is because no amount of reactive, tactical measures can be expected to compensate retrospectively for inappropriate investment in processes that do not match the market requirements in which the firm or plant is competing. Decisions have to be based on current and future market demands and counter technical or engineering indulgence or idiosyncrasy within an influential group within the firm. One of the major considerations in selecting process technology is in the amount and nature of investment necessary – the financial factor, which we shall now discuss.

The financial factor in process technology

The state of markets for most products and services means that investment in technology is seldom a question of choice of whether or not to invest; the only choice is often the *type and extent* of process technology investment. Many industrial sectors have seen the demise of firms that suffered from lack of investment over time – firms which became casualties of aggressive competitors that *were* prepared to invest in process technology. In some cases, this lack of investment has accounted for the demise of whole industrial sectors – including the British car manufacturers of the 1970s and elements of shipbuilding throughout Europe and in the USA. These industries represent a range of transformational types that fall under the title of process choice: the lack of investment has been apparent in high-volume, high-tech sectors, as well as in sectors producing low-volume products.

There are two, equally dangerous, positions that can be taken when it comes to investment in process technology. Both may seem unrealistic to the newcomer to operations management, but evidence of both is depressingly common. The first is not to invest at all; the second is to 'throw money' at technology in the hope that, somehow, this very act will ensure success for the firm. If a firm does not invest, it may be expected to grow increasingly incapable of competing against other players in its market. The temptation not to invest – management indolence – is one of *the* easiest financial traps to fall into. In the short term, the plant may survive as if no mistake has been made. More alarmingly, the firm's return on net assets – RONA, one of the most misleading of all accounting ratios if used in isolation – will appear to improve! In the longer term, the plant will undoubtedly become uncompetitive and, typically, face closure. In global manufacturing, where politics are never far beneath the surface, this strategy may be used – with stealth – to justify withdrawal from a foreign plant when conditions in the home country favour retrenchment.

Justifying investment will always be a difficult matter, relying as much on management intuition as scientific analysis: there are no calculations that can state with certainty that a specific investment will yield a specified return. In other words, we cannot say that '*x* amounts' of investment equals '*y* values of return' within a specific period of time. But we must always bear in mind that the greatest cost will arise from *not* investing. This may mean that justifying an investment is seen as a 'leap of faith' to some degree – beyond the scope of straightforward accountancy techniques. Large sums may be involved and there is often a significant period between the time of investment and the benefits that might be attained. These benefits, such as improved speed and accuracy of delivery, greater flexibility and enhanced quality, might not have an impact on the 'bottom line' for some time after the operational capabilities have been developed. Financial ratios do not always provide solutions in these cases. Various attempts have been made to justify accounting criteria, including the payback period (Monohan and Smunt, 1984; Willis and Sullivan, 1984), break-even analysis (Starr and Biloski, 1984) and net present value (Hutchison and Holland, 1982; Kulatilaka, 1984). However, the problem with these accounting measures is that there is a static and fixed 'feel' to them. For example, 'payback' criteria ignore any returns that might be forthcoming *beyond* the payback period. In addition, net present value (NPV) – a ratio that is often used to evaluate investment – assumes that factors such as market share, price, labour costs and the firm's competitive position in the market will remain constant over time. In practice, all of these factors may be expected to change. To allow for this scientifically, investment analysts would need to use parametric estimating – a complex technique only used at present for the largest, most long-term investments (such as governments' investments in major weapons systems, ship and so on). More importantly, these operational factors may be expected to degenerate if the company retains outdated production methods, preventing it from competing on key competitive bases such as cost, delivery speed and reliability, and new product innovation.

In the past, the justification for investment was that it should result in a reduction in the numbers of people employed, thus reducing labour costs. This apparently ignores the point that labour costs are typically a small proportion of product cost. There are two traditional reasons for this – the first so surprising that it is difficult to believe. Since overhead costs were traditionally recouped on the basis of a labour hour charge (e.g. overheads might be costed to a product at, say, 300 per cent of labour costs), it was hoped that a reduction in labour would result in a reduction in overhead costs. This absurdity was actually present in industry in the 1980s, revealing, perhaps, the degree to which a formulaic approach to management can result in myopia.

Just as important – especially in the justification for the vast amounts of expenditure that took place in a number of US plants on robots in the 1980s and 1990s – was the argument that technological hardware does not incur the imponderable costs associated with human employees; machines do not go on strike, have unions or pay deals, nor bring any of the other annoyances that can cause managers and directors of plants major headaches when managing human resources. Justification for investment clearly has to go beyond simply replacing labour costs to the principle of competitive advantage in other areas, such as product quality, delivery speed and delivery reliability. In addition, a major issue that has emerged is that human capability is a very necessary complementary asset to the technological hardware in flexible manufacturing systems: it appears the most complex computer control will usually benefit from a 'human break' in its control loops at some stage.

The question of how much to invest in technology is made more difficult in many Western manufacturing firms, because there is no technological or manufacturing presence among senior managers involved in business strategy decisions, whose input might help in guiding the extent and appropriateness of technological investment decisions (Brown, 1996, 1998a,b). The consequence of this in some cases is that there have been massive amounts of investment in technology that have resulted in no benefit for the firm.

For example, one of General Motors' most automated plants is in Hamtramck, Michigan, but in spite of the level of automation in place, this plant was known for having lower productivity and poorer quality performance than GM's more labour-intensive plant at Fremont, California – the NUMMI project (New United Motor Manufacturing Industry) – a joint venture between GM and Toyota in an old GM plant planned for closure.

Keller (1993, p. 169) provides insight into the inappropriate investment at General Motors:

> While Smith provided the money for automation and supported it completely, he clearly didn't understand it. ... With its 260 gleaming new robots for welding, assembling, and painting cars; its 50 automated guided vehicles to deliver parts to the assembly line; and a complement of cameras and computers to monitor, inspect, and control the process, the plant put stars in Smith's eyes. He believed it held the promise of a new era of efficiency and quality and would eventually become a model for all assembly plants. What it became was a nightmare of inefficiency, producing poor-quality vehicles despite the heroic efforts of workers to correct mistakes before they were shipped to dealers.

The NUMMI plant, meanwhile, benefited from GM's link-up with Toyota in the 1980s, in which the US giant learnt lean production from its Japanese competitor, while Toyota, in return, built a bridgehead in North America.

Between 1980 and 1995, GM is reputed to have spent $80 billion on manufacturing automation (at a time when the giant corporation's annual turnover was around $100 billion). This massive investment did not bring significant benefits to General Motors, however. In 1979, GM enjoyed a domestic market share of around 61 per cent; by the end of the 1990s this had fallen to around 30 per cent and had diminished further to around 28 per cent in 2004.

What had happened was that GM's rivals – particularly the Japanese – invested in the *right technology* for the *right reasons*. The new Japanese car transplants in the USA employed lean, flexible manufacturing techniques – a mix of human and technological capacity, which was to take the North American vehicle producers almost a decade to understand. One of the reasons behind GM's investment disaster was that the decision to invest included wanting to reduce the workforce significantly. It did just that – in a 6-year period – from 876 000 in 1986 to around 750 000 in 1992 (Brown, 1996). With the benefit of hindsight, we can see that GM's problem during this period was the lack of importance given to process technology as a *complementary* feature to skills and inventiveness of humans, rather than a wholesale replacement for them. GM learned this lesson from Toyota in the NUMMI joint venture project and later implemented it at the Saturn plant in Springhill, Tennessee.

Clearly, technology *can* replace human labour: this has been a concern since the early nineteenth century, when the British 'Luddites' destroyed the looms and 'spinning Jennies' that threatened their livelihood in the industrial revolution. Computers have also been seen as a threat. For example, in the late 1940s, Norbert Weiner, a pioneer of computing, forecast that this new technology would destroy enough jobs to make the depression of the 1930s appear tame by comparison. The case is not clear, however, as shown by this comment in *The Economist* (11 February 1995):

Are such fears justified? In one way, yes. Millions of jobs have indeed been destroyed by technology. A decade ago, the words you are now reading would have reached you from two sets of hands: those of a journalist and those of a typesetter. Thanks to computers, the typesetter no longer has a job. ... Although the typesetter no longer has that job, he may well have a different one. John Kennedy put it well in the 1960s: 'If men have the talent to invent new machines that put men out of work, they have the talent to put those men back to work.' That is as true now as it was then, and earlier.

Investment in technology can provide benefits for the firm and its workforce, principally by ensuring continued operation for a plant. The firm can gain from consistent process quality and quicker change-overs (set-up), which will result in greater flexibility. Robots can free humans from tiresome, repetitive and monotonous tasks, allowing them to do more creative activities.

With specific regard to manufacturing technology, *The Economist Manufacturing Technology Survey* (1994, pp. 8–9) noted that:

... robots have not displaced men and women ... despite the fact that their advent gave rise to yet another wave of speculation about the workerless factory. They have a role in manufacturing and have been used well in Japan. ... The Japanese have understood that, if work is designed properly for robots, they will do it well – but they are not able to replace people at jobs that have evolved to need a human's innate ability to fit the world and ideas and intentions to that of deeds and objects.

It is clear, then, that the justification for technological investment must go beyond cost reductions from reduced numbers in the workforce. Instead, it must follow on from an awareness of, and the desire to satisfy, market requirements.

Investment decisions are critical and must be made with the aim of equipping the firm or the plant to be more competitive in the market. Furthermore, wrong process choice decisions may severely reduce the company's capability to satisfy customer demands in particular markets. Process choice and technology are both vital because key competitive factors for customers, including cost, delivery speed and flexibility, can be enhanced by their combination. If appropriate investment is made in technology and process choice, the resultant capacity and capability should become a central part of the firm's competitive weaponry.

Layout

As we noted earlier, we know there have been three eras of manufacturing: craft, mass production and the current era. All three have direct relevance to the nature of the transformation process and

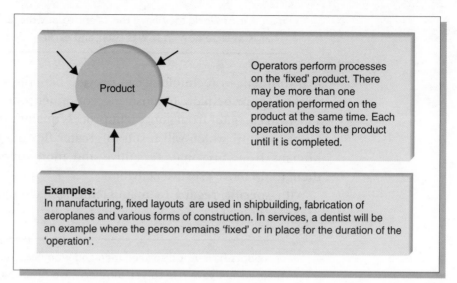

Figure 3.1
Fixed position
layouts.

process choice. They are also relevant to types of facilities layout to be understood: we start with this factor before linking layout to process choice. There are four basic layout types to be found in manufacturing and service settings:

1 Fixed position.
2 Process layout.
3 A hybrid of process and product layouts, based around cells.
4 Product layout.

Fixed layout

A fixed layout is used where a product may be heavy, bulky or fragile and in this approach operators come to the product itself. The product is completed 'on site' and is not moved during completion. The product is centred around a particular, focused area. Examples of this are shown in Figure 3.1.

Process layout

In a process layout, a plant or service location has specific activities or machinery grouped together. In manufacturing this allows a range or variety of products to be made. The machines are not laid out in a particular, sequential process. Therefore, the product does not move in a specified sequence but would go to a machine centre as and when required for the particular product. The great advantage of process-oriented

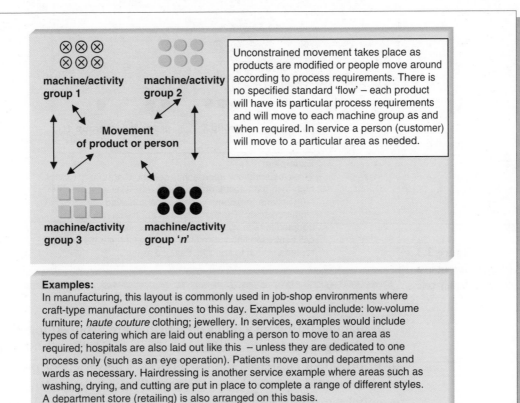

Figure 3.2
Process layout in a functional approach.

layouts is the flexibility in both equipment and labour assignments that they bring. The breakdown of a particular machine will not halt an entire process and work can therefore be transferred to other machines in the department. This type of layout is ideal for manufacturing parts in small batches – or job lots – and for producing a wide range of parts in different sizes and forms. Examples are shown in Figure 3.2.

The hybrid process/product cell

With the above approach, the machines or points of activity (operating theatres, sections in the department store) are not dedicated to a particular product family (customer) but are available for a range of products. Another approach, shown in Figure 3.3, is to group machines or activities together around a focused, product family cell.

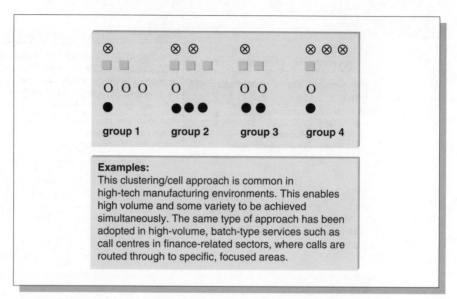

Figure 3.3
Process layout in a
product family cell.

In manufacturing, machines or activities are grouped together in a way to best support the manufacture of a particular family of products or to provide a cluster of similar services. The variety of products or services around a particular group or 'cell' may be quite large, but the essential nature of the product will remain similar and will therefore warrant a cell of its own, distinct from other product family cells.

Product layout

In a product layout, machines are dedicated to a particular product – or a very similar small range of products – and each stage of manufacture is distinct from the next, as shown in Figure 3.4.

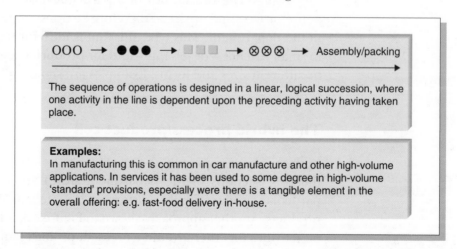

Figure 3.4
Product layout.

Each of the stations shown is laid out in an operational sequence specific to the manufacture of a particular product or the provision of a repetitious service offering.

Process choice

As we shall see, process choice will provide essential, major clues about how a firm competes and what it can – *and cannot* – do. There are five basic types of process choice:

1 Project.
2 Job.
3 Batch.
4 Line.
5 Continuous process.

The basic distinction between the five types of process choice is illustrated in Figure 3.5 and each type is discussed subsequently.

As we shall see, the choice of the transformation process choice actually dictates, to a large extent, what the company 'sells' in terms of its capabilities and how it can compete. There may be more than one process type being used within the same company, but there will usually be a dominant 'core' process that is best suited to support the company in the market. We need to be clear about the nature of each transformation process.

Project processes

In project manufacturing environments, the nature of the products is often large-scale and complex. The designs of the products undertaken in project manufacturing are, essentially, unique by virtue of their not being repeated in exactly the same way. The distinguishing

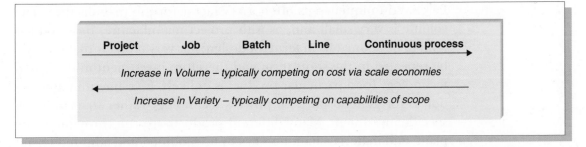

Figure 3.5
The key distinction of volume and variety outputs from process choice.

feature between project and job manufacture is that, during the process of completion, the product in project manufacture tends to be 'fixed'. Scheduling of projects tends to be undertaken in a 'phased completion' programme, where each phase of completion will be distinct and separate from other subsequent, or parallel, stages. At the simplest level of management, tools such as Gantt charts will be used. Alternatively, more complicated programmes such as project network planning will be employed.

Examples

In manufacture this includes civil engineering of various types, aerospace and some major high-tech projects – flight simulator manufacture would tend to fall into this category, for example. Projects tend to be 'one-offs', where repetition in terms of the product being exactly the same is unlikely. Construction in all forms – bridge manufacture, tunnel construction and shipbuilding – is a common application of project process choice.

In manufacturing environments, this ties the process choice (project) with the fixed type of layout. In services, all types of consulting would fall into this category. The relationship, expectations and outcomes with each client should be seen as 'unique'; each session with a client should be seen as unique. This means that the project process links to Schmenner's 'professional services' category within the matrix (see Figure 3.6).

Job processes

In manufacturing, job processes are used for 'one-off' or very small order requirements, similar to project manufacture. However, the difference is that the product can often be moved during manufacture. Perceived uniqueness is often a key factor for job manufacture. The volume is very small and, as with project manufacture, the products tend to be a 'one-off' in terms of design; it is very unlikely that they will be repeated in the short term and therefore investment in dedicated technology for a particular product is unlikely. Investment in automation is for general purpose process technology rather than product-specific investment. Many different products are run throughout the plant, and materials handling has to be modified and adjusted to suit many different products and types. Detailed planning will evolve around sequencing requirements for each product, capacities for each

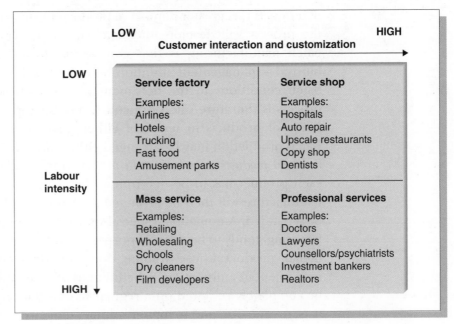

Figure 3.6
Schmenner's service
matrix (source:
Schmenner, 1986).

work centre and order priorities; because of this, scheduling is relatively complicated, in comparison to repetitive 'line' manufacture.

Examples

In manufacture, job processes are linked to traditional craft manufacture. Making special *haute couture* clothing is a clear example. Job processes are common in the following:

1 Making prototypes of new products – even if the end volume is likely to be high for the product, it makes sense to produce a 'one-off' or very low volume, which lends itself to job manufacture.
2 Making unique products such as machines, tools and fixtures to make other products. The process choice (job) is linked to the process layout.

In services, a job process is linked to the 'service shop' in Schmenner's matrix. Car repairs and many hospital service activities are job processes.

Batch processes

As volume begins to increase, either in terms of individual products (i.e. total volume) or in the manufacture of similar 'types' or 'families' of products (i.e. greater number of products in any one group or family), the process will develop into batch manufacture. The difficulty in batch manufacturing is that competitive focus can often become blurred – management attention becomes fixed upon optimizing the batch conditions to the detriment of customer service. The batch process is therefore often difficult to manage; the key is to map the range of products in terms of either 'job' or 'line' characteristics. Batch production may be arranged either in terms of the similarity of finished *products* or by common *process* groupings. As a starting point, each product has to be determined by its volume; focused 'cells' of manufacture will then be arranged so that low and high volumes can be separated. Automation, especially for lower volumes of batch manufacturing, tends to be general purpose rather than dedicated to a particular product whose volume does not demand product-specific investment in automation. Scheduling is often complicated and has to be completely reviewed on a regular basis – this applies to new products, to 'one-offs' and to higher volume, standard products: all of these types will need to be scheduled.

In batch production, operators have to be able to perform a number of functions. This is clearly also true for 'job'-type processes, but in batch this flexibility is crucial, as it allows operators to move to various workstations, as and when required. Where automation is being used, set-up times need to be short, the ideal set-up time being that necessary to accommodate run lengths of just one unit, switching over to other models and volumes as required.

Batch is the most common form of process in engineering and the most difficult to manage. Only by determining the volumes of each product and dividing these into low- and high-volume sections can a company hope to be focused and, in turn, customer driven.

Examples

Typical examples of this in manufacture will be in plastic moulding production – these would be distinguished by determining those products that need much labour input (hand laminating in glass-reinforced plastic, for example) and high-volume 'standard' products, where considerable automation would be appropriate. Other examples include bread making – where batches of similar types are produced. In general, batch processes link to process layout, although high-volume batch will tend to have a type of line (product) layout, depending upon how often the product is reproduced.

In services, 'batching a process' has become common in routing procedures for call centres. The response message to many telephone call centres is: 'press "1" for this service', 'press "2" for that service' and so on. If the service centre adds the message: 'press "0" for all other enquiries', this puts the service provision back into a job-type service. This will equate either with a mass service or a service shop in Schmenner's matrix, depending on the extent of customization involved with the customer.

Line processes

A line process becomes more appropriate as the volume of a particular product increases, leading to greater standardization than in low batch volumes. Each stage of manufacture will be distinct from the next; value and cost are added at each stage of manufacture until the product is completed. The line is dedicated to a particular product (with possible variations of models) and introducing new products that are significantly different from the former product is difficult or even impossible to realize on an existing line manufacturing process. Individual operation process times should be short – in order to satisfy delivery expectations. Competitive advantages may be gained from simplification in production planning and control, and the tasks themselves should also be simplified for each workstation (both these features were fundamental to the development of the just-in-time processes in Japan in the 1950s). In line production, there should only be very small amounts of work in process: where it does exist, it represents a poorly balanced line loading and is seen as a signal for necessary improvement. Work in process is counted as an asset by traditional accounting systems, but is actually a liability to the company as it represents unsellable materials: unmanaged, this can ruin cash-flow and stifle quick response to market requirements. Workstations should be located as closely as possible to each other to minimize materials handling between them. Materials flow and control is critical and stock-outs have to be avoided.

Since much of the discussion on automation – which appears later in the chapter – is based on developments around line processes, it is necessary for us to discuss some of the disadvantages of line processes here. The disadvantages of line manufacture include the following:

- There can often be a lack of process flexibility and introducing new products on existing technology can be difficult. This is alleviated to some degree by similar sub-components which become included in the design for new products and which then allow the new product to be made on existing lines.

■ As standardization and volumes both increase, relative to batch and job manufacturing processes, investment in technology also increases. Special product-specific technology is used and this often involves vast amounts of firm-specific investments (for example, GM's $80 billion investment in automation in the 1980s). Each workstation is dependent upon the next – consequently, the speed of the line is determined by the lowest capacity of a particular work centre; moreover, in 'standard' lines, if one set of machines is not operating, the whole line can come to a stop, thus preventing any production.

Examples

High-volume, 'standard' products – such as particular models of cars, TVs, hi-fi, VCRs and computers – lend themselves to line processes, often arranged in a U-shape. The process choice (line) ties it to the product type of layout. In services, a sequential, line-type process can be put in place where there is high standardization of the service offering. This equates to Schmenner's service factory quadrant. Where there is a high tangible element within the offering – e.g. fast foods – the back-room facilities will resemble a factory and the mode of delivery will go through specific stages. In less tangible elements, the service may resemble a line process in that there may be, for example, set procedures to adopt for a particular type of service process. For example, in dealing with high-volume, 'standard' applications – for a mortgage – there will often be set sequences of events.

Continuous processes

This is used when a process can (or must) run all day for each day of the year, on a continuous basis. The volume of the product is typically very high and the process is dedicated to making only one product. Huge investment in dedicated plant is often required. Much automation tends to be evident and labour input is one of 'policing' rather than being highly skilled as an integral input to the overall process.

Examples

In manufacturing, a chemical refining plant, a blast furnace or steel works, and very-high-volume food processing are all examples where a continuous process would be in place. In services, strictly speaking, there is no real equivalent. For example, even though technology might be in place to allow financial transactions to take place on a 24-hour basis, the amounts being transferred from one account to another would vary: it is not a case of one transaction being conducted many thousands of times.

Matrices used in services

One of the major challenges in managing service operations is to understand the nature of the service provision. This challenge is helped by using a 'mapping process' focusing on a range of factors:

- Is the labour intensity high or low?
- Is the degree of contact with the customer high or low?
- Is the interaction high or low?
- Is the degree of customization choice fixed or adaptation?
- Is the nature of the act tangible or intangible?
- Is the recipient of the act people or things?

In each factor the key issue is the degree of interaction between the service provider and the customer.

These questions help us to define the very nature of the service provision and prevent us from thinking that all services are similar. A number of matrices provide additional insights into how to map the nature of the service.

In the service literature, a useful taxonomy has been proposed by Schmenner (1986), who identified that services could be categorized, using their degree of labour intensity and level of customization, into four types called service shop, service factory, mass service and professional service. This is shown in Figure 3.6.

The Schmenner matrix links the extent of customization with the level of labour input in the transformation process. As Schmenner observes, however, a service, although essentially rooted within a particular quadrant, may wander into other quadrants, consciously or otherwise. For example, a therapist may 'batch' the same types of questions when dealing with a number of patients. The reason for doing so may well be good intentioned: namely to 'speed up' the healing process. However, in doing so the therapist is moving from the professional service quadrant into other areas and may even mimic elements of the service factory.

The Schmenner matrix is of further use because not only does it help to map the actual nature of the service, it also provides indications of the challenges that managers will face as a result of being positioned within a particular service type. This is shown in Figure 3.7.

There are other important matrices that have been provided, notably by Lovelock (1983). One of these examines whether the nature of the service offer is tangible or intangible and then contrasts this against who or what is the recipient – whether the recipient is a person or an object. This is shown in Figure 3.8.

This helps us to understand the diverse nature of services, including the issue that, in some cases, customers must be physically present to

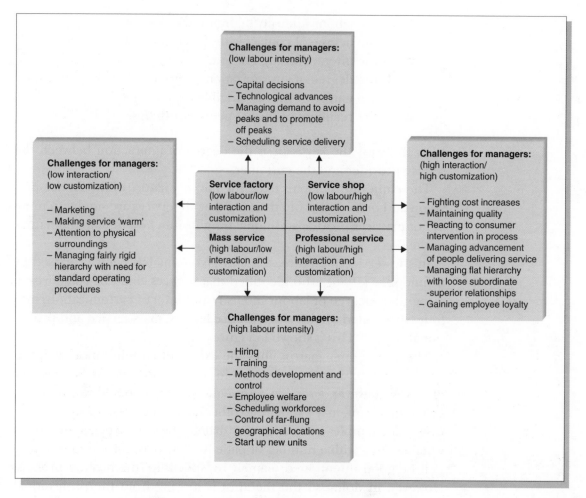

Figure 3.7
Challenges for managers in service operations (adapted from Schmenner, 1986).

receive services (where they are directed at their bodies or minds), but *need not be present* to receive other services (directed at goods or intangible assets). This will have a major impact on service design, especially the design of service facilities.

Further insight is offered by Lovelock when he states how important it is to see the dimensions of 'who does what' against the number of sites involved in the service transfer. This is shown in Figure 3.9.

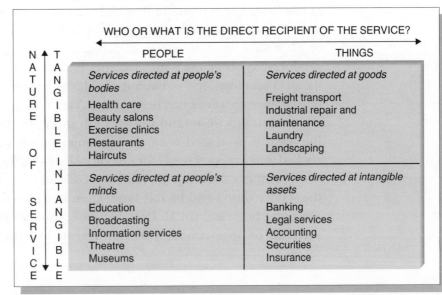

Figure 3.8
Further mapping in service operations – the degree of tangibility and the nature of the recipient in the service (from Lovelock, 1983).

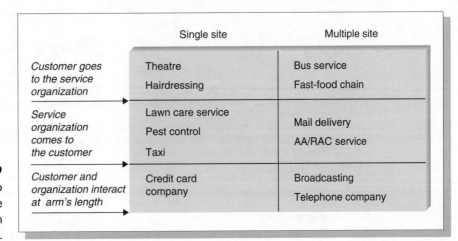

Figure 3.9
Understanding 'who does what' and the role of sites in services.

Summarizing the links between process choice and layout

As we have noted, there are clear links between the basic choice of process and type of layout. We can summarize this in Figure 3.10.

It is important to note that operations and industries are not forever tied to one type of process or one type of layout. In the early 1970s, Ted Levitt (1972) discussed the notion of production-lining service or service 'industrialization'. He illustrated this concept by discussing the concept of fast food. The innovation that lay behind the success and tremendous growth of this industry was the way in which the production and service of a hot meal was conceived and designed. Before fast food, meals were produced to order, once the customer had made their choice from the menu. This meant the restaurant could offer variety, as production only started once the order had been placed. Variety required a process layout and restaurants were (and still are) job shops. In the case of fast food, the meal is produced *before* the customer enters the restaurant. It is cooked and wrapped ready for sale on a shelf – all the server has to do is assemble the order when the customer comes to the counter. This makes the service time considerably faster than in a conventional restaurant. Since the hot meal (in McDonald's case, the hamburger) has a short shelf-life of approximately 7 minutes, in order to avoid waste the

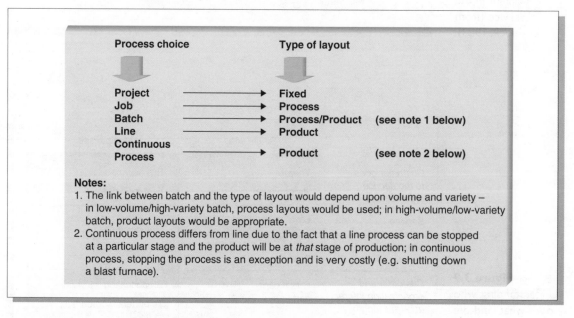

Figure 3.10
The link between process choice and layout.

restaurant needs a high volume of customers in order to ensure the stock is sold quickly. To achieve high volume the product needs to be relatively low priced and easy to eat anywhere. But also, to avoid the production of unsold stock, the menu needs to reduced down to as few items as possible. Hence a fast-food menu typically has a very small number of raw material items that can be processed in a variety of ways to produce a range of products – regular hamburger, cheeseburger, bacon and cheeseburger, etc. By increasing volume and decreasing variety, the fast-food 'restaurant' was no longer a job shop, but a line operation based on a product layout. Hence Levitt's notion of production-lining service.

However, in some industries, layout is not a matter of choice. This often applies in those operations in which the customer interacts with the service provider. The classic example of this is a hotel. Hotel rooms are cleaned in batches, each worker being allocated ten to fifteen rooms to service. Ideally, they should be organized on a process or product basis; in reality, they have a fixed position. The same is true of theme parks. The layout is fixed, although customers using the rides are processed in batches.

It is also the case that some operations do not involve one process type, nor have one layout. This is most obviously the case in those service operations which have a back and front office, such as a bank, or a front-of-house and back-of-house, such as a restaurant. In these operations it may be that customers are processed in one, typically as a job shop, whilst the materials and information processing that occurs to support the front office may be batch or even line production.

In such operations, in the past, it was typically the case that the back-of-house operation and front-of-house operation were the same process type. However, many operations have now 'decoupled' the two parts of the operation so that a *choice* can be made over the best process to use. For instance, banks continue to process customers in their branches based on job shop principles and process layout. However, in their back office, the administration has been production-lined by setting up one large data processing facility to support a very large number of branches.

Once it is possible to decouple one part of the operation from another, it then becomes possible to consider outsourcing a part of the operation. For instance, large hotels engage in two types of food and beverage operation. They have restaurants, which are job shops, and banqueting, which is batch production. In some hotels, in recognition of this, there are two kitchens, one for the restaurant and one for the banqueting suites, although this results in inefficiencies due to duplication of equipment and staff. Where there is only one production kitchen, equipment and work activities designed to cope with one operation often find it difficult to cope with the other – typically, banquet service interrupts and slows down restaurant service. Partly for this reason, many hotels now outsource the production of banquet meals to specialist cook-chill suppliers. They also outsource because the supplier can supply the meals at a lower unit cost than they themselves are able to do. This is because the supplier has a process and layout that enables lower cost production and economies of scale.

The strategic importance of process choice

As we noted earlier, the type of process choice determines to a large extent what the firm can and cannot do. This provides major clues to the actual nature of the business that the firm is in. This is shown in Figure 3.11.

One of the dangers for firms in both manufacturing and service settings is that there may be a mismatch between the type of process being used and the expectations of the customer. In services, for example, we have noted how the nature of professional services (around a job-type setting) would mean that one would expect high customization as well as high labour input. However, the danger is that, for example, lawyers,

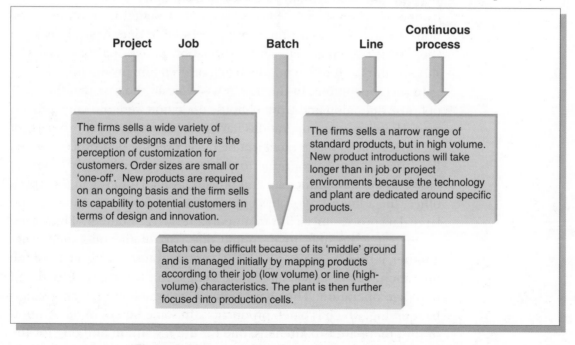

Figure 3.11
The link between process choice and marketing strategy (adapted from Brown, 1996).

doctors and other professionals might begin to batch the service process so that the customization becomes compromised in the name of gaining economies of scale or effort. This would have dangerous consequences – a clinical psychologist, for example, might batch certain questions together in order to speed up the therapy process, but in doing so may miss the deeper issues that would be expected in a one-to-one consultant/patient relationship.

Clearly, managing the process transformation is an enormously important challenge for operations managers in both service and manufacturing settings. Success does not come about purely by having the right technology. Other skills and tacit knowledge also come into play. We illustrate this with the case of Taco Bell.

Case: Taco Bell

In 1999, three out of every four Mexican fast-food meals purchased in the United States were made from one company – Taco Bell. However, this market dominance may never have come about unless the company had not transformed its operations throughout the 1980s.

In the early 1980s, Taco Bell was typical of its kind. It was essentially a job shop operation. Nearly all food production was carried out on site: foodstuffs were prepared from their raw state; food items such as ground beef for tacos were cooked for a period of several hours in vats; guacamole and other sauces were made-up; and beans were washed, cleaned and cooked. Once these items were ready for sale, they were then assembled in response to a customer order. This meant that wait time at the cash register was 105 seconds on average, and even slower during peak periods.

This type of operation led to a number of management challenges. Staff had to be scheduled and organized in shifts so that they mainly prepared food items and cleaned the unit during slack periods, whilst they assembled orders and served customers during busy times. It was estimated that the restaurant manager spent an hour each day working on this crew schedule in order to match labour supply as closely as possible to potential demand, and thereby meet the company's labour cost targets. Food cost control was also a priority, which meant that a great deal of time and effort went into ensuring no menu item was prepared in too small or too large a quantity. But the complexity of this operation lead to quite wide variations in food quality, both within single units and between units in the chain. This was not helped by inconsistency in the quality of raw materials, which were mainly sourced locally.

The emphasis on in-house food production meant that that the ratio of kitchen to dining space was 70:30. Moreover, the main assembly line where food items were made to order ran parallel to the service counter, so that employees on the line were facing away from the customers. At that time, Taco Bell did not have a drive-through window, even though 50 per cent of competitors' sales were from this source.

Beginning in 1983, the CEO of Taco Bell, John Martin, made a number of major changes to the physical layout. The food assembly line was reconfigured to have two shorter lines at right angles to the service counter. This improved product flow and improved customers' perception of the operation. The introduction of electronic point-of-sale not only improved order taking and cash handling, but also provided improved data on which food forecasting could be made. Other changes included adding new menu items, increasing the average size of new units from 1600 up to 2000 square feet, adding drive-through windows, and upgrading the decor and uniforms of staff.

However, external pressures meant that Martin also had to adopt a new operations process. By the mid-1980s, the US fast-food market had matured and competition was fierce. Previously performance was judged on growth, which could be achieved by opening new units. In the mature market-place, market share became much more significant. Labour shortages also meant an increase in labour costs, up by 18 per cent for the industry, but by 50 per cent for Taco Bell due to its relatively larger, skilled workforce. Whereas chains with burger or chicken concepts could offset this increase by taking advantage of falling food costs, Taco Bell's food cost remained at around 30 per cent of sales. So by 1989, Taco Bell was a relatively small player in the market being squeezed by rising costs.

In a series of initiatives, the operation was transformed. K-minus was a project that turned the kitchen into just a heating and assembly unit. Nearly all food preparation (chopping, slicing and mixing of vegetables and meat) and cooking was eliminated. Beef, chicken and beans arrived in pre-cooked bags, lettuce was pre-shredded, hard tortillas pre-fried and guacamole delivered in cartridges. This changed the ratio of back-of-house to front-of-house to 30:70, reduced staffing levels in each unit and increased the operational capacity of each unit. The SOS (speed of service) initiative was designed to respond to market research that showed customers wanted their food fast. Recipes were adapted and a heated staging area developed so that 60 per cent of the menu items, representing over 80 per cent of sales by volume, were pre-wrapped ready for sale. This reduced customer waiting time to 30 seconds, and increased peak hour capacity by over 50 per cent. Finally, TACO (Total Automation of Company Operations) was an IT project designed to computerize in-store operations and network each unit to headquarters. TACO provided each manager with daily reports on 46 key performance measures, assisted with production and labour scheduling, and aided inventory control. This reduced the time restaurant managers spent on paperwork by up to 16 hours a week.

These process changes and the investment in technology were also accompanied by changes in human resource management. The restaurant manager's job was now very different from what it had been due to K-minus, SOS and TACO. Taco Bell recognized that managers should now focus much more on front-of-house and on the customer. The management structure within each unit was therefore changed along with job descriptions and remuneration packages. Much more pay was performance related, so that top managers could earn $80 000 a year, a huge increase on previous salary scales. Selection criteria for new restaurant managers were also adapted to reflect the new style operation.

Between 1988 and 1994, Taco Bell doubled its sales and tripled its profits. Despite this, competition remained tough. With the right processes in place, Martin could now look to other ways in which to improve operational performance. So, in the mid-1990s, the focus switched from technology to human resources, with the growth of team-managed units and the development of the learning organization within Taco.

Process choice and competitive factors

As we saw in Chapter 2, Hill (2000) makes the very useful distinction between 'order-qualifying' and 'order-winning' criteria for a firm. Briefly put, order-qualifying criteria are those factors that a company needs in order to compete *at all* and order-winning criteria are those factors that a company needs to achieve in order to *win* in the market-place. Hill suggests that order-qualifying/winning criteria can be mapped onto process choice, as shown in Figure 3.12.

This framework can be a powerful tool for the company in 'mapping' how the process choice ties it to competitive factors. It is critically important to rank, or weight, the importance of these criteria in any specific case. It is important that firms do not see order qualifiers as inferior, because, as Hill argues, these can lose orders. A firm cannot simply 'skip over' order-qualifying criteria. For example, a PC producer, recognizing that price is an order-winner, cannot skip over order-qualifying criteria of up-to-date technology, delivery and so on in order to reduce prices still further.

	Project	Job	Batch	Line	Continuous process
Order-winning criteria	Delivery quality design capability	Delivery quality design capability	⇔	Price	Price
Qualifying criteria	Price	Price	⇔	Delivery quality design capability	Delivery quality design capability

Note: There are many more order-winning and qualifying criteria than listed – the above list is indicative only. Also, it is important to weight the criteria for specific applications or industries.

Figure 3.12
Linking process choice and order-qualifying/order-winning criteria.

Concerns with the mapping process

Although the mapping process can be useful, there are some problems with it. An excellent critique on this is given by Spring and Boaden (1997). In addition, we would add that it is important not to be too rigid with the use of this framework, for the following reasons:

■ A firm may produce the same type of product for two markets under one process choice. The particular needs of each market may differ even though the process choice is the same. For example, one of the authors acted as a management consultant for a firm producing flight simulator units. The two markets are commercial and military, and the requirements for the two are entirely different in terms of cost, delivery reliability and added features, even though each simulator product would be made under a project process choice. However, under the process choice mapping model we would expect the competitive requirements to be the same because they share the same process choice. But this is not the case.

■ In many environments, order-qualifying and order-winning criteria are often very linked, to the point where they become almost indistinguishable. For example, in the UK's public sector, price has become less of an order qualifier by itself and has been subsumed into a wider set of criteria concerned with perceived overall value, where low cost alone does not secure entry into the market. Hence hospitals will not award contracts on price alone – perceived value and reputation of the supplier are key requirements. Similarly, the 'lowest cost contract award' in public sector activities such as road-building and maintenance no longer view cost as a stand-alone factor. Rather, price is viewed as part of overall perceived value and is one of many important factors on the competitive menu.

- Hill rightly warns that what were once order-winning criteria may, over time, become order-qualifying. This may be especially so where competitors copy the technology or the firm loses control of the differentiating feature. This is where using weightings or scoring the criteria over time is very important.

- One of the key questions in this model is: 'How do products win orders in the market?' Therein lies another problem – products do not win orders, firms do, and they do so in a number of ways, including intangible but powerful factors such as reputation, perceived overall value for money and other subjective, but important, elements to the buying decision.

- The majority of manufacturing in the West is made under batch production and the model does not seem to accommodate this 'middle' path too well.

The model is still important and can clarify what are often difficult strategic decisions, but perhaps a better approach would be to add pre-qualifying criteria, as shown in Figure 3.13.

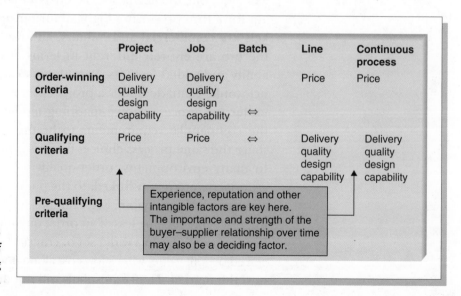

Figure 3.13
The importance of pre-qualifying criteria.

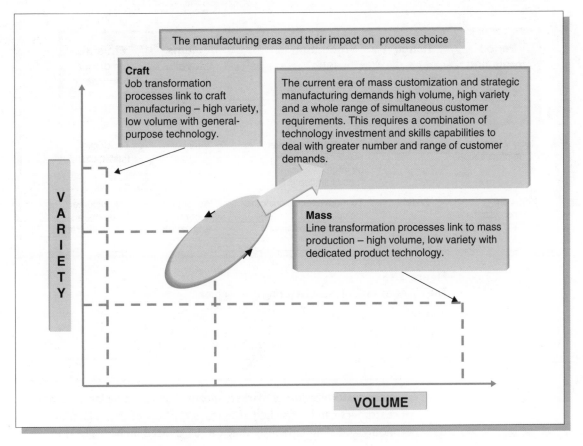

The manufacturing eras and their impact on process choice

Craft
Job transformation processes link to craft manufacturing – high variety, low volume with general-purpose technology.

The current era of mass customization and strategic manufacturing demands high volume, high variety and a whole range of simultaneous customer requirements. This requires a combination of technology investment and skills capabilities to deal with greater number and range of customer demands.

Mass
Line transformation processes link to mass production – high volume, low variety with dedicated product technology.

VARIETY

VOLUME

Figure 3.14
The manufacturing eras and their impact on process choice.

The impact of manufacturing eras on process choice

Thus far we have linked process choice to types of layout and then indicated how each process choice links to the others. We can take this one stage further by mapping the previous and current eras of manufacturing on to types of process choice, as shown in Figure 3.14.

The 'traditional' line process, which mass-produced one product in high volume, clearly fails to meet the requirement of variety. This changes the demands on manufacturing, as summarized in Figure 3.15.

Mass customization

Mass customization is not a specific type of process type; it depends fundamentally upon the transformation process. Davis (1987, p. 169)

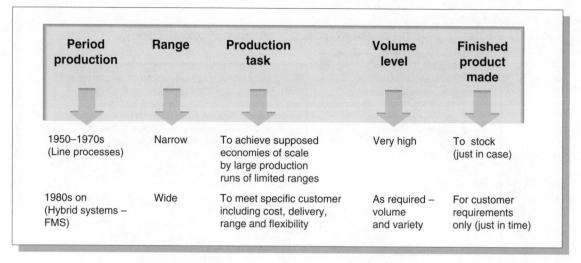

Period production	Range	Production task	Volume level	Finished product made
1950–1970s (Line processes)	Narrow	To achieve supposed economies of scale by large production runs of limited ranges	Very high	To stock (just in case)
1980s on (Hybrid systems – FMS)	Wide	To meet specific customer including cost, delivery, range and flexibility	As required – volume and variety	For customer requirements only (just in time)

Figure 3.15
The changing task of manufacturing management.

coined the term mass customization and stated:

> … mass customization of markets means that the same large number of customers can be reached as in mass markets of the industrial economy, and simultaneously they can be treated individually as in customized markets of pre-industrial economies.

In essence, this present era of mass customization combines the best of the craft era, where products were individualized but at high cost, with the best of mass production, where products were affordable but highly standardized (Fralix, 2001).

Mass customization firms comprise a diverse range of products and services, and cannot be identified as a homogeneous group. Lampel and Mintzberg (1996) illustrate the range of offers from 'pure standardization' to 'pure customization' as in Figure 3.16.

Customer involvement in the production process is argued to be one of the defining characteristic of mass customization. Mass customization overcomes what has typically been seen as a trade-off between volume and variety. It achieves this in a number of ways, such as flexible manufacturing and agile production, which we discuss below. MacCarthey *et al.* (2003) suggest that there are actually five basic ways in which mass customization can be achieved, derived

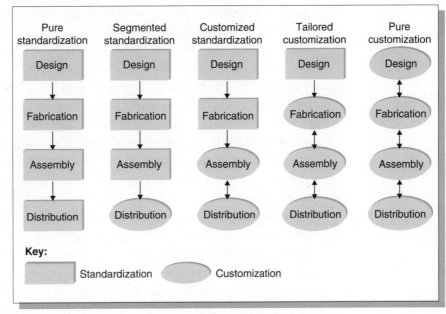

Figure 3.16 From 'pure standardization' to 'pure customization' (adapted from Lampel and Mintzberg, 1996).

from how six key operations processes are configured. The six key processes are:

1 Product development and design.
2 Product validation or manufacturing engineering (translates product design into a bill of materials and set of manufacturing processes).
3 Order taking and co-ordination.
4 Order fulfilment management (schedules activities within the operation).
5 Order fulfilment realization (manages actual production and delivery).
6 Post-order processes (such as technical assistance, warranties and maintenance).

As we have already seen, job shops make to order and line production tends to make to stock. Within some of the six processes outlined above, firms also have a choice. Thus, product development and design can be carried out before any orders are taken or in response to orders. Likewise, product validation can be established in advance or modified in relation to orders. Finally, order fulfilment realization capability can be fixed or modifiable. Hence, twelve different combinations of these are theoretical feasible, although some are mutually exclusive. For instance, if the product range is designed prior to orders being taken, it is not necessary to have modifiable product validation nor to have flexible order fulfilment realization.

Pine (1992) argues that mass production created economies of scale, whilst mass customization is based on economies of scope. So far, the approaches discussed above, such as JIT, achieve the efficiencies of mass production (volume) whilst accommodating a wide product range. But Pine (1992) goes on to suggest that 'the best method for achieving mass customization is by creating modular components that can be configured into a wide variety of end products and services'. Such standardization of parts not only reduces production costs and increases customizable output, it also reduces new product development time and accommodates short life cycles. Take-home pizza delivery has used this approach for years. The typical menu offers a range of standard pizzas using specific ingredients, but these can be customized by the consumer, who can request any one or more of these ingredients to be added to any one of the standard pizzas. So, from a range of, say, ten pizzas and less than a hundred ingredients, literally thousands of different pizzas can be produced. Other examples of this approach include house paint mixed to customer specification at point-of-sale, Black & Decker power tools, Wendy's hamburger chain, Lutron Electronics lighting equipment and Komatsu heavy equipment.

Pine (1992), building on work by Abernathy and Utterbuck (1978) and Ulrich and Tung (1991), outlines six kinds of modularity. They are not mutually exclusive and may be combined together within one operation. The six forms are:

1　*Component-sharing modularity.* This refers to the same component being used in multiple products, thereby reducing inventory costs and simplifying production. Forte Posthouse Hotels have recently redesigned the menus in their different restaurant concepts, so that the product range continues to offer a wide range of dishes, but the number of ingredients needed to make these has been reduced from over 4000 to around 1000.

2　*Component-swapping modularity.* In this instance, as opposed to different products sharing the same components (as above), the same products have different components in order to differentiate or customize them from each other. The classic example of this is Swatch, who produces a range of standard watches, but with a wide range of colours and faces.

3　*Cut-to-fit modularity.* This modularity is based around the ability to adapt or vary a component to individual needs and wants, within preset or practical limits. Pine (1992) exemplifies this through Custom Cut Technologies, who make clothing to fit; National Bicycle Industrial Co., who can produce over 11 million variations on 18 models; Peerless Saw, who use lasers to vary the dimensions of any saw.

4 *Mix modularity.* This modularity is based on the concept of a recipe, so that components, when mixed together, become something different. This can be applied to paints, fertilizer, restaurant menu items, breakfast cereals and any other process in which ingredients are mixed.

5 *Bus modularity.* This is based around the concept of a standard structure to which different components can be added. The obvious example of this is the lighting track, to which different light fittings can be attached. The term 'bus' derives from the electronics industry, which uses this as the base from which computers and other electronic devices are built up. This type of modularity allows 'variations in the type, number and location of modules that can plug into the product'.

6 *Sectional modularity.* This type of modularity is based on different types of components fitting together in any number of possible ways through the use of standard interfaces. Lego building blocks are the classic example of this. Whilst this achieves the greatest degree of variety and customization, it is the most difficult to achieve. Few products are as simple as Lego blocks (or as precisely dimensioned – total interchangeability requires very high precision manufacturing of the basic 'building blocks'), but examples include: Bally Engineered Structures (who use a standard panel to produce many different forms of refrigeration unit); Agfa Corporation's system for handling all forms and sizes of information; and American Express (who capture each transaction so that they may offer personalized products and services to match the buying needs and buying power of their customers).

Gilmore and Pine (1997) mention 'four faces of customization': collaborative (designers working closely with customers); adaptive (where standard products are changed by customers during use); cosmetic (where packaging of standard products is unique for each customer); and transparent (where products are modified to specific individual needs). By contrast, Lampel and Mintzberg (1996) discuss a continuum of various mass customization strategies, including different configurations of processes (from standard to customized), product (from commodities to unique) and the nature of the customer transaction process (from generic to personalized).

Da Silveira *et al.* (2001) provide a useful summary of perceived requirements for *mass customization*. These are:

1 Customer demand for variety and customization must exist.
2 Market conditions must be appropriate.
3 The value chain should be ready.
4 Technology must be available.
5 Products should be customizable.
6 Knowledge must be shared.

Undoubtedly, mass customization presents firms with a number of challenges. Zipkin (2001) categorizes three types of challenge:

1 *Elicitation.* The requirement of an elaborate system for eliciting customers needs and wants. Zipkin argues that capturing customer input into the production process can prove difficult.
2 *Process flexibility.* The requirement of highly flexible production technology. Zipkin argues that developing such technologies can be expensive and time-consuming.
3 *Logistics.* The requirement of a strong direct-to-customer logistics system. Zipkin argues that processing and tracking individual customer orders through the supply chain presents a variety of challenges.

Case: Mass customization

At a factory in Wichita, Kansas, run by the Cessna aircraft company, a gleaming new Citation Excel executive jet rolls off the production line roughly every 3 days. While they may look almost identical, virtually every aircraft, which sell for an average of about $10 million and are assembled from about 30 000 parts, is different, depending on the requirements of the customer.

The production line at Cessna – which is part of the Textron industrial conglomerate – is a good example of the trend in much of industry towards mass customization. This term was introduced in the early 1990s to describe how manufacturers can satisfy customer demand for product variants by introducing them into traditional factories. But they don't sacrifice manufacturing efficiencies, the absence of which can push up costs and make the company uncompetitive.

According to a seminal paper (Pine *et al.*, 1993) in the *Harvard Business Review*, mass customization requires a dynamic and flexible organization. The authors say 'the combination of how and when they (different production units) make a product or provide a service is constantly changing in response to what each customer wants and needs'. Since this paper was written, more manufacturers have realized they need to introduce variation into production as a way of keeping customers happy – but without returning to employing craftsmen to fashion items in single batches and at astronomic cost.

Cessna has introduced principles of lean manufacturing to speed up production and worker efficiency, while at the same time allowing for a large degree of product variation. Last year Cessna made 81 Excel aircraft, one of the company's best-selling models. This is a five-fold improvement on 1998, since when the number of direct assembly workers has risen two-and-a-half times. In other words, worker productivity over this period has doubled.

Behind the improvement has been a number of changes to the processes on the assembly line involving extra worker training and a reclassification of the 1000 or so individual assembly jobs that it takes to fit the parts together on an individual aircraft. The result is that production variation is catered for by substituting different parts and sub-assembly routines within a mass-production environment. According to Garry Hay, Cessna's Chief Executive, the company's ability to provide a high level of customization without overly pushing up costs is a key factor behind the company's good profits record and its likely increase in sales from $2.8 bn last year to $3.1 bn this year. This is in spite of a cooling of the world economic climate.

Also keen on mass customization is FAG Kugelfischer, a German manufacturer with sales last year of Euros 2.2 bn and which is Europe's second biggest maker of rolling bearings (devices essential to virtually all kinds of rotary motion) after SKF of Sweden. Uwe Loos, FAG's Chief Executive, suggests that how well the company can move in the direction of customized bearings that suit individual tastes will be a key determinant of future earnings growth.

Mr Loos says: 'In the bearings industry globally, 70 per cent of the sales come from standard bearings and just 30 per cent from special or customized bearings. At FAG, the ratio is closer to the other way round – 30 per cent standard and 70 per cent specials – and I want to move the ratio even further, to about 20:80, in the next few years.'

A reason for this goal is that, frequently, the profit margins on special, custom-made bearings are higher than for conventional standard bearings – a factor of their higher price. While the bearings churned out in their hundreds of thousands for car wheels might sell for tens of dollars, a high-tech bearing for a jet engine might cost $15 000.

The interest in mass customization can be seen in FAG's main German ball-bearings plant in Schweinfurt, near Wurzburg. Here, 270 people work using a high level of automated plant to turn out some 13 000 bearings a day, weighing twenty-five tonnes. While the casual observer might imagine the bearings were nearly all the same, in fact each day's output can be divided into 50 to 60 types.

The main components for each bearing – the inner and outer rings, balls and cage to hold the balls in place – are shipped in the correct quantities and dimensions to separate units or cells charged with manufacturing individual product types. As much of the detailed assembly (such as inserting balls inside a pair of inner and outer rings) is left to machinery, it is important to make the machines easy to re-programme to increase their flexibility. That, in turn, allows smaller production runs and a greater degree of product variance without unacceptable increases in costs.

Jens Krohn, FAG manager in charge of the ball-bearings plant, says: 'Increasingly we are trying to reduce the set-up times for the assembly machines, so we can change production more easily in tune with the demands of the market. The goal is to reduce set-up times by 10 per cent a year. In some cases, we can alter machinery (to make different kinds of products) in about 15 minutes when a few years ago it might have taken 2 to 3 hours.'

This kind of change allows it to be more cost-effective to make products in relatively small batches, while it used to be uneconomic to do so.

Source: Mass customization: make every one different. *Financial Times*, 21 May 2002.

Flexible manufacturing

Flexible manufacturing is an element of mass customization and the move towards flexible manufacturing was one of the major competitive advantages of Japanese car manufacturing, subsequently appearing in Western manufacturing. Segments of the car market are fragmenting as customer demands and expectations force firms to provide a wide variety of models. So whereas, at one time, a large producer could have produced 1 million of one model over its product lifetime, by the year 2000 it was rare to exceed 250 000 of a particular model. In consequence, processes that are structured around old-fashioned ideas of economies of scale and inflexible line processes must change to more 'customer-driven' processes, including flexible manufacturing systems. We should not be overly critical of past approaches around line processes; they were state of the art 100 years ago and simply no longer serve the current market requirements. Line processes (mass production) *were* entirely appropriate for past market requirements. As *Industry Week* points out:

> In the early days of the automotive industry, Henry Ford reportedly was able to produce a Model T Ford in less than 56 hours – from the conversion of iron ore into steel and through final assembly operations.

But things have changed dramatically since then (*Industry Week*, 8 June 1998):

> But when a manufacturing organization bases its competitive strategy on offering customers greater product variety, that elevates the level of product and process complexity considerably. … Supporting an endless flow of new products can trigger a chain of effects inside the organization that can burden it to the breaking point.

This is not to say that flexible production leads to a proliferation of complexity in terms of products: the trick is to offer the market 'apparent variety' while reducing it in real terms at the point of operation. This is evident in a reduction in the amount of genuine variation of products offered by manufacturing plants.

This does not mean that there is a return to mass manufacturing with its narrow, dedicated lines. Instead, production has focused on developments around the batch area – creating solutions in which flexible manufacturing systems (FMS) and group technology are employed. FMS and group technology are different approaches, or 'step changes' – not just modifications of 'traditional' batch manufacture. They are major changes whereby both variety and volume may be achieved. The mass production system has had to change to suit a volatile, changing environment with new competitors coming from all over the globe. Where mass production's process 'strategy' emphasized efficiency in production, modern world-class manufacturing firms emphasize product quality, differentiation and any other factor perceived to be important for customers.

Flexible manufacturing and its impact on competitive strategy

Flexible manufacturing can be applied to high- or low-volume batch processes. It is normally applied by installing flexible manufacturing systems (FMS) – groups of machines and other equipment that would usually include the following:

■ A number of workstations, such as computer numerically controlled machines, each performing a wide range of operations.

■ A transport system that will move material from one machine to another; loading and unloading stations where completed or partially completed components will be housed and worked upon.

■ A comprehensive computer control system that will co-ordinate all the activities.

The advantages that FMS can provide go beyond the flexibility of the hardware. The real advantage comes with the plant-specific know-how and enhanced skills that accompany FMS. Consequently, investment in technologies such as computer-integrated manufacture (CIM) and advanced manufacturing technology (AMT) is seen as *strategically* important because it can provide competitive options for the firm (Lei *et al.*, 1996):

> In most cases, AMT investments are irreversible because they are highly specialized, durable, and dependent on the firm's specific operating routines, information flows and knowledge surrounding both product design and process technology. However, the strategic options allowed by AMT help the firm recoup its investment. ... The fragmentation of markets, the development of new market segments or niches, as well as faster design ... all contribute to the need for strategic flexibility. Thus, flexible manufacturing technologies provide a strategic real option ... in which high levels of economies of scope and a 'design for response' capability position the firm to enter a broader range of different markets at its own discretion.

This learning effect is shown in Motorola's AMT investments in the flexible manufacture of components for cellular telephones, which are now being used for other electronic component applications. This is typical of the sort of strategic opportunities that technology investment can present to the firm. As a result, AMT investments can enable the firm to provide a range of products or components based on group technology .or shared design characteristics. This in turn provides strategic options based on economies of scope, rather than economies of scale.

Moreover, investment in FMS and other advanced manufacturing technologies provides strategic scope for the firm (Honeycutt *et al.*, 1993):

> Flexible manufacturers are in a rather interesting position in the market-place. When non-flexible manufacturing firms are asked, 'What business are you in?', they list the products they produce. When flexible manufacturers are asked the same question, they respond, 'Whatever business you want us to be in!' In a rapidly changing market-place, the ability to almost instantly change what the firm can offer its customers can be a formidable competitive weapon.

This has to be treated with some caution: it is clearly not realistic for a firm to claim that it is *any* business that *any* customer wants. Toyota might be able to produce many variations around a single platform but the auto giant could not respond to a customer who asked for, say, an aeroplane or a ship, because Toyota's technology remains focused on car production. So the term 'flexible' has to be seen within product-specific boundaries. (At a corporate group level, however, some technology transfer may enable sister divisions to excel at different products or services. The Toyota group, for example, has a division that makes pre-fabricated houses; Saab makes aircraft as well as cars, and almost every large firm provides some sort of financial services.)

FMS allows the firm to compete on *economies of scope* rather than economies of scale. Because technologies are more flexible, allowing numerous product variations to be made, the overall volume achieved can be almost as great as manufacturing large volumes of standardized products. This means that the basis of competition moves from a strategy of low-priced, commodity products to an emphasis on low-cost special options and customized products.

This profoundly changes the rules of the game. As we saw in Chapter 2, Porter (1980) had stated in *Competitive Strategy* that in order to be profitable, firms were faced with two options: *either* low cost *or* differentiation. This reflected industrial economic theory at the time, but now firms have to compete on both fronts – amongst a range of other customer requirements. Due to the nature of competition, what were once differentiated features, able to provide sustained competitive advantage (for some time at least), have become the 'level playing field' (basic expectation) in many markets. This is because technology is often easy to copy. The computer industry exemplifies this. For years, Apple was able to charge premium prices for its 'differentiated' products. Once others emulated the technology, however, price became critical and the differentiating software became available on all PCs. So neither low cost nor differentiation is sufficient by itself. Instead, a range of new competitive requirements including speed, flexibility and customization, have emerged as the key competitive drivers. Flexibility has become a central capability of world-class manufacturers.

Flexibility has spilled over to customer response times. In the past, in addition to the old 'any colour so long as it's black' mentality in manufacturer's (mass production marketing to an immature market), there was also the mentality of 'you'll have the product when we're ready' (mass production lack of customer orientation). In modern markets, this has had to change, because if the firm does not respond quickly, it must be assumed that another will. Computer-integrated manufacture (CIM), originally a matter of information and control systems linking items of production technology, has grown to embrace electronic data interchange and other information technology tools, including intranets, resulting in the ability to provide greater speed of customer response. *Fortune* magazine (30 March 1998) described how Ford has made great use of intranet:

> Ford Motor's intranet is an example of a bigtime manufacturer getting the technology right. The intranet connects about 120 000 of Ford's computers around the world to Web sites containing proprietary company information such as market research, rankings of suppliers' parts and analyses of competitors' components. The network has enabled Ford to bring new models into full production in 24 months compared with 36 months before. The intranet is expected to save the company billions of dollars during the next few years. Ford plans to use its intranet to move closer to manufacturing on demand, a process that involves co-ordination of delivery and assembly of thousands of components. The company plans to manufacture most of its vehicles on a demand basis by 1999, requiring linking of its 15 000 dealers around the world via its intranet.

Fortune also mentioned how Ford has had to speed up its customer response and provide greater choice for customers simultaneously:

> ... this is all part of a sweeping manufacturing re-engineering process that Ford has undergone in the past couple of years. The results are clear: in 1996 ... it took more than 50 days to get the Mustang of your

choice delivered from the plant to the dealer; today you'll get that Mustang in 15 days. Ford's goal is to manufacture the majority of its vehicles on a demand basis by the end of 1999, with delivery in less than 2 weeks after the order. This would save billions of dollars in current inventory and fixed costs.

The actual arrangement of production cells provides insight into how manufacturing becomes flexible. Flexible manufacturing systems are typically arranged in small, U-shaped cells, as illustrated in Figure 3.17. The reasons for this shape include:

- reduction of space;
- shorter workflow paths;
- increased teamwork and better communication and motivation brought about by seeing a completed product in the cell.

Workers are arranged into teams to operate the cells. A single cell can manufacture, inspect and package finished products or components. Every cell is responsible for the quality of its products and each worker

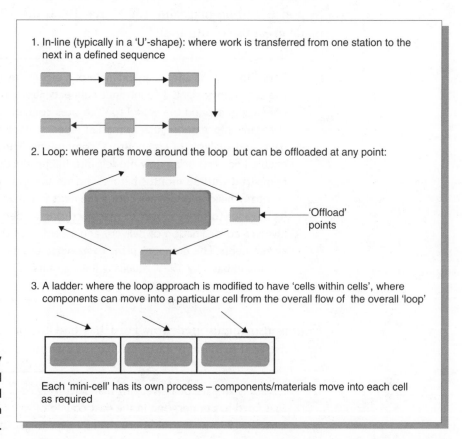

Figure 3.17
Layout of a typical U-line or cell (adapted from Brown, 1996).

will normally be able to perform a range of tasks. Once again, process choice is the key insight in cell arrangements; under line processes, introducing variety or changing the product meant stopping the entire assembly line. Such breakdowns and shortages are very costly overheads for mass-producers, intent on low-cost production. To compensate for this, they have to carry large stocks of parts and spares, 'just-in-case'. We shall discuss the critical importance of just-in-time – which is linked to cell manufacturing – in Chapter 5, but we can say here that stocks of partly finished products also tend to be high under traditional line processes. Components that have undergone part of the production process often sit idle, waiting for the next stage. This is a major source of waste. Large amounts of inventories, some sitting in large warehouses, are a feature of mass production. By contrast, flexible manufacturing, via U-shape cells, and low inventory levels go hand in hand.

Agile production

Like mass customization, agile production is not a particular process choice but it is wholly dependent upon the transformation process for agility to become a reality within the offer to customers. It is clear that we are in an era that has evolved from mass production offering 'any colour of car as long as it is black' to that of customer-centric offerings, as indicated by Ridderstrale and Nordstrom (2000): 'Let us tell you what all customers want. Any customer, in any industry, in any market wants stuff that is both cheaper and better, and they want it yesterday.' This comes under the umbrella of mass customization and agile production. There is some confusion about both of these terms, as Brown and Bessant (2003, p. 708) explain:

> … there seems to be no firm agreement as to the definitions for, and major differences between, the paradigms of *mass customization* and *agile manufacturing*. For example, Feitzinger and Lee (1997) in their discussion on *mass customization* also include 'Agile Supply Networks' as a necessary factor. In addition, Da Silveira *et al.* (2001) mention *agile manufacturing* as a feature within their summary on the literature on *mass customization*. We suggest that although it might be important to understand both, we add that *agile manufacturing* and *mass customization* are not mutually exclusive paradigms. Instead, we argue that *mass customization* is best viewed as a powerful example of a firm's ability to be *agile*.

Bessant *et al.* (2001, p. 31) offer the following definition of *agility*:

> *Agility* in manufacturing involves being able to respond quickly and effectively to the current configuration of market demand, and also to be proactive in developing and retaining markets in the face of extensive competitive forces.

Gunasekaran and Yusuf (2002, p. 1357) add:

> Agile manufacturing can be said to be a relatively new, post-mass-production concept for the creation and distribution of goods and services. It is the ability to thrive in a competitive environment of continuous and unanticipated change and to respond quickly to rapidly changing markets driven by customer-based valuing of products and services. ... It includes rapid product realization, highly flexible manufacturing, and distributed enterprise integration. ... Technology alone does not make an agile enterprise. Companies should find the right combination of strategies, culture, business practices, and technology that are necessary to make it agile, taking into account the market characteristics.

Bessant *et al.* (2001) offer an emerging model of *agile manufacturing capabilities*, consisting of four key interlinked parameters. The four major dimensions of the reference model are:

1 *Agile strategy* – involving the processes for understanding the firm's situation within its sector, committing to *agile* strategy, aligning it to a fast-moving market, and communicating and deploying it effectively.
2 *Agile processes* – the provision of the actual facilities and processes to allow agile functioning of the organization.
3 *Agile linkages* – intensively working with and learning from others outside the company, especially customers and suppliers.
4 *Agile people* – developing a flexible and multi-skilled workforce, creating a culture that allows initiative, creativity and supportiveness to thrive throughout the organization.

Figure 3.18 shows the reference model for agile manufacturing practices.

Further insights are provided by understanding the configurations and dimensions of agility and some of the theoretical underpinnings. Figure 3.19 shows the dimensions of agility.

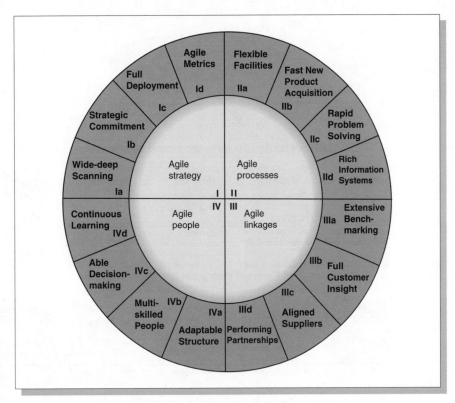

Figure 3.18
A reference model for agile manufacturing practices (from Bessant *et al.*, 2001).

Of course, there is considerable overlap between mass customization and agile practices, and one will feed the other. It is best, therefore, not to see these paradigms as conflicting and competing approaches to 'best practice', but rather as complementary sets of skills and abilities that need to be in place for today's highly competitive and demanding conditions.

Putting it all together

There are no hidden secrets to running successful transformation processes in either manufacturing or service settings. There are, of course, many companies that will fall into the trap of purchasing 'instant solutions' via the latest technological offerings. However, these can, at best, mask what are fundamental mistakes in understanding the basics of the transformation processes within organizations. The following, although focused on manufacturing plants, has much that can be applied to service settings as well.

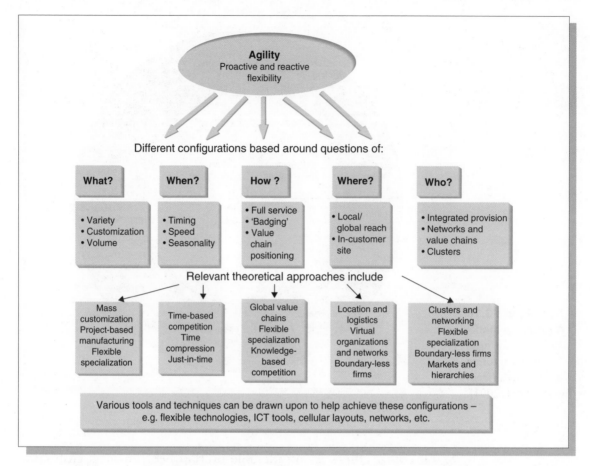

Figure 3.19
The dimensions of agility (adapted from Brown and Bessant, 2003).

Case: How Nissan laps Detroit – its *manufacturing* flexibility makes for a huge advantage over the Big Three

Jonathan Gates slaps a wide slab of tan-coloured, hard foam rubber on his workbench. He fastens a numbered tag in one corner and some black foam insulation at the edges. As soon as he puts a number on the piece of foam, which will become the top of a dashboard for a Nissan Quest minivan, the vehicle has an identity. All of the parts for a big chunk of the minivan's interior, decked out with the customer's choice of colours, fabrics and options, will come together in the next 42 minutes.

Gates and his co-workers fill a crucial role at Nissan Motor Co.'s new Canton (MO) assembly plant: almost everything a driver touches inside a new Quest, Titan pickup or Armada sport-utility vehicle is put together in a single module, starting at Gates's workbench. 'This is the most important job,' he says. And yet, amazingly, Gates doesn't even work for Nissan. He works for Lextron/Visteon Automotive Systems, a parts supplier that also builds the centre console between the front seats and a sub-assembly of the car's front end. The finished modules pass over a wall to be bolted into a car or truck body rolling down the assembly line. Lextron/Visteon does the work faster than Nissan could and pays $3 an hour less than the carmaker pays assembly workers. Nissan is using a similar strategy for its vehicle frames, seats, electrical systems and completed doors.

It's a level of efficiency that Detroit auto makers are only beginning to attempt. Along with other features in Nissan's 8-month-old, $1.4 billion factory, the wholesale integration of outside suppliers is another reason why

General Motors, Ford and Chrysler are still playing catch-up with Japanese car manufacturers. The Big Three have made great strides in productivity in recent years: General Motors Corp.'s best plants now actually beat Toyota's factories. But overall, every time Detroit gets close, the competition seems to get a little better. 'The Japanese are continually improving,' says Michael Robinet, Vice-President of CSM Worldwide, an industry consultant.

Nissan has been the best example of that in North America for years. The Canton plant was designed with the same flexibility, shopfloor smarts and management-dominated work rules that made Nissan's 20-year-old plant in Smyrna, TN, the most productive factory in North America year after year, according to Harbour & Associates. The Smyrna plant builds a car in just under 16 labour hours – six fewer than the average Honda or Toyota plant, eight fewer than GM and ten fewer than Ford. Its profit per vehicle of $2069 is the best in North America.

The Canton plant, which opened in May, will almost certainly top that. Nissan's secret? Sure, its plants use cheaper, non-union labour. Besides lower wages, the Smyrna workers get about $3 an hour less in benefits than Big Three assemblers represented by the United Auto Workers. But there's more to it. Outsourcing offers huge savings, whereas the Big Three must negotiate the outsourcing of sub-assembly work with the union. And Nissan's plants are far more flexible in adjusting to market twists and turns. Canton can send a minivan, pickup truck and sport-utility vehicle down the same assembly line, one after the other, without interruption.

Manoeuvring room

The payoff: Nissan plans to build an impressive five different models in the Canton plant. And, like Toyota and Honda, Nissan will have more financial room to manoeuvre as it pushes aggressively into segments like pick-ups and SUVs. That is already putting pressure on Detroit's few remaining areas of dominance. When it launched the new Titan pickup this November, Nissan set the price at $22 000, undercutting the Ford F-150 by at least $2000 while still maintaining a healthy profit margin.

At first glance, a Nissan factory does not look much different than one you would see in Detroit or St Louis. But talk to the workers and it soon becomes clear how relentlessly the company squeezes mere seconds out of the assembly process. 'There's no silver bullet,' says Emil E. Hassan, Nissan's Senior Vice-President of Manufacturing. 'It's really just following up every day with improvements.'

On the Smyrna passenger-car line, for instance, a worker stands on a moving platform, called a lineside limo, that inches along the body of an Xterra SUV. The limo carries all the tools and parts he needs. The assembler grabs a seat belt from a bin next to him, bolts it in, then moves along and installs the rear struts – all without having to make what used to be a twenty-foot walk back and forth, three times per car. Nissan started installing lineside limos 13 years ago at the suggestion of a line worker; GM and other auto makers also use these limos, but not as extensively. 'We don't have to do a lot of walking,' says Smyrna Vice-President of Manufacturing Gregory Daniels.

Still, there are some big differences between domestic and foreign plants in the USA. The United Auto Workers is slowly allowing more outsourcing. But the UAW wants to outsource work only to union-friendly suppliers. And even then it has to be negotiated. Nissan, meanwhile, has free rein to outsource jobs. Two of Smyrna's vehicles – the Maxima and Altima sedans – were engineered to be built using modules built by suppliers. Every vehicle built in Canton was designed that way. All together, buying modules saves 15–30 per cent on the total cost of that section of the car, according to the Center for Automotive Research (CAR) in Ann Arbor, MI. And the Big Three? GM is the most 'modular' of the domestic manufacturers, but only a few of its plants have been designed to build cars using many big modules.

Making headway

One of the biggest advantages the Japanese have is that they can keep their plants busy pretty much no matter how the market shifts. In Nissan's case, if demand for the Titan surges it could cut production of, say, slower-moving Altima sedans. That means its workers are rarely idle and the company doesn't need rebates to keep its plants busy. This flexibility means that Nissan, Toyota and Honda all run their plants at 100 per cent capacity or higher, once overtime is figured in. GM, Ford and Chrysler, on the other hand, use about 85 per cent. 'The key to making money in this business is running plants at 100 per cent capacity,' says Sean McAlinden, Chief Economist with CAR.

Toyota is probably the most flexible auto maker in North America, according to Prudential Securities Inc., with five of its seven North American assembly lines building more than one vehicle. When Canton starts building the Altima, three of Nissan's four lines will be fully flexible. What that means on the factory floor is that Canton's body shop can weld any of four vehicles – two SUVs, a pickup and a minivan – on the same line. Robotic arms can be quickly programmed to weld in the spots needed for different vehicles.

Detroit is slowly making headway. Prudential says half of GM's 35 North American assembly lines can make multiple vehicles. GM's 2-year-old Cadillac plant in Lansing, MI, will make three luxury vehicles – the CTS and STS sedans and SRX SUV. It has also been designed to get some large, preassembled modules from suppliers. GM is using the Cadillac plant as a model for upgrading other plants. 'We're getting much more flexible,' says Gary L. Cowger, President of GM North America.

But it's much easier to design a new factory to be flexible from the ground up than to refurbish those built 30 or more years ago. And with so much excess capacity, the Big Three have no room to build new plants. Even if they could match the Japanese in productivity, they would have to account for the costs of laid-off workers, whose contracts entitle them to 75 per cent of their pay.

By contrast, Nissan runs a tight ship and works its employees harder. During the UAW's failed attempt to organize Smyrna in 2001, workers told the union that line speeds were too fast and people were getting injured, says Bob King, the UAW's Vice-president of Organizing. The union says that, in 2001, Nissan reported 31 injuries per 1000 workers – twice the average at Big Three plants – according to logs reported to the Occupational Safety and Health Administration.

Squeaks and rattles

Nissan does not dispute the OSHA figures, but it denies its assembly lines are any less safe than Detroit's. Although the company won't release current numbers, executives do say that they have taken steps to reduce injuries. For instance, the company has workers do four different jobs during a typical 8-hour shift, to try to cut down on repetitive-motion injuries. Nissan claims that injury rates have fallen 60 per cent in the past 2 years.

As for the finished product, the real test is still to come for Nissan. The company has yet to prove that the popularity of its Altima and G35 Infiniti sedans can carry over to minivans, big pickups and big SUVs. The company's quality rating is below average, and critics say the Quest has squeaks and rattles that need to be worked out at the factory. Trucks are Detroit's last bastion of dominance, and it will fight to maintain an edge. But at least in terms of efficiency, each new Nissan is rolling off the line with a huge headstart.

A second wave of efficiency

Here's how Nissan pushes its productivity edge at auto factories in Canton, MI and Smyrna, TN:

- *Body shop*. Nissan can weld bodies for different cars and trucks using the same machines. Computer-controlled robots quickly change weld points to adjust.
- *Paint shop*. Nissan's plants have highly automated processes to paint all kinds of vehicles one after the other, with no downtime for reconfiguration.
- *Outsourcing*. Nissan uses lower wage suppliers to build the frame, dashboard and seats. They are shipped right to the assembly line.
- *A moving stage*. Assembly workers can stand on a 'lineside limousine', which moves them, their tools and parts along with the car. That eliminates having to walk back and forth to the parts bins and tool racks.
- *Elbow grease*. Nissan works its staff hard. Critics say injury rates are high, though Nissan counters that it has been making ergonomic improvements.

Playing catch-up on the factory floor

General Motors has made great strides in efficiency, but Nissan still operates the most efficient auto plant in North America:

Best plants	Hours per vehicle*	Product
Nissan: Smyrna, TN	15.7	Altima, Maxima
GM: Oshawa, Ont. 1	16.4	Chevrolet Monte Carlo, Impala
GM: Oshawa, Ont. 2	17.1	Buick Century, Regal
Worst plants	**Hours per vehicle***	**Product**
Ford: Wixom, MI	44.2	Lincoln Town Car, LS, Ford Thunderbird
Chrysler: St Louis North	33.8	Dodge Ram pickup
GM/Suzuki: Ingersoll, Ont.	29.9	Suzuki Vitara, Chevrolet Tracker

*Average labour hours spent on vehicles made in 2002.

Source: Business Week, 22 December 2003, pp. 58–61.

Summary

- Layout and process choice are of major strategic importance to manufacturing and services operations. The options to choose from are also essentially similar – it's not an infinite variety but a small number of options, and switching between one and the other is by no means cost free – so there is an important strategic objective to align the transformation process with market requirements and to understand the implications of changing.
- The five basic types of process choice are project, job, batch, line and continuous process.
- The basic types of layout are fixed, process, hybrid (cell) and product.
- There are links between the layout (the physicality of operations) and process choice (the transformation).
- A process choice will indicate what a firm *can and cannot* do. Process choice may significantly influence what the company sells and what it is able to offer.
- Increasingly, because of the need to satisfy volume and variety requirements, production technology is centred on the middle of the continuum between volume and variety.
- Process technology is not a quick-fix solution and investment must be made alongside skills and capabilities. Any investment has to be made to support the company in its chosen market and should not be at the whim of a particular technical specialist, but should be a holistic decision for the company.
- Vast amounts of investment have been made in some plants with little competitive advantage being gained as a result. However, when appropriate investment is made it should allow the firm to operate at world-class levels, provided that it is used to meet the needs of the markets in which the firm is competing.
- Process technology is a requirement in order to meet the demands of the needs of markets. In order to meet these needs, technology can be used for rapid changeover and set-up times, volume and variety mixes, delivery speed and reliability requirements, and for ensuring process quality. However, technology must not be seen as a replacement for human resource capability.
- Investment in technology is a strategic decision. Investment must be made to enable the firm to support the markets in which the firm is competing.

Key questions

1. Describe how types of layout are often linked to process choice.
2. What clues does process choice provide concerning how a company competes?
3. Why is investment in process technology often a difficult decision to make?

References and further reading

Abernathy, W.J. and Utterbuck, J.M. (1978) Patterns of industrial automation. *Technology Review*.

Bessant, J., Brown, S., Francis, D. and Meredith, S. (2001) Developing manufacturing agility in SMEs. *International Journal of Technology Management*, 28–52.

Brown, S. (1996) *Strategic Manufacturing for Competitive Advantage*. Hemel Hempstead: Prentice Hall.

Brown, S. (1998a) Manufacturing strategy, manufacturing seniority and plant performance in quality. *International Journal of Operations and Production Management,* **18**(6).

Brown, S. (1998b) New evidence on quality in manufacturing plants – a challenge to lean production. *Production and Inventory Management Journal,* **39**(1), 14–22.

Brown, S. and Bessant, J. (2003) The strategy–capabilities link in mass customization. *International Journal of Operations and Production Management,* **23**(7), 707–730.

Business Week, 22 December 2003.

Da Silveira, G., Borenstein, D. and Fogliatto, F.S. (2001) Mass customization: literature review and research directions. *International Journal of Production Economics,* **72**, 1–13.

Davis, S. (1987) *Future Perfect.* Reading, MA: Addison Wesley.

The Economist Manufacturing Technology Survey, 5 March 1994.

The Economist, The celling out of America, 17 December 1994.

The Economist, Technology and unemployment: a world without jobs?, 11 February 1995.

Financial Times, 21 May 2002.

Forbes, Custom-made (PCs made to order), 6 November 1995.

Fortune, 16 November 1992.

Fortune, Ford's intranet success, 30 March 1998.

Fralix, M. (2001) From mass production to mass customization. *Journal of Textile and Apparel, Technology and Management,* **1**(2), 1–7.

Gilmore, J.H. and Pine, J. (1997) Beyond goods and services. *Strategy and Leadership,* **25**(3), 10–18.

Gunasekaran, A. and Yusuf, Y. (2002) Agile manufacturing: a taxonomy of strategic and technological imperatives. *International Journal of Production Research,* **40**(6), 1357–1385.

Hill, T. (1995) *Manufacturing Strategy,* 1st Edition. Basingstoke: Macmillan.

Hill, T. (2000) *Manufacturing Strategy,* 2nd Edition. Basingstoke: Macmillan.

Honeycutt, E.D., Siguaw, J.A. and Harper, S.C. (1993) The impact of flexible manufacturing on competitive strategy. *Industrial Management,* **35**(6), 2–15.

Hutchison, G. and Holland, J. (1982) The economic value of flexible automation. *Journal of Manufacturing Systems,* **1**(2), 215–227.

Industry Week, The search for simplicity, 8 June 1998.

Keller, M. (1993) *Collision.* New York: Currency Doubleday.

Kulatilaka, N. (1984) Valuing the flexibility of flexible manufacturing systems. *IEEE Transactions on Engineering Management,* **35**(4), 250–257.

Lampel, J. and Mintzberg, H. (1996) Customizing customization. *Sloan Management Review*, **38**, 21–30.

Lei, D., Hitt, M.A. and Goldhar, J.D. (1996) Advanced manufacturing technology: organizational design and strategic flexibility. *Organization Studies*, **17**(3), 501–524.

Levitt, T. (1972) The production-line approach to service. *Harvard Business Review*, **50**(5), 20–31.

Lovelock, C.H. (1983) Classifying services to gain strategic marketing insights. *Journal of Marketing*, **47**(3), 9–21.

MacCarthey, B., Brabazon, P.G. and Bramham, J. (2003) Fundamental modes of operation for mass customization. *International Journal of Production Economics*, **85**, 289–304.

Monohan, G. and Smunt, T. (1984) The flexible manufacturing system investment decision. *Proceedings of ORSA/TIMS Conference*, November.

Porter, M. (1980) *Competitive Strategy*. New York: Free Press.

Pine, B.J. (1992) *Mass Customization: The New Frontier in Business Competition*. Cambridge, MA: Harvard Business School Press.

Pine, B.J., Victor, B. and Boynton, A. (1993) Making mass customization work. *Harvard Business Review*, September–October.

Ridderstrale and Nordstrom (2000) *Funky Business*. London: FT Books.

Schmenner, R.W. (1986) How can services business survive and prosper? *Sloan Management Review*, **27**(3), 21–32.

Spring, M. and Boaden, R. (1997) One more time: how do you win orders?: a critical reappraisal of the Hill manufacturing strategy framework. *International Journal of Operations and Production Management*, **17**(8).

Starr, M. and Biloski, A. (1984) The decision to adopt new technology. *Omega*, **12**(4), 353–361.

Ulrich, K.T. and Tung, K. (1991) Fundamentals of product modularity. Working Paper No. 3335-91-MSA, Sloan School of Management, MIT.

Willis, R. and Sullivan, K. (1984) CIMS in perspective. *Industrial Engineering*, February, 28–36.

Zipkin, P. (2001) The limits of mass customization. *Sloan Management Review*, **42**(3), 81–87.

CHAPTER 4

Innovation – managing the renewal of the business

Introduction – the innovation imperative

It's a disturbing thought – but the majority of companies have a life span significantly less than that of a human being. Even the largest firms can show worrying signs of vulnerability – for example, of the top names in the *Fortune* 500 list for 1985, less than half were still there by 1995. For the smaller firm, the mortality statistics are even more worrying. For instance, in 2003 over 200 restaurants were declared bankrupt in London alone.

Sometimes it's individual firms which face the problem – sometimes it is whole sectors. We only have to consider the sad fate in the United Kingdom of industries like motorcycles, machine tools, coal mining and toys, to realize how shaky the foundations of most of our industrial base really are. What goes up can come down just as fast.

It is not all doom and gloom though – there are also plenty of stories of new firms and new industries emerging to replace those which die. And in many cases the individual enterprise can renew itself, adapting to its environment and moving into new things. Consider a firm like Nokia – once a humble boot and shoe maker and now the number one player in the global business of mobile telephones. Arie de Geus (for many years the planning director for Shell and responsible for helping that company navigate the turbulent waters of the oil business) cites the example of the Stora company in Sweden, which was founded in the twelfth century as a timber cutting and processing operation but which is still thriving today – albeit in the very different areas of food processing and electronics (de Geus, 1996).

The purpose of this chapter is for the reader to:

- understand the strategic importance of innovation;
- realize that operations management can play a central and pivotal role in the innovation process;
- appreciate how operations 'lines up' within the innovation process.

Business success through rewriting the rules of the game

There are plenty of examples of firms that have made an impact in established sectors through doing something differently – either in what they offer or how they produce that offering. For example:

- Amazon.com revolutionized the world of publishing and bookselling by the early adoption of the Internet as a mechanism for advertising, ordering and distributing books. So successful has the project been that now almost all the major booksellers have added Internet operations to their existing physical bookshops.
- The Body Shop broke new ground in the well-established cosmetics and toiletries field of retailing by a strategy based on environmentally friendly products and a strong commitment to international development aid. Again, their success caused other players in the field to alter their own behaviour and to produce products and redesign packaging and retailing operations to match.
- Dell Computers have redefined the computer as a consumer product, taking advantage of several technological and social changes. They offer not only a rapid delivery and low price, but also customization – each machine is built to an individual customer specification. Achieving this is done through a mixture of careful modular design and the management of an extended web of outsourced capabilities – in manufacturing, distribution, service, etc. The result is a highly successful mass customizing company that operates from a tiny core – a true virtual business.
- Easyjet have innovated in services with their low-cost scheduled flights (in fact, their in-flight literature includes a detailed description of airline economics and how they have changed the rules of the game!).

Underpinning all of this is a simple point. Firms need to innovate – to change what they offer and how they produce that offering – to survive. History is very clear on this point; survival is not compulsory, but those enterprises that do survive and grow do so because they are capable of regular and focused change. It is worth noting that Microsoft – currently one of the biggest and most successful companies in the world – takes the view that it is always only 2 years away from extinction!

On the plus side, innovation can be about more than simple survival – it is also strongly associated with growth. New business is created by new ideas, by the process of creating competitive advantage in what a firm can offer. Economists have argued for decades over the exact nature of the relationship, but they are generally agreed that innovation accounts for a sizeable proportion of economic growth in a country or at the level of the firm. Marx called technological change 'the locomotive of growth', whilst Joseph Schumpeter developed a whole school of economic thought based on this principle (Schumpeter, 1950). More recently, studies by the OECD have highlighted the strong correlation between innovation and economic growth.

This chapter explores the challenge of innovation, arguing that it is not a luxury or optional extra but a core part of what the organization does. Managing this central process of renewal is one of the most important challenges facing the strategic operations manager.

Looking back ...

Perhaps the most telling difference between past approaches to innovation and the present day is provided by the eminent management writer, Peter Drucker (*Business 2.0*, 22 August 2000), who describes how:

> My ancestors were printers in Amsterdam from 1510 or so until 1750 ...
> *and during that entire time they didn't have to learn anything new.*

Drucker is not being critical of his ancestors, nor is he accusing them of not being innovative, nor is he stating that such an approach was 'wrong'. Indeed, it might well be argued that in previous times such an approach would have been entirely appropriate. The issue is: in today's competitive arena it is not appropriate.

Innovation has been with us since the earliest days, when our ancestors began experimenting with different ways of hunting, of fighting, of cooking and generally trying to survive in the hostile prehistoric environment. New tools, new materials, new methods – all of these things on which our civilization was founded did not happen by accident but by a gradual process of learning and capturing of knowledge. History is punctuated by periods in which new ideas drove society forwards – for example, the Renaissance or the Industrial Revolution – and it is clear that technological change continues to be a powerful force in all aspects of our lives.

Whilst innovation has been the mainspring of development in society, our understanding of it has, until recently, been somewhat poorly developed. Much thinking assumed relatively simplistic and linear models of the process – for example, that all it takes is a good idea for successful innovation. Emerson's famous quote about the world beating a path to the door of the inventor of the better mousetrap has never really been a good description of what actually happens in innovation – but that has not stopped many people trying and failing to introduce new ideas.

Innovation today

Our view of innovation today no longer sees it as an occasional event but a core part of what organizations do to survive. Nor is it the province of a few gifted specialists – it is too important to be left to them. Rather it is at the heart of what organizations do to renew themselves in terms of what they offer and how they create and deliver that offering. For this reason, it is of central concern to strategic operations managers whose role is co-ordinating the development and deployment of capabilities that make innovation happen.

It will be worth spending a little time looking in more detail at what innovation involves, and from that identifying the key levers with which we can try and manage the process.

What is innovation?

Innovation can take many forms. It could be in the equipment used to produce the product or service, or it could be in the way in which the process is organized and structured. It could be in the repositioning of an existing idea – for example, an established product in a new market. (Think about the cellular phone, originally sold as a business tool but with suitable packaging and advertising now sold to concerned parents as a safety aid to give to their children when out alone at night.) The case of McDonald's expanding internationally into such diverse markets as France, China and the Middle East demonstrates the extent to which global brands need not adapt to reflect local needs. Likewise, Harley-Davidson motorcycles have had great success in selling their products to the 50+ age group. And occasionally it can involve a complete reframing of the way in which we see the world – a 'paradigm shift'. The transition to steam power and mechanization underpinning the first Industrial Revolution, the emergence of mass transportation with the railways and the motor car and, more recently, the radical changes in computing and communications are all examples of this kind of innovation.

Transforming industries through innovation

Two examples of recent innovations that are likely to transform industries or whole segments of society will be considered. The first is in the field of music, where the complex web of products and services involved from creating and performing and the accompanying recording and distribution now represents one of the world's biggest industries. Much of this has grown up around the physical capture and distribution of music on a variety of media – from graphite cylinders, through to vinyl discs, magnetic tape and, most recently, various forms of laser-written discs. Around this set of technologies an industry grew up to control the production and distribution of music – and collect revenues from its sale. But now, with the advent of the Internet and with technologies like MP3 that enable anyone to create and distribute music – and indeed to copy and pirate it! – the foundations of this industry are beginning to shake. It is not clear who will be the eventual 'winners' in this process – needless to say the major music industry players are taking the whole challenge very seriously and responding with a mixture of technological and legal changes. But what is clear is that the music business will never be the same again – it is being transformed through innovation.

A second example concerns an everyday object – the light-bulb. Ever since Edison and Swann took the ideas of nineteenth-century physicists and managed to produce a working and reliable light-bulb, we have relied on some variant of their basic device. Whilst bulbs may come in different shapes, sizes, colours and have different energy efficiencies, they are still fundamentally based on glowing filaments in a glass container. But all that is about to change.

Light-emitting diodes (LEDs) are familiar to everyone in the form of little red or green lights that tell us whether our various electrical devices are working. This technology has been around since the 1960s, and is widely used and understood. But most scientists have accepted that it has its limits, one of them being that LEDs can only be made in certain colours – red, orange, yellow and light green. White light – the kind we use in light-bulbs – is made up of many colours and the missing one as far as LEDs was concerned was always blue.

A small chemicals firm in Japan, and a dedicated scientist by the name of Shuji Nakamura, have changed that perception. Twenty years of work and considerable investment by the company in what seemed at the time to be high-risk research is about to transform the electric light industry – because Nichia have developed blue LED technology. More importantly, they have solved the manufacturing problems associated with producing such LEDs successfully, and have moved on to produce prototype light sources. In 1995, they made the first prototype for what will replace Edison's design – a blue diode with a phosphor coating on top of the semiconductors, which converts the frequency of light emitted into white light.

Devices of this kind will use around 85 per cent less power and last sixteen times longer; the market for them is estimated at around £8 bn per year! Nichia invested around £2 m in their original research project on the technology, and the work has led to around 300 patents, which provide them with a significant degree of protection from which to exploit this potential. Once again this demonstrates the potential transformation of an industry through technological innovation.

Changes do not always have to be great leaps forward or involve radical new ideas. Most of the time change is more gradual, moving incrementally forward with a sequence of little, cumulative improvements. For example, although the invention of the electric light-bulb was a dramatic breakthrough, little improvements in the design of the bulb and in the process for manufacturing it led to a fall in price of over 80 per cent between 1880 and 1896. In recent times, the dramatic growth and success of the Japanese car manufacturing industry is primarily the result of a 40-year programme of systematic and continuous improvement of product and process design.

Innovation depends on attitudes to change, as shown in Figure 4.1.

Whatever form it takes, innovation is at least a survival imperative and it can also offer real opportunities for growth. But the choice of whether or not to innovate remains at the level of the individual enterprise.

For some firms the challenge is obvious – take, for example, the printing industry. Here the entire rules of the game are being rewritten – by technological and market changes that have turned the industry

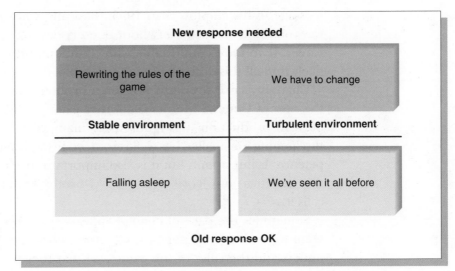

Figure 4.1
Contrasting
attitudes to
innovation.

upside down. Firms that don't recognize the need for change simply disappear – whilst those that recognize that 'we must change' can use this to build new and growing businesses. The kind of transformation described in the box cannot be ignored; firms making light-bulbs need to adapt rapidly to enter the new technology or they will not survive. It is instructive to look, for example, at the names of the firms that were active players in the early days of electronics, when valves were the dominant products. If you compare this list from around 1948 to the list some 6 years later – after the advent of solid-state electronics – there are quite a few omissions. New firms moved into the new technology and exploited the opportunities emerging; older firms often failed to see the change coming or to respond quickly enough (Braun and Macdonald, 1980).

But not all firms recognize the need to change; for some there appears to be security in size or in previous technological success. Take the case of IBM – a giant firm which can justly claim to have laid the foundations of the IT industry and one which came to dominate the architecture of hardware and software and the ways in which computers were marketed. The trouble is that such core strength can sometimes become an obstacle to seeing the need for change – as proved to be the case when, in the early 1990s, the company moved slowly to counter the threat of networking technologies – and nearly lost the business in the process. (In 1993, IBM lost nearly $8 bn and global lay-offs of employees ran close to 100 000. Its subsequent return to good health under a new Chief Executive, ex-consultant Lou Gerstner, is reflected in his public message to his employees in 1993: 'Basically, you need to change the way you think and act, every hour of every day for the rest of your IBM career. If you are comfortable with tradition and procedure, you will likely find all this difficult, if not impossible, to accomplish.')

Changing core strengths is often a problem for large companies – the case of General Motors is another example, where the challenge of 'lean production' was ignored for many years – but it can be life threatening for smaller, less well-resourced firms. Building on 'core competence' is important, but it is also important to remember how easily this can turn into 'core rigidity', as Dorothy Leonard-Barton (1995) calls it.

Sometimes the pace of change appears slow and the old responses seem to work well. It appears, to those within the industry, that they understand the rules of the game and that they have a good grasp of the relevant technological developments likely to change things. But what can sometimes happen here is that change comes along from outside the industry – and by the time the main players inside have reacted it is often too late. For example, in the late nineteenth century there was a thriving industry in New England based upon the harvesting and distribution of ice. In its heyday it was possible for ice harvesters to ship hundreds of tons of ice around the world on voyages that lasted as long as 6 months – and still have over half the cargo available for sale. By the late 1870s, the 14 major firms in the Boston area of the USA were cutting around 700 000 tons per year and employing several thousand people. The industry made use of a variety of novel techniques for cutting, insulating and transporting ice around the world. But the industry was completely overthrown by the new developments that followed from Linde's invention of refrigeration and the growth of the modern cold storage industry. The problem – as Professor Utterback of MIT points out in his book studying a number of industries – is that the existing players often fail to respond fast enough to the new signals coming from outside their industry. Yet three-quarters of the industry-changing innovations that he examined originated from outside the industry itself! (Utterback, 1994).

Other examples of this kind of change include:

- The shift from valve to solid-state electronics (where few of the original producers and especially the industry leader, RCA, were able to make the transition).
- The emergence of digital watches (which nearly destroyed the traditional Swiss watch industry).

■ The emergence of low-cost airlines has led to several major airlines declaring, or being close to declaring, bankruptcy. Whilst traditional airlines, so-called 'flag carriers' such as British Airways and KLM, have experienced falls in passenger demand, budget operators such as Ryanair and Easyjet have experienced significant growth.

■ In the UK, McDonald's entered the market in 1974, but most restaurant operators with hamburger-based products did not adopt their process technology (which puts the fast in fast food) until the mid-1980s, by which time McDonald's was already close to achieving dominance in the market-place.

■ Currently, Kodak is facing a major challenge as the traditional fields in which it has been strong give way to completely new technologies – and unless the company can succeed in re-inventing itself as a digital image operation rather than a mechanical and physical chemistry firm, its survival may be in doubt.

Of course, for others these conditions provide an opportunity for moving ahead of the game and writing a new set of rules. The case of banking is an example; for many years the banking industry in the UK was a relatively stable environment. Small changes took place but each of the major players kept up and maintained their market shares. But in the 1980s, following developments that had radically shaken up the insurance industry, one or two banks began to rewrite the rules of the game by introducing telephone banking services backed up by sophisticated information technology systems. The results, as far as the customers were concerned, were massive improvements in perceived levels of service; no longer did they have to wait until the banks were open but instead they had 24-hour access every day of the year. The range of services that could be offered was increased so that the telephone became a 'one-stop shop' for a range of banking and other financial services. And, as far as the banks were concerned, the reduction in their cost base was enormous, switching from an expensive physical infrastructure with branches on the streets of most towns and many staff to run these, to a streamlined and professional call centre in one city handling all the business in the UK. So innovation is not a luxury or an optional extra – it is essential to the firm's survival. But simply changing things for their own sake is not necessarily the answer. The problem with innovation is that it is uncertain – by its nature, it involves risks and there are no guarantees of success. This makes its *management* a primary strategic task for the enterprise.

Innovation as a process

If someone asked you 'when did you last use your Spengler?', they might well be greeted by a quizzical look. But if they asked you when you last used your 'Hoover' – the answer would be fairly easy. Yet it was not Mr Hoover who invented the vacuum cleaner in the late nineteenth century but one J. Murray Spengler. Hoover's genius lay in taking that idea and making it into a commercial reality. In similar vein, the father of the modern sewing machine was not Mr Singer, whose name jumps to mind and is emblazoned on millions of machines all round the world. It was Elias Howe who invented the machine in 1846 and Singer who brought it to technical and commercial fruition. (Of course, not all great entrepreneurs put their own name to someone else's invention. For instance, it was Ray Kroc that made the restaurant concept invented by the McDonald brothers what it is today.)

Perhaps the godfather of them all in terms of turning ideas into reality was Thomas Edison, who during his life registered over 1000 patents. Products for which his organization was responsible include the light-bulb, 35-mm cinema film and even the electric chair. Many of the inventions for which he is famous were not in fact invented by him – the electric light-bulb, for example – but were developed and polished technically and their markets opened up by Edison and his team. More than anyone else, Edison understood that invention is not enough – simply having a good idea is not going to lead to its widespread adoption and use. Much has to be done – the 99 per cent perspiration in his famous dictum – to make ideas into successful reality. His skill in doing this created a business empire worth, in 1920, around $21.6 billion. He put to good use an understanding of the interactive nature of innovation, realizing that both technology push (which he systematized in one of the world's first organized R&D laboratories) and demand pull need to be mobilized.

Take the light-bulb, for example. To bring that to fruition required enormous technical development on both the product and the process to produce it at the right cost and quality, and it required the creation and development of a market into which it could be sold. But Edison also recognized that, although the electric light-bulb was a good idea, it had little practical relevance in a world where there was no power point to plug it into. Consequently, his team set about building up an entire electricity generation and distribution infrastructure, including designing lamp stands, switches and wiring. In 1882, he switched on the power from the first electric power generation plant in Manhattan and was able to light up 800 bulbs in the area. In the years that followed he built over 300 plants all over the world.

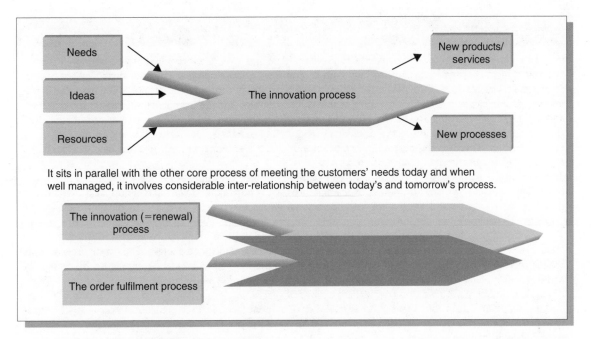

Figure 4.2
The process of innovation.

In other words, invention is just the first step along an extended process of translating ideas into reality and it is of central concern in operations management. Innovation can thus be represented as a process – a sequence of activities which lead to an outcome. In the organization it is a core process concerned with renewal – translating ideas and resources into new products and processes that will underpin the future of the business, as shown in Figure 4.2.

It is a process triggered by many things, but these stimuli can be resolved into two components – pull and push. The 'push' comes from the gradual accumulation of ideas through technological research and development; these create a range of opportunities that might be exploited in new or improved products or processes. The 'pull' comes from the influence of different kinds of demand (market, social, regulatory, etc.) that bring new responses – essentially the 'necessity is the mother of invention' model. Arguments have raged between those who see one or the other as the prime driver of change; experience tells us that, whilst the balance may vary widely under different circumstances, both are involved in triggering innovation. One of the most helpful analogies is that of the blades of a pair of scissors – both need to work together to ensure that cutting takes place. The challenge for the firm is to pick up these signals and respond to them to create relevant new responses and exploit relevant new opportunities.

Case example: the pre-filled drinking glass

In 1973, an inventor patented the concept of a pre-filled glass and in 1990 approached a West London firm specializing in flight catering for airlines to help with its commercial development. The standard inflight approach to drinks service is to serve the passenger a glass and a separate miniature bottle of spirits. The patented product was a tumbler pre-filled with a measure of spirits. This tumbler is made from a high-quality plastic that feels and looks like glass. Around the inside, a few millimetres from the base, is a rim to which is attached a foil disc, thereby sealing the alcohol inside the tumbler. A strip up and over the side of the glass allows the seal to be removed when served to the customer. For promotional and identification purposes, the seal has the name and logo of the spirit in the tumbler printed on it.

The design not only enables the spirit to be packaged but also the tumblers to be stacked one inside the other. This provides two key advantages over miniatures – it is both space-saving and lighter than the conventional approach. Space and weight are key operational issues for airlines in order to maximize passenger capacity and minimize fuel consumption. The stackable, pre-filled glass takes up the same amount of space as a conventional glass, but without the need to stock, handle and dispose of miniature bottles of spirit.

This new product concept was easy to describe, but technically difficult to achieve. The major problem was sealing the foil disc to the inside rim. Both the sealant and the foil had to be strong enough to be rigorously handled whilst being transported to the point of sale and distributed to customers. A great deal of investigation and experimentation went in to alternative types of seal, which is now subject to patent protection.

But even when this problem was overcome, the development faced further problems in turning the prototype product into one that could be mass-produced. To make the pre-filled glass commercially, the process had to be automated along production-line principles. This meant tumblers had to be moved along a line for filling with spirit before being sealed. But the seal was ineffective if the rim was contaminated by alcohol. The need to ensure a dry rim radically affected the speed of the line and the method of dispensing the alcohol, and consequently the unit cost of production. Then, in 1995, it was found that the shelf-life of spirits stored in this way was only 6 months, considerably shorter than bottled storage. This lead to a further redesign of the adhesion of the foil seal, in order to make it more airtight.

Even after these technical problems were overcome, the pre-filled drinking glass did not go in to commercial production. Airlines and other potential users of the product, such as railway caterers and vending machine operators, saw the advantages of the product, but also some difficulties with its use. For instance, there were service problems on aircraft if passengers wanted ice and lemon with their drink; some passengers ask for miniature spirits on board for consumption after the flight is over; and distillers like their miniatures on aircraft as they see it as a major form of product placement. Trials on the ground by one caterer were highly satisfactory, but bar staff were highly resistant to the product, claiming the seals were too easily broken and that customers did not like the pre-filled glass. Such resistance might have been due to the fact that stock security was greatly improved by using this instead of miniatures!

Hence caterers were reluctant to commit themselves to this revolutionary product, with its many desirable features. But large-scale commitment was necessary if the product was to be produced commercially. Four assembly lines producing 8 million pre-filled tumblers a year would only be twice as expensive to set up as one line predicting only 2 million units. Such economies of scale could not be ignored. Twenty-five years after its invention, and with more than 5 years of product testing and development, along with considerable investment, the tumbler was still not in production.

Innovation and operations management

As we saw above, innovation is a risky and uncertain process, but it can be managed. At its heart it is about disposing resources and controlling activities – in other words, it's about operations management. It may seem somewhat strange since 'mainstream' operations management is often preoccupied with capacity, with production flow and control, and other themes – but managing innovation is fundamentally about the same set of challenges – of co-ordination and disposition.

Indeed, we could argue that one reason why innovation is often poorly managed in organizations is precisely because of a *lack* of an integrated operations management perspective. There is a tendency to see it in limited terms and to manage that bit of it well – but at the expense of the bigger picture. For example, if innovation is viewed simply as invention, then firms will tend to organize and manage it as if R&D (the part of the firm associated with generating ideas) is all that matters. But unless we connect these ideas to other parts of the firm – the marketing, the production, the quality, etc. – then the chances are that we will end up with a better mousetrap that nobody wants and that we can't make in volume.

Similarly, if we only see it as a demand-led process where signals from the market pull through innovations, then we risk the danger of only offering me-too products and of failing to lead. One of the most famous examples here would be the Sony Walkman – a product for which no market existed and about which the marketing department were deeply sceptical during the early days of development! (Nayak and Ketteringham, 1986).

Table 4.1 indicates some of the problems of managing with only a partial view of what innovation process involves.

So what is needed in successful innovation management is a strategic, integrative and systemic approach. Before we look at how this might be achieved, it will be worth reminding ourselves about *what* has to be managed. In process terms, we need to look at the structure of the process itself, the inputs/outputs that are involved and the factors that can influence in positive or negative fashion the workings of the process. Figure 4.3 provides a simple process model of these factors.

A key issue for us is that, although a number of important contributions to the literature see innovation as a strategic issue (e.g. Hamel, 2001; Christensen, 1997; Henderson and Clark, 1990; Nelson and Winter, 1982; Tushman and Anderson, 1987; Utterback, 1994), we suggest that the specific role of operations is underplayed in much of the literature. Of course, it is axiomatic that operations personnel will be involved in innovation simply due to the fact that they will be charged with producing or assembling the new product. But the assertion that operations personnel should be involved in innovation, particularly with new product development, is not enough because the specific role and contribution from operations personnel in

Table 4.1

Problems of partial views of innovation

If innovation is only seen as	The result can be
Being good at invention – and therefore having strong R&D capability	Technology which fails to meet user needs and may not be accepted
The province of specialists in white coats in the R&D laboratory	Lack of involvement of others, and a lack of key knowledge and experience input from other perspectives
Meeting customer needs – and therefore emphasizing good market research and hearing 'the voice of the customer'	Lack of technical progression, leading to inability to gain competitive edge
Technology advances	Producing products which the market does not want or designing processes which do not meet the needs of the user and which are opposed
The province only of large firms (with the resources to carry through technological and market research)	Weak small firms with too high a dependence on large customers
Only about 'breakthrough' changes	Neglect of the potential of incremental innovation. Also an inability to secure and reinforce the gains from radical change because the incremental performance ratchet is not working well
Only associated with key individuals	Failure to utilize the creativity of the remainder of employees, and to secure their inputs and perspectives to improve innovation
Only internally generated	The 'not invented here' effect, where good ideas from outside are resisted or rejected
Only externally generated	Innovation becomes simply a matter of filling a shopping list of needs from outside and there is little internal learning or development of technological competence

innovation is still far from clear in spite of the plethora of articles related to the subject.

One of the key areas of dialogue in the innovation process is between operations and marketing personnel, and the areas of interface between the two is shown in Figure 4.4.

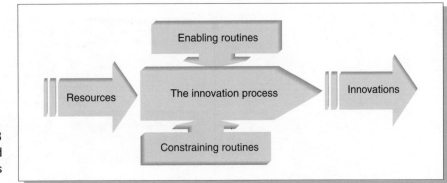

Figure 4.3
Enabling and
constraining factors
in innovation.

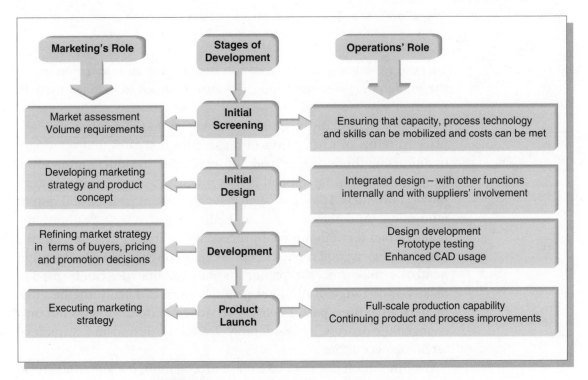

Figure 4.4
The interface between marketing and operations in the innovation process
(adapted from Brown, 2000).

Types of innovation

Innovations come in various configurations – some radical and highly
visible (like the examples of new light sources or of robots in industrial
processes), but others less visible or dramatic. The challenge for

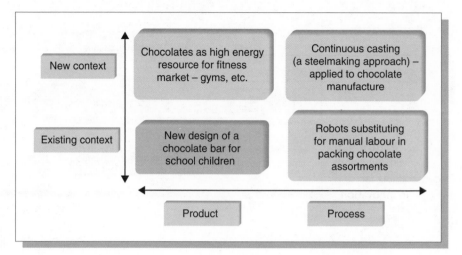

Figure 4.5
Types of innovation.

effective management of innovation begins with an understanding of the whole range of innovation types and the need to manage them in different ways.

The first helpful distinction is to recognize that innovation can take place in terms of what a firm offers or how it creates that offering – traditionally, these are termed 'process' and 'product' innovation, although they can be applied just as much to a service context as to physical products. Hence we shall refer to these as process and output innovation. And they are not mutually exclusive. For example, the budget hotel was a new way of processing the hotel guest stay, but the basic output – a good night's sleep – remains unchanged. On the other hand, the same process capability in food manufacture can be used to make a wide range of different product outputs. Finally, the development of an express parcel delivery service by Federal Express not only changed the process, it considerably altered the output and customers' service expectations.

But innovation does not take place in a vacuum; it involves taking an idea (invention) and developing it to the point where it is adopted and used by others. This could be a new product in the market-place or a new way of working being adopted and used by the workforce inside an office. So we also need to consider innovation in terms of the context into which it is applied; an old idea in a new context is still an innovation. Figure 4.5 shows these types of innovation.

The second major distinction concerns the degree of novelty involved in an innovation. At one end of the spectrum we have tiny, incremental changes which take place every day and which represent minor improvements – 'doing what we've always done a little bit better'. But at the other end of the spectrum we have innovations which are major changes, often representing significant shifts in what we offer or how we create that. At the limit there is 'discontinuous' change, where innovation involves a jump to something completely different and rewrites the rules of the game.

We can see this pattern better if we consider some specific examples. In the field of glass-making, for example, the traditional method of making window glass was to grind and polish sheets of glass produced in moulds. This was a labour-intensive process whose performance was gradually increased through a long series of incremental innovations, punctuated by more radical changes as, for example, the process was mechanized and then new generations of machine came along. But in the 1960s a radical jump took place with the development of the 'float glass' process by Pilkingtons. Here the whole concept of flat glass-making moved from grinding and polishing to a new approach in which molten glass was continuously extruded from a furnace and floated on a bath of molten tin so as to give a very flat, high-quality surface without the need for polishing. This process became the dominant model for the industry and almost all window glass in the world is now made by licensees of the Pilkington process (Nayak and Ketteringham, 1986).

Another example in process innovation is that of the automobile. When Henry Ford and his team of engineers began looking at the motor car in the late nineteenth century the process was essentially one of craft manufacture. Skilled men working in small groups would more or less hand build a car, fashioning components one by one on general-purpose machines, where the key to what was produced lay in the operator's head and hands. The cars took weeks to build and each was slightly different – very much as a hand-made suit is built up and shaped to an individual client. Not surprisingly, this process was expensive and slow.

It was not without change; there was a continuous stream of minor incremental improvements in the ways in which craft production operated – for example, in the materials used or the machinery involved. But the shift that Ford and his team introduced was fundamental – a radical jump from craft production to an early version of what we now term 'mass production'. The combination of new organizational practices (based on Taylor's 'scientific management' ideas) and standardization of product and process elements meant that huge increases in productivity were possible – for example, an 800 per cent jump in productivity in engine building between 1912 (craft) and 1913 (early mass production) (Womack *et al.*, 1990).

We can see other examples in the field of products – for example, the telephone. This moved through a phase of radical innovation

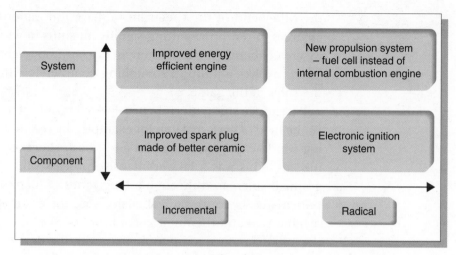

Figure 4.6
Incremental and
radical innovations.

when it was first invented and then stabilized into a pattern of incremental improvements – both in terms of the external styling and shape and the internal electromechanical functioning. Throughout its life there have been long periods of such incremental development, punctuated by surges of radical change – for example, the move to electronic mechanisms and, in recent years, the advent of mobile phones.

In recent years, major impacts have been felt across information-intensive sectors like banking and insurance as a result of the impact of information and communications technology development. Until the bursting of the 'dotcom bubble' there were dire predictions about the fate of many other industries with an information handling component – for example, travel, media, retailing, etc. – but the impact on these has varied widely (Evans and Wurster, 2000). Customer processing operations, on the other hand, have experienced much less innovative turbulence. A range of sectors continue to use processes and offer outputs that are little changed – hotels, cinemas, hairdressers, schools and so on.

The line between incremental and radical innovation is hard to fix – not least because novelty is in the eye of the beholder. For some firms an innovation may be a simple and logical next step in an incremental process of improvement. But for others it may represent a major shift.

It may also be that innovation is confined to the level of the firm, but there are occasions where it influences and shapes a whole sector – as in the case of the glass industry. (Other examples of such radical change include the shift in steel-making technology enabled by the Bessemer process, or in chemicals by the continuous Solvay process replacing the batchwise Leblanc for the manufacture of soda ash and other key alkali products.) And periodically something comes along which has an impact across sectors and affects whole societies – for example, the advent of steam power in the first Industrial Revolution or the current 'revolution' that the convergence of computing, communications and electronics has brought about.

Why is it important to think about the different types of innovation? Put simply, they need different ways of managing. An incremental change in process in a familiar context is not a high risk and can probably be managed in day-to-day fashion – for example, as part of a shopfloor daily 'review and improve' activity. Equally, a radical new product being launched in a new market will require care and attention to manage the risks and resource flows – and will probably form the basis of a special project teams' work. At the limit, radical change in product, process and context may offer the chance to change the rules of the business game – but it will need very careful and focused management. For successful strategic operations management of the innovation process we need a portfolio approach.

The innovation process

Innovation, as we said earlier, is not just about invention but about a sequence of activities involved in turning ideas and possibilities into reality. We can map this process in terms of a number of discrete phases or stages (Tidd *et al.*, 2001). (This is, of course, an oversimplification, but helps focus our attention on the different management issues and needs at each stage of the 'journey' through the process.) It involves:

- scanning the environment (internal and external) for and processing relevant signals about threats and opportunities for change;
- deciding (on the basis of a strategic view of how the enterprise can best develop) which of these signals to respond to;
- obtaining the resources to enable the response (through creating something new through R&D, acquiring something from elsewhere via technology transfer, etc.);
- implementing the project (developing the technology and the internal or external market) to respond effectively.

We should also add the point that enterprises can learn from progressing through this cycle so that they can build their knowledge base and can improve the ways in which the process is managed, as illustrated in Figure 4.7.

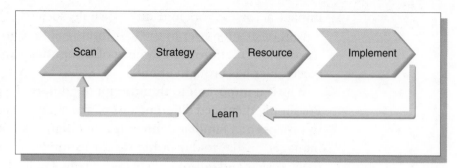

Figure 4.7
Learning from
innovation.

Whatever their size or sector, all firms are trying to find ways of managing this process of renewal. There is no right answer, but each firm needs to aim for the most appropriate solution for its particular circumstances. For example, those firms concerned with large, science-based activities – like pharmaceuticals or electronics – will tend to develop solutions to the problem of managing innovation, which include formal R&D inside and outside the firm, patent protection and searching, internationalization, etc. By contrast, a small engineering subcontractor might develop very different solutions that aim at creating a capacity to respond very quickly. Firms in the retail sector may not invest much in formal R&D, but they are likely to stress scanning the environment to pick up new consumer trends, and to place heavy emphasis on marketing. Heavy engineering firms involved in products like power plant are likely to be design intensive, and critically dependent on project management and systems integration aspects of the implementation phase. Consumer goods producers may be more concerned with rapid product development and launch, often with variants and repositioning of basic product concepts.

Although each firm is, in this way, unique in coming up with its own solution to the problem of configuring and managing the innovation process, the underlying pattern of phases in innovation remains constant. For example, developing a new consumer product or service proposition will involve picking up signals about potential needs and new technological possibilities, developing a strategic concept, coming up with options and then working those up into new products that can be launched into the market-place.

By the same token, deciding to install a new piece of process technology also follows this pattern. Signals about needs – in this case internal ones, such as problems with the current equipment – and new technological means are processed and provide an input to developing a strategic concept. This then requires identifying an existing option or inventing a new one, which must then be developed to such a point that it can be implemented (i.e. launched) by users within the enter-prise – effectively a group of internal customers. The principles of needing to understand their needs and to prepare the market-place for effective launch will apply just as much as in the case of product innovation.

It is worth looking at the question of services a little more closely. Traditionally, it is argued that they are different – because they are intangible and because production and consumption often take place simultaneously. But if we look more closely at what is going on, the same underlying process can be seen. For example, when an insurance or financial services company launches a new product the innovation process will follow a path of signal processing, strategic concept, prod-uct and market development, and launch. What is developed may be less tangible than a new television set, but the underlying structure to the process is the same. Similarly, restaurant chains develop new con-cepts and adapt an existing site into a prototype on a trial basis before deciding whether to develop the new brand.

Another apparent exception to the rule is the case of what can be termed 'complex product systems'. These are typically the kinds of product that bring together many different elements into an integrated whole, often involving different firms, long time scales and high levels of technological risk. Although such projects may appear very different to the core innovation process associated with, for example, producing a new soap powder for the mass market, the underlying process is still one of careful understanding of user needs and meeting those. There are differences in intensity of key stages – for example, involvement of users throughout the development process, with the close integration of different perspectives being of particular importance – but the over-all map of the process is the same.

A number of factors may affect the specific process adopted by an organization. Based on case study research in the tourism and hospi-tality industries, it is suggested (Jones, 1996; Jones *et al.*, 1998) that these factors derive from features of the product/service, the organ-ization and the environment. Product factors include the degree of originality, the extent of patent protection, the level of capital invest-ment, the range of professional expertise required and the potential life cycle of the product. Organizational factors include the size of the organization, organizational culture, in-house capability and organiza-tional design. Finally, environmental factors relate to the maturity of the market-place, nature of the supply chain, structure of the industry, and the roles of trade associations and related trade shows in fostering innovation.

Table 4.2

Key activities in innovation management

Stage in the process	Critical activities
Scanning	Scanning the environment for signals about triggers for innovation – market research, competitor analysis, technology scanning, etc. Forecasting – scanning ahead in time for technological and market developments
Strategy	Strategic analysis of what could be done in response to the trigger signals Strategic choice – what will we do, given our previous experience and knowledge, our business strategy and the likely costs and benefits of particular choices? Strategic planning – how are we going to turn the idea into the reality of an innovation?
Resourcing	Where and how will we obtain the key knowledge resources to make the innovation happen?
Implementation	How will we manage the project? How will we manage the technological and market development leading up to launch? How will we balance the risks and costs, and decide whether to continue or stop the project?
Learning	Having launched the innovation, how can we learn from the process? Technological knowledge Managerial knowledge Continuous improvement – how can we make it better?

A formal, systematic approach to innovation is likely to be adopted when:

- a new product, with a major process impact, is being developed;
- a number of interrelated innovations are being developed simultaneously;
- the product's life cycle is long – it can be protected by patent or licence;
- the innovations are original or new to the world;
- competitors are unlikely to enter the market with a similar product.

If innovation is a process then we should be able to model it – and this is very much the case. One of the most-cited models for product innovation is due to Booz, Allen & Hamilton, whilst Robert Cooper's work suggests a slightly extended view with 'gates' between stages which permit management of the risks in the process (Booz, Allen & Hamilton, 1982; Cooper, 1988a,b). There is even a British Standard (BS 7000) that sets out a design-centred model of the process. A number of authors have also developed models for new service development (Easingwood, 1986; Cowell, 1988). These models are reviewed and integrated by Scheuing and Johnson (1989) into a 15-stage process, which emphasizes the involvement of the marketing and human resource functions as well as operations.

The danger in models of the process is that we risk confusing them with what really happens. In practice, most innovation is messier, involving false starts, recycling between stages, dead ends, jumps out of sequence, etc. But thinking about it in process terms can help us identify particular stages and activities on which we can focus particular kinds of management effort. Table 4.2 highlights some of the key activities associated with each stage.

This can be further demonstrated in the following mini-case.

Case: Developing a short break tour to Poland

Travel companies and tour operators routinely engage in new product development and 'Magic Tours' is no exception. It specializes in short break holidays to major cities, and from 1992 to 1996 it won the UK travel trade's top awards for this. The company's mission statement makes no reference to innovation, focusing on quality and service. But each year, during the firm's annual strategic planning round, new holiday ideas and destinations are mooted and investigated.

The tour package to Warsaw and Krakow was generated at a senior management meeting in the Spring of 1995. It built on an existing programme of short breaks to Prague and Budapest. Over the next 3 months, the idea was screened in a number of ways. The contracts manager visited Poland on familiarization trips; airlines were contacted; and volume forecasts developed in consultation with the Polish Tourist Board.

Informal approval was given in July to further develop the product over the next 6 months. Visits were made to the destination by the marketing, contracts and transportation managers. The tour price was established by the marketing team, along with a sales forecast. Copy was prepared for inclusion in the 1996 corporate brochure. Reservations staff were briefed on the new product but no formal training took place.

The destination was formally launched in October 1995, as part of the firm's 1996 product range. To support the launch, the firm's PR manager successfully placed articles in the trade press. Since then, little or no formal evaluation of the product has been carried out.

Managing innovation

Table 4.2 sets out the key challenges at different stages in the process but says nothing about *how* these things might be achieved. This is the core problem in managing innovation – every firm has to do these things but each finds its own particular solutions to the problem. Firms develop their own particular ways of doing things – sometimes called 'firm-specific routines' – and some work better than others. It is quite possible to find two firms trying to innovate the same thing, but one succeeds whilst the other fails – indeed, this is a common approach to studying success and failure in managing innovation.

Any organization can get lucky once, but the real skill in innovation management is being able to repeat the trick. And whilst there are no guarantees, there is plenty of evidence to suggest that firms can and do learn to manage the process for success – by consciously building and developing their firm-specific routines. Take the case of 3M, a company whose commitment to innovation is such that it bases its branding in advertisements on themes like 'Innovation – working for you'. 3M see strategic advantage in their being able to come up with a regular stream of product innovation, so much so that they have a policy that 50 per cent of sales should come from products invented during the past 3 years. In practice, this means that they are betting on their ability to bring new ideas to market not once or twice but consistently and across a range that now numbers around 60 000 products worldwide. Underpinning this is a particular set of firm-specific routines that 3M have learned, adapted and developed over time – and that seem to work more often than they fail. There are some problems and the occasional disaster, but the company's track record on innovations (from sandpaper, through Scotch tape, overhead projection film, magnetic tape and discs to the 'post-it' notes) strongly supports their particular ways of doing things.

One important feature about firm-specific behaviour of this kind is that it can't be copied easily – it has to be learned the hard way, through experience, trial and error. Many firms have tried, for example, to emulate 3M's famous 15 per cent rule – a policy that encourages experimentation and curiosity by allowing staff to 'play around' with ideas and hunches for up to 15 per cent of their working time. This helps create 'space' in which innovative ideas can flourish within 3M – but it doesn't necessarily transplant to other companies. Instead, they need to develop their own particular way of making some 'space' (Augsdorfer, 1996).

The particular bundle of structures, policies, procedures and other 'ways of working' – essentially the organization's behavioural routines – which define the 'way we manage innovation' in a particular firm can be called its 'innovation capability'. For example, at Hewlett Packard researchers are encouraged to spend up to 10 per cent of time on their own pet projects, and have 24-hour access to laboratories and equipment. The company tries to keep divisions small to focus team efforts.

In the pharmaceutical company Merck, researchers are given time and resources to pursue high-risk, high-pay-off products, whilst in Johnson & Johnson the principle of 'freedom to fail' is a core corporate value. General Electric lays particular stress on jointly developing products with customers – for example, this approach helped develop the first thermoplastic body panels for cars through joint work with BMW (Mitchell, 1991).

So what are the key routines? What do strategic operations managers need to consider in tackling the problem of managing innovation? In essence, the task is one of developing capability so that the organization has appropriate and effective structures and procedures for making the process work. Table 4.3 lists some of the main capabilities required.

For each of these areas there is now a wealth of experience about how other organizations have tackled the problem – some more successfully than others. There are also many tools and techniques that can be used to help with the process. For example, the problem of scanning the environment for signals about relevant triggers can be dealt with using an extensive armoury of tools, ranging from various kinds of market and competitor analysis (e.g. benchmarking, market surveys), through forecasting tools (technological, market, social, etc.) to complex procedures for 'hearing the voice of the customer' and translating this into action plans throughout the organization.

Similarly, the question of strategy formulation is one of analysis (what could we do?), fit (given our positioning and our resource/experience base, what should we do?), choice (what are we going to do and what are the opportunity costs of particular commitment decisions?) and planning (how are we going to do it?). Again, there are many tools and techniques available to help with each of these issues, and the same is true of the remaining stages in the innovation process.

We can break this capability analysis down further, into four key areas, as shown in Table 4.4. From this we can begin to focus on some key tools, techniques, structures and other enabling routines that can be deployed to help manage the process. (We do not have the space to discuss them in depth in this chapter, but references to further information are given.) It is also possible to use this research-derived model to develop frameworks against which innovation management can be audited and through which learning can be facilitated by looking at examples of firms who manage particular aspects well. Examples of such audit frameworks include process models, innovation climate audits, innovation performance measures and innovation network maps (Ekvall, 1990; Chiesa *et al.*, 1996; Francis, 2001; Tidd *et al.*, 2001; Design Council, 2002).

Table 4.3

Capabilities in innovation management

Basic capability	Contributing capabilities
Recognizing	Searching the environment for technical and economic clues to trigger the process of change
Aligning	Ensuring a good fit between the overall business strategy and the proposed change – not innovating because it's fashionable or as a knee-jerk response to a competitor
Acquiring	Recognizing the limitations of the company's own technology base and being able to connect to external sources of knowledge, information, equipment, etc. Transferring technology from various outside sources and connecting it to the relevant internal points in the organization
Generating	Having the ability to create some aspects of technology in-house – through R&D, internal engineering groups, etc.
Choosing	Exploring and selecting the most suitable response to the environmental triggers that fit the strategy and the internal resource base/external technology network
Executing	Managing development projects for new products or processes from initial idea through to final launch Monitoring and controlling such projects
Learning	Having the ability to evaluate and reflect upon the innovation process and identify lessons for improvement in the management routines
Implementing	Managing the introduction of change – technical and otherwise – in the organization to ensure acceptance and effective use of innovation
Developing the organization	Putting those new routines in place – in structures, processes, underlying behaviours, etc.

Managing discontinuous innovation – moving beyond the 'steady state'

The only certainty about tomorrow's environment is that it will be more uncertain than today's! This flash of the blindingly obvious reminds us of a major difficulty in managing innovation – the fact that we are doing so against a constantly shifting backdrop. And it is

Table 4.4

Four key areas in innovation

Capability area	Key capabilities	Enabling routines
Strategic focus and direction	Inspiring 'visionary leadership' Targeting key strategic areas Making strategy Communicating and deploying strategy	Top teamworking (Francis and Young, 1988) Benchmarking, competitor analysis, customer focus (Camp, 1989; Voss, 1992) Strategy process (Porter, 1985, 1990; Francis, 1994) Policy deployment (Bessant and Francis, 1999)
Implementation	Managing projects Managing risk Developing technology and market in parallel Cross-functional working	Appropriate project structures (line, matrix, project, heavyweight project) (Wheelwright and Clark, 1992) Project team building (Thamhain and Wilemon, 1987; Kharbanda and Stallworthy, 1990) Stage gate process (Cooper, 1988a,b) Early involvement (Souder and Sherman, 1994) Cross-functional working 'Simultaneous' engineering
Innovative people and organization	Structuring Teamworking Managing knowledge Participating in continuous improvement Empowering	Appropriate design (Mintzberg, 1979) Team building (Bixby, 1987; Holti et al., 1995) Knowledge management tools (Nonaka, 1991; Pisano, 1994; Quintas et al., 1997) Training and development Continuous improvement tools and techniques (Lillrank and Kano, 1990; Robinson, 1991; Bessant, 1999)
Effective linkages	Active networking Involving customers and suppliers	Customer involvement tools and procedures, QFD (Akao, 1990; Shillito, 1994) Supplier development (Lamming, 1993) Technology transfer (UNIDO, 1995; Rush and Bessant, 1998)

clear that some trends in the current environment are converging to create conditions that many see as rewriting the rules of the competitive game.

Certainly there are big changes taking place in the environment in which we have to try and manage innovation, and in this unit we will look at some of the major forces underpinning such change. Whilst there is no room for complacency, we should also not be in a hurry to throw away the basic principles on which innovation management is based; they will certainly need adapting and configuring to dramatically new circumstances, but underneath the innovation management puzzle is what it always was – a challenge to accumulate and deploy knowledge resources in strategically effective fashion.

Innovation involves some change in either the thing that is offered (product innovation) or the ways in which that offering is created and delivered (process innovation). Change in these takes place mostly in a continuing, incremental way, but sometimes in a radical and discontinuous jump. Occasionally, the two take place simultaneously – and under these conditions particularly we are likely to see the rules of the game shifting.

Consider the current emergence of the Internet and related information and communication technologies (ICTs) as examples of the powerful forces shaping the competitive environment and arguably rewriting the rules of the game. Let's look, for example, at their impact in the world of publishing.

On the one hand, we have an industry that was, until recently, based on very physical technologies and a complex network of specialist suppliers who contributed their particular parts of the complex puzzle of publishing. For example, copy – words or pictures – would be generated by a specialist journalist or photographer. He or she would then pass this on to various editors, who would check, make choices about design and layout, etc. Next would come typesetting, where the physical materials for printing would be made – hot metal would be cast into letters and grouped into blocks to form words and sentences within special frames. Pictures and other items would be transferred on to printing plates. The type frames or printing plates would then be fixed to presses, these would be inked and some test runs made. Finally, the printed version would appear – and pass on to someone else to distribute and publish it.

Such a method might still be recognizable by Messrs Caxton and Gutenberg – the pioneers of the printing industry. But it is a fair bet that they would not have a clue about the way in which publishing operates today – with its emphasis on information technology. Now the process has changed such that a single person could undertake the whole set of operations – create text on a word processor, design and lay it out on a page formatting program, integrate images with text and, when satisfied, print to either physical media or, increasingly, publish it worldwide in electronic form.

There are plenty of examples of firms that have exploited the opportunities that this kind of change creates (Evans and Wurster, 2000;

Pottruck and Pearce, 2000). The challenge of disruption has prompted many others to rethink the business models that operate – and to try and rewrite the rules of the game. The author Stephen King, for example, has made a number of attempts to move beyond the traditional relationships between writers and publishers, and particularly to publish directly via the Internet. In his latest venture, he has taken this a step further; his new book is being written chapter by chapter and will only appear if enough people ask for it. He has moved from the traditional model of writing in the hope of readers, to the point where he is effectively writing on demand – much like a factory nowadays often operates on a make-to-order basis only.

There are winners in this game but also losers. People still think of the *Encyclopaedia Britannica* as a household name and the repository of useful reference knowledge that can be trusted. It is a well-established product – in fact, the original idea came from three Scottish printers back in 1768! The brand is fine – but the business has gone through dramatic shifts and is still under threat. From a peak of sales in 1990 of around $650 m its sales have collapsed – for example, by up to 80 per cent in the USA. The problem is not the product but the way in which it is presented – all the hard copy encyclopaedias have suffered a similar fate at the hands of the CD-ROM-based versions like *Encarta* (which is often bundled in as part of a PC purchase).

We could go on looking at the publishing industry but the point is clear – when technology shifts dramatically it opens up major opportunities but also poses major threats to players in the industry and to those who might want to enter from outside. Under these conditions simply being an established player – even with a centuries-old brand name and an excellent product – is not enough. Indeed, as firms like Amazon.com (an online bookstore) have shown, it is at times like these that coming from outside and starting fresh may offer significant advantages.

What is going on here is clearly not conforming to a stable, big-is-beautiful model, nor is it about historically important emphasis on core competence. The foundations of a business like publishing become shaken and many of the famous names disappear, whilst other unknown upstarts become major industry players – in some cases overnight! (To put that in perspective, Amazon.com was at one time worth more than established businesses like British Airways!) Turbulence like this throws a challenge to established models of managing – not only is it a question of urgently needing to change, but the very models of change management on which many traditional players rely may not be sufficient or appropriate.

Perhaps the hardest challenge is that 'more of the same' may not be enough under these conditions. Even firms that have a good track record in innovation and who seek regularly to improve their products and processes are vulnerable. Doing what you do better may not always work – sometimes you have to look to do different things. This is not to say that we have to rewrite the entire rule book – if we do that we risk throwing the baby out with the bathwater. Closer examination of the above successful cases – and many others that have been researched – shows that those firms that do well look to merge new ideas and models about how to do business with established good practices. For example, Amazon have succeeded not only by exploiting the new opportunities created by the Internet, but also by employing well-established principles like listening to their customers, ensuring a total quality approach in their dealings with them, encouraging widespread incremental innovation to continuously improve their service offering, etc.

Innovation theory is helpful here, at least insofar as showing that change of this kind is not uncommon. Indeed, it is a consequence of Schumpeter's concept of 'creative destruction'. (Joseph Schumpeter was a famous economist who, more than anyone else, worked on the economics of innovation and established much of the theory that underpins its management.) Entrepreneurs in his model are constantly seeking for ways to achieve an edge that no one else has in the competitive market-place. This could come from a new product or process, or at least a better one than the rest can offer. The result is that for a short time, if successful, he or she will be able to reap a handsome rent – what Schumpeter calls monopoly profits. Of course, sooner or later many imitators come in, copying or finding better alternatives, often ingeniously getting round patent and other protection – but the overall effect is to create a swarm of innovations and to drive the economy forward (Freeman, 1982; Coombs *et al.*, 1985).

Implicit in this model is the idea that if the entrepreneur is lucky, he or she may come up with a 'killer application' – a product or process innovation that not only offers something dramatically new, but that simultaneously makes the old ones obsolete. Under these conditions the rules of the game are rewritten – and there is a shakeout of the old and new winners and losers.

Experience and theory tells us that (a) this kind of discontinuous change happens regularly, often at the level of a sector or branch, less so at the level of the whole economy, and that (b) when it does the old incumbent players are often not very successful at making the transition. New entrants tend to thrive partly because they are small and fast moving (and have little to lose), and partly because they do not come encumbered with the baggage of their past experience. They only have to learn new tricks, whereas old players have to unlearn old ones as well (Utterback, 1994; Christensen, 1997).

But it isn't just a form of corporate Darwinism in which the thrusting young players overturn the old order; history suggests that a significant number of older players do survive and prosper through discontinuity. And we shouldn't forget that we hear about the few small new firms that enter successful, but conveniently ignore the large number of failures amongst this size range. (Think about the current crop of Internet fatalities – boo.com, clickmango.com, etc. Small businesses are easy to start but also very vulnerable to even minor infections.)

We have learned that under discontinuous conditions there are strategies and responses that can help. Although the technological and market shifts are dramatic, the basic innovation management issues remain. In particular, impacts vary, from niches where the rules change through to sectors through to – very occasionally – the whole economy. It is important to be clear about what's going on and its implications – and this means that firms will need sensitive antennae and a strong future orientation. If anything, effective management of the scanning phase becomes even more critical.

We have seen that even large and long-established firms are not immune from the forces of disruptive change. It's worth reflecting on the fact that most firms don't live all that long – for example, of the firms comprising the Dow Jones index of the largest businesses in the USA in 1900, only one firm (out of 250) made it through to the year 2000! But equally there are survivors and firms that have managed to stay around and to thrive and prosper. When we look more closely at these, we can see two important themes for our interest in managing innovation (de Geus, 1996).

First, these firms do not survive because of their scale or their physical assets. The thing that enables them to survive is a deep knowledge base – a core competence that defines what they're distinctively good at and that others find hard to match. This could take many forms. It might be a specific technology – for example, the Pilkington Company in the UK has the patents on the process by which most of the world's flat glass is made – so it has some measure of defence against shocks by virtue of this knowledge base. In most cases, the core competence of a firm is much more than just a set of patents or a specific knowledge set – for example, Sony's skills lie in being able to link electronics, miniaturization, design and good customer understanding to make them the respected player they are in consumer electronics. Canon does the same in imaging because of competence built up from mixing electronics and optics. 3M have deep skills in coating technology down to sub-molecular level – but they are also extremely capable in the field of regular product innovation, so their competence lies in being able to build a business out of technological knowledge (Hamel and Prahalad, 1994).

The second point is even more important, though. What separates the survivors from the rest is not just that they have core competence, but that they actively manage this side of their business. And a key feature in such management is knowing when you have to build it (for example, by making strategic investments in R&D or in acquiring knowledge which you need to add) – but also when you have to let it go. Letting go of knowledge you no longer need is simple in concept but very hard to achieve in practice.

We can see this in the case of a firm like Nokia – a large company that began as a forestry business in the nineteenth century. It diversified and acquired many different areas of knowledge – some would say too many, since its product range at one time ran from pulp and paper right through to Wellington boots! But in the late twentieth century it focused on electronics and particularly on mobile communications – and let the other competencies go. By the year 2000 it was entirely a mobile telecommunications business.

Table 4.5 gives some other examples of firms that have survived but that have done so by being prepared to take on new knowledge and to let go other sets of knowledge when needed.

An important piece of work was done on this theme of competence by two US writers, Tushman and Anderson (1987). Their paper looked at the historical evidence from a wide range of industries that had faced discontinuous change and they identified that there were two ways in which a new technology could affect an industry. On the one hand, it could be what they called 'competence enhancing' – that is, it actually extended the range of things a firm could do and built on what they already knew. Examples might be the jet engine, which didn't knock aircraft makers out of the sky but rather enhanced their ability to deploy what they knew about aerodynamics, control systems, etc.

On the other hand, there are technologies that they term 'competence destroying' – which have the capacity to make redundant all the knowledge that a firm has accumulated over many years and on which it has built its business. A good example here would be those printing and publishing firms we looked at earlier, where much of what they knew about how to make physical printing plates and typesetting operations becomes irrelevant in an era of digital imaging and communication.

Kodak faces a significant challenge of this kind. Founded around 100 years ago, the basis of the business was the production and

Table 4.5

Examples of radical transitions in business

Company	Origins	Current basis of business	How they moved
Preussag	Prussian state-owned mining and smelting company	Largest integrated tourism operator in Europe – owns Thomas Cook, Hapag-Lloyd, Thomson Holidays, etc.	Had transport interests to move coal, iron ore, etc. Moved into shipping and other transport. From there, into airline business and exploiting growth of leisure and service industry
ICI-Zeneca	19th century UK chemical industry – alkalis	Major international pharmaceutical firm (Astra-Zeneca)	Demerger of heavy chemicals and commodity businesses and concentration on high-value 'precision' chemistry business
Mannesman	19th century inventors of the seamless steel tube – basis of all pipes	Major European player in mobile telephones – sold to Vodafone in 1998	From steel pipes to steel production and downstream applications. Let go of steel and concentrated on increasingly sophisticated downstream machinery and from there moved into control technology. From there into data communications and from there into mobile phones

processing of film and the sales and service associated with mass-market photography. Whilst the latter set of competencies are still highly relevant (even though camera technology has shifted), the move away from wet physical chemistry in the dark (coating emulsions onto film and paper) to digital imaging represents a profound change for the firm. It needs – across a global operation and a workforce of thousands – to let go of old competencies that are unlikely to be needed in the future whilst at the same time rapidly acquiring and absorbing cutting-edge new technologies in electronics and communication.

What does this mean for our question of how to manage discontinuous innovation? The challenge posed by this model is one of making sure firms understand the nature of the changes coming at them. If they are competence enhancing, the innovation management questions are around how best to build on this new opportunity, how to acquire complementary and new competence, and to merge these with what already exists. But if the technology is competence destroying, the challenge is how to let go of redundant competencies and move quickly into the new era.

History tells us that such strategic riding of the waves of change is possible – but not for everyone. Typically, when discontinuous change happens, most of the incumbent firms don't make a very good show of moving forward. This is partly because they are so committed – not just in terms of fixed assets but also in terms of their underlying psychology – to the old model. Letting go is not easy – shrugging off the knowledge base that might have been the original source of strength for the company is not something that comes easily. For the same reason, new entrants usually do well under conditions of discontinuity – because they are carrying less baggage and have nothing to let go of.

Figure 4.8 summarizes the key dimensions associated with this view of change.

The idea of looking at technologies in terms of whether they are likely to enhance or destroy our existing competencies has a lot of power. But we need to be careful – as two US writers, Henderson and Clark (1990), point out. Change, whilst dramatic, may not affect the entire business. Their concept of component and architectural innovation is relevant here – firms need to develop the ability to see which parts of their activity are affected by technological change and to react accordingly.

They suggest that we need to recognize that in most industries the core product or service is not a single thing, but actually made up of different components configured into a system or architecture. For example, a motor car is not a single thing but a complex assembly of chassis, wheels, engine, body and control systems. A bank is not simply a building where money is kept, but a complex arrangement of

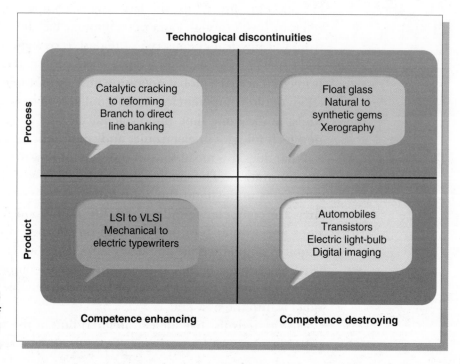

Figure 4.8
Dimensions of technological discontinuity.

components concerned with customer service, information processing, inter-bank transactions, etc.

Viewed in this way, we can see that even major technological changes do not necessarily destroy the whole business – they may only affect one part of it. Our example of Kodak earlier is correct in that the film manufacture and processing side of the business is facing competence-destroying change in the shift from wet chemistry to digital imaging. But this does not necessarily threaten other aspects of the business – for example, the camera and photographic equipment side. In fact, the impact of technology here is probably competence enhancing – digital technology opens up the chance to configure lenses and other elements in new and more powerful ways.

So, in managing discontinuous changes we need to learn not only to assess whether or not they are competence enhancing or destroying, but also which parts of our business are affected in which ways. In some cases, change at the component level opens up new opportunities – for example, new materials or propulsion systems like fuel cells – may open up new options for vehicle assemblers, but will not necessarily challenge their core operations. However, the shift to MP3 as an alternative way of creating and distributing music via the Internet poses challenges to the whole system of music production and publishing, and may require a much more significant response.

Figure 4.9 highlights the key dimensions here and gives some examples.

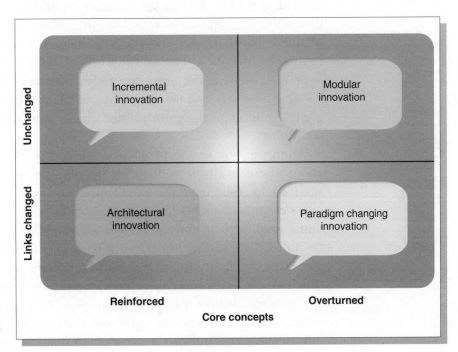

Figure 4.9 Architectural and component innovation.

An example of where change that is discontinuous and competence destroying for some businesses whilst opening up opportunities for others can be seen is the case of Internet retailing. Although much of the discussion of the Internet and innovation focuses on new services and processes enabled by the network, we should not forget the new opportunities opened up around the edge of this phenomenon. Much potential exists for innovation in the products and technologies sustaining the network itself – for example, the fibre optics, switches, routers, etc. that make the Internet physically possible. One of the problems posed by the Internet revolution, especially in the area of online retailing, is the so-called 'last mile' question. Even for conventional mail- or telephone-order shopping, one problem is the fact that you need to be at home or arrange for someone to sign for/receive/store your package of books, computer parts, CDs or whatever. And very often the suppliers won't commit themselves to a definite time for the delivery but only to, at best, a time window.

Don't forget the demand side!

The danger in spending all our time looking at technological discontinuities is that we forget the key point about innovation – that it always arises out of a combination of needs and means. Sometimes the main impetus comes from the opportunities created by a new technological discovery, but sometimes it will be the emergence of strong signals about demand. Under these circumstances, necessity becomes the mother of invention. Part of the problem with much of the Internet hype at present is the absence of clear demand for all the wonderful new products and services that can be configured to exploit the great technological opportunities made available by information technology.

When we look at the problem of discontinuity – and particularly about where and how we look for signals – we need to be aware that these could come from the market-place as much as from the technology development labs. This point comes through very clearly in influential work by Christensen (1997). He made a detailed study of the hard disk drive industry and how it has evolved and changed over the past 30 years. His argument is that this represents a good test case from which we can learn some valuable lessons about how innovation works and particularly how disruptive technologies operate.

Although perhaps not on a par with the complete redefinition of an industry that the Internet represents to many service businesses, the pattern of change in disk drives has been dramatic. It is possible to identify several generations – but more importantly the transition between them has not been smooth. The size and shape of the drives and the underlying technologies have all jumped – and significantly the firms associated with leading the change at each wave were different. So too was the industry structure – firms that were leaders in one generation did not always do well in making the transition.

This partly confirms the theme we have already explored – that old-established players find it harder to move than newcomers do. But Christensen adds another important dimension. He suggests that the good business practice of staying close to your customers may not always be the best strategy in times of rapid technological development. If you work closely with a major customer you will soon become part of a closed system in which innovation happens but at a pace and in a direction that is defined by the users in terms of their prior experience and the technology suppliers in terms of the problems they already know how to solve.

Christensen's point is that the significant jumps in disk drive technology arose not from listening to these markets, but rather from picking up on weak signals from customers and potential customers right at the fringe. These players weren't large and were often not particularly well known in their sector. They were essentially working at the fringe and had requirements that were not of interest to the mainstream players – for example, for smaller size, higher capacity or access speed. But it was their ideas that actually set the pace of change to the next generation, with the result that what began as fringe concepts became mainstream designs.

He introduces two useful concepts to our discussion – those of 'sustaining' and 'disrupting' technologies. Sustaining technologies enable continuous progress within an existing set of market relationships and it is here that staying close to the customer works well as a recipe for continuing successful innovation. But 'disrupting' technologies do just that – they threaten to change the rules of the game and to open up opportunities for new markets to emerge.

Once again, in innovation management this places the emphasis on building effective scanning mechanisms, and for ensuring that the signals generated get heard within the organization and not filtered out because they conflict with the established view – the 'not invented here' problem. This is by no means an unfamiliar problem – imagine a well-established company in the photocopier business being faced with two proposals on a Monday morning. One is from a salesman who is working closely with a big corporate client and has brought back some ideas from a meeting with that client that could lead to modifications and improvements to the existing range of copiers. His views are likely to be taken seriously, the procedures for transmitting them to the design and development team are in place, and the whole proposed innovation has an aura of managed risk about it. It will probably succeed – at least as far as getting a product on the market that the client likes.

But consider another salesman who spent Friday night in a bar with a couple of computer whiz-kids with some crazy ideas about the hand-held device of the future. Their view is that incorporating scanning and printing technology into the package would give it a sharp edge in the emerging market for portable and personal computing/commun-ications. The challenge would be to make a copier much smaller and that would demand very different power and other arrangements. Presenting these ideas on a Monday morning would probably incur disapproval and they could well be dismissed as the dreams of a couple of cranks. The salesman would not be encouraged to do this – either by his unreceptive colleagues or by the reward system, which may well be based on sales targets that are easier to achieve by working with established customers on incremental innovation.

In fact, this demonstrates well Christensen's principle. In the first case, the salesman's proposals are for innovation – but in a controlled sense, working to clearly specified user needs and within a sustaining

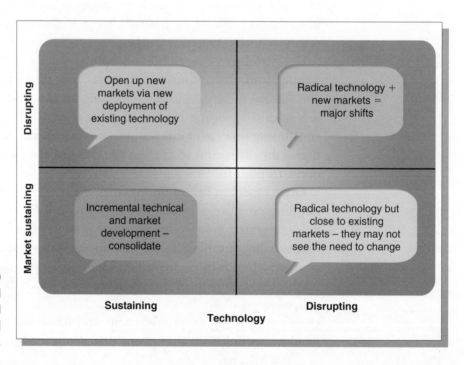

Figure 4.10
Christensen's model of market and technological disruption.

technology envelope. But in the second, we are in the realms of high risk and uncertainty, and with a requirement for a technology that – if it is eventually feasible – might well disrupt the industry.

Sticking close to the customer remains a good prescription, but innovation managers need to complement it with additional structures or mechanisms that also allow the possibility of disruptive technology. Firms have to find a way of resolving what Christensen calls 'the innovator's dilemma' – otherwise, they risk being caught out when disruption occurs. Figure 4.10 summarizes the key points of this approach.

Looking forward ...

We have seen in this chapter the growing recognition of innovation as a core business process, something essential to the renewal and indeed the survival of the enterprise. Our thinking has moved it from the periphery of the organization to the centre of the stage, and the creation and management of suitable routines and structures to enable innovation is a key role for strategic operations. But we need in the future to look more closely at the key components of innovation – and to manage these for competitive advantage.

Knowledge management

Three themes are worth mentioning here. First, we need to recognize that innovation is always a race in which front runners are constantly being chased and caught. Finding something that confers sustainable and protectable competitive advantage is a key challenge – and we have come to realize that in a global economy this is not an easy task. In particular, advantages of location, of access to cheap labour or raw materials is not often sustainable – because globalization means that others can move somewhere with similar or better factor endowments. Even technology is not a good solution – having a machine with powerful and clever capabilities is not really an edge, since anyone else with deep enough pockets can also buy such a machine or, if the underlying technology is protected, they can reverse engineer or even steal the ideas!

For these reasons we are beginning to think of competitive advantage as lying fundamentally in knowledge – in what we know about and can deploy in new products or processes. This places emphasis on the aspects of innovation to do with acquiring, capturing and managing the knowledge bases of the firm as the key task (Teece, 1998). Thinking in this way brings a new perspective to the task of managing innovation – we need to recognize that innovation is essentially a knowledge creating and deploying process (Leonard-Barton, 1992). Developing the capacity to learn becomes central to strategic operations management.

Involvement

The second challenge for the future lies in the area of involvement. In the past, and still to a large extent in today's innovation operations, there is an emphasis on specialists – those who, by virtue of possessing particular skills or experiences, are 'licensed' to participate in the innovation process. It is true that such people have been central to the creation of all the radical innovations we have been speaking about in this chapter – but they represent a small part of the total workforce in most organizations. Yet innovation is primarily the application of a fundamental human skill – that of creative problem-solving. This is something with which everyone in the organization could potentially make a contribution – and the relatively few studies that have been done on high levels of involvement in innovation support this view. In recent years, we have seen some dramatic examples – for instance, the transformation of Japanese manufacturing from its weak base in the 1950s to world-class by the 1980s – and we now understand that much of this can be related to high involvement of people in the innovation process. Where a firm like Toyota receives over two million ideas per year and does so over a 30-year period it becomes clear that it has learned to harness considerable innovative resources.

The challenge for strategic operations management is making high involvement a reality. It sounds simple. As one manager put it, 'now I see the potential – with every pair of hands you get a free brain!' The difficulty is finding ways to mobilize such involvement and to sustain it in the long term.

Sustainability

The final area in which there are significant future challenges for the strategic operations manager in managing the innovation process lies in the concept of sustainability. One of the implicit problems in innovation is that it assumes anything is possible, that there is always something new in product or process. The trouble with this view is that it ignores the fact that we live on a planet with finite resources, many of which are not renewable. Increasingly, there is public concern about changes that appear to have negative effects on the world we live in or on quality of life – not just for ourselves but throughout the value chain from raw material to finished product. People like new designs in furniture, for example – but are no longer so interested when they find that such innovative products are made by destroying a non-renewable teak forest in Indonesia.

Thinking about more sustainable products and forms of consumption is becoming increasingly important and affecting many aspects of operations management. The challenge in the context of innovation is to harness the creativity within the organization to find product and process ideas that contribute to sustainability whilst also preserving and developing business opportunities.

Case: Bags of ideas – the case of James Dyson

In October 2000, the air inside Court 58 of the Royal Courts of Justice rang with terms like 'bagless dust collection', 'cyclone technology', 'triple vortex' and 'dual cyclone' as one of the most bitter of patent battles in recent years was brought to a conclusion. On one side was Hoover, a multinational firm with the eponymous vacuum suction sweeper at the heart of a consumer appliance empire. On the other a lone inventor – James Dyson – who had pioneered a new approach to the humble task of house cleaning and then seen his efforts threatened by an apparent imitation by Hoover. Eventually the court ruled in Dyson's favour.

This represented the culmination of a long and difficult journey that Dyson travelled in bringing his ideas to a wary market-place. It began in 1979, when Dyson was using, ironically, a Hoover Junior vacuum cleaner to dust the house. He was struck by the inefficiency of a system that effectively reduced its capability to suck the more it was used, since the bag became clogged with dust. He tried various improvements, such as a finer mesh filter bag, but the results were not promising. The breakthrough came with the idea of using industrial cyclone technology applied in a new way – to the problem of domestic cleaners.

Dyson was already an inventor with some track record; one of his products was a wheelbarrow that used a ball instead of a front wheel. In order to spray the black dust paint in a powder-coating plant they had installed a cyclone – a well-established engineering solution to the problem of dust extraction. Essentially a mini-tornado is created within a shell and the air in the vortex moves so fast that particles of dust are forced to the edge, where they can be collected whilst clean air moves to the centre. Dyson began to ask why the principle could not be applied in vacuum cleaners – and soon found out why. His early experiments – with the Hoover – were not entirely successful, but eventually he applied for a patent in 1980 for a Vacuum Cleaning Appliance using cyclone technology.

It took another 4 years and 5127 prototypes, and even then he could not patent the application of a single cyclone, since that would only represent an improvement on an existing and proven technology. He had to develop a dual cyclone system, which used the first to separate out large items of domestic refuse – cigarette ends, dog hairs, cornflakes, etc. – and the second to pick up the finer dust particles. But having proved the technology, he found a distinct cold shoulder on the part of the existing vacuum cleaner industry represented by firms like Hoover, Philips and Electrolux. In typical examples of the 'not invented here' effect, they remained committed to the idea of vacuum cleaners using bags and were unhappy with bagless technology. (This is not entirely surprising, since suppliers such as Electrolux make a significant income on selling the replacement bags for their vacuum cleaners.)

Eventually Dyson began the hard work of raising the funds to start his own business – and it gradually paid off. Launched in 1993 – 14 years after the initial idea – Dyson employed 1800 staff producing around 10 000 cleaners every day in their factory in Malmesbury in Wiltshire. (However, pressures on costs eventually led him to relocate production to the Far East, although investment in R&D was increased in the UK. This demonstrates the need for continuing innovation and for action across both product and process dimensions.)

The Dyson empire is worth around £530 m and has a number of product variants in its vacuum cleaner range; other products under development aim to re-examine domestic appliances like washing machines and dishwashers to try and bring similar new ideas into play. The basic Dual Cyclone cleaner was one of the products identified by the UK Design Council as one of its 'Millennium Products'.

Perhaps the greatest accolade, though, is the fact that the vacuum cleaner giants like Hoover eventually saw the potential and began developing their own versions. Although Hoover lost the case, they are planning to appeal, arguing that their version used a different technology developed for the oil and gas industry by the UK research consultancy BHR. Whoever wins, Dyson has once again shown the role of the individual champion in innovation – and that success depends on more than just a good idea. Edison's famous comment that it is '1 per cent inspiration and 99 per cent perspiration' seems an apt motto here!

Summary

- Innovation is not a luxury but an imperative; it is essential for survival and growth.
- Although the process is uncertain, it is not a lottery; evidence shows that it can be managed to competitive advantage.
- The key to this lies in recognizing that it is a *process* like any other in organizational life, the difference being that this process is concerned with renewing the things an organization offers and the ways in which it creates and delivers them.
- Managing the process is thus of central concern in strategic operations management.
- Operations management plays a central and pivotal role in the development process within innovation.

Key questions

1   'Invention is not enough' was the response given by a major designer/manufacturer when asked about the secrets of successful innovation. What other factors need to be managed to ensure a good idea makes it through to successful implementation?

2   We have only scratched the surface of the topic of innovation in this chapter and have presented a general model of how the process works. What factors (for example, sector, type of product, etc.) might shape the ways in which a particular firm needs to go about the process? How might they affect its management?

3   Introducing process innovation – change in 'the way we do things around here' – can be thought of in the same way as trying to

launch a new product in the commercial market-place. What similarities and differences might there be between the two, and what messages emerge for successful management of both?

4   'Innovation is a survival imperative, not a luxury!' Thinking of an organization with which you are familiar, think about whether this statement applies – and if it does, what kinds of innovation can you trace in its history? What triggered them, and what difference did they make?

5   In this chapter we have positioned innovation as a core process in the business, concerned with renewing what the organization offers and the ways in which it does so. This process operates in parallel with those concerned with the present-day operations – managing supply through to satisfying customers. Inevitably, there will be points of conflict between managing today and building for the future. Where do you think these 'flashpoints' might emerge – and how would you deal with them as an operations manager?

References and further reading

Akao, Y. (ed.) (1990) *Quality Function Deployment – Integrating Customer Requirements into Product Design.* Cambridge, MA: Productivity Press.

Augsdorfer, P. (1996) *Forbidden Fruit.* Aldershot: Avebury.

Bessant, J. (1999) Developing continuous improvement capability. *International Journal of Innovation Management,* **4**(2), 409–430.

Bessant, J. and Francis, D. (1999) Policy deployment and beyond. *International Journal of Operations and Production Management.*

Bixby, K. (1987) *Superteams.* London: Fontana.

Booz, Allen & Hamilton (1982) *New Product Management for the 1980s.* Booz, Allen & Hamilton Consultants.

Braun, E. and Macdonald, S. (1980) *Revolution in Miniature.* Cambridge: Cambridge University Press.

Brown, S. (2000) *Manufacturing the Future – Strategic Resonance for Enlightened Manufacturing.* London: Financial Times/Pearson Books.

Business 2.0, 22 August 2000.

Camp, R. (1989) *Benchmarking – The Search for Industry Best Practices that Lead to Superior Performance.* Milwaukee, WI: Quality Press.

Chiesa, V., Coughlan, P. and Voss, C. (1996) Development of a technical innovation audit. *Journal of Product Innovation Management,* **13**(2), 105–136.

Christensen, C. (1997) *The Innovator's Dilemma.* Cambridge, MA: Harvard Business Press.

Coombs, R., Saviotti, P. and Walsh, V. (1985) *Economics and Technological Change*. London: Macmillan.

Cooper, R. (1988a) The new product process: a decision guide for management. *Journal of Marketing Management*, **3**(3), 238–255.

Cooper, R. (1988b) *Winning at New Products*. London: Kogan Page.

Cowell, D. (1988) New service development. *Journal of Marketing Management*, **3**(3), 296–312.

de Geus, A. (1996) *The Living Company*. Cambridge, MA: Harvard Business School Press.

Design Council (2002) Living innovation. Design Council/Department of Trade and Industry website: www.livinginnovation.org.uk, London.

Easingwood, C.J. (1986) New product development for service companies. *Journal of Product Innovation Management*, **4**, 264–275.

Ekvall, G. (1990) The organizational culture of idea management. In: Henry, J. and Walker, D. (eds), *Managing Innovation*, pp. 73-80. London: Sage.

Evans, P. and Wurster, T. (2000) *Blown to Bits: How the New Economics of Information Transforms Strategy*. Cambridge, MA: Harvard Business School Press.

Francis, D. (1994) *Step by Step Competitive Strategy*. London: Routledge.

Francis, D. (2001) *Developing Innovative Capability*. Brighton: University of Brighton.

Francis, D. and Young, D. (1988) *Top Team Building*. Aldershot: Gower.

Freeman, C. (1982) *The Economics of Industrial Innovation*. London: Frances Pinter.

Hamel, G. (2001) *Leading the Revolution*. New York: New American Library.

Hamel, G. and Prahalad, C.K. (1994) *Competing for the Future*. Boston, MA: Harvard Business School Press.

Henderson, R. and Clark, K. (1990) Architectural innovation: the reconfiguration of existing product technologies and the failure of established firms. *Administrative Science Quarterly*, **35**, 9–30.

Holti, R., Neumann, J. and Standing, H. (1995) *Change Everything at Once: The Tavistock Institute's Guide to Developing Teamwork in Manufacturing*. London: Management Books 2000.

Jones, P. (1996) Managing hospitality innovation. *Cornell HRA Quarterly*, **37**(5), 86–95.

Jones, P., Hudson, S. and Costis, P. (1998) New product development in the U.K. tour operating industry. *Progress in Hospitality and Tourism Research*, **3**(4), 283–294.

Kharbanda, O. and Stallworthy, M. (1990) *Project Teams*. Manchester: NCC-Blackwell.

Lamming, R. (1993) *Beyond Partnership: Strategies for Innovation and Lean Supply.* Hemel Hempstead: Prentice Hall.

Leonard-Barton, D. (1992) The organisation as learning laboratory. *Sloan Management Review,* **34**(1), 23–38.

Leonard-Barton, D. (1995) *Wellsprings of Knowledge: Building and Sustaining the Sources of Innovation.* Cambridge, MA: Harvard Business School Press.

Lillrank, P. and Kano, N. (1990) *Continuous Improvement; Quality Control Circles in Japanese Industry.* Ann Arbor: University of Michigan Press.

Mintzberg, H. (1979) *The Structuring of Organisations.* Englewood Cliffs, NJ: Prentice Hall.

Mitchell, R. (1991) How 3M keeps the new products coming. In: Henry, J. and Walker, D. (eds), *Managing Innovation.* London: Sage.

Nayak, P. and Ketteringham, J. (1986) *Breakthroughs: How Leadership and Drive Create Commercial Innovations that Sweep the World.* London: Mercury.

Nelson, R.R. and Winter, S.G. (1982) *An Evolutionary Theory of Economic Change.* Cambridge, MA: Belknap Press.

Nonaka, I. (1991) The knowledge creating company. *Harvard Business Review,* November–December, 96–104.

Pisano, G. (1994) Knowledge, integration and the locus of learning: an empirical analysis of process development. *Strategic Management Journal,* **15**, 85.

Porter, M. (1985) *Competitive Advantage: Creating and Sustaining Superior Performance.* New York: Free Press.

Porter, M. (1990) *The Competitive Advantage of Nations.* New York: Free Press.

Pottruck, D. and Pearce, T. (2000) *Clicks and Mortar.* San Francisco: Jossey Bass.

Quintas, P., Lefrere, P. *et al.* (1997) Knowledge management: a strategic agenda. *Long Range Planning,* **13**(3), 387.

Robinson, A. (1991) *Continuous Improvement in Operations.* Cambridge, MA: Productivity Press.

Rush, H. and Bessant, J. (1998) Innovation agents and technology transfer. In: Miles, I. (ed.), *Innovation and the Service-based Economy.* London: Frances Pinter.

Scheuing, E.E. and Johnson, E.M. (1989) A proposed model for new service development. *Journal of Services Marketing,* **3**(2), 25–34.

Schumpeter, J. (1950) *Capitalism, Socialism and Democracy.* New York: Harper & Row.

Shillito, M. (1994) *Advanced QFD: Linking Technology to Market and Company Needs.* New York: John Wiley.

Souder, W. and Sherman, J. (1994) *Managing New Technology Development.* New York:, McGraw-Hill.

Teece, D. (1998) Capturing value from knowledge assets: the new economy, markets for know-how, and intangible assets. *California Management Review,* **40**(3): 55–79.

Thamhain, H. and Wilemon, D. (1987) Building high performance engineering project teams. *IEEE Transactions on Engineering Management,* **EM-34**(3), 130–137.

Tidd, J., Bessant, J. and Pavitt, K. (2001) *Managing Innovation,* 2nd Edition. Chichester: John Wiley.

Tushman, M. and Anderson, P. (1987) Technological discontinuities and organizational environments. *Administrative Science Quarterly,* **31**(3), 439–465.

UNIDO (1995) *Technology Transfer Management.* United Nations Industrial Development Organization.

Utterback, J. (1994) *Mastering the Dynamics of Innovation.* Cambridge, MA: Harvard Business School Press.

Voss, C. (1992) *Manufacturing Strategy.* London: Chapman & Hall.

Wheelwright, S. and Clark, K. (1992) *Revolutionising Product Development.* New York: Free Press.

Womack, J., Jones, D. and Roos, D. (1990) *The Machine that Changed the World.* New York: Rawson Associates.

Managing inventory, MRP and JIT

We have stated throughout the text that it is important to think of manufacturing *and* services as a *total offering* to customers simply because wonderful services without excellent products will count for nothing; conversely, excellent products without good service is also not acceptable for customers. When problems occur in the interface between the two, the 'moment of truth' that we discussed in Chapter 1 becomes a major disappointment, as shown in the following mini-case.

Case: ToysRUs.com

'eToys SUCKS!!!' one customer shouts on a thread dubbed 'Online Shopping Hell'. Another rants, 'I doubt I will ever shop again online for Christmas. It is not worth the wait, lies, ill-informed customer service reps, and the hassle and stress.'

No brand did more to infuriate shoppers than toysrus.com. It kicked off the season with a big ad campaign that lured thousands to the site – traffic jumped more than 300 per cent. But midway through the holidays, the company announced it could not guarantee delivery by Christmas day. When Shaun Lawson learned his orders wouldn't arrive on time, he e-mailed the company to cancel. He received a form e-mail from toysrus.com telling him orders could only be cancelled within 30 minutes of the time they were placed. After several more attempts and a slew of form e-mail responses, an apoplectic Lawson fired off an e-mail he was sure the company couldn't ignore: 'Your form letter is grossly insulting. Cancel the ****ing order (yes, that means do not ship) and never bother me again.' He posted his rant on a website so 'others have an opportunity to learn from my mistake'. Toys 'R' Us's response came a few days later: 'Dear Shaun Lawson: Thank you for contacting toysrus.com. Our records indicate that your order was shipped … and is en route to you!'

Source: The nightmare before Christmas, *Fortune*, 24 January 2000, **141**(2).

Managing inventory successfully is not about technical solutions; rather a key factor to bear in mind with inventory management is that much of it is service related – it has to do with managing relationships throughout the supply network (which we explore further in Chapter 6) and this is fully linked to service operations.

The purpose of this chapter is for the reader to:

- understand the strategic significance of managing inventory;
- gain insights into why tactical 'solutions' do not work;
- appreciate how MRP (materials requirement planning), MRPII (manufacturing resource planning) and JIT (just-in-time) can be successful only if they are expertly managed within networks, which we will discuss in depth in Chapter 6.

The problem – the tactical 'solution' to managing inventory

Many Western firms have tended to view inventory management as a 'tactical' activity – this same 'tactical' attitude has also applied to operations management in general. Consequently, purchasing and supply management has been performed, in the main, at lower levels of the organization and has been relegated to a reactive function – again, much like operations itself. In the West this has meant that purchasing has been seen as a 'buying function' responding to production requirements – after they have been, in turn, determined by marketing. This mentality has changed to some degree, as *Industry Week* pointed out:

Heading for box?

There was a time when top-ranking executives in manufacturing tended to distance themselves from such operational details as supply chain management or information sharing with upstream and downstream partners in the 'value chain' – that continuum of activities that ultimately delivers something of value to an end customer. In the past, company presidents and CEOs were more inclined to fret about internal politics and bottom-line earnings than plunge into the various intercompany relationships that can either elevate or undermine the ultimate success of a business. But, like last month's stock price, that's history.

Today, in many firms, executives at the highest corporate levels are driving the development of value-chain strategies to enhance interactions with business partners. They've seen, for example, what innovative business models have done for leading companies like Dell Computer Corp. and Cisco Systems Inc., shrinking inventory costs and accelerating the cash-to-cash cycle.

In adopting elements of the so-called virtual corporation – often through outsourcing – they are trying to leverage the efficiencies of their value-chain partners. And they are beginning to understand that all of this requires a higher level of collaboration and information sharing if they expect to improve not only the performance of their own companies, but also the overall performance of the value chains in which they participate. To varying degrees that's true, whether their companies are 'chain starters' that supply raw materials and components, mid-chain suppliers, finished-product manufacturers, distributors or direct marketers.

Executives in each of those segments – including 1309 who lead finished-product firms – were among the more than 2000 respondents to an *Industry Week* survey designed to assess the impact of effective value-chain strategies and identify major obstacles to optimizing the performance of a value chain.

Among the major findings of the extensive research project, conducted in association with Ernst & Young, the New York-based management consulting firm, were these:

- Nearly one-third of the survey participants (31.2 per cent) said that, in their companies, the CEO or president is 'most responsible' for value-chain-improvement initiatives. Another 33.6 per cent indicated that responsibility rested at the vice-president level.
- More than half of the executives said that their firms have adopted – or are in the process of developing – formal value-chain strategies. Of the 36.7 per cent who now have formal strategies in place, a heavy majority believe their efforts have been at least 'somewhat effective' – although only 26.1 per cent think the strategies have been 'highly effective'.
- Only 13.3 per cent of the respondents rate the overall performance of the primary value chain that they participate in as 'very good' or 'excellent' – indicating that there is considerable room for improvement.
- Companies that have adopted formal strategies – and especially those with highly effective strategies – tend to be more successful in growing top-line revenues.
- Intercompany pressures on pricing issues are the most common stumbling block to value-chain optimization. Fully 44.2 per cent of the executives cited pricing issues as a 'major' barrier, while 39.7 per cent blamed poor communication.

A strategic imperative

Considering the level of executive involvement, value-chain management has clearly become 'a strategic imperative' in most companies, observes Robert Neubert, Ernst & Young's national director of automotive and industrial products services. 'It is not something that is being left to the purchasing department. It has reached the highest levels in the corporation,' he says. 'People see it as a key element of strategy.'

In smaller companies – those with revenues of less than $100 million – the president or CEO is most likely to bear the primary responsibility for value-chain improvement, the IW survey found, while large companies more frequently assign vice-presidents the leading role.

Source: Industry Week, Now it's a job for the CEO, 20 March 2000, p. 22.

The degree to which a strategic view is really embraced by firms is still unclear, although there is some evidence that there is a shift in emphasis in how inventory is managed. This will be developed further in the next chapter, but we will explore the strategic issues surrounding inventory in this chapter as well.

Looking back ...

The perceived management wisdom between the 1950s and 1980s was that a firm should try to vertically integrate as much as possible. So, looking at Figure 5.1, the former desired aspiration was that, wherever

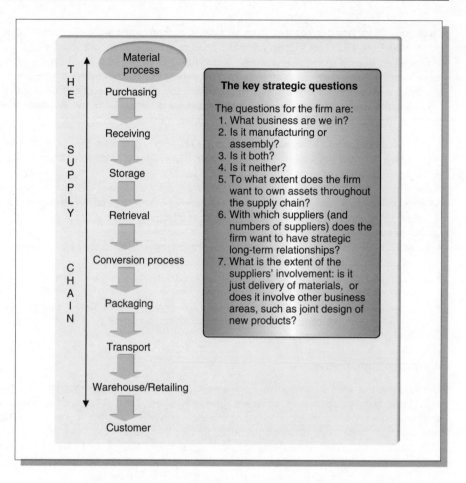

Figure 5.1
Questions within
the 'supply chain'
(from Brown, 2000).

possible, a firm would own all of the 'supply chain', or network. We use the term 'chain' here because it is commonly used but, as we shall see in Chapter 6, firms typically operate within networks, which are often complex, rather than within linear, 'chains'.

The reasons for the strategy of vertical integration were complex, but included the following factors:

■ the need for control (including costs, assurance of delivery and perceptions of quality) within the supply chain;

■ the possibility of diversification of business activities within the firm's business portfolio;

■ there was a commonly held belief that the 'bigger we are, the better we are' and that owning activities – including entire firms – within the supply chain could then be shown on the balance sheet as an asset.

The rationale behind this strategy was captured by Wise and Baumgartner (1999, p. 133):

> Ever since the birth of the modern industrial corporation in the 1920s, manufacturing strategy has been built on three foundations: the vertical integration of supply and production activities to control the cost and maintain the predictability of raw materials and other inputs; disciplined research to create superior products; and a dominant market position to provide economies of scale. With these in place, manufacturers could be assured of a durable cost advantage, steady revenue growth, and substantial scale barriers to competition. The usual reward was double-digit margins and returns on capital.

What became clear over time, however, was that this strategy had major flaws. This was brought to light in the 1980s, when Western firms began to understand how Japanese companies managed buyer–supplier relationships. We shall discuss this in greater detail in the following chapter, but as Brown (1996, p. 224) commented:

> Nowhere has the contrast between Western and Japanese manufacturing been more evident than in materials – or inventory – management. This area has also been one of the great areas of organizational learning by the West in terms of how it has tried to emulate some of the Japanese practices which have underpinned Japan's success in key industries.

The major shift in thinking since the 1980s has been to move away from the idea of inventory as an asset (which can be shown on a balance sheet as part of the firm's 'worth') to the idea, instead, that inventory can become a huge liability for the firm, the bad management of which (especially in production/operations areas) will weaken competitive capability in terms of delays, increased costs, reduced output and poor responsiveness to market requirements. As we shall see in Chapter 6, the sheer cost of bought-in materials from suppliers reveals how important inventory is to the buying company.

Inventory as an indication of world class

Inventory is not about 'buying things'; rather, its management goes right to the core of world-class practice in both manufacturing and services, and it is used as a key parameter in assessing capabilities, as can be seen in Figure 5.2.

Value chain	Raw material turns		WIP turns		Finished goods turns		Total inventory turns	
	Median	Upper quart.	Median	Upper quart.	Median	Upper quart.	Median	Upper quart.
Aerospace	6.8	13.0	10.0	20.0	8.5	15.0	6.0	10.0
Automotive	16.2	30.0	20.0	40.0	19.0	30.0	12.0	22.0
Chemicals	12.0	24.0	20.0	55.0	12.0	30.0	8.0	20.0
Construction	8.5	15.5	20.0	51.2	11.0	27.5	6.4	12.0
Consumer packaged goods/non-durables	15.0	45.0	24.0	81.5	13.0	38.0	10.0	23.0
Consumer product durables	10.0	20.0	20.0	38.4	12.5	24.0	8.0	17.3
High tech	8.0	22.0	12.0	30.0	10.0	24.0	7.0	10.0
Industrial equipment and machinery	8.0	13.0	12.0	20.0	10.0	12.0	6.0	10.0
Pharma, biotech, medical devices	8.7	15.0	11.0	18.5	8.0	13.0	5.0	10.0
Printing and publishing	12.0	20.0	25.5	90.5	15.0	88.0	10.0	16.0
Other	12.0	26.3	15.5	49.5	12.0	40.8	6.8	12.0
All	**11.6**	**22.0**	**16.0**	**38.2**	**12.0**	**25.0**	**8.0**	**13.0**

Note: Upper quart. equals upper quartile.
Raw material turns is cost of goods (COGS) sold divided by average raw materials.
Work-in-process (WIP) turns is COGS divided by average WIP value.
Finished goods turns is COGS divided by average value of finished goods.
Total inventory turns is COGS divided by average value of total inventory.

Raw material turns – a median of 11.6 for all plants, with 16.2 being the high for automotive – indicate how well manufacturers are working with suppliers to deliver needed material when it is needed. Finished goods turns – 12.0 or once per month for all plants, with 19.0 being the high, again in automotive – offers a sign of how customer responsive manufacturers are, and how quickly they're moving what they make out the door.

Figure 5.2
US manufacturing scorecard. (*source*: IW/MPI Census of Manufacturers shows challenges, reality and, yes, even optimism. *Industry Week*, 1 January 2004).

The scorecard in Figure 5.2 is typical of the measures that are used and the parameters have been central to lean production since the publication of *The Machine that Changed the World* (Womack *et al.*, 1990). However, as we shall see, although inventory management has strategic consequences, it has sometimes been managed in a tactical fashion. One of these has been in the EOQ formula.

The poor solution – the economic order quantity (EOQ) 'fix'

As can be seen from the Toys'R'Us case earlier, having stock-outs or zero-inventory for customers is not acceptable. However, there is a tension here because holding too much inventory can also cause major problems for firms.

All operations have to hold levels of inventories. The typical reasons for this are (Waters, 2003, p. 7):

- to act as a buffer between different operations;
- to allow for mismatches between supply and demand rates;
- to allow for demands that are larger than expected;
- to allow for deliveries that are delayed or too small;
- to avoid delays in passing products to customers;
- to take advantage of price discounts;
- to buy items when the price is low and expected to rise;
- to make full loads and reduce transport costs;
- to provide cover for emergencies.

Many of the above reasons are, however, no more than excuses, either for bad in-house performance or for poor buyer-supplier relationships. Similarly, work-in-process and finished goods inventories tend to act as covers or 'buffers' for possible failures. If finished goods inventories are held in order to 'supply the good product quickly to the consumer', then action should be taken to ensure that speed is improved within the in-house process, rather than keeping large quantities of finished goods, 'just in case', due to the current process being incapable of rapid response. In addition, keeping finished goods in inventory in high-tech markets is dangerous, due to rapid product/component obsolescence. Admittedly, there are industries that are seasonal or extremely erratic and where the threat of obsolescence is low, in which case holding raw materials and finished stock makes some sense – this approach makes little sense in many industries, however. One of the problems in the car industry is in levels of finished goods, as can be seen in Figure 5.3. As we shall see in our discussion on just-in-time, there are major challenges that need to be addressed in managing inventory.

There are problems with holding inventories:

- storage costs;
- interest is tied up – therefore, a loss on capital;
- obsolete stock;
- less money is available for the business;
- prices fall on held items;
- deterioration, theft, damage.

Conversely, there are problems with inventory 'stock-outs':

- failure to satisfy customer demands;
- costly emergency procedures to rectify situations;
- higher replenishment costs for stock replacement.

Figure 5.3
A telling example of finished goods inventory in the car industry (courtesy of Dr Howard and Professor Graves, University of Bath, 2004).

There are also the costs associated with inventory management, with the option of ordering large quantities infrequently, thereby keeping order costs down and increasing bulk discounts, or ordering small quantities frequently, to keep storage costs down and improve cash flow. The 'solution' to this was seen to be in the economic order quantity (EOQ), which *de facto* is the order size that minimizes both total stock holding and ordering costs.

However, it should be noted that the EOQ is based on weak assumptions, including the idea that demand is constant, there is little uncertainty, only order and storage costs are relevant, and orders are placed for only single items. Furthermore, the EOQ only identifies how much to order, not when to place the order. Two approaches to this may be adopted: the continuous review system or periodic review system. Under the continuous review system, the order is placed when the stock held is at a pre-designated re-order point. The re-order point is determined by calculating the average use of stock over time compared with the expected lead time between the order being placed and materials being delivered.

There are major problems with the EOQ formula. It is based on the following assumptions (Brown, 1996):

1   All costs are known and do not vary – demand for an item is also similarly known and will not vary.

2 As a result of point 1, both the unit cost of an item and the reorder costs are fixed and do not change according to quantity.

3 There is only one delivery for each order – this is fine on an as-required basis for JIT, but under the EOQ approach this 'one delivery' means that the buyer will incur stockholding costs until the materials are actually required and then decline over a period of time. The delivery will not necessarily act as a driving force to speed up its use and, even if it did, it might merely encourage forcing a material onto a work area before it is required. This will create a bottleneck and act to increase work in process.

The EOQ formula glosses over important issues, including:

- *The ordering cost.* In the EOQ formula, this is seen to be constant, regardless of the distance in placing the order, the mode of communication (phone, fax, EDI) and the time spent in placing the order, and the salary cost of the particular person(s) who placed the order.
- *The cost of stockholding.* Trying to determine this value is – for all practical purposes – impossible. Waters (2003) suggests that: 'The usual period for calculating stock costs is a year, so a holding cost might be expressed as, say, £10 a unit a year.'

Another approach is to charge a percentage (25 per cent, for example) against the actual cost of a bought item. A £100 item, therefore, will have a storage charge of £25. The problem with this is that holding an item for any period – particularly if the item is a high-tech component – will run the risk of obsolescence, which makes the unit itself redundant. Moreover, trying to work out a 'standard time' that an item might be expected to be in stock is at best pseudo-scientific and at worst becomes a means of providing an overhead cost on a unit component in order to fund another major overhead cost – warehousing. The EOQ approach is alien to just-in-time management that, as we shall see, seeks to 'pull' the exact number of materials or components to a particular work station only when it is required and not before. The EOQ formula encourages buffer stock and endorses a 'just-in-case' mentality rather than a just-in-time approach.

Usually, a buffer stock is added to cope with uncertainties, such as higher than average usage or delayed stock delivery. Under the periodic review system, there is no fixed order size, as orders are placed routinely at fixed time intervals, with order size being determined by comparing planned stock levels and actual stock levels. For instance, most pubs and bars have an identified 'par stock' level and re-order this once or twice a week. In practice, there are many combinations of these two basic approaches to inventory management, including base stock, optional replenishment and visual systems.

It should be clear, then, that the EOQ 'solution' is not really a solution at all. What this approach shows is that academics and practitioners alike are, perhaps, fond of seeking answers to what are often complex, dynamic variables. The impact of managing inventory is summarized by Lee and Schniederjans (1994, p. 323):

> Implementing a new inventory system takes more than a commitment from the inventory manager. It takes a commitment from the entire organization, from purchasing to shipping and from top management to the workers at the shop floor level of the organization.

A good starting point for an inventory manager intent on managing inventory in a strategic manner is to assess the range of inventories in an 'ABC' analysis.

ABC analysis

An ABC analysis is a surprisingly accurate, although simplistic, approach to managing inventory. It is based on the reality that components within the firm's total inventory range have various values or costs. ABC analysis can be undertaken in two ways. First, it can be done by focusing on a particular product and analysing its costs. Second, it can be undertaken by looking *across* the complete range of products within the firm (this is done where there is a large range of products) and analysing costs of components across the range.

In ABC analysis, the basic rule is: if we were to dismantle a finished product into a 'bill of materials' (which we shall discuss later) and lay out all of the components and then group them in terms of cost, we would find that around 20 per cent of the number of components account for 80 per cent of the costs of the product. This 'rule of thumb' is not fixed, of course; it might well be that 17 per cent of the components account for 76 per cent of costs, for example. ABC analysis is important because it helps to focus on the key issues in inventory management. The Class A components are those that need to be managed within strategic buyer–supplier relationships that we will discuss in this chapter and then develop further in Chapter 6.

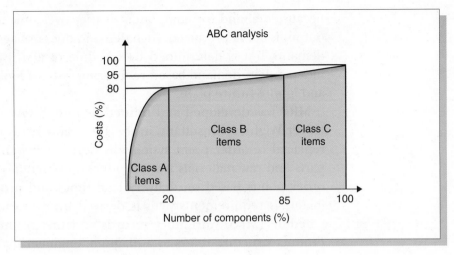

Figure 5.4
A simplified ABC
analysis.

A basic ABC analysis is shown in Figure 5.4.

Once we have undertaken ABC analysis we can then manage inventory by using powerful systems. Some of the most important in recent times have included MRP, MRPII and ERP.

The emergence of material requirement planning (MRP) manufacturing

Material requirement planning (MRP) came about with the recognition that, in high-volume manufacturing environments, assumptions that underpinned materials management in the craft era did not apply in the mass production era. The inventory control systems of the earlier era treated demand as if it were *independent* – that is, it is externally generated directly by the customer – and as a consequence, due to the aggregation of demand over time, it is generally smoother. Whilst demand from one customer may be 'lumpy', demand from many customers may create relatively uniform demand. Such independent demand is still relevant today to many kinds of operations, especially those mass retailing directly to the public, such as supermarkets, restaurants, department stores and so on. Indeed, 44 per cent of the inventory held in the US economy is wholesale and retail merchandise (Krajewski and Ritzman, 2001). However, this notion of relatively uniform and continuous demand is not likely to apply within organizations as far as demand for parts or components is concerned. In this context, demand is *dependent*. This means demand is lumpy because demand for components varies over time according to what output is being produced; such demand does not aggregate to smooth demand, but is determined by schedule of activity planned. Finally, independent demand-based reordering systems look at historic usage and ignore future plans.

MRP was developed and refined by Joseph Orlicky at IBM and by Oliver Wight, a consultant, in the 1960s and 1970s (Orlicky, 1975). It replaced re-order point systems by deriving dependent demand for parts and raw materials from production schedules and determining order points based on delivery lead times and production needs. A materials requirements plan is derived from the master production schedule (MPS), inventory records and the product structure. The product structure refers to a diagram, engineering drawing or list of materials and their quantities, usually called a bill of materials (BOM), needed to produce one item of output. The structure is often shown as a hierarchy of levels or 'parts explosion' (see Figure 5.6). For instance, the end product (level 0) may be made up of assemblies (level 1), each of which is made up of sub-assemblies (level 2), each of which may be made up of component parts (level 3).

MRP systems are often in the form of commercial software. Such commercialization has led to different terminology for similar aspects of the system, although there are some common terms in use. Generally, all MRP systems would involve the management of the following:

- gross requirements, i.e. the total quantity of material needed to produce planned output in a given period;
- available inventory, i.e. actual stock available for use in any given time period;
- allocated inventory, i.e. stock not available as part of the plan since it has been allocated to another use, such as spares;
- safety stock, i.e. stock not available for the plan as it exists to cope with uncertainty;
- net requirements, i.e. the quantity of material needed to meet scheduled demand;
- scheduled receipts, i.e. inventory already ordered and expected to be received from suppliers, which can be assumed to be in stock for planning period;
- planned ordered receipts, i.e. quantity of material planned to be received to meet net requirements or greater than net requirements if required by order size limitations;
- planned ordered releases, i.e. the quantity of output planned for a given time period to satisfy planned ordered receipts.

In essence, MRP is very simple. It seeks answers to the following questions:

1 How many products are to be made?
2 When do these products need to be made?
3 What is the finished product composition in terms of materials and components?
4 What are the numbers and types of components and materials currently in stock?

A figure is determined (by subtracting the answer to question 4 from the answer to question 3) to then ask:

5 How many items have to be ordered from suppliers?
6 What is the lead time for suppliers and, consequently, when do orders have to be placed?

Once these questions have been answered, the 'number crunching' begins on a component basis. The basic calculations are shown in Figure 5.5.

Another feature of the MRP system is the 'parts explosion', whereby a finished product is 'exploded' into 'levels' of components so that it becomes clear which components are dependent upon others. For example, in Figure 5.6 it is clear that some parts of the tricycle are level 1 only, whereas others are level 2. This is important in tracing components in terms of where they 'line up' across the range of the firm's products.

Using these data, these computerized systems typically produce a material requirement plan, priority reports, performance reports and

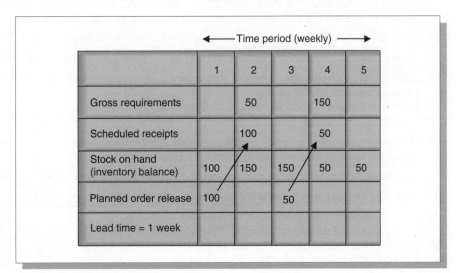

Figure 5.5
The basic MRP calculation (adapted from Brown, 1996).

action notices, which draw management attention to exceptions. In fact, one of the requirements of successful MRP is that it should be an integrated, cross-functional process. Oliver Wight listed 25 key points – which he called the ABCD checklist – against which firms could rate their level of adoption of MRP. It was clear from this that this was meant to encourage close liaison between operations, marketing and financial functions. The ABCD checklist is shown in Table 5.1.

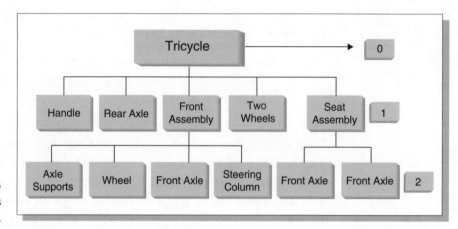

Figure 5.6
A simple parts explosion.

Table 5.1
ABCD checklist

1 Company has a formal monthly sales and operations planning process chaired by the Managing Director.
2 Company has a business planning process that is fully integrated with its operating system.
3 All functions within the company use a common set of numbers to drive the business.
4 There is a single database that drives all material and capacity planning.
5 System supports daily planning buckets and may be run daily (i.e. MPS, MRP and CRP).
6 Company has the appropriate levels of data accuracy to support business excellence: (a) Stock records 98–100 per cent; (b) Bills of material 98–100 per cent; (c) Routings 98–100 per cent.
7 The master production schedule is realistic in that there are no plans to produce items that have dates in the past and there are no overloads against critical resources.
8 Valid material plans exist for all components and ingredients of master schedule items.
9 Valid capacity plans exist for all work centres.
10 Company is committed to schedule achievement. It achieves: (a) On time in full delivery to customers 98–100 per cent; (b) Factory schedules on time 98–100 per cent; (c) Vendor schedules on time 98–100 per cent.

11	Forecasts are updated at least monthly and customer order promising is directly related to the master schedule.
12	New product introductions and engineering changes are managed effectively within the common system.
13	Company has a programme to reduce lead times, batch quantities and inventory to gain competitive advantage. Results are visible.
14	Company has sufficient level of user understanding to support business excellence: (a) Initial education of 80 per cent of all employees; (b) A structured ongoing education programme.
15	Company is working in partnership with its vendors through use of vendor scheduling and associated techniques.
16	Company is working in partnership with its customers through closer linkage and shares information.
17	Company monitors that it is improving its level of customer service and increasing inventory turns.
18	Company uses performance measurements as the mechanism for monitoring and improving all business processes.
19	Company uses such measurements to continually monitor and improve its competitive position in the market-place.
20	Company is committed to continuous improvement to maintain competitive advantage.

A Class 'D' user is typically one where either MRP is not operated or, if it is, no-one believes the MRP figures. Frequently, the storeman will have a manual record that anyone will refer to if they want to find out what is really in stock. Manual records and schedules are a dead give-away to poor data accuracy and a Class 'D' level of performance. Even if all the MRP II bits were in place, the lack of accurate data would render the output worthless. A Class 'D' user uses the MRP package as a (very expensive) typewriter!

A Class 'C' user may have a pretty good MRP system as was common in the 1950s and 1960s. The system will launch orders and progress chasers will expedite them according to which customers shout the loudest. They can never be better than Class 'C' because they do not attempt to manage the MRP according to the resources available. The lack of a managed master schedule and integrated capacity planning are Class 'C' indicators.

A Class 'B' user will have capacity resource management in place via a sales and operations plan and a managed master scheduling process, but the failure to properly control all the elements of ERP/MRPII will typically be shown up by the necessity to have secondary priority information to get the 'hot' jobs through production.

A Class 'A' user will score 18 or more on the check sheet and will need neither shortage sheets nor progress chasers. Instead, production control and monitoring will typically be carried out using the output from the planning system. The 98 per cent, or better, on time delivery to customers will soon become an accepted part of the company's culture. A missed shipment or even a stock error will become a major cause for concern instead of just a way of life.

Source: BPIC, The Manufacturing Planning Resource: www. BPIC.co.uk.

MRP, however, is not a magic solution. Oliver Wight thought that less than 10 per cent of companies were what he termed 'Class A' users – i.e. firms scored at least 18 or more from the above checklist. Cerveny and Scott (1989) identified 40 per cent of firms they surveyed had adopted it, but only 67 per cent regarded it as success.

MRP operates best under four conditions:

1 High-volume line processes.
2 Product structure is complex and there are many levels of bills of materials.
3 Production is carried out in relatively large batch sizes.
4 There is limited volatility. Bottlenecks, rush jobs, high scrap rates and unreliable suppliers create volatile conditions unsuited for the MRP system.

MRP also requires high data integrity – that is, the accuracy of the data must be high and consistent. Since inventory level data is traditionally poor and quoted lead times from suppliers even worse, the general failure of MRP should not surprise us. The precision was also inherently poor: a lead time for delivery of a component, for example, might typically be quoted – and entered into the database – as, say, 14 weeks. There are several problems with this: the suggestion that anyone can predict what materials will be needed in 14 weeks' time, and the excessively loose unit of a week for a delivery promise.

From MRP to MRPII

MRP evolved into MRPII which, in essence, *included* MRP and added other management ingredients such as tooling, routing procedures, capacity availability and man-hours requirement. MRP is therefore a subset of MRPII, as shown in Figure 5.7.

Often, plant managers will refer to MRP when, in fact, the system they have is MRPII – the terms have become almost interchangeable. When executed properly, MRPII can make a powerful contribution to materials planning and capacity management. However, both MRP and MRPII have been severely criticized, as Luscombe (1994, p. 123) observes:

> One article referred to 'disillusionment with existing MRPII-based production planning tools', another stated that MRPII implementation methodologies 'belong to a different era' whilst a third offered reasons why 'so many large-scale MRPII systems failed'.

But, as Luscombe (1994, p. 123) also suggests:

> Those who abandon MRPII in search of some form of instant-response, shopfloor-driven system are likely to be disappointed, as they ignore

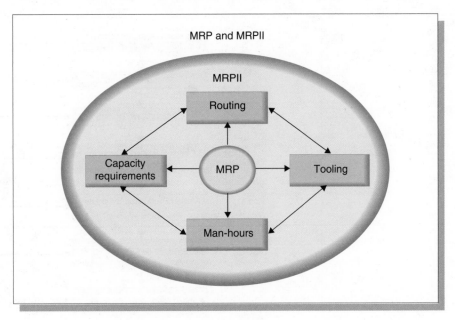

Figure 5.7
MRP as a subset of MRPII.

the realities of manufacturing as reflected in both MRPII and leading Japanese production systems.

The real problem is that often managers expect an instant solution to poor management of inventory. They suspect that software alone, via MRP/MRPII, will solve these problems. The lack of strategic importance given to materials management by senior managers becomes a key reason for failure. But when there is a strategic and holistic approach to managing inventory, the 'closed loop' system becomes a reality, as shown in Figure 5.8.

In addition, MRP should facilitate better relationships with suppliers because, in theory, all lead times are known and therefore unreasonable delivery requirements are not made on suppliers. Admittedly, shorter lead times are preferable, especially when MRP is used alongside JIT, but that has more to do with an ongoing pursuit of improvement in delivery performance via relationships with suppliers than as a reflection on MRPII itself.

Resolving problems of MRP

There is nothing to stop MRP being used as the planning system, and then for the tools and techniques of JIT to be used to actually 'pull' the

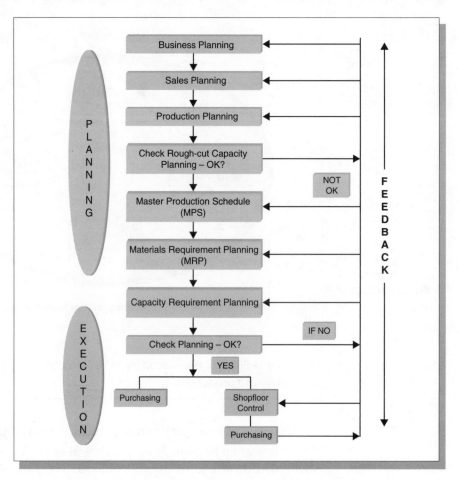

Figure 5.8
MRPII: the closed
loop system.

materials only when needed. At any rate, there must be some sort of master plan for a given time period in order for the firm to know what is to be made in a particular time. MRP can therefore be used as an exhaustive management tool whereby numbers of products and, consequently, sub-components can be determined and tracked throughout the process. MRP should not be used to 'push' components or materials onto a workstation before they are required. Advocates of JIT (and critics of MRP) have stated that MRP is inclined to do this (Plenert and Best, 1986) – but, again, this has more to do with management's failure in terms of using MRP rather than the system itself. MRP can provide a discipline so that key areas such as master production schedules, bill of materials, lead times with suppliers and other data integrity are reliable, accurate, relevant and known to all parties, which is essential to any well-run management information system.

MRP encourages an holistic approach within the firm itself. As Waters (2003, p. 279) states:

> The introduction of MRP needs considerable changes to an organization and these require commitment from all areas.

The MRP system can also serve to highlight business performance problems with delivery speed and reliability. As Schmenner (1990, p. 487) suggests:

> Not only can an MRP system detail what should be ordered and when, but also it can indicate how and when late items will affect other aspects of production. It can signal ... how tardiness will alter the existing production schedule.

Since delivery speed and reliability are crucial in many markets, it is clear that MRP can play an important role in achieving these market requirements. MRP also becomes a powerful ally to just-in-time management. As Karmarker (1989, p. 125) states:

> MRPII ... initiates production of various components, releases orders, and offsets inventory reductions. MRPII grasps the final product by its parts, orders their delivery to operators, keeps track of inventory positions in all stages of production and determines what is needed to add to existing inventories. What more could JIT ask?

The answer to this question is twofold:

1　Much better internal quality control systems to enable JIT to become a reality.
2　A strategic vision with suppliers – a vision of shared destiny between them rather than the buyer versus supplier relationship that pervades in much of Western manufacturing.

The linkages within MRP are shown in Figure 5.9.

MRP became an important step in the evolution toward the strategic management of inventory, as shown in Figure 5.10.

Enterprise resource planning (ERP)

Enterprise resource planning (ERP) systems go beyond MRP and MRPII to integrate internal and external business processes. SAP AG, a German software company, sells the most popular ERP system, R/3. Although

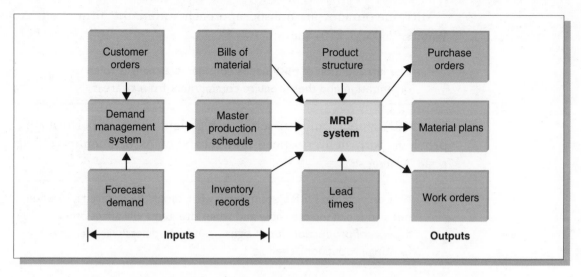

Figure 5.9
Linkages within the MRP system.

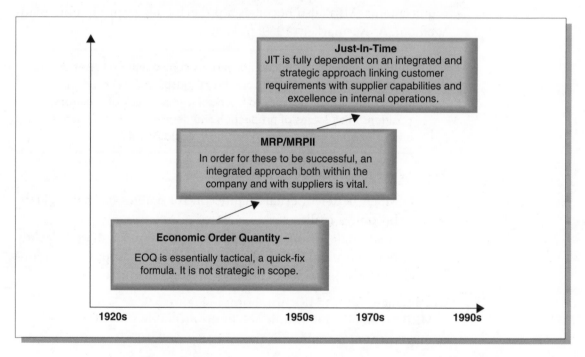

Figure 5.10
The development of the strategic importance of inventory management.

ERP systems have become popular, implementing ERP is time-consuming and costly. Like all software 'solutions', ERP has its advocates and critics alike. The basic flow of the system is shown in Figure 5.11.

ERP has gained in popularity over MRP to some extent, although MRP and MRPII remain in use. The basic problem with MRP is that it

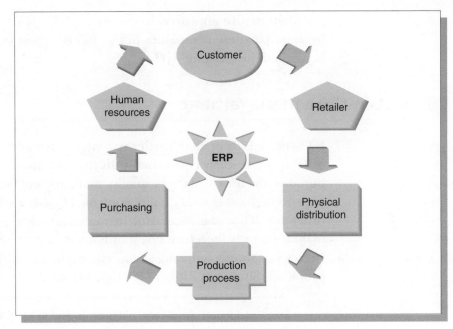

Figure 5.11
How enterprise resource planning (ERP) systems link the supply chain (from Brown *et al.*, 2001).

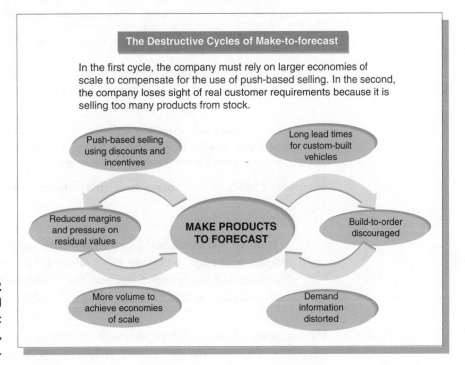

Figure 5.12
Push versus pull strategies (*source*: Holweg and Pil, 2001).

can be a 'push' system of inventory management. This means that there can be a danger of ordering materials and then 'pushing' them through the system before an operator is ready. The danger of a 'push' system is shown in Figure 5.12.

An alternative approach based on a 'pull' approach was developed by some Japanese companies in the 1950s – most famously by Toyota. It is called 'just-in-time' (JIT).

Just-in-time management

JIT is more holistic than earlier systems of inventory management and MRP. It is not solely concerned with capacity, materials and inventory, but also includes aspects of quality management, such as continuous improvement and total quality control. TQM is a vital prerequisite in order for JIT to be successful in manufacturing plants. Just-in-time management is therefore not simply an inventory reduction exercise. In fact, just simply reducing stocks will, in the first instance, *create* major problems. Shingo in Zipkin (1991, p. 44) states:

> Stock reduction should not become an end in itself, however, since cutting stock blindly may cause delivery delays. ... Rather the conditions that produce or necessitate stock must be corrected so that stock can be reduced in a rational fashion.

Just-in-time is a complete shift away from traditional Western manufacturing. Hutchins (1999, p. 11) narrates how:

> JIT is part of a fundamentally different approach to management which when fully developed will help to create a totally new industrial culture.

Harrison (1992, p. 24) shows how this fundamental change works in Japan:

> In Japan, JIT has developed into a total management system from marketing through to delivery. It has diffused through suppliers and distributors. It has provided Japanese companies with a formidable competitive advantage over their Western rivals.

JIT includes elements of production scheduling and inventory management. This approach identified for the first time that trade-offs were not an essential aspect of operations. JIT is linked to capacity management. For example, Toyota creates a fixed monthly production schedule each month. The production level will change each month, but what Toyota is doing by adhering to the monthly production schedule is to manage the uncertainty of capacity by making the production 'fixed' for a given month. This schedule is then communicated to

Toyota's suppliers. This then means that capacity has become synchronized between Toyota and its suppliers so that deliveries can be planned with a great amount of certainty to manufacturing operations.

JIT enables improvements to be made to costs, delivery times and quality. It is for this reason that we shall consider it in more detail in discussion of the mass customization era. Perhaps the most fascinating aspect of JIT, in retrospect, is that it was developed entirely without computers (although latterly much computerization has been incorporated into it). At a time when managers in the West were fixated with the computer programs in MRP, missing the absurdity of relying on data such as '14 weeks lead time', the Japanese were dealing with immediate requirements – making a virtue out of living from hand to mouth and employing common sense, not rocket science.

Just-in-time production (JIT) was conceived by Taiichi Ohno, the former head of production at Toyota, in the 1980s. World-class JIT streamlines production, exposes problems and bottlenecks, and attacks waste. Suzaki (1987) quotes Jujio Cho of Toyota, who identifies seven types of waste; these are shown in Table 5.2.

Table 5.2
Seven categories of waste

1. **Overproduction**	5. **Stock on hand**
■ More than customer needs ■ Out of sequence ■ The wrong part ■ Early or late	■ Buffer against variability ■ Store excess parts ■ WIP deadens responsiveness ■ Money tied up
2. **Waiting**	6. **Motion**
■ By people ■ By products ■ By machines (bottlenecks) ■ By customer	■ Process choice ■ Efficiency of task ■ Maintain operator flow ■ Maintain work flow ■ Improve the method first, *then* inject capital
3. **Transportation**	7. **Defective goods**
■ Not value added ■ Effort and cost ■ Inventory ■ No control, no ownership	■ Cost of scrap ■ Creates inventory (just in case!!) ■ Cost of rectification ■ Causes poor delivery performance
4. **The process itself**	
■ Basic raw material ■ Basic process ■ Value eng, value analysis ■ Make/buy ■ Why do it at all? ■ Process choice	

True JIT operation does not employ safety stocks, therefore, as they are wasteful. At the heart of the system is the *kanban*, the Japanese word for card; in practice, these take many forms – cards, magnetic strips, plastic containers and so on. They are the means for communicating to, from and within work centres. Information about the part is written on the *kanban*, including reference number, storage area and associated work centres. These days, much of this information is now in barcode form. In a JIT system, parts can only be used, moved or produced if accompanied by a *kanban*. Movement of parts is further simplified by bins or containers of fixed size, designed to hold a specific and relatively small number of units of the same part. Different parts are never put into the same containers. In a typical production situation, an operator at a workstation has one or more *kanban*. When one is empty, this is authorization to obtain a full *kanban* from either the storage area or the next workstation up the line. The arrival of an empty *kanban* at a workstation is authorization for that operator to produce sufficient parts to refill it. Thus, production activity is generated by demand from the next operator down the line ('downstream'), which is why it is a 'pull' system. MRP and JIT systems are not mutually exclusive. Many operations operate a hybrid of these two in an attempt to take advantage of the best elements of both. MRP/MRPII will be used to plan materials; JIT will then 'pull' materials as required.

Another element of the Japanese approach to manufacturing has been to dampen the impact of variations in the production schedule, by producing relatively small quantities of the same mix of products. Operations schedules are planned on a daily basis to achieve monthly planned output. The adoption of uniform plant loading may have the impact of increasing the frequency of machine set-ups, however, as the plant switches from producing one output to another. Hence the Japanese, notably Shigeo Shingo in Toyota, spent many years seeking to achieve a 'single digit' set-up – the ability to change a machine tool from one set-up to another in less than 10 minutes. By the late 1970s, a Toyota team of press operators was able to change over an 800-ton press, from one part to another, in less than 10 minutes, compared with 6 hours for the same activity (i.e. the same two parts) in a US car plant. They achieved this simply by differentiating between external set-up, which can be carried out whilst the machine is running, and internal set-up, which requires the machine to be stopped. External set-up may include transfers of dies or moulds from a storage area to the machine and preheating the machine or its component up to operating temperature. Set-up time may also be reduced by standardizing the set-up function of the machine, conveyors and cranes to move dies, eliminating unnecessary adjustments, synchronizing operator tasks and automating some of the procedures, such as feed and position work, if possible. Furthermore, in Japanese factories, change-over teams would go into the factory at weekends, when production was shut down, to practise set-ups. This same approach can be observed during Formula 1 races, when the pit team changes tyres. They can change all four wheels and put large volumes of fuel into the tank in under 10 seconds, whereas the average motorist can take up to half an hour to change one wheel!

The challenges of JIT

Just-in-time is a very simple idea which has been extraordinarily difficult for many companies to implement. Zipkin's (1991, p. 40) statement is pertinent here:

> ... a storm of confusion swirls around JIT. Ask any two managers who have worked with it just what JIT is and does, and you are likely to hear wildly different answers. Some managers credit JIT with giving new life to their companies; others denounce it as a sham ....

The essence of JIT is that the exact number of components will arrive at a workstation exactly at the time required and, in JIT, the *supply* of materials will exactly match the *demand* of materials both in terms of quantity and time.

Although the just-in-time management approaches emanated from Japan, it is clear that the techniques have been transferred – with varying degrees of success – to the West. For many companies just-in-time will present a massive challenge to the way in which the firm will operate its business. These factors will include both internal and external factors: the internal factors will include an obsession with quality – 'getting it right first time' – because JIT cannot tolerate re-work and scrap, since only the exact amount of materials will be 'pulled' to satisfy the component requirements for a particular workstation. The internal challenges of JIT are shown in Table 5.3.

One of the main factors in just-in-time is in the elimination of waste, resulting in measurable benefits, not always centred on costs: areas such as flexibility, rapid response to customer requirements, innovation, and delivery speed and reliability.

Table 5.3

The effect of JIT on operations (adapted from Brown, 1996)

	Traditional manufacturing	**JIT/enlightened approaches**
Quality	'Acceptable' levels of rejects and rework – an inevitability that failures will occur. A specialist function	'Right first time, every time', constant, ongoing pursuit of process improvement. Everybody responsible for ensuring quality
Inventory	An asset, part of the balance sheet and therefore part of the value of the firm; buffers necessary to keep production running	A liability, masking the operational performance by hiding a number of problems
Batch sizes	An economic order can be determined to show the balance between set-up time and production runs	Batch sizes must be as small as possible, aiming toward a batch size of 1
Materials ordering	Determined by the economic order quantity	Supply exactly meets demand, no more no less, in terms of quantity; delivery is exactly when required, not before and not after
Bottlenecks	Inevitable; shows that machine utilization is high	No queues – production is at the rate which prevents delays and queues
Workforce	A cost which can be reduced by introducing more automation	A valuable asset, able to problem solve, and should be supported by managers

The Japanese have insisted that, in their plants, there should not be idle time, waiting or buffers. The Japanese terms for these are:

Muda   waste
Mura   inconsistency by machines or workers
Muri   excessive demands upon workers or machines

When there is little 'buffer' inventory, these three factors become prominent. Conversely, these three factors are disguised by holding amounts of inventory. Holding inventory – at any stage – can serve to 'cover' poor operational performance and reducing inventory will, in the first instance, cause these problems to surface, which will then focus the firm in having to make improvements in production/operation areas, as shown in Figure 5.13.

Interestingly, when these problems appear, the *strategic* importance is revealed. Instead of a 'quick fix', tactical approach – buying more

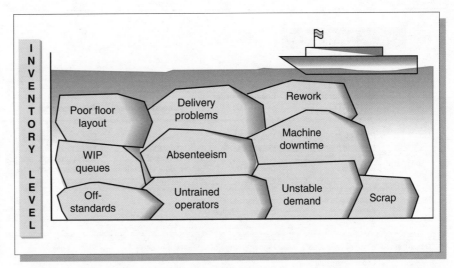

stock to cover problems – the firm must take strategic measures: continuous and ongoing improvements in-house to reduce stock levels, coupled with strategic alliances with suppliers to enhance delivery, innovations and reduce total costs.

We hinted at the differences between push and pull earlier in the chapter. The challenges and benefits of this transition to JIT are shown in Figure 5.14.

As well as the internal requirements for JIT, there are also external factors: a major failure of some Western companies in terms of implementing just-in-time is their inability to forge long-term, strategic partnerships with their suppliers. We shall discuss this in depth in the next chapter, but a note is pertinent here in our discussion on just-in-time.

You will recall how, earlier in the chapter, we stated that the former perceived wisdom within management was for the firm to own as much of the supply chain as possible for the reasons that we listed. Over time this perception changed, although this did not mean that there were mutually beneficial strategic relationships in place between buyers and suppliers within the supply network. Indeed, Porter (1980, p. 125) had pitched the buyer–supplier relationship in, largely, adversarial terms – the buyer, for example, should pursue the 'threat of backward integration' and 'use of tapered integration' according to Porter. This has changed over time, although there are many firms who remain routed in this approach. However, buyer–supplier relationships had changed over time, as Turnbull *et al.* (1993, p. 51) commented:

In Japan, the actual contract between motor manufacturer and supplier is based on co-operation, a full exchange of information, a commitment

Push vs. Pull Strategies

PUSH ◄───────────────────────────────────► PULL

	Make-to-forecast (MTF)	Locate-to-order (LTO)	Amend-to-order	Hybrid Build-to-order	True Build-to-order (BTO)
Goals	▪ Produce standard products from long-term-demand forecasts ▪ Manage stock reactively to allow for efficient production	▪ Use MTF, but increase stock visibility (through the internet, for example) to enhance customer choice	▪ Provide custom orders when specifications of product in system can be easily amended	▪ Rely on forecasting for high-volume, stable products, and build low-volume product to order	▪ Build products only after the customer orders them ▪ Make customer needs visible to all parts of the value chain
Benefits	▪ Efficient production ▪ Local optimization of factory operations	▪ Higher chance of finding right product in stock ▪ Inexpensive to implement	▪ Higher degree of custom-built vehicles in production	▪ Stable base production ▪ Relatively short order-to-delivery times on average ▪ Less inventory ▪ Less discounting	▪ No stock apart from showroom and demonstrators ▪ No discounting
Weakness	▪ High levels of finished stock in market ▪ MTF requires alternative product specifications and discounting to sell ageing stock ▪ Customer orders compete with forecast for capacity ▪ MTF loses sight of real customer demand	▪ High stock levels remain ▪ Discounting still required ▪ Custom orders still compete with forecast for capacity ▪ Extra cost to transfer product to location close to customer	▪ Customer orders built only when they fit ▪ Unsold orders are built anyway ▪ High temptation to revert to MTF if demand drops	▪ Stock is still in market ▪ Still requires discounting to cope with forecast error ▪ Danger of reverting to pure MTF when demand shifts	▪ System is sensitive to short-term demand fluctuations, so will not work without proactive demand management ▪ Active revenue management required to maximize profit

Figure 5.14
Key factors in push versus pull strategies (*source*: Holweg and Pil, 2001).

to improve quality, and a recognition … that prices can (and will) be reduced each year … bargaining is not simply focused on price *per se* but on how to reach the target price while maintaining a reasonable level of profit for the supplier.

That is not to say that the partnership is based on complacency and ease as a result of the partnership deal having been made. Rather, demands are made on the supplier, but these are made achievable as a result of the Japanese buyer helping the supplier to improve its business in terms of lower cost and faster delivery. The partnership approach is summarized by Schonberger and Knod (2001, p. 291):

> In the partnership approach, the idea is not to change suppliers. The rule is: stay with one, in order that it may stay on the learning curve, get to know the customer's real requirements, and perhaps participate with the customer on product and process improvements.

The benefits of buyer–supplier collaboration are stated by Carlisle and Parker (1991, p. 5):

> Co-operation between industrial users and sellers is a far more powerful strategy for making them both more profitable in the long term than any adversarial approach yet devised.

In order for buyer–supplier relationships to be strong there has to be considerable trust shown between both parties. Sako (1992) suggests that three types of trust need to be in place:

1 *Contractual trust* – which is the adherence to formal, legal promises.
2 *Competence trust* – that either side is capable of providing what has been promised.
3 *Goodwill trust* – which borders on 'ethics', trusting that appropriate behaviour will ensue.

As we shall see in the next chapter, the ability to form such partnerships, essential to successful JIT, is a major challenge and calls for the very best of management expertise. It is clear that, sometimes, this expertise is not in place. *Business Week* (8 August 1994, p. 26) noted how:

> GM's relations with its suppliers remain the worst in Detroit. … An electronics supplier tells of a $30 part he developed jointly with GM. He says that after he slashed the price to $15, the GM purchasing agent demanded more cuts, citing a $9 bid from a Chinese company that had never made the part in question. … One parts maker that does $600 million in business with car makers says it is focusing its efforts on selling to GM's rivals.

Fortune (15 May 2000) too, added how buyer–supplier relationships within the car industry have not improved across many companies:

> The relationship between an auto-parts company and its customer, the automaker, is like the relationship between a masochist and a sadist. Really. The parts maker slashes margins to the bone to get a contract in which the difference between a winning bid and a losing one may be one-thousandth of a cent. Then the real pain begins. The manufacturer demands that the parts maker meet rigorous schedules, adjust to wide fluctuations in production, and cut prices by several per cent every year that a contract runs. If a part turns out to be defective, the parts maker may have to share in the manufacturer's added warranty costs – or perhaps pay damages from a class-action lawsuit.

The *Financial Times* (29 January 2003, p. 19) commented how buyer–supplier relationships were far from perfect in retail services:

> From September 2001, the report says, they operated a programme called – almost comically – Project Slow It Down. Payments to suppliers were systematically delayed or reduced, suppliers were denied access to computer records of accounts payable and were deceived about why they were not being paid.

Even though JIT was pioneered within the car industry, there are still problems in place. One of this relates to the time taken for a car to be transferred from customer order to delivery to the customer. The problem is captured in Figure 5.15.

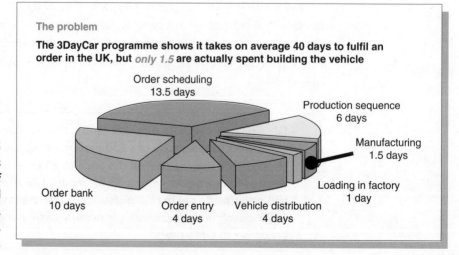

Figure 5.15
Ongoing problems with JIT (courtesy of Dr Howard and Professor Graves, University of Bath, 2004).

The problem

The 3DayCar programme shows it takes on average 40 days to fulfil an order in the UK, but *only 1.5* **are actually spent building the vehicle**

Order scheduling
13.5 days

Production sequence
6 days

Manufacturing
1.5 days

Loading in factory
1 day

Order bank
10 days

Order entry
4 days

Vehicle distribution
4 days

Another challenge with JIT is that even when there are mutually beneficial relationships in place, with both parties striving to continuously improve their operations in order to outperform other such relationships within the same industry, unforeseen problems may occur. These can have a devastating effect upon JIT, which although vastly superior to the just-in-time scenario under traditional mass production, is a very fragile, almost delicate phenomenon.

Clearly, the management of inventory has developed over time, from a largely tactical activity to a senior-level strategic position within firms. Changes from EOQ to MRP and JIT have shown profound developments over time. JIT is more than inventory management because it represents a fundamental change in how firms produce goods by utilizing a 'pull' system that we discussed earlier.

A key issue in inventory is in managing buyer–supplier relationships within networks and we discuss this in depth in the next chapter.

Case: The virtues of vertical integration

Crown Equipment Corp. seems on first impression to be a company that time forgot. Tucked away in the small Ohio town of New Bremen (population: 2909), which prides itself on its nineteenth-century streetscape, the company has leveraged vertically integrated manufacturing facilities to produce products for the mature material-handling industry. Yet with its passionate attention to the products it makes and uncommon attention to the needs of the people who use them, the company represents at least one aspect of US manufacturing's future: the ability to design, manufacture, distribute and service innovative, high-tech products in mature segments for which buyers are willing to pay a little bit more.

Crown's FC4000 series sit-down counterbalanced electric lift truck, a recent Industrial Design Excellence Award (IDEA) winner, was developed along with a three-wheel model. Having in-house manufacturing, design and engineering helped the company leverage its product development investment over the two products.

Consider Crown's achievements: the privately-held company entered the material-handling industry late, in the early 1950s. The last North American entrant to the lift-track manufacturing market, the company thrived amid a consolidating industry, rising to become the fifth largest lift-truck company in the world and capturing the top spot in the electric lift-track segment. It's now a $1 billion company.

Its financial success is complemented by its innovation and design accomplishments, represented by a substantial list of design awards – including an international award that ranks Crown ahead of such design stalwarts as Audi, Jaguar and Porsche.

Company executives insist that no grand strategy or implementation of the latest management trend drives their success. They contend that what might be considered their 'management strategies' are simply work processes that work for them, given the company's mission. Take the vertically integrated manufacturing 'strategy', for example. The fact that Crown plants produce 85 per cent of the parts in its products came about not because of 'some big strategic thing that we want to be vertically integrated and by golly that's what we're going to do,' says Senior Vice-president Don Luebrecht. He notes that executives rarely even employ the term 'vertical integration'. Rather, the company's bias toward in-house manufacturing evolves from a 'product-focused, product passionate' mindset, says Mike Gallagher, Vice-president, Crown Design Center. Vertical integration gives the company 'the ability to cook more of ourselves and this passion into the product', enabling them to build a product that is more central to the Crown brand.

Both men are quick to point out that they and other executives at the company are not adamantly opposed to outsourcing manufacturing and other functions. 'We do tend to review these things, and revisit them to make sure we're still competitive,' says Luebrecht.

Most often though, says Gallagher, 'It would be harder to achieve the brand promise with everyone else's supplied content.' Both executives stress that the company's focus on meeting the forklift operator's needs and their emphasis on ergonomics and safety has set Crown apart from its competitors. But it's also created the type of manufacturing challenges that few or no outside vendors address. He explains that the company's breakthrough product, Crown's first counterbalance truck introduced in the 1970s, is a good example. In developing the lift, the first in the industry to combine a multi-function control handle with a side-stance operator position, Crown could have found suppliers to contribute components to the control device, but no supplier had the technology to build it. Says Luebrecht, 'That first multi-function handle was an incredible mechanical and electronic combination of things. That combination of things just wasn't around in those days.'

Ultimately, says Luebrecht, the company's intense customer and product focus inspires designers, engineers and production employees at the company to be 'more willing to be challenged and find new ways of solving problems – to sweat the details of each component – than somebody else who is one or two times removed from that feeling. I think at times we've found ways of doing things that weren't impossible in other ways, but [most companies] wouldn't have had the patience or taken the time to get there.'

Tight integration between the design and production also accelerates product innovation, say company executives. They note that once they've solved technological or ergonomic challenges for one product, they can quickly adapt the innovation to other products. When the company started development of its three-wheel sit-down counterbalance lift track, the design team all had in mind the future development of a four-wheel model. This allowed them to consider design challenges associated with both applications and essentially address them for both models at the same time.

One question that remains to be answered is whether low-cost, overseas manufacturers will redefine competition in the electric lift-truck industry and render the vertical manufacturing approach obsolete, as it has in so many other industries. The executives readily admit they are very aware of the possibility, noting that they do not only compete on price: 'We're at the higher end of the price continuum,' notes Joe Ritter, Director of Marketing. They also allow that they've been somewhat insulated from low-cost competition from overseas: 'The electric lift-truck industry has not been impacted over the years nearly the way the internal combustion industry has with offshore products,' says Ritter. He notes that while low-cost, overseas manufacturers tend to be good at mass manufacturing, 'electric lift trucks tend to be more specialized. Our products are not cookie cutter and that's a different challenge for manufacturers, and those challenges have not created opportunities for those other countries in the electric lift-truck industry.'

No one can say for sure, but many speculate that US manufacturers will survive by producing highly specialized products that do not compete on price, but rather better meet customer needs and provide better customer service. Who knows? Maybe this smallish company, steeped in history and practising what many think is an outmoded vertical manufacturing strategy, just might represent US manufacturing's future.

Source: Panchak, P. (2003) The virtues of vertical integration. *Industry Week*, September, pp 50–52.

Key question: What role does strategy have in the above case?

Summary

- For many years, inventory management was one of the major contrasts between the Japanese and Western approaches to manufacturing, although there is evidence that many Western firms are improving in the area of inventory management.
- Inventories can, if badly managed, serve as a means of covering problems both in terms of in-house operations and poor supplier performance.
- 'Quick-fix' purchasing formulas (such as EOQ) do not provide any strategic advantage for the firm.
- The firm must concentrate on improving operations performance in order to avoid a 'just-in-case' approach. In this way, inventory costs will decrease and, just as important, the firm's capabilities in terms of delivery reliability, rapid response and flexibility will be greatly enhanced.

- Material requirement planning (MRP), manufacturing resource planning (MRPII) and enterprise resource planning (ERP) can be powerful means of controlling inventory. However, MRP should not be used to 'push' materials through the production system; rather, MRP is a management planning system whereby all components can be planned in advance for a particular time period.
- Just-in-time is part of world-class, strategic manufacturing. However, JIT is not simply about inventory reduction; it is a complete shift from traditional 'push' approaches based around production of large batches (made to stock). Instead, a 'pull' system based upon 'make to order' for customers becomes the focus of production.
- A vital feature of just-in-time is the buyer–supplier relationship. The 'traditional' buyer versus supplier approach makes little sense; instead, the manufacturing firm must concentrate on focusing on key suppliers and forming strategic partnerships with them.

Key questions

1 Why has inventory management emerged as strategic factor?
2 What is the main difference between push and pull systems?
3 What internal and external capabilities need to be in place for successful JIT?

References and further reading

Brown, S. (1996) *Strategic Manufacturing for Competitive Advantage.* Hemel Hempstead: Prentice Hall.

Brown, S. (2000) *Manufacturing the Future – Strategic Resonance for Enlightened Manufacturing.* London: Financial Times/Pearson Books.

Brown, S., Cousins, P., Blackmon, K and Maylor, H. (2001) *Operations Management – Policy, Practice and Performance Management.* Butterworth-Heinemann.

Business Week, 8 August 1994.

Carlisle, J. and Parker, L. (1991) *Beyond Negotiation.* Chichester: Wiley.

Cerveny, R.P. and Scott, L.W. (1989) A survey of MRP implementation. *Production and Inventory Management*, **30**(3), 177–181.

Financial Times, 29 January 2003.

Fortune, 24 January 2000.

Fortune, 15 May 2000.

Goldratt, E.M. and Cox, J. (1986) *The Goal.* Great Barrington, MA: North River Press.

Harrison, A. (1992) *Just-in-Time Manufacturing in Perspective.* Hemel Hempstead: Prentice Hall.

Holweg and Pil (2001) Successful build-to-order strategies start with the customer. *Sloan Management Journal*, Fall, 74–83.

Hutchins, D. (1999) *Just in Time,* 2nd Edition. London: Gower Books.

Industry Week, 20 March 2000.

Industry Week, IW/MPI Census of Manufacturers shows challenges, reality and, yes, even optimism, 1 January 2004.

Lee, S. and Schniederjans, M. (1994) *Operations Management.* Boston, MA: Houghton Mifflin.

Karmarker, U. (1989) Getting control of just in time. *Harvard Business Review,* September–October, 122–131.

Krajewski, L. and Ritzman, L. (2001) *Operations Management: Strategy and Analysis.* Englewood Cliffs, NJ: Prentice Hall.

Luscombe, R. (1994) Getting better all the time. In: *Proceedings of BPICS Conference,* Birmingham.

Orlicky, J. (1975) *Material Requirements Planning.* New York: McGraw-Hill.

Plenert, G. and Best, T.D. (1986) MRP, JIT and OPT. What's best? *Production and Inventory Management,* **27**(3), 22–30.

Porter, M. (1980) *Competitive Strategy.* New York: Free Press.

Sako, M. (1992) *Prices Quality and Trust: Inter-firm Relations in Britain and Japan.* Cambridge: Cambridge University Press.

Schmenner, R. (1990) *Production/Operations Management.* Macmillan.

Schonberger, R. and Knod, E. (2001) *Operations Management: Improving Customer Service.* New York: Irwin.

Suzaki, K. (1987) *The New Manufacturing Challenge: Technqiues for Continuous Improvement.* New York: Free Press.

Turnbull, P., Delbridge, R., Oliver, N. and Wilkinson, B. (1993) Winners and losers – the 'tiering' of component suppliers in the UK automotive industry. *Journal of General Management,* **19**, Autumn, 48–63.

Waters, D. (2003) *Operations Management: Producing Goods and Sevices.* Harlow: Addison Wesley.

Wise, R. and Baumgartner, P. (1999) Go downstream: the new profit imperative in manufacturing. *Harvard Business Review,* **77**(5), 133–142.

Womack, J., Jones, D. and Roos, D. (1990) *The Machine that Changed the World.* New York: Rawson Associates.

Zipkin, P. (1991) Does manufacturing need a JIT revolution? *Harvard Business Review,* January–February.

CHAPTER 6

Supply management

Definition and development

In the first edition of this book we started this chapter by remarking: 'It is perhaps necessary to explain at the outset why we have dedicated a whole chapter to the subject of supply management, and what we mean by the term.' Since the mid-1990s, the importance of understanding the supply chain has become accepted in every part of business and the subject is now amongst the most popular in research in the area.

The purpose of this chapter is for the reader to:

- understand how supply management has changed over time;
- gain insights into the strategic importance of supply within operations;
- appreciate the importance of lean supply.

In the last quarter of the twentieth century, the perception of what takes place in the transactions between organizations and their suppliers – of materials, component parts, services, information and utilities – changed profoundly. When, in 1997, the *Harvard Business Review* published its 75-year review of management thinking, the central theme of 'production' (as it was called in 1922) had become 'adding value' in modern times, and featured prominently in the mid-1990s was 'supply chain management'. The expression 'supply chain management' is now over 20 years old and probably reaching the limit of usefulness as a metaphor: it is now recognized that strategists in supply must embrace the concepts of supply *networks* (another metaphor). It is still appropriate, however, to begin by exploring supply *chain* management and explaining the reason we prefer to focus on *supply* management. In particular, we should focus on the implications for operations strategists.

In this chapter, we shall first explore the nature of supply chains and supply bases. This will be followed by a discussion on the essential factors in developing a comprehensive supply strategy. These are: a policy on supply positioning, with a strategy to implement it; an internal strategy on the location of the purchasing and supply process within the organization; and a set of techniques for managing relationships between organizations – the essence of supply.

Strategic supply and focused operations

Supply management has a significant role to play in focusing operations. All organizations have to focus to some degree as they do not have limitless resources and cannot, therefore, provide a limitless range or volume of products or services around the world. However, focus is much more specific than this and can have profound importance for the firm. The organization can focus in a number of ways, including:

- Choosing the customer groups and market segments which it serves.
- Adopting a particular type of manufacturing process – as we saw in Chapter 3, the choice of process determines to a large degree what the firm can and cannot do.
- Focusing the plant into a number of different, but specific, allocated areas – these cells of production or service units can be focused by customer, process, product or service.
- Outsourcing non-core areas of the business, which in turn will impact on operations management.
- Concentrating on a specific activity within the supply chain and forming strategic buyer–supplier relationships with other players in the supply chain. For many years, this has been a key strategic factor in the success of firms in the aerospace industry, where as much as 85 per cent of the value of an aircraft is derived from the supply base.

The last two points clearly relate directly to management of supply.

Focus is concerned with what the organization chooses *not* to do itself – and must therefore obtain from its supply network. This choice forms part of its strategic intent. For example, focus within the supply network played a key part when, in 1991, Hewlett Packard decided to enter the PC market. HP did this with great intensity and was one of the top four PC producers by 1997. Later, HP decided to move away from being a manufacturer to being *an assembler* of products. This shift in focus placed even greater emphasis on the need for excellent supplier relations throughout the supply chain, especially with those suppliers on whom HP greatly depends. It also freed the firm from unnecessary investment in manufacturing plant to focus on investment in assembly technology. Subsequently, even the assembly of finished units was considered non-core and was widely outsourced to suppliers. Today, the impacts of strategies such as this, which have been followed by all the well-known computer companies, have led to a major reframing of the industry, so that now the majority of laptop computers are manufactured by a handful of companies, operating globally, the equipment being badged for marketing by the big brands.

Focusing operations means concentrating on specific aspects of the entire process of production or provision of a service to see where the organization can really add value and make money for itself; other areas may be outsourced, responsibility for them (including conducting parts of a service, manufacturing parts of a product or system, and the management of further input resources, such as supplies of raw materials) being given to suppliers. Of course, such suppliers become much more significant players in the process and may be expected to employ more sophisticated management skills, rather than simply doing what they are told.

Focus may even mean that the firm becomes a *virtual* organization, employing far fewer people then before but achieving similar business goals. For example, TopsyTail, a small Texan company, sold $100 million worth of its hairstyling equipment during the mid-1990s, although it had virtually no permanent employees of its own. Subcontractors handled almost all of the organization's activities – design, manufacturing, marketing. The Italian motorcycle manufacturer, Aprilia, sources all parts for its bikes and scooters from suppliers in the region around its home in Mestre, near Venice, simply assembling to order and managing its supplies accordingly. Its own organization is small, representing the hub of a network that forms a virtual organization.

Supply and outsourcing

Whereas focus includes divesting business assets that were once part of the firm's attempts to diversify, outsourcing is more often associated with the configuration in which the firm finds itself within the supply chain. The perceived wisdom was formerly that a firm should own all activities within the supply chain. For example, at one time, Ford made almost everything that went into its cars, including the steel and glass. In 1980, it made about 87 per cent of a car itself. Now it makes less than 40 per cent. Similarly, in the past, IBM produced the silicon as well as the software and hard drives for its computers. This approach – one of vast amounts of vertical integration – has been replaced by outsourcing strategies. As a result, by the end of the century a new group of 'contract manufacturers' had emerged in the PC industry – companies such as SCI Systems, Celestica, Solectron, Merix, Flextronics, Smartflex and Sanmina – who now manufacture products for major PC players including IBM and Hewlett Packard, as we saw above. Some of these firms have become very large (typically over $10bn in sales turnover) and together represent a new business sector.

In the USA, such outsourcing has seen a remarkable growth of small manufacturing enterprises so that, by the mid-1990s, companies with fewer than 100 employees comprised some 85 per cent of the USA's 370 000 manufacturing firms (*The Economist*, 27 January 1996). Service industry soon followed manufacturing, with the development of call centres (for sales enquiries and customer service) sited offshore. These are typically moving from the USA or the UK to countries such as India or Malaysia, where international English is spoken. In 2002, a report on 'offshoring' by the Forrester research group in the USA estimated that 3.3 million white-collar American jobs (500 000 of them in IT) would shift offshore to countries such as India by 2015. Stephen Roach, the Chief Economist at Morgan Stanley, described the opportunity represented by outsourcing as a 'new and powerful global labour arbitrage' that has led to an accelerating transfer of high-wage jobs to India and elsewhere. While the dominant trend has been USA/UK to India, there are also cases of Japan 'offshoring' to North-East China (where Japanese is spoken), Russia to Eastern Europe and Switzerland to the Czech Republic. In addition to the low costs of labour in such countries, the logic of offshoring is boosted by the drop in the cost of international phone calls. However, such activities have not always been successful, as the following case demonstrates.

Case: Hang-ups in India call centre backlash!

India isn't the answer say some firms

Last year, after reading about Indian call centres in a magazine, Web.com CEO Will Pemble decided to 'offshore' his Internet hosting company's customer service. This November, plagued by cultural misunderstandings and lost customers, Pemble brought all of Web.com's calls back from India to Brookfield, CT.

In the end, Pemble concluded, it was costing his company more to send work to India than to do it in one of the highest-cost states of the Union. Dell made a similar – if much more widely publicized – decision in November, routing calls from some high-end business customers back to Texas from its Indian call centre in Bangalore. None of this means that the great migration of service jobs to India and other low-cost overseas locations (see 'Where Your Job Is Going' on fortune.com) is about to come to a halt. It is an indication, though, that there are limits to offshoring. The most obvious have to do with politics and public opinion: corporations are having to tread more gingerly on the outsourcing front for fear of backlash from elected officials and customers. If the US economy keeps strengthening, that backlash should fizzle. But CEOs are being forced to realize that, while their shareholders may think it's swell that customer calls can be routed seamlessly to people in India making $2000 a year, many customers are less pleased.

In Web.com's case it wasn't so much anti-foreigner sentiment among customers as frustration with tech-support people who were simply too far from headquarters to reach the people who could solve problems quickly. 'If it's a binary decision process – yes or no – then you should consider outsourcing,' says Pemble. 'But if there's a maybe in there anywhere, then you can be sure that all your customer-support difficulties will gravitate to that like iron filings to a magnet.'

As a result, many larger companies – like Dell – are developing a hierarchy of which calls get shunted overseas and which don't. 'Not everything is moving offshore,' says Amit Shankardass, Solution-Planning Officer at ClientLogic, a Nashville-based call centre outsourcing company. 'Airline companies would not move management of high-yield customers offshore.' Instead, they practise, to follow industry jargon, 'onshoring' or 'near shoring' – which means sending calls to Canada.

Meanwhile, back in India, the vaunted limitless supply of well-educated young English speakers willing to answer phones is looking slightly more limited. Much of the IT work outsourced to India in recent years benefits from the 10½-hour time difference with the Eastern USA – Indian programmers can work while their American counterparts sleep. But call centres and back-office operations that offer real-time service need peak staffing in the middle of the Indian night, and many providers are already struggling with high turnover (upwards of 20 per cent a year) among their urban, just-out-of-college workforce. As a result, Indian operators are beginning to eye older workers living in the provinces. Translation: get ready for an even wider cultural and language gulf between workers and Western customers.

Source: Fortune, 22 December 2003, **148**(13), p. 16.

Not surprisingly, outsourcing strategies have sometimes seen major negative reactions from what were once seen as 'core' employees. For example, in 1996, there was a major strike at General Motors (Leslie, 1996):

> … when GM workers went on strike, the term 'outsourcing' became a dirty word. Widely used when describing GM's tactic of contracting out for the manufacture of certain automobile components that it had been manufacturing in-house, 'outsourcing' in this context meant knocking yet another raft of auto workers off GM's assembly lines.

and (*Financial Times,* 26 June 1996):

> The United Auto Workers Union used the 17-day strike to complain that jobs were being threatened and technological leadership put at risk by the increased shift towards outside suppliers.

In the UK, throughout the 1990s, the compulsory tendering of service contracts by local government led to services such as street cleaning, maintenance, security and even such practices as planning permission, being outsourced to private sector organizations – many from outside the UK. At the national level, outsourcing information systems in central government departments have recently been conducted but without any clear (or 'joined-up') policy. This resulted in contracts for over three-quarters of the central administration's information systems being placed with one, North American, company – but this only became apparent later, causing much dismay.

A similar reaction has been seen in the USA, in some cases eliciting a strong response. For example, in November 2002, the state government in Indiana withdrew from a $15 million contract with the American subsidiary of a leading Indian IT outsourcing firm. Governor Joe Kernan said that the contract did not fit with Indiana's 'vision' of providing better opportunities to local companies and workers.

So although the decision to outsource has become a popular one, it can cause unrest and strategic problems if it is poorly managed. But simply divesting part of what was previously an owned asset is only part of the puzzle. For such outsourcing to be successful, strategic buyer–supplier relationships need to be in place, as we shall see.

The nature of supply

Looking back ...

The practice of buying and selling is one of the oldest 'professions' in the world. In the remains of cities within Mesopotamia (modern-day Iraq) there are records of transactions that took place 6000 years ago – bearing chilling resemblance to today's purchase orders and materials schedules. What has changed recently is the scope of concern that the purchaser and seller must have in order to ensure their organization survives. The copper traders in Ur may have paid the merchants from Dilmun (Bahrain) for minerals from Makan (Oman), and considered they were doing business over great distances. Today, the same distance takes a couple of hours by air and traders in the modern equivalent of each of these countries are dealing by Internet and mobile, wireless telephony with collaborators, customers and competitors in every part of the globe. Thus, managing the provision of the resources necessary to conduct the operations of the organization – latterly called purchasing, procurement, buying and materials management – is now a matter of competing for scarce commodities that may differentiate the product or service in the eyes of the consumer. It is a short, simple step to connect such activity with the operations strategy for an organization.

The current position

The term 'supply chain' is now about 25 years old, having being coined in the early 1980s by consultants (Houlihan, 1992) in various parts of North America and Europe to crystallize the concept of managing an organization in the light of the activities, resources and strategies of other organizations on which it relies. Individual supply relationships between pairs of organizations – sometimes called 'dyads' – were addressed by economists such as Williamson (1975), Williamson and Masten (1999), and Granovetter (1985) in the development of 'transaction costs economics', but the idea of going beyond the immediate relationship to manage remote links (i.e. between one's suppliers and their suppliers) came later. The term 'chain' may have originated in the concept of the 'food chain' (humans may like these because they are at the 'top' of one) or simply the attractive causal image of a chain of events. A contemporary of the supply chain was the value chain (Porter, 1980), which we have discussed in Chapter 1.

The chain, however, is clearly an imperfect metaphor: even a cursory attempt at mapping the process of supply (for anything other than the simplest logistical transportation activities) reveals that there is little about it that is linear. This is illustrated in Figure 6.1.

Supply is actually carried out in a network – or, perhaps, a mess! One example of this complexity is given by the case of Octel Network Services, Electronic Data Systems (EDS), Xerox and Motorola. EDS is a major client of Octel Network Services, a firm in Dallas that operates more than 1 million electronic voice 'mailboxes'. EDS, in turn, has a $3.2 billion contract to run Xerox's computer and telecoms networks,

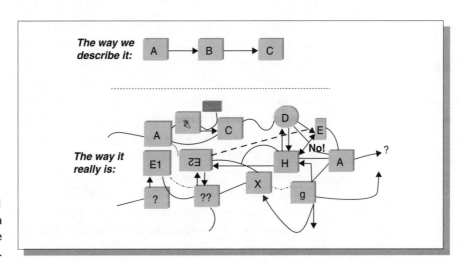

Figure 6.1
The supply chain metaphor may be inappropriate.

a deal that involves some 1700 of Xerox's employees transferring to EDS. Xerox itself provides invoicing and billing services for Motorola, which in turn designs and makes parts of Octel's voice-messaging systems, and thus the circle is completed. Such supply configurations do not fit into neat, simplistic models of the supply chain.

There are different types of supply networks and attempts have been made to classify them (see Lamming *et al.*, 2000). Management practice has sometimes struggled to deal with this problem, developing models for controlling supply chains based upon the assumption that one organization can intervene in the business relationships of another. We shall examine this later. The process of forming a strategy for the operational concerns of the organization outside its boundaries of ownership and physical presence cannot rely upon a concept of remote control, however: some better theory is required for managers to employ.

Research over 20 years by a group of academics from around the world, known as the Industrial Marketing and Purchasing group, has concluded that it is not possible to manage in supply networks – instead, it is suggested, organizations may only seek to manage *within* it (Ford, 1997). So far, research in the area does not refute this conclusion and, in discussing supply strategy within operations strategy, we shall retain this assumption: forming supply strategy, as an accompaniment to operations strategy, begins with managing the relationships between the organization and other organizations with which it deals directly; as a result of this management, influence may be exerted on the activities of organizations elsewhere in the network that are involved in delivering the goods and services that form the focus of the supply strategy. Some of the strong *keiretsu* networks formed in Japan during the twentieth century do appear to be controlled by their principal firms, but research in 1999 showed that this was changing profoundly as Japan weathered 10 years of recession and the impacts of global operations (see Lamming, 2000).

This makes sense for the strategist – form a plan for one's own activities and then try to influence others (either directly or indirectly) so that it may be complemented and therefore successful.

So, it isn't a chain, and you can't manage it, but 'supply chain management' is the term that has become common parlance around the world – for managers, academics and politicians. We shall use it here, but focus particularly on *supplier relationship management* – the management of supply relationships between two organizations (including the activities that one might term 'purchasing') and the network perspective.

Managing supply – the objective

For many organizations, the major proportion of value offered to the customer is actually derived not from doing things, but from adding value to things that have been bought. This is sometimes referred to as the 'purchasing ratio'. In our fast-food example in Chapter 1, the cost of the components of the meals sold by Sunnyside Up was around 30 per cent of the meal itself. The component parts of an aeroplane often add up to over 80 per cent of the total sale price: the aircraft assembler is adding less than a fifth of the value, for all its labour, design, sales effort and administration, etc. Many manufacturers of consumer durable products have a purchasing ratio of over 70 per cent. If the unit cost may be thought of as a pie chart, a typical manufactured product might appear as shown in Figure 6.2.

Clearly, efforts to reduce the size of the pie – and thus the cost of the item – should concentrate on all three aspects. A 10 per cent reduction in labour costs would result in a 1.5 per cent reduction in overall cost; 10 per cent off overhead costs would lead to 3.5 per cent reduction. A similar reduction in material costs would reduce the overall pie by 5 per cent. This simple point leads to the conclusion that control of material costs may actually be more important than savings on labour or overheads. As purchasing people like to point out, such savings go directly to the bottom line for the company and improve profits in a way that increased sales could rarely achieve.

In practice, however, materials costs result from a series (or chain) of events – the supply chain. Reducing them is thus not simply a matter of attacking the immediate target – the price paid for the goods or services – but a more complex task of analysing the build-up of value,

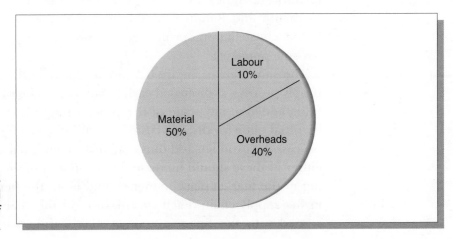

Figure 6.2
A traditional representation of product unit cost.

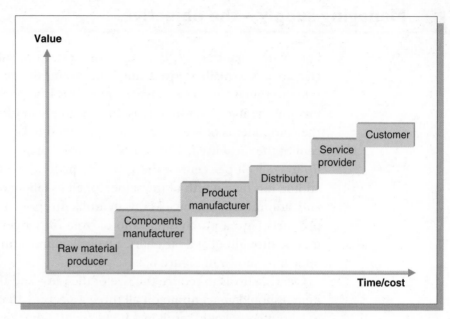

Figure 6.3
Build-up of value
and cost in the
supply process.

cost and time that has resulted in the material cost as it is experienced by the organization.

As we have seen earlier, the materials are actually part of a service provided by the supplier: materials surrounded by delivery, presentation, treatment, aftercare and so on. It follows that one is not simply buying a product but paying for a service; this must be borne in mind when considering the value being purchased.

Figure 6.3 provides a view of the way in which firms in the supply chain may be viewed in the context of progressive value addition. (Note that the customer is a part of this process and can be required to add value for which they pay – for example, the total value of 'flat-pack' furniture includes the value which the owner adds by constructing it. Normann and Ramirez (1993) suggested this might be termed the 'value constellation' principle, although this has not subsequently become popular.)

The simplicity of Figure 6.3 should not hide the complexity of the supply process, as discussed earlier, but it does show how an increase in value added at any stage of the process might lead to an increase in eventual value for the end customer, while a reduction in time taken to process the product, and thus cost, may be lessened at any point. Since either of these should increase the likelihood of the product succeeding in the market-place, either should be to the benefit of all parties in the supply chain. Each organization in the chain is naturally concerned with the financial gain it makes from adding value in the process – in effect, the value it receives itself. Each organization must thus have a supply strategy in order to operate within the chain, and in order for the chain itself to operate competitively.

The players in the chain thus have two concerns: for the overall competitiveness of the chain and for their own prosperity within it. Since they derive their income from the value they add, each firm may be expected with the others to add more of the total value. It follows that the customers and suppliers at each stage in the chain are actually competing for the value: they are competitors as well as collaborators. Where the boxes in Figure 6.3 overlap there lies an arena for this competition – the value should be great, the time/cost small. This leads to a set of dynamic partnerships in the chain, which, if it works efficiently in market terms, should lead to individual and mutual prosperity.

So much for the concept: how does it work in practice? Each organization is driven by its owners – shareholders in the case of a limited company, public offices in the case of, say, a government department. In either case, the responsibility of the directors and managers in the organization is to their stakeholders: their shareholders, employees, customers and members of the community affected by the activities of the organization. The dominant force here has traditionally been the first one: the owners. Recently, the stakeholder concept has been extended to include suppliers to the organization; the actions of the organization may have an adverse effect upon the suppliers in the short term and on the supply chain (and thus the organization itself) in the long term. This domination has led managers to be concerned principally (often exclusively) with their own organization – especially in the case of a limited company, where shareholders are most directly aware of the results of any strategy.

Structuring the supply base

Observers of Japanese industrial structure coined the term 'first tier' to describe the powerful, large suppliers that supported the household-name manufacturers of cars, consumer durables and capital equipment that were such a part of Japan's revival in the post-war period. The structure of supply 'base' – a sort of pyramid of firms upon which the final product assembler sat – was a feature of the historical Japanese social structure and key to the formation of the giant groups (known as *zaibatsu* in the first half of the twentieth century and *keiretsu* in the second half). As Nishiguchi (1986) pointed out, these supply structures should not be seen as separate 'mountains' but as a sort of

Alpine structure – a great base of manufacturing companies, from which peaks (the well-known product assemblers) emerge (the point being that components from any of the firms in the substructure might end up in a product of any of the 'peak' organizations).

In Japan, the tiers are clearly marked (and documented). Elsewhere, they do not exist, simply because the historical development of firms has been more autonomous. The image of tiers is so strong, however, that there is a tendency to call suppliers 'first tier' and 'second tier' without a logical basis. A tier, after all, is a very specific feature of a structure: it has a hierarchical position (in this case, the first being above the second, since the referencing is done from the top – the customer – but it could easily be the reverse, in a different situation) and lateral links to other items in the same tier (like seats in a stadium or theatre – arranged in integrated rows).

The danger of referring to organizations in the supply chain, base or network as 'first tier' (or second tier, and so on) is that the expectations thus created bear no actual resemblance to the activity that will be addressed by the organization in question, since the lateral links, which may be essential for the expected activity, do not exist. Thus, a vehicle assembler may require a major supplier to buy components from other suppliers, and construct and deliver complete 'systems' (e.g. an entire engine cooling system, consisting of the radiator, hoses, brackets, sensors, etc., ready to fit into the car). The system supplier might be called 'first tier' but have little link-up with other suppliers, with whom their supply of systems must be interfaced. It is now common to hear supply strategists speak of 'tier-half', referring to suppliers to whom so much responsibility (e.g. for design and production) has been given that they must be seen as not entirely separate from the customer. This rather odd terminology fits well with the concept that a relationship as close as this is actually an overlap between the two organizations, rather than a bridged gap.

During the 1980s, supply strategists began to realize that they had, in general, too many suppliers. It was not unusual for an organization (of any size) to have more suppliers than employees. A practice emerged for reducing the number of suppliers with whom the organization dealt on a regular basis, in order to focus the cost of dealing with them on a smaller number, who would therefore benefit from the customer's attention. This was usually termed 'supply base rationalization'. In fact, it seldom appears rational in practice – a common problem being that illustrated in Figure 6.4. In the second diagram (post-rationalization), there are in fact just as many suppliers involved in the supply base, despite the number of direct suppliers being reduced by two-thirds.

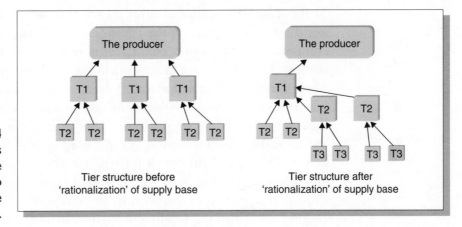

Figure 6.4
Tiers in supply bases and the flaw in some approaches to supply base rationalization.

Moreover, the ex-first-tier suppliers, now called second tier by the 'Producer', are likely to be demoralized, and possibly dissatisfied with supplying to the remaining first-tier supplier. In many cases, the Producer will stipulate that the first-tier supplier must purchase from specific ex-first-tier suppliers, for political reasons, leaving the remaining first-tier organization in a commercial trap. The supply strategist must avoid this situation and devise a more rational approach if this practice is to produce genuine benefits.

The Japanese tiered system was formed and maintained by a technique known in the West as 'supplier associations' (in Japanese: *kyoryokukai*); this is discussed later in this chapter.

Setting up a supply strategy

In forming a supply strategy, there are four requirements, the first two of which may be considered together:

- a general policy on how the organization is to engage with its external activities, accompanied by a suitable strategy for implementing it;
- an internal strategy for the role that the purchasing process (and thus the functions associated with it) should play;
- a set of specific approaches to managing supply relationships.

Supply policy and strategy

A policy is concerned with clarifying an organization's position on a specific matter – an articulation of the way it feels about something.

In this case, the matter is supply. Directors of the organization may decide that the nature of their business means that they must be very competitive in the supply chain (i.e. in terms of controlling the value-adding process) rather than collaborative. This would be the case where the resources needed for the business (including skills, materials, information, locations, equipment and finance) were scarce and the number of suppliers or subcontractors with whom one might work was high. In this case, simply getting hold of – or controlling – what Cox (1997) called the 'critical assets' in the supply chain might be enough to ensure success for the organization, and simultaneously causing one or two other firms in the chain to suffer fatal difficulty, causing them to exit, might not matter. In other circumstances, the resources needed might be plentiful and the number of firms with whom one might work small. In this case, the policy might be more collaborative, since success might only come from differentiating the product or service through imaginative and creative development, in which the organization and its suppliers would need to work together. As industries tend to become more concentrated (i.e. mergers and acquisitions are frequent) to support the costs of global operation, so aligning oneself with the right supplier becomes an increasingly important factor. In the aerospace industry, for example, there are three manufacturers of engines for large passenger jets: Rolls Royce, General Electric and Pratt & Whitney. For aircraft manufacturers, the supply of engines is a vital area, but it is not a simple case of, say, Boeing acquiring General Electric's engine business, since the latter requires non-Boeing business to support its research and development and production activities. Such a strategy should not be seen as a soft position for the supplier, however: in the large engines business of the aircraft industry, a supplier must commit to achieving 7 per cent per annum 'cost-out' just to remain in the supply base (even as a half-tier supplier). If this is not accepted, the customer will bring in another company that can do so.

The supply policy might also include meddling with the resources issue – to create scarcity and thus influence the degree of competitiveness or collaboration in the chain. This is a central theme of Cox's (1997) approach, one that he suggests is universally applicable. It naturally includes acquisition, so that one might become the owner of assets required by a competitor, and thus hold the whip hand. Other commentators argue that there are cases in which the immediately apparent benefits of controlling all the assets may lead to longer-term dysfunction in the supply markets as players upon whom the organization must rely (for activities that may not be appropriate for it to conduct itself) are starved and exit the field. This might mean that the meddling organization is left to buy the products and services from a reduced number of suppliers (who will feel little sympathy with it) or make the items for itself. The investments necessary for the latter may not be possible, or sensible, for the organization and it is thus left with an inappropriate portfolio of activities to manage. In practice, the reverse of this strategy is increasingly in evidence, as witnessed by the growth in contract electronics manufacturers in the early 1990s, fuelled by computer and other electronic product manufacturers selling their production facilities and setting up supply contracts with their former in-house divisions – so-called 'outsourcing'.

All this assumes that the organization is in a competitive situation and has the ability to acquire and shed activities and businesses strategically. If this is not the case, the strategic potential for supply may be limited.

Other factors come into the policy-making process, such as ethical and environmental issues, social considerations and the nature of the organization, including the constraints on its freedom of action (now discussed under the general title of 'corporate social responsibility'). This will entail a series of trade-offs, such as the commercial benefits of sourcing in low-labour-cost countries, versus the issue of child labour, which may form a part of the low-cost labour.

Once policy is set, an overall strategy for supply requirements may be formed. This will include matters such as 'make or buy' (or 'do or buy'), location and alliances. In the first of these, the organization must decide whether or not it wishes to carry out a process itself, or have it done by an outside party. This may be a simple matter of subcontracting (having something done for you that you could do yourself but choose not to) or outsourcing (setting up an external resource that does something for you in which you choose not to become expert). This is clearly fundamental to the organization's success and is not usually left to traditional supply managers – e.g. purchasing directors.

The mass production approach to this was neatly summed up by Henry Ford, who said: 'If you need a machine and you do not buy it, you will eventually find that you have paid for it but do not have it.' With the long product lives and controlled sales markets of mass production, the logic of this statement is powerful. As the useful lives of product and process technologies shorten, however, with the opening of markets and the need to recognize the 'voice of the customer', so the wisdom of buying 'the machine' may be less clear. Put briefly, it may be a choice between, on the one hand, operating without a critical resource by buying in the service (thereby risking paying too much for the service and losing competitiveness, or even having to do without it) and, on the other, being caught with a sunk cost investment in a technology that is no longer commercially valuable (and thus paying off the investment long after it has ceased to provide the necessary revenue). The former problem (which would be avoided by acquiring the resource 'in-house') may lead to a cost penalty and loss of sales, while the latter (which could be avoided by outsourcing) might lead to a cash flow crisis and insolvency. In fact, either could prove fatal. Once again, the answer might be to meddle in the supply market, suppressing technologies that appear (e.g. by buying them) in order to increase the period of 'economic rent' – and thus recouping the investment. The extreme form of this would be monopoly – at least temporarily – in which case, the organization's concerns would be reduced. However, the rate of technological change in many sectors makes monopoly a difficult concept: examples such as Microsoft Corp. are rare exceptions.

Policy may lead to the strategies of outsourcing, as we saw earlier. The policy evident in Nintendo and Sega, for example, is that the natural dynamism of their products should not be reduced by heavy corporate inertia. The strategy associated with this is to outsource everything and concentrate on the competence of marketing. They are thus never left with production competences that are out of date (including the mercurial resource of software writing) and can switch to a new idea with only minimal costs.

Sourcing strategy

Much has been written about ways of deciding where to procure products and services. The most well-respected modern approach was published in the *Harvard Business Review* as long ago as 1983, by Peter Kraljic, a senior member of the consultants, McKinsey. Kraljic's sourcing 'tool' is shown in Figure 6.5.

Kraljic's argument is that, for any item, the risk of being caught without it (and thus, for example, stopping the production line or failing to fill an order) may be high or low. Kraljic calls this risk of exposure. The cost to the organization (of the procured item) may also be dichotomized into high and low. Cost may include many factors in addition to purchase price – for example, the cost of acquiring, storing, insuring and maintaining the item. Combining these two factors enables the supply strategist to decide on what approach should be taken to managing the item; those in the top right-hand box may be treated as strategically important and thus managed through close collaboration

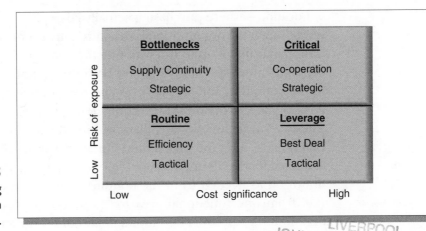

Figure 6.5
Kraljic's sourcing
tool (adapted from
Kraljic, 1983).

with the supplier, while those in the bottom left may be dealt with via, say, automated buying and stock control. Taking its origins clearly from such ideas as the famous Pareto '80–20' effect (which observes, in this context, that 80 per cent of expenditure on goods and services supplied to the organization will probably be accounted for by 20 per cent of the suppliers from whom these things are bought), Kraljic's tool has encouraged supply managers in many sectors to consider more than the immediate aspects of their sourcing decisions. Its simplicity has appealed to supply strategists over two decades and many modern strategies consist of little more than this diagram – almost always with different wording, as the analysis has been customized to a specific organization's situation. Anyone wishing to be taken seriously as a professional purchaser must be able to recognize and use this tool – as a basic skill. As with all 'two-by-two' analysis methods, the tool is open to criticism for oversimplification – there are other variables involved in sourcing. There has also been recent discussion over the appropriateness of the boxes – an item that is low in cost and has little risk of exposure attached to it may still be a vital part, without which the organization cannot function – the traditional 'halfpenny's worth of tar which (by its absence) spoiled the ship'.

Internal strategy for the role of the purchasing process

Having built a strategy for supply itself and a way of understanding the management of sourcing decisions, the supply strategist must decide how purchasing is conducted within the organization. This has two parts: location and process.

Location – where purchasing actually takes place – depends upon the way in which the organization is structured. In a general sense, the organization may be set up to run with functional departments, each of which contains career specialists who are both the operational competence of the organization and also its 'eyes and ears' in that specialism (i.e. they ensure that the organization's competence in their area is up to date). These vertical, functional pillars within the organization (sometimes called 'silos', after the agricultural storage device in which materials such as animal foodstuffs are delivered into the top of an upright cylinder, and drawn off as needed from the bottom) form its structure. Across them (i.e. from one functional area to another) flow the processes of the organization – product development and order fulfilment being the two basic activities. In recent years, many firms have removed their functional silos and organized themselves along process lines, supporting the processes with the necessary functional expertise at the appropriate points. The operational manifestation of this is cross-functional teams, in which experts with a variety of functional and commercial skill are put together (often 'co-located' in one office) to take responsibility for a specific process – such as bringing a new product to market on time.

Thus, purchasing, as the traditional home of responsibility for supply management, may be located as a separate functional department, with processes passing into and out of it (in which case the management role is to ensure that the interfaces with other departments do not delay communications or add cost to the process) or as part of a cross-functional team within a process-oriented organization, where there are no clear 'departments'. There are, of course, many hybrid arrangements. Either way, the organization will need a strategy for the way in which the purchasing process takes place, which will influence the way in which it is organized.

The best-known and practiced strategy for this was developed by Reck and Long in 1988. Like the Kraljic model, this useful approach has survived from the 1980s, developed many times in practice but still respected. It is a four-stage, hierarchical process with which managers may compare themselves as they develop purchasing's role and position in the supply management of the organization. At all times, of course, this needs to be conducted in the light of the policy and strategy discussed above. Reck and Long's model is shown in Figure 6.6.

The Reck and Long model enables the supply strategist to define the role of the purchasing process and the function (i.e. the department). It may be used first to identify the present situation and then to define the appropriate position. Moving from one to the other then becomes a project of change.

Stage	Definition
Passive	No strategic direction: primarily reacts to requests from other functions
Independent	Adopts latest purchasing techniques and practices, but strategic direction is independent from the organization's competitive strategy
Supportive	Supports the organization's competitive strategy by adopting purchasing techniques that strengthen its competitive position
Integrative	Purchasing strategy is fully integrated with the organization's competitive strategy and constitutes part of an integrated effort among functional peers to formulate and implement a strategic plan

Figure 6.6
Reck and Long's model for developing the role of purchasing (adapted from Reck and Long, 1988).

Other writers have constructed similar, multi-level models for explaining the ways in which purchasing may be positioned to ensure the best use is made of the expertise and the best 'fit' with corporate purposes is maintained. Naturally, supply strategy must be made to fit with higher level direction in the company, and thus the Reck and Long model is used in the context of corporate strategy.

Two developments have fundamentally affected the way in which purchasing is positioned as part of the supply process: information technology (IT) and global expansions of business organizations. The two are, of course, related. IT has made possible practices such as electronic purchasing (i.e. paperless and instant), sharing scheduling information with suppliers via access to the organization's intranet (leading in some cases to the removal of the need to schedule deliveries, simply asking the supplier to monitor stock levels of their products within the organization's stores and replenish them as necessary), and information through intranet and Internet technologies. In some cases, this has been combined with Kraljic's model to encourage people within the organization to purchase their own requirements, using electronic catalogues that maintain a corporate knowledge of 'best buys'. This is used to cover everything from travel to electronic components, and takes the purchasing activity away from the specialist and into the hands of the first-line manager. The purchase may be made with a corporate credit card, so that the budget holder can monitor expenditure against the plan and be accountable for it. This 'atomization' of purchasing responsibility has the benefit of leaving the specialists to concentrate on strategic matters (including setting up the framework agreements for the supply of the items covered) and relationship management on strategic items. The potential problem is that control of expenditure will be lost; despite the rigour of budget management, individuals given autonomy for purchasing their requirements may not adhere to corporate guidelines in practice. If the individual is a line manager who needs replenishment of production components, there may only be one or two specified sources that can be used (controlled by the information system). If the item required is a laptop computer, however, there may be dozens – the proliferation of suppliers of such items, accessed through catalogues, is precisely the type of uncontrolled activity that results in administrative congestion within an organization.

This may be controlled, however, as in the case of the British–American global medical and foods manufacturer, GlaxoSmithKline. In the late 1990s, GSK (in its former name of SmithKline Beecham – SB) put in place a worldwide IT system that allowed any budget holder in the corporation, anywhere in the world, to find the best buy for any item, and to understand the corporate policy associated with the purchase they are about to make. Thus, a manager wishing to buy a laptop computer in Australia will know what it should cost to SB (global price from the laptop manufacturer) and also what specification of machine will be appropriate to ensure that it could be repaired in London or Chicago, when the user is attending an SB meeting there. The technicalities are endless; the principle is clear. Giving responsibility for sourcing to non-specialists throughout the organization requires discipline and support, but can lead to a reduction in formal (centralized) purchasing departments, thus actually saving the organization money.

GSK were also one of the first companies to become expert in the use of online auctions, in which suppliers bid for business in a live, onscreen event, run by the customer or their agent. Online auctions (once called 'reverse' auctions, because the prices are driven downwards in the bidding) are now commonplace, either within Internet exchanges or simply as tools within the sourcing process. The initial concerns for suppliers' interests have largely abated and such methods are seen simply as the way in which sourcing will be done in future (as often seen, electronic communication replaces paper). In practice, however, the online auction only replaces part of the sourcing process – it is still important in many cases for purchasers and prospective suppliers to discuss details of the contract personally. This may be a complication where the customer has chosen to run the online auction worldwide.

Globalization of operations and markets leads to further challenges for positioning supply management. The customer for a manufactured product expects it to operate efficiently in any country, and to be compatible with other items that may have been made in a different part of the world. The same expectations of consistency exist for international hotel chains, courier services and airlines. In global manufacturing, the production system costs (which include supply of materials and components) for an item made in, say, Latin America, need to be as close as possible to those in, say, Korea, in order for location decisions to made on the simplest basis possible – the logic of position (wage level, subsidies, logistics, etc.). To address this need, global operators have developed global purchasing and supply – dealing with other global players on a worldwide level. One way of managing this is to assign responsibility for technical expertise in a particular product or commodity area to a specific geographical office, e.g. the global head of purchasing for a computer manufacturer might say 'Our purchasing expertise in DRAMs (dynamic random access memory chips) is located in Singapore: anyone who needs to purchase DRAMs has only to speak to Singapore in order to get the best deal from our global supply partners.' (Of course, 'speaking' is done via intranet.) In this case, Singapore might be called the 'lead buyer' for DRAMs.

An alternative way of addressing this supply management need is to set up what IBM calls 'Commodity Councils' – working groups with members drawn from all operating divisions around the world that are in constant touch with each other, meeting in person occasionally, as well as via intranet and telephone or video conferences. The group becomes the organization's knowledge base and develops expertise and 'good deals' in purchasing and supply. The advantage over the 'lead buyer' approach is that the expertise is spread around the divisions and may grow from a multiplicity of inputs and perspectives, rather than the narrowly focused efforts of one group.

The following case shows how supply policy and strategy for acquiring pharmaceuticals has been developed recently, in the highly complex environment of the UK National Health Service.

Case: The supply of pharmaceuticals in NHS hospitals – setting up a strategy

The English National Health Service spends over £11 billion per year on goods and services purchased from commercial companies. Of this, hospitals' spend on pharmaceuticals is worth over £1.6 billion p.a. Traditionally, hospital pharmaceutical departments have been accountable for their own purchasing and contracting. This had the key benefit of allowing them to accommodate the needs of their individual trusts, but had the disadvantages of high transaction costs, duplication of effort and fragmentation of purchasing leverage, in a market characterized by powerful suppliers. It also constrained effective information sharing, and the dissemination of good contracting practice. To deal with this, regional groups were established to co-ordinate purchasing activities. Variation in practices between groups meant, however, that the disadvantages were only partially resolved.

Following the publication of a key report in 1998, the Pharmaceutical Contract Review Group, with hospital pharmacists and executives from the NHS Purchasing and Supply Agency, was established to recommend how to improve the situation. The Group developed a 'selective competitive tendering' (SCT) model for contracting and guidelines, based on 2-year initial contracts, with options to extend for two further periods of 2 years (2 + 2 + 2). Under this model, tendering follows a 4-monthly cycle and is staggered across the country, with regional contracting groups being allocated specific dates on which to tender. The arrangement allows full compliance with EU public procurement regulations, whilst reducing trusts' and suppliers' transaction costs. This not only spreads the workload for suppliers and buyers, but the spacing of activity and the carefully planned timetable allows time for market analysis and information exchange between groups. Adoption of the SCT model necessitated the co-operation of over 300 trusts, and required a carefully managed transition process to co-terminate existing contracts whilst ensuring continuity of supply.

The Group also produced a guide setting out standards of behaviour required from NHS Trust personnel and contracting groups, pharmaceutical suppliers, and the NHS Purchasing and Supply Agency, whose personnel support the contracting process and act as information brokers.

Co-ordinated and standardized contracting is necessary for effective information sharing, which in turn is critical for better decision-making by buyers. The recent improvements in contracting are, however, not just about improving operational performance and generating cost savings. They also provide the basis for a much longer-term and more strategic approach to managing the supply of pharmaceuticals into the NHS, and promoting dialogue with the supply market. Recognizing this, the Pharmaceutical Contract Review Group recommended the establishment of the Pharmaceutical Market Support Group because 'the NHS must seek to assure the supply of pharmaceuticals so that patient care is not compromised. A healthy, competitive and innovative market will remain key in achieving this objective.' (NPSG, 2000, p. 7).

Reference: National Pharmaceutical Supplies Group (NPSG) (2000) *Review of NHS Pharmaceutical Contracting*. Reading: NHS Purchasing and Supply Agency.
For further information, see: www.pasa.nhs.uk/pharma.

Case authors: Samantha Forrest and Howard Stokoe, NHS Purchasing and Supply Agency (an Agency of HM Government's Department of Health), Reading, UK and Dr Louise Knight, Centre for Research in Strategic Purchasing and Supply, University of Bath School of Management, Bath, UK.
Used with permission of the case authors.

We now have the basis for a supply strategy in place:

- a policy on what our supply market looks like and how we should try to operate within it;
- a strategy for carrying out this policy;
- a way of deciding on sourcing activities, categorizing items in the light of their significance to the organization;
- an internal strategy for the management of supply – including how the organization's purchasing expertise is positioned and the process managed;
- a way of dealing with the needs of global supply, including sharing expertise between regional offices and ensuring information systems support purchasing decisions.

All that remains is to do the purchasing and supply management!

The process of purchasing and supply

The purchasing and supply process is one of responding to demand for products and services from within the organization by providing the necessary resources to specification. This involves competences, action and knowledge. Identification of the services and products that the organization requires, and their sources, may stem from any of three directions.

The first is the user of the product or service. Clearly, a designer of a product will be concerned for the parts that fit within it and will keep a close eye on the possible sources of supply. Similarly, budget holders who want items of capital equipment will have clear ideas of the models they would like to get. The manager of a hotel within a global group will know which laundry service works best for him or her; the catering manager at a company restaurant will be aware of the best place to buy fresh vegetables. The risk here is that the budget holder may not be in touch with the commercial consequences of specifying a particular supplier for the parts; the same may apply to the purchase of capital equipment (it is less likely that the problem would arise for the hotelier or catering manager, who may be expected to be very much in touch with the immediate commercial consequences of their sourcing decisions). However, the user is the traditional origin of the requirement for purchased resource and will often go beyond identifying the generic resource, suggesting or even specifying the supplier of the item with whom purchasing should place the contract for supply.

The commercial problems of this should be obvious: the suppliers know that the buyer must get the item from them and will negotiate accordingly. It is not surprising, therefore, that it is the dream of every sales representative in the manufacturing industry to have their component specified by the designer of a product before purchasing becomes involved. The potential problem may be addressed strategically by deciding that purchasing should be involved early, perhaps advising the designer on potential suppliers that might be considered. The strategic supply manager must thus develop and maintain a knowledge of the supply market as good as that concerning the sales market which would be expected of a marketing manager. If this is done, the supply manager becomes a genuine source of ideas in the decisions about what resources to use in the organization's business.

The third origin of ideas for such resources comes from outside the organization – the supply base. Suppliers of services and products to an organization are often able to use their expertise, developed from working with a variety of customers, to the benefit of the organization.

Managing this resource must be done with care, since the organization must retain its own strategic choice, rather than become dependent upon suppliers for its resource management. Others within the organization may suspect the supply manager's introduction of a supplier's idea into, say, a design discussion (especially if it conflicts with the preference of the designer, even without technical problems) and tension in the internal relationships between functional specialists is apparent in practice in almost any case of integrating external and internal resource management. Nevertheless, if the full strategic advantages of a properly managed supply process are to be realized, the ideas and expertise of the supply base must be tapped. As Gene Richter, Head of Global Procurement at IBM, told every one of his 2400 staff (by e-mail) in December 1997:

> Our suppliers are often more aware than we of technology developments, what our competitors are doing, and where the industry is going. We must learn to listen to them and act on what they tell us.

At the time, this was seen as a new responsibility for supply managers. Most of their training has been to do with telling the supplier what to do and managing the problems that result from this rather arrogant posture. Suppliers, after all, work with lots of customers and know their own business (service or product) well: if the customer tries to manage them, they are likely to defend themselves against the cost and strategic implications of the customer's demands, setting up a traditional relationship battlefield. In mass production this was the general *modus operandi*: a battle of wits in which the supplier (who may be assumed to be in league with other suppliers, through trade associations and other mechanisms) would build-in costs to the transaction to pay for the difficulties the customer caused through arrogance. In post-mass production days, where customers demand what they want, rather than accept what providers offer, the costs of this battlefield may be punitive for the supply chain. The listening to suppliers that Richter evangelized has become a common aim for purchasers. The head of Ford followed IBM's lead 5 years later, with COO Sir Nick Scheele encouraging all personnel (in an e-mail) to work towards closer relationships with suppliers. So, the company that invented the old way, 100 years before, now sought a new way. Some better ways of working were required, starting with recognizing and managing supply relationships.

Supplier relationship management

In the next part of this chapter we shall look at the ways in which supply managers try to deal with their relationships with other organizations (suppliers of materials, components and services to the organization) and explore some ways in which these may need to be developed in order to ensure the supply chain is effective. This is known as supplier relationship management, or SRM, and has a direct resemblance to CRM, or customer relationship management, which is a core feature of marketing. In doing so, we shall touch upon the principles of lean supply – the supply management activity necessary to provide a lean supply chain within a lean production system. We shall not concern ourselves with semantic differences between 'lean', 'agile' and 'mass customization' for these purposes: the focus is on developing strategies to ensure that supply functions perfectly. The three aspects of SRM that we shall use in exploring the move from mass production thinking to lean supply are: how performance in the supply chain is assessed; how development is approached and conducted; how information and knowledge are shared within the supply chain. Sometimes this relationship places enormous stress on suppliers, as the following case demonstrates.

Case: Wal-Mart keeps the change

Suppliers pay for new technology, but Bentonville really benefits

Imagine strolling into Wal-Mart to buy the new DVD of *The Matrix*. As you take it off the shelf, a radio signal alerts an employee to restock, telling him where in the backroom to find *The Matrix* and giving a warning ping if he mistakenly slides it onto the *Legally Blonde* shelf. Meanwhile, forget going through the checkout line: an electronic reader scans the items in your cart and automatically charges your debit card.

Sound far-fetched? The future is closer than you think. Wal-Mart, the company that almost singlehandedly made the bar code ubiquitous by demanding 20 years ago that suppliers use it, is promoting a new tracking and identification system. Called radio frequency identification (RFID), the geeky-sounding technology – already used by Exxon Mobil Speedpass and E-ZPass – will revolutionize both the way stores sell and the way consumers buy.

On 4 November, Wal-Mart's top 100 suppliers are convening near Bentonville, AR, for what amounts to a United Nations of retail. Everyone from Procter & Gamble, which sells 17 per cent of its goods to Wal-Mart, to Unilever, which sells 6 per cent, will attend the 2-day meeting. They'll discuss plans for attaching RFID tags by January 2005 to every box and pallet shipped to Wal-Mart (smaller suppliers have until 2006). Wal-Mart CIO Linda Dillman is expected to explain what needs to be tagged (high-volume products may be targeted first), where it will be rolled out (chances are it will happen by region) and how RFID will tie into existing delivery systems. Flout Wal-Mart's orders, and 'you potentially get thrown off the shelf of the largest retailer in the world,' says Banc of America household-products analyst William Steele.

Dozens of RFID component manufacturers – from tiny startups to tech titans like IBM, Intel, Microsoft and Philips Semiconductor – will also be at the Bentonville meeting, vying for a piece of the action.

Because of cost and privacy concerns, Wal-Mart plans to start using RFID just in its backrooms and distribution centres, not on individual products or at checkout. But wider use of the technology is inevitable. The Defense Department already uses it internally to track some 400 000 items – from air-cargo containers to Hummers – and last month the DoD issued a Wal-Mart-like edict to suppliers to be RFID-ready by 2005. Metro, Germany's leading retailer, opened an RFID-rich Future Store in April.

Retail analysts at Sanford C. Bernstein estimate that Wal-Mart could save $8.35 billion annually by using RFID – mostly in labour costs from not having to manually scan the bar codes of incoming goods. While other analysts believe the $8 billion figure is optimistic, there's no doubt RFID can help solve retail's two biggest problems: out-of-stock items and shrinkage – products lost to theft or supply-chain snafus. Theft costs Wal-Mart alone an estimated $2 billion a year; a legitimate business of that size would rank No. 694 on the *Fortune* 1000.

Though few suppliers will say so publicly, many are less than thrilled with the RFID mandate – they see costs, not benefits. Only about two dozen companies have conducted meaningful pilots, and most analysts say RFID is still too expensive and full of bugs for widespread use. AMR Research estimates that a typical consumer-products company will spend $13–23 million just to meet Wal-Mart's 2005 demands. True, Larry Kellam, Director of Supply-network Innovation at P&G, notes that reducing out-of-stock products by 10–20 per cent could boost its annual sales by anywhere from $400 million to $1.2 billion. But benefits of that magnitude will come when companies start analysing their data to reduce inventories and respond better to fluctuations in consumer demand.

For now, it seems, RFID is just the latest cost of living in a Wal-Mart world.

Source: Fortune, 10 November 2003, **148**(10).

SRM and performance assessment

Measurement of performance is an important part of strategy. This requires prior identification of the criteria for success, disciplined monitoring of performance against the criteria and their component parts, and careful interpretation of results. In the field of supply management, this process has become established over three decades and is typified by schemes that are generally known as 'supplier (or vendor) assessment'. The principle of supplier assessment is that the customer sets up an articulation of its expectations and requirements, monitors the supplier's performance against them and then converts the results into an assessment of the supplier's performance, complemented in some cases by suggested paths towards improvements.

Supplier assessment began in the 1960s, tracing its origins to the quality management movement that grew from the work of Walter Shewart in North America in the 1930s. The development of quality management in Japan following the Second World War was supported by the American consultants such as Deming and Juran, itself leading to a renaissance of concern for quality in the West. Part of this concern focused upon the quality of incoming goods and materials. In the defence (aerospace) and automotive industries, schemes began to appear for, typically, 'supplier quality assurance'. These schemes generally employed some statistical analysis of data concerning performance criteria set by the customer – 'hoops' through which the supplier must 'jump'.

The focus on product quality was gradually replaced (on both sides of the Atlantic and in the other areas of the industrialized world that took their steer from the USA and Europe) by a focus on service and on appropriate management approaches in the supplier organizations. Thus, schemes emerged with complex algorithms for calculating the supplier's performance, often accompanied by annual reward ceremonies and all the trappings of celebration that are associated with project management.

In the 1980s, some companies began to institute schemes that involved two-way assessment: the customer would tell the supplier how well or poorly they were performing and seek the supplier's view of them as a customer in return. Suppliers would naturally tend to be complimentary, fearing retribution from the customer for a criticism, and the resultant good feedback from suppliers would encourage organizations to refer to themselves, rather naively, as 'preferred customers'.

Supplier assessment, however, has a basic flaw: responsibility for the performance of the supply activity cannot simply be laid at the door of the supplier. The manner in which the customer (and not just its purchasing department) conducts itself in the transaction is also heavily influential on the smooth running, or otherwise, of supply and the related costs. Thus, vendor assessment, born of a time when the cracks in the mass production paradigm were beginning to show, results not in the improvements in supply that are expected (and may indeed be shown and measured by proud customers), but in a systemic corruption of the process, as suppliers learn how to deal with dozens of different customers' assessment schemes, managing by guile to avert the commercial disaster that full compliance with all of them would almost certainly entail.

The principle of supplier assessment is logical but limited. There are many different types of scheme in operation and it is clear that, in some cases, the suppliers are actually helped by them. However, the area of assessment is thus one in which supply strategists should be employing their imagination and creativity. If it is not worthwhile to measure the individual performance of the supplier (which results, almost always, in a game of blame and defence) nor even that of the two separate parties (customer and supplier – again, this becomes a game of blame and counter blame, if, indeed, it ever moves beyond the blame and pleasantry model), then some other focus must be found for the performance measurement that is a critical part of strategic management.

One approach to this has been to use a facilitator between the two parties who provides the rationale in assessment. The Relationship Positioning Tool, developed by academic consultants at Glasgow Business School in the 1980s, does just this (Macbeth and Ferguson, 1994). Using a common framework for assessment, the performance of each organization is mapped independently (by the consultant/facilitator) and then a comparison and discussion takes place to identify ways forward.

A further development of this is to manage the unique relationship that is shared by the two parties as an entity itself; that is, the overlap of operational value adding between one stage in the chain and the next (as shown in Figure 6.3) is seen as a jointly owned activity with 'fuzzy' responsibility instead of a clean division, at least for operational purposes. The legal difficulties with this may be small or great, depending upon the situation. In the early 1990s the expression 'partnership' became popular within this context, with organizations professing mutual interest embodied in the relationship of partners. This served well in terms of awareness of shared responsibility but raised potential problems, especially when things went wrong. In the UK, under the 1891 Partnership Act, any two parties acting as if they are one entity become jointly responsible for one another's liabilities (as partnerships in, say, the legal profession do). Two companies acting this way may therefore incur unwanted liabilities – even if they do not actually call their relationship a partnership, or even claim that it is not (the interpretation is left to the courts). It may be that the only way around this is actually to form a third party – a joint venture company. When the stakes are high, this is precisely what some firms have done.

Assuming that the customer and supplier do not need to go to quite these lengths, it is reasonable to view the joint operation of organizing supply as a shared responsibility, and measuring its performance becomes a mutual interest. Since the activity of either party to the relationship (customer or supplier) might affect the performance, there is clearly no point in one of them simply blaming the other (other than as a tactical ploy in the 'competition' part of the relationship). Instead, the two can jointly assess the relationship and take appropriate action to reduce the difficulties it is experiencing, thereby improving the efficiency and cost-effectiveness of the value-adding process. This technique was pioneered by researchers at the University of Bath, in the form of the relationship assessment process (RAP), and subsequently, in the UK aerospace industry, as the relationship assessment process. The RAP is shown in Figure 6.7. In the early years of the new century, the field of management consultancy in purchasing and supply abounds with relationship assessment models: a good example of practice (via consultancy!) following academic research by about ten years.

SRM and development

The development of supplier assessment over three decades reveals a worrying assumption on the part of supply strategists that Gordon

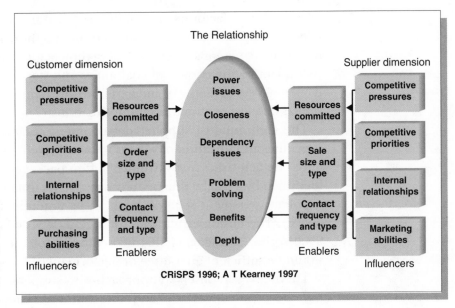

Figure 6.7
The relationship
assessment process
(adapted from
Lamming *et al.*,
1996).

Selfridge's famous aphorism 'The customer is always right' is a truism rather than the retailing sales tactic that it really is. The extension of this suggestion to commercial and industrial supply has left a legacy of techniques in which the customer assumes the role of infallible despot, while the suppliers become wily and resourceful, living on their wits and tricks.

As supplier assessment needs revision for post-mass production supply strategy, so its close cousin, supplier development, is also ripe for new perspectives. The idea that the customer could blame the supplier for all the shortcomings in the supply process led not only to the assessment mentality, but also to a view that customers might tell suppliers how to run their businesses – under the banner of development. Growing in popularity on the back of supplier assessment in the 1980s, this approach meant that by the mid-1990s many customers were seeking to 'develop' their suppliers in industries far from the origins of the approach (once again, aerospace and automotive). While some logic may be seen in, say, a global automotive company telling a small components manufacturer how do adopt statistical process control, the rationale for an airline telling its bakery supplier how to make its bread rolls is difficult to see. The latter example is real, however, and illustrates how far a fashionable idea can drift from its relevant basis.

Supplier development is actually a 'developing countries' strategy – used when an organization from a developed country wants to set up supply lines in a new, foreign venture. This also applies in the case of redeveloping economies and was evident in the strategies of the Japanese television manufacturers moving into South Wales in the 1980s. The UK television industry at the time was in ruins and the arrival of three of the top Japanese manufacturers in an area replete with labour recently made redundant by the closure of coal mines and steelworks resulted in fundamental regeneration of industrial wealth (coupled, as it was, with a similar development in the automotive industry in the region).

The technique of supplier development consists of the customer providing an indication of what is to be achieved, in terms of performance characteristics and attributes, often packaged into a campaign – identified by a catchy title or acronym. This is usually integrated with a supplier assessment scheme (with all its potential flaws, as discussed above). The customer may opt for a generic scheme, such as the ISO 9000 series, considering that accreditation of the supplier's systems would be sufficient guarantee of performance.

There are two observed approaches to supplier development: they have been called 'cascade' and 'intervention' (Lamming, 1996). They are illustrated in Figure 6.8. In the first, the customer organization develops a new concept that it would like to have adopted throughout its supply chain, formulates it in some way (often with the help of consultants) and cascades it 'down' to its direct, or first-tier, suppliers. It is either implicitly or explicitly expected that the direct suppliers will cascade the idea on 'downwards' to their own suppliers (the supposed 'third tier'). The mechanisms for doing this vary, but are seldom more than documentation and presentation (sometimes given at the award for 'supplier of the year', as part of the supplier assessment programme). Suppliers see many of these schemes and have to adopt a strategy that enables them to survive in the messy and sometimes contradictory combination of them all: the supplier may be expected to

Figure 6.8
Cascade and intervention strategies in supplier development (source: Lamming, 1996).

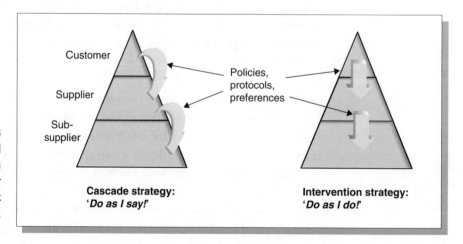

develop expertise in dealing with such complexity, appearing to comply with all but in fact approximating each to a common model.

The second strategy has the same basis as the first – the good idea (perhaps termed 'best practice') stems from the customer and is passed on down to the suppliers. However, in this case, the customer 'intervenes' into the business of the supplier, actually working at the operating level to help the supplier to develop specific skills. In this case, the customer is clearly making a real investment in the process, and this is likely to be more respected by the supplier as a valuable contribution (rather than simply issuing edicts *ex cathedra*). From the customer's point of view, it may actually be possible to make ideas 'stick', by working alongside the supplier's personnel in implementation.

The problem with intervention strategies is that the supplier may simply become dependent upon the customer for new ideas – a 'sheep'. The strategy should be used with care, therefore, and for a limited period only. This path was followed by the Japanese vehicle assemblers on coming to the UK and the USA: the intervention was for a limited period, following which the supplier was expected to develop their own competences, although the customer still brought new challenges and initiatives, to ensure the suppliers (of components, materials and services) were aware of the pressures in the end markets, which had to be transmitted all the way back along the supply chain.

In the course of time, one might expect the advanced supply strategist to construct a way of capturing the learning available from the interaction with suppliers so that the customer also sought to develop, not just the supplier. This might be a two-way, 'vertical' activity or perhaps, recognizing the complexity of the actual situation, a case of network development, where any player might learn from, and help to develop, any other. This situation, which is illustrated in Figure 6.9, is rarely found as yet, although one good example is the Supply Network Innovation Programme at British Nuclear Fuels plc in the UK in the following case.

Case: The Supply Network Innovation Programme at British Nuclear Fuels plc – an example of radical thinking in supply management

British Nuclear Fuels plc (BNFL) is an international business employing 23 000 people in 16 countries. Their activities span the entire nuclear energy cycle, from reactor design and fuel manufacture, generating electricity in nuclear power stations to spent fuel recycling and decommissioning, and cleaning up redundant nuclear facilities. The company has a large supply base, providing materials and services, many of a very specialized high-technology nature.

In 1998, BNFL decided to develop a 'supplier of the year award' scheme, to reward outstanding suppliers for their achievements over the past year, on an annual basis. This was seen as a normal approach to supply management, underway in many industries, but before they embarked upon it BNFL purchasing strategists did some deep thinking. They brainstormed, workshopped, consulted widely and talked to their suppliers. They realized that to go this route would simply be following an old-fashioned idea – treating the performance as the responsibility of the supplier alone, whereas, in fact, it reflected on the customer as well. Rather than development being something that should be done *to* suppliers, they realized that *they* should develop too, as part of the process. Leaving the outdated, mass production idea behind, BNFL began to work on a radical, lean idea; the supply network, they argued, could develop in many ways, using good relationships between BNFL and suppliers (singly and in groups) as the means for delivering mutual benefits and removing noise from the supply network. They designed and implemented a new scheme – the Supply Network Innovation Programme (SNIP). Within this programme, project teams would form, consisting of people from BNFL and a supplier (in practice, this sometimes became two or three suppliers at once – a mini-network). Each team would be set up on the basis of an identified development project that would provide benefits and learning for BNFL and the supplier. Where investment was required (people's time, etc.), a cost-benefit analysis would be drawn up to show the business logic for both parties – and identify the criteria for success (in fact, this became the norm). The projects would be intended to run for about 9 months, at which point their success would be assessed. (In practice, many projects have continued well beyond this period, delivering joint benefits for several years.) The most impressive projects would then be presented to an annual celebration event, attended by a broad range of suppliers and funded by BNFL, at which those involved in the projects (the BNFL people as well as those from the supplier) would be given physical records of the celebration – such as small, specially commissioned sculptures – not awards but symbols of the team's success. The intrinsic reward to suppliers and BNFL of being celebrated for their achievements, in front of 200 representatives of many industry organizations, was significant.

The scheme was a resounding success, resulting in major financial benefits for BNFL and its suppliers. Many of the projects (some 30 celebrated between 1999 and 2003) provided significant cost savings for BNFL and increased business or improved terms for the supplier. It is an example of lean supply at work: mutual benefits through *network development*, getting away from 'the customer's always right' and cutting the noise or waste in the system that results from the mass production attitudes to performance measurement.

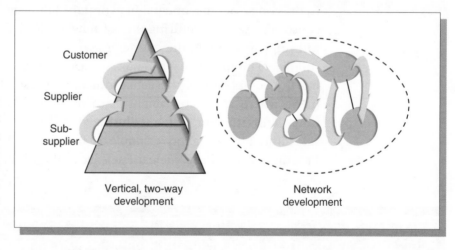

Figure 6.9 Two-way vertical development (customer and supplier) and network development (*source*: Lamming, 1996).

Whichever ways the development of skills, knowledge, learning and techniques is fitted into a supply strategy, it is important not to lose sight of the degree to which the customer, as well as the supplier, should seek to improve in all aspects; not to do so represents a waste of resources – something that lean supply cannot tolerate. It is a question of retaining strategic autonomy in both the supplier and the customer, recognizing the fundamental competition that exists between the supply chain 'partners', and managing the limitations to both so that each exploits the business opportunity to the level necessary to ensure their continued, combined activity.

One way of approaching this problem is through mimicking the Japanese technique of bringing suppliers together into a supplier association (the Japanese word is *kyoryokukai*). In this approach, the customer sets up a series of meetings between suppliers that it wants to form into a development group – the objective being to improve the overall situation in supply for the customer's products (with consequent benefits for all in the supply chain). These meetings may take place on neutral territory, and it may be necessary for the customer to be absent, at least after an initial 'bonding' has taken place. Supplier associations are a central feature of the Japanese system and have been adopted in the West successfully in several industries, the first European example being set up by Canon in France (for more information on this, see Hines, 1994).

SRM and information sharing: open-book negotiation

Recently, the practice of requiring a supplier to reveal all sorts of sensitive information to the customer, in the interests of joint competitive position, has become popular. The principle is that, if the supplier shows the customer how the costs are structured for a particular product or service (including, sometimes, their profit margins), the customer will be able to help the supplier to reduce costs, and thus prices. Sometimes this is dressed up as part of a joint effort, i.e. amid claims that the customer's own product or service might become more competitive in the market-place, thus ensuring the supplier's business too.

The principle of open-book negotiation is sound, but in practice it appears to be flawed – something the supply strategist must clearly understand. The supplier must manage resources to meet corporate objectives – generally a matter of shareholder value and return on capital employed. To do so, it has to manage risk and reward. Business is all about taking risks (i.e. making investments) and then ensuring that the reward is sufficient to justify having done so. When two parties compete, one will try to ensure that the other does not receive adequate reward for the risk and suffers accordingly. If they are collaborating, however, it is in the interests of both that they each receive appropriate reward – although for truly strategic operations to be conducted, each party must be free to decide its own rate or return.

In the supply chain, the organizations are both competing and collaborating. Thus, they must ensure that each makes appropriate reward, but there will be constant tension over who actually takes what risk and how the rewards (which are clearly jointly generated – each party is dependent upon the other) are shared.

A supply strategy that requires one side of a supply relationship to take a risk while the other does not, with the second seeking to articulate in heroic terms what the reward should (or might) be for the former, appears unlikely to succeed. When a customer stipulates to a supplier, therefore, that private information must be revealed (i.e. the supplier must take a very great risk) and also what the reward should be (i.e. the supplier is not allowed the strategic determination of the vital risk–reward business balance), it is probable that the supplier will take the only sensible business action, and cheat. Information will be distorted and misrepresented, incomplete and arcane. The customer, believing that they have extracted valuable information, will act accordingly and may only find after some time that they are not deriving the value from the transaction that they expected. (The failure of some European automotive manufacturers to make profits after a decade of such – publicly declared – initiatives may be related to this.)

The only solution to this is to manage the risk in some way, so that it makes economic sense for the supplier to share information. If the customer takes a risk, as well as requiring the supplier to do so, there may be a chance of genuine information and knowledge emerging. Thus, for a worthwhile supply strategy, exchange of sensitive information must be two-way – the customer must share information as well as demand it. Such 'transparency' may result in focused activity towards real improvements, but it will often require a great deal of confidence on the part of the supplier, that the customer has really taken a risk. Research on this has developed the management technique of 'value transparency' – now in use in manufacturing firms in the UK and USA and under consideration in the healthcare industry. For an explanation, see Lamming *et al.* (2001). It is not currently a common-place practice, however, and is actually considered impossible in some instances. It is, perhaps, an area in which the supply strategist must explore and innovate.

SRM: policy and strategy

Equipped with a policy, general strategy, structure plan, internal strategy for the purchasing and supply process, and set of techniques for managing relationships, the supply strategist can make a significant contribution to operations strategy – in both financial and technical terms. The structure of the organization may change fundamentally as a result, perhaps leading to more dissipated, decentralized activity, in which case the activity of supply management becomes even more important.

This may challenge or even threaten some traditional approaches to strategy and organizational analysis. When it is stripped of its mass production baggage, however, supply management consists of a cold logic and pragmatism that cannot be ignored for long.

Case: Facing the complex problems of managing supply

In order to illustrate the differences between lean supply and intervention strategy in supply chain management, we may consider the case of a Spanish manufacturer, identified here as 'Nunca'. This company is located in north-east Spain and manufactures a high-technology, high-complexity consumer product to which its clients add finishing touches (only a few features, in some cases) before selling the product as their own, to be marketed through distributors to end customers.

Nunca's unit cost for the product includes approximately 70 per cent bought-in components and materials. In addition to these, Nunca often receives materials 'free-issue' from its clients.

The Nunca name is well known – especially for design. Many of the items of equipment that they make for their client are actually Nunca designs, and the consumers who buy them appreciate this. The famous Nunca insignia is displayed on the product in addition to that of the client.

Nunca's clients are all skilled in manufacturing processes similar to those conducted by Nunca but are accustomed to work in high volumes. Nunca, on the other hand, has chosen to specialize in making high-profile niche products (or equipment that constitutes a large part of the finished product) for its clients to market. The components that are issued free of charge to Nunca are generally those the client purchases for use on a high-volume product, which are also fitted to the low-volume niche model made by Nunca.

In 1996, a very large French client ('Choux') that had been dealing with Nunca for many years began to treat the Spanish firm as 'a partner'. Although the equipment that Nunca made constituted almost the total value of Choux's product, in some cases (i.e. the 'package' that Choux sells to consumers is basically the Nunca product with the Choux badge added), the relationship had been one of master–servant, with Nunca allowed to make only minor decisions in sourcing components. This was a very limited expectation for Choux to exhibit in respect of a 'first-tier' supplier.

As part of its supplier development programme, Choux started to intervene in Nunca's supply operation. Nunca had its own supplier accreditation (vendor assessment) scheme, but Choux insisted on visiting the second-tier suppliers itself. Nunca understood lean production and supply but Choux did not take them seriously when Nunca's management team explained its plans for implementing the latter. It was true, however, that Nunca had sometimes experienced problems in maintaining the required levels of manufacturer quality or timeliness.

This was an intervention strategy that may only be considered as part of a collaborative approach if it is conducted in a co-operative manner. In this case, however, the visits to second-tier suppliers were characterized by Choux's representatives insisting on activities being done in the way they stipulated, often embarrassing Nunca in front of its suppliers.

Nunca could not refuse Choux's proposals, even though it could often see a better way to solve a particular problem. It also needed to develop its relationships with suppliers but found Choux's intervention disruptive in this respect.

Finally, Choux exhibited nationalist tendencies, often refusing to condone Nunca's choice of supplier (not just the Spanish ones), requiring instead that a French firm was awarded the business – especially one from which Choux already bought. If Nunca persisted and did manage to gain agreement for one of its partner suppliers to supply a component in preference to Choux's choice, it knew that the French were 'just waiting for something to go wrong – to say "I told you so".'

Choux was using a vantage point intervention strategy in this case. As a result, it was unable to develop lean supply, since the potential contribution of Nunca was not valued. It could not afford to lose Nunca in the short term, however. Nunca's strategy was to develop lean production in its own operation and to demonstrate to the client – and others – that it was capable of running its own lean supply base, perhaps with co-operative, rather than dictatorial, intervention from the client.

In the end, it took several visits by the most senior managers in Nunca (including the Chairman and CEO) to Paris to convince Choux that their supply management was counter-productive. As a result, Choux altered the words of its contracts to allow more scope for Nunca to contribute to technology and logistical matters. By that time, however, Nunca had begun to court a new set of clients (non-European) who valued the company's contribution more highly.

Summary

- The strategic management of supply is a critical part of managing the operations of an organization, and may represent the most critical part.
- The supply process is not a chain – it is a network, possibly even a mess. It is not possible to manage it in a straightforward manner; it may only be possible to manage *within* it, pursuing strategies for one's own activities that influence rather than control the activities of others.
- The term 'supply chain management' is in common parlance and may be used as an approximation to the actual situation, as a point of departure. In fact, *supplier relationship management* offers a more realistic focus for managing the process of supply.
- The organizations within a supply chain are both competitors and collaborators. Their operations are interdependent but they must also compete for the available value-adding business from which profit may be made.
- The structuring of supply 'bases' may include assumptions and expectations that are not backed up in practice. Simply calling a supplier 'first tier' may not bring the benefits expected of a structure supply base, such as that observed in post-war Japan.
- In order to develop a supply strategy, it is necessary to have a policy on how the organization should behave in the supply chain, a strategy to implement that policy, an internal strategy for the positioning of the purchasing and supply process, and a set of techniques for managing relationships within the supply chain.
- Some currently available and practised techniques for supplier relationship management are based upon mass production thinking and may not be appropriate for the post-mass production era. Techniques that form parts of lean supply – the removal of noise or waste from the supply relationship and process – can provide alternatives to such outdated approaches, especially those based on the mass production idea that the customer is always right.

Key questions

1   What are the challenges facing operations managers in obtaining competitive advantage from proficiency in supply management? Use examples from a heavy manufacturing industry (e.g. steelmaking), a light manufacturing industry (e.g. televisions), a service sector organization using materials (e.g. catering) and a service organization with almost no materials (e.g. finance).

2   Give examples of ways in which organizations might achieve differentiation in their own sale market by managing supply in new ways.

3   Trace the influence of Henry Ford to today's supply relationships: what techniques may be attributed to his ideas and in what ways are they now being questioned?

4   In what ways are customers and suppliers competitors and collaborators? How would this apply if one of them has a monopoly?

References and further reading

Cox, A.W. (1997) Relational competence and strategic procurement management: towards an entrepreneurial and contractual theory of the firm. *European Journal of Purchasing and Supply Management,* **2**(1), 57–70.

The Economist, 27 January 1996.

Financial Times, 26 June 1996.

Ford, I.D. (ed.) (1997) *Understanding Business Markets,* 2nd Edition. London: Dryden Press.

Granovetter, M. (1985) Economic action and social structure: the problem of embeddedness. *American Journal of Sociology,* **78**, 481–510.

Hines, P. (1994) *Creating World Class Suppliers: Unlocking Mutual Competitive Advantage.* London: Pitman.

Houlihan, J.B. (1992) International supply chain management. In: Christopher, M. (ed.), *European Logistics: The Strategic Issues.* London: Chapman & Hall.

Kraljic, P. (1983) Purchasing must become supply management. *Harvard Business Review,* **61**(5), 109–117.

Lamming, R.C. (1996) Squaring lean supply with supply chain management. *International Journal of Operations and Production Management,* **16**(2), 183–196.

Lamming, R.C. (2000) Japanese supply chain relationships in recession. *Long Range Planning,* **33**(6), 757–778.

Lamming, R.C., Cousins, P.D. and Notman, D.M. (1996) Beyond vendor assessment: the relationship assessment process. *European Journal of Purchasing and Supply Management,* **2**(4), 173–181.

Lamming, R.C., Johnsen, T., Harland, C.M. and Zheng, J. (2000) An initial classification for supply networks. *International Journal of Operations and Production Management,* **20**(5/6), 675–691.

Lamming, R.C., Caldwell, N.D., Harrison, D.A. and Phillips, W.E. (2001) Transparency in supply relationships: concept and practice. *Journal of Supply Chain Management,* **37**(4), Fall.

Leslie, W. (1996) High order strategy for manufacturing. *Journal of Business Strategy,* **17**(4), 21–36.

Macbeth, D.K. and Ferguson, N. (1994) *Partnership Sourcing: An Integrated Supply Chain Approach.* London: Pitman.

Nishiguchi, T. (1986) Competing systems of automotive components supply: an examination of the Japanese 'clustered control' model and the 'Alps structure'. In: *First Policy Forum, International Motor Vehicle Program.* Cambridge, MA: MIT Press.

Normann, R. and Ramirez, R. (1993) From value chain to value constellation: designing interactive strategy. *Harvard Business Review,* July–August, 65–77.

Porter, M.E. (1980) *Competitive Strategy: Techniques for Analysing Industries and Competitors.* New York: Free Press.

Reck, R.F. and Long, B.G. (1988) Purchasing: a competitive weapon. *International Journal of Purchasing and Materials Management,* Fall, 2–8.

Williamson, O.E. (1975) *Markets and Hierarchies.* New York: Free Press.

Williamson, O.E. and Masten, S.E. (eds) (1999) *The Economics of Transaction Costs.* Cheltenham: Elgar.

CHAPTER 7

Capacity and scheduling management

Introduction

Managing capacity is a central feature of strategic operations management. In some ways managing and understanding capacity is twinned with process choice that we discussed in Chapter 3, because understanding both areas can then enable the firm to make informed decisions about what it can and cannot do in the market.

The purpose of this chapter is for the reader to:

- understand the strategic importance of capacity;
- be able to utilize specific approaches to managing scheduling.

Adding capacity allows firms to position plants and service outlets in key areas around the world. In some cases location may be influenced by industry trends (e.g. in order to develop a fluid labour pool in a certain geographical area). For example, in the mid-1990s, before its merger with Hewlett Packard, Compaq invested $90 million in order to double its capacity at its Singapore manufacturing plant. In addition, the firm injected a further $11 million into its manufacturing plant in Scotland to enhance the manufacturing capabilities there. These additions to capacity formed part of Compaq's pronounced plan to become the world's leading PC manufacturer. The extent to which this will be realized after its merger with Hewlett Packard remains uncertain in the mid-2000s. The strategic importance of capacity for the computer industry was evident at the same time that Compaq expanded its capacity, when Dell Computers doubled the size of its manufacturing plant in Ireland as part of its long-term strategic positioning in Europe.

Japanese firms have clearly understood the strategic importance of capacity in their transplants operations. For example, the expansion by Nissan when it enlarged its Tennessee plant by 1.7 million square feet in order to allow a further 200 000 vehicles to be manufactured there in the mid-1990s was typical of many such aggressive expansions (Brown, 2000). This, and the other massive investments in North American capacity by Japanese firms, employed the technology advantage of lean production to exploit a window of opportunity – indolence in American management.

More recently, Intel showed the importance of capacity (*Fortune*, 11 November 2002):

> Intel is gambling that by pushing the state of the art in chipmaking faster than rivals are able to, it will reach a point where it can use sheer manufacturing prowess and capacity to undercut any competitor in price, performance, and variety. That means not just fending off would-be arch-rival Advanced Micro Devices and continuing to dominate the business of making chips for PCs, but also challenging Texas Instruments, IBM, Motorola, and a spate of smaller competitors in chips found in everything from cellphones to cars. 'Capacity is strategy,' says Andy Grove, Intel's Chairman and former CEO. 'Henry Ford used it to revolutionize the automobile industry; the Japanese used it to push us out of the memory-chip business 25 years ago; we used it a decade ago to ignite the explosion of the PC industry. Now we're using it again so we can broaden our business beyond the PC.'

Capacity expansion can often be targeted within specific countries, as illustrated in the example of Pepsi-Cola (*Business Week*, 6 September 2003):

> What the Chinese want now are more bottles of Mountain Dew. At least that is the hope of PepsiCo, which says it plans to spend $150 million to expand bottling capacity by a third. That will mean 100 million more cases of Pepsi, 7 Up, and the caffeine-charged Mountain Dew. While the company's annual sales in China have grown at around 10 per cent in recent years, it still has only about half the penetration of rival Coca-Cola. PepsiCo executives say they are determined to increase their beverage presence in China, despite the threat of severe acute respiratory syndrome (SARS).

Capacity has to be seen within the specifics of industry characteristics. For example, in the year 2004 the car industry had about 40 car producers. The likelihood is that there will be ten or even as few as six car producers by 2010. The reason for this is overcapacity within the industry. However, this means that the current car producers are seeking to expand capacity still further, as can be seen in the following (*The Economist*, 2 January 2003):

> Almost nobody, not even the giant western carmakers that have been dreaming about China for two decades, was prepared for today's boom. Ford, a latecomer which opened its first car factory in China in January, says that it expects China to become a larger market than Germany and perhaps even Japan in the next 3 to 5 years. For Volkswagen, whose joint ventures still dominate even though their market share has fallen from 55% to 41% in the past 2 years, China is already the biggest market outside Germany, its home. And in China, where fewer than 2% of urban residents have cars, this take-off phase could last a while – in Germany and America, by comparison, about half the population now owns a car. Shanghai Automotive Industrial Corp (SAIC), the largest domestic car company, has joint ventures with both Volkswagen and GM, as well as with other domestic firms. … The capacity that investors are now building will outstrip demand by 20% at least.

These examples clearly show the strategic intents of those companies who utilize capacity to achieve aims of growth and expansion into existing or entirely new areas.

Capacity defined and measured

Capacity can be considered as:

> The potential output of a system that may be produced in a specified time, determined by the size, scale and configuration of the system's transformation inputs.

At all stages of any process, limitations are placed on capacity. A machine has a maximum output per hour, a truck has a maximum load, a production line has a limit to its speed of operation, an aeroplane has a certain number of seats for passengers, a computer processes a specified number of bytes per second, and so on.

Capacity is therefore normally measured by considering how much can be processed in any given time period. This is commonly the case in materials processing operations, many information processing operations and some *customer processing operations* (CPOs). For example, a car plant is designed to produce a certain number of cars per shift; the work pattern of an insurance company worker is designed to process a certain number of claims per hour, and fast-food stores expect to be able to serve a certain number of customers in a defined time period (typically at a rate of one every 90 seconds).

Waters (2001) suggests that there is a difference between 'designed capacity', defined as 'the maximum output of a process under ideal conditions', and 'effective capacity', defined as 'maximum output that can be realistically expected under normal conditions'. He explains that, usually, effective capacity is less than designed capacity, due to set-up times, breakdowns, stoppages, maintenance, and so on. Whilst this is true in many cases, especially in materials processing operations, there are instances in which effective capacity may be greater than designed capacity. For example, there are many mass transit systems around the world, such as the London Underground and metropolitan railways in the Far East, where more passengers routinely travel than the system was designed for. Likewise, under normal conditions it might be thought a hotel could sell its rooms only once in a 24-hour period but some hotels, those at airports for instance, routinely sell their rooms more than once per day. Overbooking can be an issue, as in the case of one of the authors' experience with two airlines. The following are extracts from two letters from one of the authors.

Case: Overbooking and poor capacity management in the airline industry – the case of the angry passenger

Case 1
XXX Airlines,
Customer Care Department,
16 June 2003.

Dear Sir/Madam,
It is with much regret that I am writing to you to convey our disappointment with the lack of customer care and poor quality of service that we encountered in our last flight from Gatwick to Newark. The facts are as follows:

1 We booked a flight with XXX from Gatwick to Newark on the morning of 29 March. This booking was for two adults (my wife and I) and our baby daughter, and we had specified that we needed a bassinet for our baby.

2 When we checked in, we were told that that the bassinet would not be offered because we had 'requested' but not 'booked' it – I am at a loss as to what this really means and the distinction between the two terms is meaningless.

3 What became annoying was the dismissive attitude, with comments from your staff that included 'you're not the only family with children' (we didn't assume that we were!) and 'all seat allocations are made on a first come, first served basis'. If this is the case then the question is: what is the point of requesting a bassinet (which in turn demands allocations to specific seating areas on the plane that can house this unit) if this is overridden with a first come, first served basis, regardless of need?

4 More annoying was that we were informed that seats had already been allocated to families with children who had booked in earlier. However, as we later discovered on the plane, when we walked round the body of the plane, this was clearly a lie.

5 When asked why our request had not been honoured, I also had to endure standard nonsense statements about how all airlines overbook. I am a Professor of Business Management with a very good knowledge of the airline industry, and I really do not need to be lectured on the industry.

6 Finally, at the departure gate we were told that we were 'lucky' because the airline had managed to persuade a couple of other passengers to change seats.

To summarize, the issues are as follows:

- We had ordered a bassinet, which was evident from the onscreen data, but were then told we had not.
- We were, frankly, misled and lied to about seat allocations having been given to other families in the two rows of seats where bassinets can be located. This was clearly not the case.

I have travelled with XXX on many occasions. However, the nature of the response to this letter will determine the extent to which I, my family and colleagues will continue to book with you.

We look forward to hearing from you.

Yours sincerely,

To the airline's credit, there was a response dated 1 July, which included the following:

'Because we value you as a customer, I will forward a tangible token of goodwill under separate cover.'

However, by November, no such 'tangible token' had been offered. Consequently, another letter was sent:

XXXX Airlines,
Customer Care Department,
5 November 2003

Dear
You may recall that I wrote to you on 16 June and that you responded to my concerns about poor service quality that my family and I were exposed to on the Gatwick/Newark flight in your letter, dated 1 July 2003.

I appreciate that fact that you responded and in your letter you stated:

'Because we value you as a customer, I will forward a tangible token of goodwill under separate cover.'

As of today, nothing has been forthcoming. This is highly disappointing given the tone and content of your letter.

I trust you will respond by return and I look forward to hearing from you.

Yours sincerely,

A week later, a $50 gift voucher to be redeemed within the airline's shop was sent.

Case 2
XXXX Airways,
Customer Relations Department
PO Box

12 March 2004

Dear Sir/Madam,
I am writing to you to convey my huge disappointment in the poor service quality offered by XXXX on our recent flights to Athens. The facts are as follows:

Flying to Athens, 4 March

1 We booked a flight with XXXX from Heathrow to Athens, for 4 March, returning on 8 March. This booking was for two adults (my wife and I) and our baby daughter, and we had specified that we needed a bassinet for our baby. The reservation for the bassinet was confirmed.
2 When we checked in, we were told, initially, that we would not be able to sit together and the plan was that I would be in row 20 and my wife and child would be in row 27.
3 We were then told that XXXX would be able to accommodate us in row 27, where the bassinet would be.
4 When we boarded the plane we found, to our annoyance, that our seat allocations in row 27 were not where the bassinet would be! It took about 15 minutes of fuss, arguments and conflict in order to move seats.
5 To (your) credit we were, finally, moved to the Business Class area and the bassinet was brought on board.
6 The net result to our flight was that we had to endure considerable and unnecessary stress in order to have what had been agreed. It gets worse …

Flying to Heathrow, 8 March

1 Again, we confirmed that we needed a bassinet for our return flight on 8 March.
2 When we boarded the plane we found that, again, there was a problem. This time there was no bassinet on the plane and we were told, wrongly I believe, that the 757 could not accommodate a bassinet (even though our seats were in front of what was, clearly, a bassinet holder).
3 Your flight attendant (name provided) showed a great deal of empathy and tried to diffuse the problem.
4 However, again after a great deal of fuss, we were moved to Business Class but this time there was no bassinet and my wife was left carrying our child for the full 4-hour flight!

Clearly, the above is unacceptable. We were promised that a bassinet would be available for both flights; we endured a great deal of fuss and stress, which was avoidable, and we were left with a poor sense of service quality from XXXX. The fact that we were moved to Business Class did not solve the problem. Indeed, on the return flight we would have preferred to have been in Economy Class with a bassinet, as clearly agreed, booked, confirmed and paid for!

I have travelled with XXXX on many occasions. However, the nature of the response to this letter will determine the extent to which I, my family and colleagues will continue to book with you.

We look forward to hearing from you.

Yours sincerely,

On 17 March, the following standard reply was provided. It had no address on it and no details of the person who sent the letter:

17 March 2004

Dear
Thank you for completing our comment card on your flight from Athens.

I understand your disappointment, and I am sorry we could not arrange for you to have the bassinet seat for your child, which you had asked for. We try and make your time in the air as relaxed and comfortable as possible, but I'm afraid we cannot positively guarantee a particular seat to anyone. I do hope you will choose to fly with us again soon.

Yours sincerely
Customer Relations

Key questions: Why do airlines typically overbook and what does this say about how they manage capacity in relation to customer expectations? Given the nature of the replies from both of these airlines, which would you choose to fly with and why?

Waters (2001) suggests that 'actual output will normally be lower than effective capacity'. This will certainly be the case if capacity is not managed well. As we shall see, managing capacity is a challenging task, because matching output with effective capacity is very difficult. However, by distinguishing between designed capacity and effective capacity, we can establish the difference between 'utilization' and 'efficiency'. Utilization is the ratio of actual output to designed capacity, whilst efficiency is the ratio of output to effective capacity. In some operations, management focuses very much on utilization. For example, key performance measures in many capacity-constrained services, such as hotels, airlines and theatres, are utilization measures, namely room occupancy, passenger load and seat occupancy. In other operations, especially those adopting high-volume production processes, the focus is often upon efficiency measures.

The importance of capacity management

Strategic capacity management – i.e. knowing the *maximum* as well as the *attainable* input and output capabilities within a period of time – enables the firm to make vital strategic decisions. One of these is to reject potential opportunities. Hill (2000) describes how many firms suffer from the 'can't say no syndrome'. By that he means that, sometimes, firms embark on growth and expansion and take on business for which they have neither the capability nor the capacity to satisfy customers.

So, capacity management becomes an important means by which important, valid, business decisions can be made. Capacity also becomes a means by which both entrance and exit barriers to industries are put in place. Setting up new plants is a matter of managing strategic capacity.

That is, these decisions are made at senior levels of the firm; the amount of investment can be large; they are intended to provide competitive advantage – possibly by destabilizing the industry – or, at least, to allow the firm to remain in a position to compete.

In this book, we argue that the aim of operations management is to deliver an offer (a product or service) to consumers at the time they need it, to an appropriate quality standard, and at a price they are prepared to pay. The role of capacity planning and scheduling management in making this aim possible is to ensure the products and services are available when needed by the consumer. This is achieved by managing processes as efficiently as possible.

The management of capacity focuses on two aspects of the operation:

1 Transformation inputs and their organization into processes. Transformation inputs are those resources used to process the final output. They comprise both hard systems such as plant, machinery and technology, and the so-called soft systems, which are essentially work processes and the workforce. Capacity planning is largely focused on the effective and efficient utilization of these transformation inputs. In operations management terms, at the operations level, this is typically and variously referred to as capacity planning, aggregate planning or master scheduling. For separate processes within an operation, capacity management includes activities such as production control, loading or activity scheduling.

2 Ensuring the transformation inputs are utilized efficiently depends on the flow of inputs through the system. This requires the adoption of an appropriate strategy for inventory management. As we saw in Chapter 5, such strategies include inventory management, material requirement planning/ manufacturing resource planning (MRP/MRPII) and just-in-time (JIT) production.

Inputs and outputs of capacity

We need to make a distinction between outputs and inputs of capacity. They are linked, of course, but we need to focus on each because inputs can act as *constraints* on outputs. One of the key constraints that needs to be managed in capacity is bottleneck problems.

Schmenner and Swink's 'law of bottlenecks' states that productivity is improved if the rate of flow is consistent throughout the whole process. Applying this to engineering and manufacturing in job shops has led to the emergence of a number of rules:

- throughput is governed by the capacity of the bottleneck;
- balance material flow rather keep all resources fully occupied;
- inventory will accumulate at the bottleneck;
- any decrease in the output of a bottleneck will be a decrease in the output of the whole system;
- any increase in the output of a non-bottleneck will not increase the output of the system as a whole.

Managing bottlenecks is an important feature of scheduling. One solution to this comes from Goldratt and Cox (1986), who speak of optimized production technology (OPT). OPT is, essentially, based around software, aimed at locating and dealing with possible bottlenecks in the system. There are ten principles to OPT:

1 Balance flow, not capacity.
2 The level of utilization of a non-bottleneck is determined by some other constraint in the system, not by its own capacity.
3 Utilization and activation of a resource are not the same thing.
4 An hour lost at a bottleneck is an hour lost for ever out of the entire system.
5 An hour saved at a non-bottleneck is a mirage.
6 Bottlenecks govern throughput as well as inventory in the system.
7 The transfer batch may not, and at times should not, equal the process batch.
8 The process batch should be variable, not fixed.
9 Lead times are the result of the schedule and cannot be pre-determined.
10 Schedules should be established by looking at all constraints simultaneously.

The capacity challenge

From an internal, resource management point of view, the first challenge of capacity planning is to maximize utilization, and if this is constrained by process capability, to maximize efficiency. However, there is not much point in producing output if it cannot be sold. The second major challenge of capacity management is therefore fundamentally about matching the productive output of the operation with market demand. These challenges interact. Fluctuating demand increases the challenge of utilization and managing capacity efficiently.

There are two principal variables that need to be managed. These are the total demand for the product/service offering and the range of different product/service offerings being made available to consumers. The former defines the size of the productive capacity of the operation, the latter defines the scope of this capacity. Both of these may change over time. These can be considered as the four Vs, as shown in Figure 7.1.

In addition to the four Vs, there are two other factors that impact on capacity management that may increase its complexity. These are the predictability of demand and the 'perishability' of the output. In markets where there is high variation and variability, the complexity of capacity management can be reduced if there is a high degree of certainty about what demand will be. Some firms manage this by 'fixing' the amount that will be produced in a particular period of time, thus creating certainty. This will be made possible by having a master production schedule within a 'time bucket' – a week or month – in which output will be determined and information will then be provided to both suppliers and customers. Likewise, variation and variability are less problematic if the product is non-perishable, since a long shelf-life may enable stocks to be built up as a buffer against variability, even though this may add to costs. These key aspects of capacity planning are summarized in Figure 7.2.

The four Vs of capacity	
Volume	– total demand for output
Variety	– range of output
Variation	– change in total demand
Variability	– change in demand for each type of output

Figure 7.1
The four Vs of capacity.

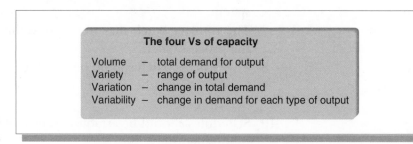

Capacity management		
Capacity Factors	**Straightforward**	**Complex**
Variety	Low	High
Variation	Low	High
Variability	Low	High
Predictability	High	Low
Perishability	Low	High

Figure 7.2
Factors affecting complexity of capacity management.

Back in 1967, Thompson wrote: 'the ideal operation is one in which a single kind of product is produced at a continuous rate and as if inputs flowed continuously at a steady rate and with specified quality' or, in other words, a continuous flow process. In this 'ideal' operation, capacity management is simple – volume is stable; there is no variety (and hence no variability or variation).

Continuous flow processes tend to produce outputs, like petroleum, that are commodities with relatively long shelf-lives for which demand is reasonably predictable over the medium term. A key point to note is that variation, variability and predictability are inherent features of market forces, whilst perishability is an inherent feature of the output. Firms may try to smooth demand and make their markets more predictable by, for example, introducing a reservation system, but they can only do so if consumers are prepared to accept such influence. Likewise, firms often seek to make their product less perishable to facilitate smoothing production capacity, but their ability to do so is constrained by the physical properties of the output. Variety, on the other hand, is a strategic choice that firms make in relation to the scale and scope of their operations. In the very early days of manufacturing, it was recognized that variety added costs, which is one reason Henry Ford only wanted to make black cars. This is the law of variability, which states 'the greater the random variability, either demanded of the process or inherent in the process itself or the items processed, the less productive the process is' (Schmenner and Swink, 1998).

So far this discussion of capacity has focused on aggregate demand. We know, however, that many operations are made up of complex processes that can be divided into subsystems. The four Vs, predictability and perishability also affect the utilization and efficient performance of each subsystem. Hence capacity and scheduling management becomes more complex the greater the number of different subsystems and the greater the flexibility of their use.

Capacity in services

It is in the nature of some services, specifically customer processing operations, that scale economies are limited, because in some cases the firm's physical assets have to be located where the customer is. Thus, whilst manufacturers may be highly selective as to the countries in which they locate their plants, from which to ship their products elsewhere, service firms often need a physical presence wherever they identify sufficient demand for their services. For example, of more than 2 million hotel rooms operated by the world's major hotel chains, 89 per cent are in just 1200 locations, typically capital cities, gateway cities (with an international or national airport) and major industrial centres.

Multi-unit operations

A key strategic issue for firms in managing capacity is the extent to which they own and operate their own assets. This is a particularly important issue for firms that need to utilize a large number of assets, specifically buildings. Such firms tend to be in the consumer service, companies that operate 'chains' of hotels, restaurants and retail outlets. In this instance, the property itself and its location are essential elements of the operations strategy. For instance, in the hotel industry, Conrad Hilton is famous for identifying the three keys to success in the business – 'location, location, location'.

Such chains have specific characteristics and face particular operational challenges. First, production is geographically dispersed across many units because these are sited close to their market. Second, most of these units are small. By definition they cannot be centralized into one large unit in order to achieve economies of scale. Third, production is local. Whilst some back-of-house activity or operation may be centralized, all front-of-house delivery is carried out at the point of contact with the consumer. Fourth, each outlet will be operated within the brand standards established by the chain. Just as manufacturers use brands to assure consumers of the quality of the product wherever it may be bought and consumed, service chains also use branding to assure consumers of the conformity of service in whatever outlet they visit.

Localized, small-scale operations of multiple units present both a challenge and an opportunity (Jones, 1999). The three major challenges are growing quickly, finding the right sites and ensuring each outlet satisfies its local market whilst conforming to brand standards. Amongst consumer service firms, rapid growth is desirable for two main reasons. First, new service concepts are easily copied by competitors. Unlike new products, which may be patent protected, it is very difficult to define a service concept and to legally protect this from commercial exploitation by others. In most cases, all consumer service firms can do is copyright the brand name they adopt, and some firms, such as McDonald's, are highly proactive in protecting their brand. Second, sites are difficult to find and rapid growth is desirable to get these before the competition does.

But rapid growth is difficult because the firm may lack the capital and cash flow needed to fund this. Property construction or acquisition is highly capital intensive. A relatively simple new-build 100-room hotel may cost 6 million Euros and a roadside restaurant with 80 covers in the region of 900 000 Euros (Jones, 1999). Many firms therefore have adopted franchising as a means by which they can grow rapidly. However, there is evidence to suggest that the higher the investment cost, the higher the risk (Brickley and Dark, 1987). As a result of this, single franchisees (so-called 'mom and pop' operators) may be replaced by corporate franchisees. For instance, the British company Whitbread is a corporate franchisee of US-based Marriott Hotels, owning and operating a number of hotels under the Marriott flag throughout the UK.

Franchising has three main advantages. First, the franchisee typically 'owns' and develops the unit. Hence they provide the funding to enable rapid expansion. Second, the franchisee is typically local to the community, region or even country that the franchisor is expanding into. This local knowledge greatly assists with regards the findings of a suitable site for the outlet. Third, this same local knowledge should also ensure that operations are managed effectively – both in terms of serving local customers as well as operating within the local labour market.

Operations management in multi-unit firms

The third issue faced by multi-unit chains is to ensure each unit is operated effectively and efficiently. In chains which own and operate outlets directly, the operations function has total control over performance in each of the units, usually through the 'area manager' role. How this is specifically achieved depends on a number of dimensions:

- job scope – this is the range of tasks and responsibilities at area management level;
- organizational congruence – this is the extent to which all managerial levels within the firm share a common vision and work together towards a common purpose;
- geographic density – this is the number of units in an area relative to the size of the area;
- unit conformity – this is the extent to which units within an area are identical or not.

When Sasser *et al.* (1978) first proposed the concept of the service firm life cycle, they drew heavily on the growth of fast-food and restaurant chains in the USA. Such chains demonstrated characteristics of high market penetration, strongly branded identical units, tightly and narrowly defined job descriptions for area managers, tightly specified standards of performance, effective organization-wide systems and strong organizational culture. The archetype of this kind of multi-site business is McDonald's. At that time, it can be inferred that area manager effectiveness required relatively narrow, tightly defined job scope; a high degree of organizational congruence; high geographic density; and high unit conformity.

But there is growing evidence from the USA that chains are abandoning these established traditions of multi-site management. For instance, at a conference in 1993, the CEO of PepsiCo outlined how he was refashioning the management of Pizza Hut, KFC and Taco Bell by increasing dramatically (from twelve to twenty-four) the span of control of area managers, empowering managers and employees, flattening the hierarchy, and investing in information technology.

It does not appear that the orientation towards a strategic role for the area manager versus an operational role is sector specific. In one UK study (Goss-Turner and Jones, 2000), the *job scope* of area managers appeared to vary greatly – from those who clearly had a narrowly defined operational role as a line manager, with tasks focused around unit inspection and control, to those with a broad range of responsibilities for developing the business. Indications were that there are two alternative business strategies adopted by firms. The first focuses on achieving high levels of profit through tight control of operating units. The second is more concerned with sales growth and market share through a strategic service vision related to customer service, hence a differentiation strategy. It would appear that multi-unit managers from firms in the first category have a narrower job scope. Again, this is not necessarily sector specific. Although the hotel area managers in this study tended to have a narrower job scope than restaurants or pubs, this appears to be a reflection of their strategy, rather than related to the relative complexity of the business at unit level.

An alternative explanation may not be the strategy adopted by the firm but the attitude of the firm to operating in a mature market-place. Certainly hotels and pubs are mature UK businesses, with some kinds of restaurant less so. Baden-Fuller and Stopford (1994) suggest two alternative mindsets towards this context. 'Mature businesses' perceive the industry as stable, believe profitability derives from giving stakeholders less value, regard themselves victims of external economic forces, strive for market share, and seek economies of scale. 'Dynamic businesses', however, seek new ways of operating, give better service to customers, believe profit derives from their own ability to control events, see market share as the reward for creating value not the means of achieving it, and use innovation to compete. There is some evidence that firms like Taco Bell in the USA have adopted this dynamic perspective.

Such a shift may have implications for *organizational congruence*. New ways of thinking and operating take a while to develop within firms. This concept of congruence is largely concerned with organizational systems or culture. In the UK study (Goss-Turner and Jones, 2000), formal systems were most evident in those firms operating UK corporate franchises of international brands originating in the USA. On the other hand, one firm stood out as a firm in which cultural norms rather than formal systems were dominant. It appears that rather than having both strong systems *and* culture, as is the case with the US archetypes, most firms were strong in one but weaker in the other. The relative lack of strong cultures may relate to the British approach to business, a lack of clear identity in businesses that were franchises of concepts (in restaurants), a very strong tradition of management (in pubs) and few firms operating single concepts. The relative lack of strong systems, especially integrated IT support, may be due to the age of the infrastructure and lack of new build units in the UK compared with the USA. Most firms in the study were investing in IT to address this issue.

Business units may vary in a number of different ways: sales volume, sales revenue, operating capacity, number of employees and so on. There tends to be a close fit between these factors, i.e. the larger the physical capacity of the unit, the larger its sales revenue. In firms which have units that vary in size, there is a tendency to adapt the size of an area to reflect this. However, there is no evidence of any formal method, such as a formula or statistical analysis, used to determine the size of areas. According to Goss-Turner and Jones (2000), firms with the highest level of *unit conformity* are those that have grown through new-build or green field site development. But most UK chain hospitality businesses, unlike the USA, have a relatively old property portfolio, especially in the pub and hotel sectors, which significantly reduces unit conformity.

Reflecting the diverse range of operations within firms, many UK hospitality chains have developed brands, notably in the hotel and pub sectors. Hence there is potential trade-off in these large firms between geographic density and unit conformity. Areas may be organized with high density but low conformity, or low density and high conformity.

Based on their work (Goss-Turner and Jones, 2000), firms have a *strategic* choice as to how they should organize the operation function in multi-unit chains. There are four types of area manager.

The archetype

Area management in the archetypal multi-site service firm conforms to the McDonald's model – strongly branded identical units, tightly and narrowly defined tasks for area managers, tightly specified standards of performance for units, and an emphasis on operational control over units. The job scope of this type of multi-unit manager is relatively narrow and there is a high degree of organizational congruence, with a focus on operational performance. Firms would like to have high geographic density, as they believe their area managers should be in the units as much as possible.

The entrepreneur

Entrepreneurial area managers are responsible for a single concept, also tightly branded, but are expected to develop the potential of each unit as a business. It is possible in this context for control to be exerted over and by the area manager entirely through cultural norms. Organizational congruence also tends to be culturally driven. Such managers therefore have wide job scope, applying a range of skills to operating units to reflect local and regional influences.

Multi-brand manager

The area manager in the multi-brand context has more than one concept to manage but does so by applying almost identical 'rules of the game' to them all – namely, tight cost controls, standards conformance and revenue growth. Job scope remains quite narrow, but because the manager is responsible for more than one brand or type of operation, there is more flexibility. In this context, achieving high levels of organizational congruence may be difficult. Typically, geographic density is high as the rationale for defining an area is based on this.

The business manager

The 'business manager' is responsible for more than one brand and applies creative solutions to each of their units within the context of over-arching policy guidelines and marketing strategies. Such managers, like their firms, need to be dynamic. They coach and influence their unit managers, rather than control them. Geographic density is not too great an issue for them as they do not believe they have to spend a lot of time in each unit.

Goss-Turner and Jones (2000) suggest that individual managers could not easily move from one firm to another with different characteristics. For instance, area managers used to operating with high geographic density might dislike managing a large area with long drive times; those used to tight control over a single brand may be challenged by more strategic responsibility for a number of brands; and those used to a clearly defined job may find a lack of definition and emphasis on cultural norms disquieting. This appears to be confirmed by industry practice, which is for most firms to appoint area managers from within.

Franchisor–franchisee relationships

In firms that have adopted franchising as their approach to growth, the firm still requires units to be operated effectively and efficiently. They want units to be profitable as franchise fees are often based on a proportion of profits, whilst they also want to ensure brand standards are maintained. Rather than have area managers, such firms have franchise managers. Whilst the role these managers play is essentially the same, the means by which they do it is quite different. Franchise managers have to operate in the context of the legal franchise agreement agreed between the firm and its franchisees.

Franchise contracts have many similarities whatever market they may be applied to and whatever country they operate in. The franchisee agrees to operate the business according to policies and procedures laid down by the franchise 'system'. Such a system typically stipulates the products to be sold, inventory items, opening hours, plant maintenance, staffing levels, insurance cover, accounting procedures and auditing processes. In return, the franchisor provides national brand marketing, along with a range of managerial assistance, such as help with site selection and development, training, standard operating manuals and financing. The franchise fees for the right to operate the system and have access to assistance are usually in the form of royalties, such as a percentage of sales. In addition, franchisees are usually required to purchase their raw materials from the franchisor or designated suppliers. The contract will also have clauses in relation to the termination of the agreement by either party. The franchisor typically may terminate the contract if the franchisee operates the unit outside the parameters of the stipulated 'system' and terms of the contract, and there will be constraints on the franchisee in terms of opening a competing business.

In the popular press, the relationship between franchisor and franchisee is often portrayed as coercive – big business controlling and coercing the little guy. For instance, in his book *Fast Food Nation*, Eric Schlosser (2001, p. 99) talks about conflicts between franchisor and franchisee as 'commonplace', franchisees being 'afraid to criticize their chains' for fear of reprisals or termination of contract, and firms anxious to expand 'encroaching' on the territories of their franchisees. This relationship tends to be further supported by the approach adopted by multi-unit firms to monitor and regulate quality in their operations (owner or franchised). The typical approach is to have a mystery shopper scheme, whereby each unit is visited on a random basis by an incognito quality inspector posing as a typical consumer.

In reality, the relationship between the two parties is much more complex than this and firms have a *strategic* choice with regard to how they work with their franchisees. Hunt and Nevin (1974) argued that the franchise relationship is a specific type of distribution channel and that, as such, power in the relationship may be exercised by the franchisor in five ways – by *coercive* sources (typically enshrined in the contract), and four non-coercive sources, namely reward, expertise, legitimacy and identification (or referent power). *Reward*-based power derives from one party being able to reward the other to their mutual benefit. A relationship based on *expertise* derives from one party sharing its expertise with the other. *Legitimate* power is based on the one party accepting the right of the other party to exert power over it, whilst *identification* means 'a feeling of oneness' or desire for it between the two parties. Hunt and Nevin (1974) showed that those franchisors that used non-coercive approaches had franchisees that were more satisfied than those who were contracted to 'coercive' franchisors.

It is suggested that the non-coercive style and resultant higher levels of franchisee satisfaction lead to considerable benefits. First, franchisees will have higher morale. Second, co-operation between the two parties will be better. Together, this should lead to both better business performance as well as compliance with system requirements. Furthermore, the non-coercive approach will reduce the likelihood of legal action by either party to terminate the contract, file suits or take out class actions.

Capacity and scheduling in mass services

During the mass production era, service operations began to be addressed, initially from the viewpoint that they were becoming more like manufacturing. This view was seminally articulated by Ted Levitt, of Harvard Business School, who wrote two key articles in 1972 and 1976 – 'The production-line approach to service' and 'The industrialization of service'. The success of hamburger fast-food chains, notably McDonald's, in the late 1950s partly derived from appearing to offer a reasonably wide range of products at different prices, made from a small stock of 'components' and using a small number of processes. So from the same food items (meat pattie, bun, salad items and sauce), based on identical processes (grilling, toasting, assembly and wrapping), the basic hamburger could be turned into a cheeseburger by adding a slice of cheese, a Big Mac by including two patties instead of one, and so on. Meanwhile, in manufacturing, many operations required variety reduction programmes in order to remove redundant processes and duplicated components.

In contrast to Levitt's perspective, Sasser *et al.* (1978) suggested some different and new ideas about services. These new ideas originated from their analysis of services as being intangible, heterogeneous, perishable and 'simultaneous'. Services are 'perishable' in the sense that those not consumed today cannot be stored until tomorrow. As Sasser *et al.* put it: 'a hotel room unused today cannot be sold twice tomorrow'. This perishability derives from the fact that production and consumption of many services are simultaneous; 'production' only occurs when a consumer arrives to use the service facilities. Such facilities may also have a fixed capacity that derives from the physical infrastructure that delivers the service offer. For instance, aircraft or cinemas have a defined number of seats, hotels a certain number of bedrooms, and schools an optimum class size. Due to the perishability of the service offer and fixed capacity, there is greater emphasis in services capacity management on managing demand. Hence, from the 1980s onwards, there has been a growing synergy between the operations and marketing functions of organizations, especially those delivering services.

These developments lead to a paradox. On the one hand, a growing number of authors and researchers were actively developing theories and models based on the idea that services and manufacture were different. On the other hand, a growing number of practitioners and operations managers were using similar ideas and methods irrespective of whether they were engaged in goods production or service delivery. The reason for this confusion is clear. Often, the examples of industrialized services cited in the literature were not pure customer processing operations (CPOs), but had strong elements of materials processing as with fast food, or information processing as with automatic teller machines. Hence it is not surprising that they could be managed like batch production operations. Those that were more CPOs continued to be operated as job shops like they had always done, albeit with better utilization than before due to better forecasting and priority management. The adoption of yield management in hotels is a good example of this. In discussing 'priority management', Westbrook (1994) identifies that it is a key element of batch production operations, so that organizations 'pursue certain kinds of order to fill capacity ... and choose which customer orders are to have priority'. A hotel is a particular kind of batch production operation in that it produces every 24 hours a number of rooms available for sale. Its output is therefore highly perishable. Yield management is an approach to priority management that comprises a range of systems and procedures designed to maximize sales of a product or service under more or less fixed supply conditions, where the revenue producing ability diminishes with time. The following case illustrates this.

Case: Hotel yield management

The Portsmouth Hotel is part of an international chain. It has 160 rooms and is located on the South Coast of England. The General Manager's performance and that of his hotel are evaluated by the company on the basis of profitability, sales revenue, customer satisfaction and employee satisfaction. Thus, yield management is the key tool for delivering revenue and contributing to profitability. The General Manager emphasizes the role that strategic decisions have in the yield management system. On an annual basis, a business plan is drawn up that sets sales targets for seven market segments ('premium', corporate, conference, leisure, promotions, tours/groups and 'special company'). These targets derive from an analysis of the hotel's previous performance, analysis of achieved rate per segment, a competitor analysis and an environmental analysis. This leads to the setting of rates for these segments, designed with the overall aim of increasing the overall average rate performance. In 1996, a key decision was made to lower the rack rate significantly, adjust sales mix and reduce the number of special companies (those with specially negotiated, discounted rates) from 200 down to just 20. This has led to an increase of £4.00 in the average room rate achieved, even though the rack rate is £10.00 lower. The aim is to establish what the manager calls a 'fair price' (or price–value relationship), thereby attracting the right volume of business and negating the need to negotiate price.

The business plan is reviewed on a quarterly basis by the full management team. Rooms performance is specifically reviewed by a group comprising the General Manager, Sales Manager, Reservations Manager, Front-Office Manager and Financial Controller. This group also convenes weekly for a Sales Strategy Meeting. The routine agenda for this weekly event is based around a review of the previous week's performance (rooms sold, occupancy rate, actual revenue, average rate achieved, lost potential sales from declines/denials); competitor review (five hotels regarded as direct competition are telephoned twice per day to establish room availability and rack rate offered); 35-day occupancy forecast by market segment; monthly financial forecast; 3-month forecast of occupancy. The meeting analyses the reasons for any deviation from plan and proposes action to ensure future plans are achieved. Special events, such as, in the case of this hotel, the Whitbread Round the World Race, are also considered and responses to these considered.

These annual, quarterly and weekly planning meetings enable the Reservations Manager, who is largely responsible for managing the yield management system, to take appropriate action on a daily basis. Over 80 per cent of the hotel's reservations are taken in the reservations office in the hotel, comprising the manager and two full-time reservationists. Each day, the yield management system presents a report showing the current level of bookings for the next 7-day period by each 'rate category'. These categories are related to, but not identical to, the seven market segments. A is the rack rate and B–H are different levels of discount on this rate. It is possible for a 'special company' to pay a significantly discounted rack rate, but still be categorized as A, due to the volume of business they provide the hotel. The system also provides a breakdown of what would be 'acceptable' lengths of stay that could be accepted by each of seven rate categories, A–H. In response to an enquiry, the reservationist establishes the rate category and desired length of stay. If the hotel is near capacity, lower rate categories, such as D–H, are likely to be blocked out, so the reservationist will identify this rate is unavailable and offer occupancy at whichever category rate is the minimum available. The reservationist may also turn away business at these lower rates if the requested length of stay spans a period during which higher rates are forecast to be achievable. The system can be overridden by anyone taking a booking. A detailed record is kept of these denials (due to the hotel being fully booked or length of stay mismatch) and decline (due to the customer not accepting the rate offered). These are regarded as 'lost sales opportunities' and are analysed at the weekly meeting against the actual occupancy achieved. Such sales may be acceptably 'lost' if the hotel was fully booked or the enquiry was made some time in advance. Recent denials and recent declines (in the previous week) are reviewed if the hotel did not achieve full occupancy. The daily demand forecast can be adjusted by the Reservations Manager in the light of adjustments to the overbooking policy and policy decisions made at the weekly review meetings. The system also has a subsystem that enables decisions to be made about conference or group bookings. Based on demand forecasts, the subsystem predicts the sales mix and identifies the potential level of displacement of rack rate. On this basis it advises what rate to propose for the conference.

The core team engaged in yield management is the Reservations Manager and two reservationists. In terms of strategic decision-making, the Reservations Manager has strong support and encouragement from the General Manager, as well as effective co-operation with other members of the hotel's management team. Operationally, the Reservations Manager liaises with the Front-Office Manager and her team, especially with regards to the 10–15 per cent of reservations taken through the front office. There is a clear distinction between the level of knowledge and skill displayed by the reservationists compared with the receptionists. The Reservations Manager undertook a 2-week induction course based on simulation exercises before taking up his post, but believes that it took him a further 6 months to really understand the system. He has personally supervised the training of the reservationists, who also have taken months to become fully competent. The receptionists, on the other hand, have had a minimum level of training. A high proportion of their 'reservations' are actually 'walk-ins' on nights when rooms are available. Given the emphasis on keeping 'lost sales' to a minimum, the Reservations Manager always follows up a reservation taken by a receptionist that has overridden the system (usually by accepting a lower rate category).

The yield management team is not directly incentivized. The hotel's management team have a bonus based on their performance, whilst employees are able to collect points towards household goods and other consumables based on their individual performance. However, this company's emphasis on employee satisfaction and the prevalent corporate culture creates an environment in which good performance is recognized and praised by the General Manager down. The technology that supports yield management is based around a central reservations system that enables bookings to be made in the central sales office or in each individual property. This system advises reservationists on room availability and rate (as described above), and records all the relevant data for a booking to be made. A number of subsystems use this data to facilitate yield management. These comprise a demand forecasting system, a decline/denial model, guest history database, group demand forecasting system and a travel agency commission system. The chain also has a hotel information system that supports accounts, guest check-in and check-out, audit and payroll.

Strategies for managing capacity

Over time it became clear that there were two basic strategies that operations could adopt when managing capacity. Starr (1978) proposed an 'aggregate planning model' that led to two strategies: either

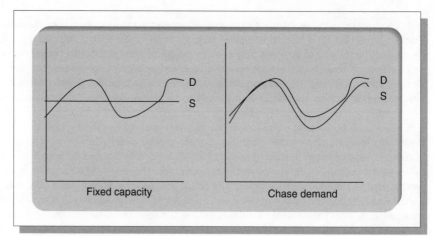

Figure 7.3
Fixed capacity and
chase demand.

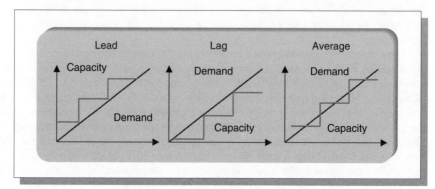

Figure 7.4
Three strategies in
managing capacity.

'vary W [the workforce] so that P [production] matches the demand as closely as possible' or 'do not vary the workforce, thereby keeping P constant over time'. This is illustrated in Figure 7.3. Sasser *et al.* (1978) identify that these same strategies may be applied to service operations. Under a chase demand strategy, the emphasis is placed on matching output to demand and hence there is a need to forecast demand. In the level capacity strategy, the emphasis is on maximizing utilization.

Managers are faced with decisions about matching demand with supply in capacity and these are for both short-term and longer, more strategic, decisions on capacity. The three types of capacity are:

- lead – adding capacity in advance of demand growth;
- lag – adding capacity after demand growth;
- average – trying to maintain average capacity.

These are illustrated in Figure 7.4.

The first of these, 'lead' capacity, can be a sign of aggressive growth from an organization whereby it will 'stake out a position' geographically

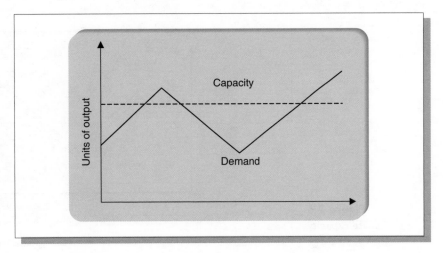

Figure 7.5
A level capacity
strategy.

and actively create demand. Japanese transplants have been hugely successful at doing this; some types of pharmaceutical and biotechnology capacity management is handled in this way. 'Lead' capacity can be viewed as a 'risk-seeking' strategy.

The second, 'lag' capacity, is a more reactive, risk-averse approach whereby an organization responds to specific demands. It is, none the less, a powerful approach. For example, the tragedy of the Aids epidemic has caused some pharmaceutical companies to increase capacity in response to this tragic phenomenon.

The third type, averaging capacity, is typically used within service organizations to smooth out the relationship between demand and supply. As we have mentioned earlier, some services cannot store capacity and so the key task is to match demand with supply so that capacity requirements are met on both sides.

Further strategies that are used across organizations to manage fluctuations in demand and supply are:

- Providing the same level of supply, no matter what demand level. This strategy may be called *demand smoothing* in service operations, or *level production* in manufacturing operations.
- Exactly matching the level of supply to the level of demand. This strategy is usually called *chase demand.*
- Adjusting demand to better match supply. This strategy is called *demand management.*

Level capacity strategies. One strategy that organizations use to match demand and supply is to produce and store outputs in advance of demand. These strategies rely on building inventory. Other types of operations – such as service operations – have only limited recourse to

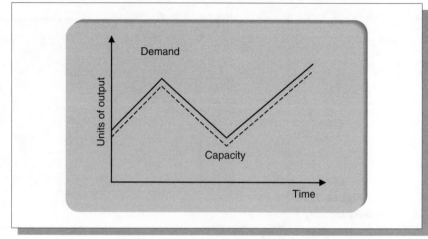

Figure 7.6
A chase capacity
strategy.

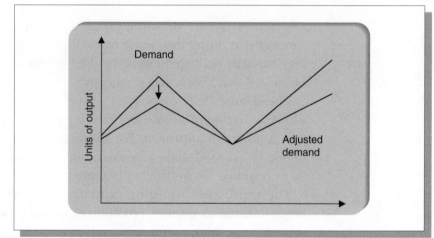

Figure 7.7
A comparison of the
three types of capacity
management policies.

inventory-building strategies. In many service organizations, mismatches between supply and demand will result in queues.

Chase strategies. Organizations that use chase strategies adjust their activity levels to reflect the fluctuations in demand.

Demand management strategies. Organizations that use demand management try to change demand to smooth high and low periods.

According to Shore (1973), the 'essence of aggregate planning is to devise a strategy by which fluctuations in demand can be economically absorbed'. In this sense, this approach to capacity management is largely concerned with managing volume and reducing or controlling the impact of variation through improved predictability. The focus is therefore on forecasting.

The two stages of aggregate planning are first to add together all productive output to arrive at a total level of production (the equivalent of what we have called 'volume') and second to predict or forecast the fluctuations in this output (what we have called 'variation'). *De facto*, therefore, this approach eliminates, or rather ignores, variety and variability.

Once a strategy or aggregate plan has been drawn up, it has to be put into practice. In manufacturing, especially where high-volume batch or line processes are in place, this is usually through a master production schedule. Such a schedule includes information about promised delivery dates, resources and materials needed, assembly capacity, set-up costs, and inventory. The particular approach will depend on the competitive priorities of the organization. Those with a make-to-stock strategy schedule production of output or end items, those with a make-to-order strategy schedule inputs or purchase items, and those with an assemble-to-order strategy schedule assemblies to capitalize on making common components for various output items.

Although volume, variety, variation and variability are derived from finished output, they feed back through each stage in the production process. Likewise, prediction about finished output leads to prediction about each stage of the process, whilst there may be perishability of components at each stage of the process. The 'make or buy?' approach to capacity management reduces variety with regard to inputs and in-process activity by shifting production to suppliers. Often, the final stage of the process is the assembly of components. Hence the 'make or buy?' decision identifies the extent to which a process should also include the 'manufacture' of these components. By outsourcing the production of some or all of component production, the variety of sub-processes within the operation is reduced, and just as capacity may be more easily managed if the variety of output is reduced, so it is if the variety of process is reduced.

The profound implication of outsourcing for capacity planning is the shift from a process that is controlled within the operation to one that requires co-ordination with suppliers. The growth of so-called 'supply chain management' during the 1980s (although, as we saw in Chapter 6, it is perhaps better to think in terms of networks rather than chains) indicates the extent to which this was increasingly identified as a key aspect of operations management. Operations have always been faced with the challenge of deciding whether or not to use raw materials or processed materials supplied by intermediaries. Even the archetypal job shopper, the blacksmith, did not smelt his own ore to produce iron. The key difference in managing capacity that was adopted was the idea of a strategic approach to outsourcing, from which supply chain management emerged. Decisions about whether to make or buy therefore shifted from consideration about individual items on a piecemeal basis

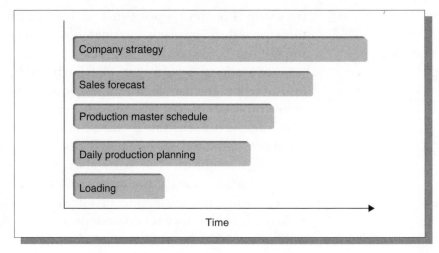

Figure 7.8
Links between
long-term capacity and
daily scheduling.

to decisions about whole groups of components and whole sets of processes. We saw in Chapter 3 how Taco Bell had reconfigured its processes. Taco Bell also made changes to how they managed scheduling, as the study illustrates.

The capacity/scheduling interface

We have deliberately spent much of this chapter discussing types of capacity. Capacity has clear strategic consequences, but it is also linked to day-to-day scheduling. In essence, the link between capacity and scheduling is one of timing, as can be seen in Figure 7.8.

Scheduling methods

Given that operations scheduling is so important for utilization and efficiency, order sequencing, or as Westbrook (1994) terms it 'priority management', is essential. From the craft era onwards, order sequencing has been determined using a range of criteria. Informal scheduling methods include the following:

- Giving priority to the best customer. For instance, hotel clients (often large companies) that provide a high number of bed nights are not only given a discounted room rate, but also 'last room' availability.
- Prioritizing emergency cases. This applies particularly in medical circumstances, such as accident and emergency departments, which often have a 'triage' system.
- Giving in to pressure from the most demanding customer.

Other 'good ideas' of scheduling based on systematic order sequencing can include the following:

- First come, first served. This is the fairest system, and is often applied where people are processed through the operation.
- Earliest due date.
- Shortest or longest total processing time. This is based on the idea of getting jobs that take the least, or most, time out of the way.
- Least slack time. This sequencing is based on matching process time to the due date so that the finished output can be shipped to the customer as quickly as possible.
- Least change-over cost. Jobs are selected on the basis that they require little or no machine set-up or change-over.
- Shortest first/last operation first – the 'shortest first operation first' approach enables jobs to become active and aims to make good utilization of plant. The problem is that it can create work in process and bottlenecks at later stages. Loading jobs according to their shortest last operation attempts to ensure that jobs are not held up at the point where most cost has been accrued – i.e. at the last stage. Once again, though, this can cause bottlenecks at earlier stages of the overall process.
- Critical ratio. This is determined by dividing the time to due date by the process time. Less than 1 means that the job will finish after the promised delivery date. In this situation, steps can be taken to reduce process time through employee overtime and so on. Orders are sequenced by the lowest critical ratio.

Case: Financial services

The provision of financial services such as banking, mortgages and insurance has been transformed in recent years by the increase in power of desktop computing and the development of the information superhighway. Many 'virtual' firms have entered the market, without the physical retail infrastructure of their predecessors. These firms have radically transformed this sector.

They have been able to handle significantly higher volumes of business through access to sophisticated databases. Customers making a telephone enquiry need only cite their post code (or zip code) for detailed information about the enquirer to be revealed to the tele-sales operator. This also reduces the transaction time through accelerated data entry.

But the same databases may also hold considerably more information. Insurance companies are now able to 'customize' individual home insurance policies based on post code data that identifies the level of crime and hence risk for any given area, along with the detailed information provided by the customer as to the content of their properties. Again, standardized data entry enables swift data entry, along with highly individual policy production.

Claim processing has also been very much more flexible and responsive to customer needs, whilst at the same time reducing costs. Claims settlements have traditionally comprised two stages: an assessment of the damage sustained, usually determined in the field by a loss adjuster, and processing of the associated paper-work and issuance of the cheque, usually centrally processed in batches back-of-house. Today, it is possible for loss adjusters to be equipped with technology that enables them to respond to claims immediately, travel to the claimant, assess the claim, process the documentation and issue the cheque, all within 3 hours of the accident occurring. This combination of mobile computing and telephony also enables the adjuster to liaise with other service providers that the claimant may need, such as in the case of a car accident, a towing vehicle, medical treatment, overnight accommodation or whatever. This form of provision adds considerable value, customizes the experience and is relatively cheap to provide with the right kind of technological support.

The same information that enables insurance policies or mortgages to be customized also enables these firms to engage in more effective marketing of other products or services, to the point where the concept of one-to-one marketing has emerged. Information about the age, sex, residence and most especially spending habits of the customer identify key lifestyle changes that may trigger new sales opportunities for financial services firms. For instance, the regular purchase of airline flights might signal the opportunity to sell travel insurance or travellers' cheques.

Summary

- Capacity management is based on understanding the specific characteristics of volume, variety, variation, variability, predictability and perishability.
- There are two main strategies available for managing capacity – level capacity or chase demand.
- Early operations management approaches to capacity were based on order sequencing, scheduling activities and process control, whilst materials management was based around economic order quantities, standardized components and inventory control.
- It is erroneous to assume that because some approaches to capacity planning were developed early in the twentieth century, they are no longer relevant to today. There are many operations, businesses and even sectors that continue to need and indeed use these methods.
- Such operations are often small scale and owner operated in sectors with some technology that has remained largely unchanged.

Key questions

1. How well do firms really understand the four Vs of their business and the concepts of perishability and predictability?
2. How should firms go about making the choice between improving their existing approach to capacity and scheduling management or radically changing their process to reconfigure the notion of capacity?

References and further reading

Baden-Fuller, C. and Stopford, J. (1994) *Rejuvenating the Mature Business.* London: Routledge.

Brickley, J.A. and Dark, F.H. (1987) 'The Choice of Organisational Form: The Caso of Franchising'. *Journal of Financial Economics*, **18**, 401–421.

Brown, S. (1996) *Strategic Manufacturing for Competitive Advantage.* Hemel Hempstead: Prentice Hall.

Brown, S. (2000) *Manufacturing the Future – Strategic Resonance for Resonant Manufacturing.* London: Financial Times/Pearson Books.

Business Week, 6 September 2003.

The Economist, 2 January 2003.

Fortune, Intel's $10 billion gamble, 11 November 2002.

Goldratt, E.M. and Cox, J. (1986) *The Goal.* Great Barrington, MA: North River Press.

Goss-Turner, S. and Jones, P. (2000) Multi-unit management in service operations: alternative approaches in the UK hospitality industry. *Tourism and Hospitality Research: The Surrey Quarterly Review,* **2**(1), 51–66.

Hill, T. (2000) *Manufacturing Strategy.* Basingstoke: Macmillan.

Hunt, S.B. and Nevin, J.R. (1974) Power in a channel of distribution: sources and consequences. *Journal of Marketing Research,* **11**, May, 186–193.

Jones, P. (1999) Multi-unit management in the hospitality industry: a late twentieth century phenomenon. *International Journal of Contemporary Hospitality Management,* **12**(3), 155–164.

Levitt, T. (1972) The production-line approach to service. *Harvard Business Review,* **50**(5), 20–31.

Levitt, T. (1976) The industrialisation of service. *Harvard Business Review,* **54**(5), 32–43.

Sasser, W.E., Olsen, M. and Wyckoff, D.D. (1978) *The Management of Service Operations.* Boston, MA: Allyn & Bacon.

Schlosser, E. (2001) *Fast Food Nation.* London: Penguin Press.

Schmenner, R. (1990) *Production/Operations Management.* Macmillan.

Schmenner, R.W. and Swink, M. (1998) On theory in operations management. *Journal of Operations Management,* **17**, 97–113.

Schonberger, R. (1986) *World Class Manufacturing.* New York: Free Press.

Shore, B. (1973) *Operations Management.* New York: McGraw-Hill.

Starr, M.K. (1978) *Operations Management.* Englewood Cliffs, NJ: Prentice Hall.

Suzaki, K. (1987) *The New Manufacturing Challenge: Techniques for Continuous Improvement.* New York: Free Press.

Thompson, J.D. (1967) *Organisations in Action.* New York: McGraw-Hill.

Waters, D. (2001) *Operations Management: Producing Goods and Services.* Harlow: Addison Wesley.

Westbrook, R. (1994) Priority management: new theory for operations management. *International Journal of Operations and Production Management,* **14**(6), 4–24.

CHAPTER 8

Quality and BPR

Introduction

This chapter looks at the key issues in quality. We discuss its strategic importance, track its evolution through the various stages of manufacturing, and provide details of important research in an important aspect of quality – continuous improvement.

The purpose of this chapter is for the reader to:

- understand the strategic importance of quality;
- realize that it remains a central feature of strategic operations in manufacturing and service settings in private and public sectors.

Quality is not an option in most walks of life. For example, it would be unthinkable for airline pilots or hospital midwives to aim for anything less than perfection in what they do, and nonsense to think of only trying for an 'acceptable' level of failure – one plane crash in 100 or one baby dropped per 500 deliveries! In similar fashion, no artist who is serious about his or her work would think of producing something that did not reflect their best endeavours and provide an object or artefact of lasting value.

One of the annoying factors about quality is that seemingly unimportant details can have an astonishing impact on how quality is perceived. For example, when Concorde crashed it was as a result of a lack of attention to a piece of debris on the runway. The consequences to this were both profound and fatal. Concorde had not suddenly become a poor-quality product, but the issue of safety (the most important element of travel in our evaluation of service quality) now became paramount.

On the positive side, it is Disney's obsession with keeping the theme park clean that has been seen as a key issue in our view of quality.

Of course, we don't go to a theme park just because we want to see how clean it is; none the less, this detail has become a source of advantage for Disney – 'other theme park operators can copy Disney's technology with its theme rides but nobody can figure out how to keep the damn park clean!' (Peters, 1990).

Yet until recently these ideas of quality were not common in the world of business. Indeed, much of the early theory of manufacturing operations contains terms and concepts such as 'acceptable quality level' and an underlying philosophy that assumes mistakes will happen and that things will go wrong. For much of the twentieth century, the question of quality was recognized as an issue, but the assumption was also made that with complex products and manufacturing processes there would inevitably be defects and problems that could not be predicted or prevented. There is some truth in this at the most basic statistical level; in any population of events there will be an element of random variation, but this level is very small – and even then action can be taken to ensure this does not adversely affect the perception of overall quality.

As a result, whole departments of specialists were developed to manage the effects of having problems with quality as an endemic part of business life. This included inspectors whose job it was to catch defective products before they left the factory; customer support staff, processing complaints and warranty claims; and an army of people running around the factory trying to repair or replace the faulty items.

Needless to say, all of this quality 'management' results in extra costs, and they may be considerable. It is not just the cost of the direct employees involved that we have to consider, it is also the disruption, the wasted effort producing something of poor quality in the first place, the risk to reputation and goodwill, the wasted time and effort in attracting customers who then become dissatisfied and tell their friends, and so on. One of the noted quality writers of recent years is Philip Crosby, who began working on quality issues within the giant ITT Corporation. He tried to put some numbers to the real costs of quality, and realized to his – and the company's – horror that these could account for as much as 40 per cent of sales revenue! (Crosby, 1979).

For example, back in 1984, when IBM first began looking at this problem, they estimated that $2bn of its $5bn profits was due to improved quality – not having to fix errors. But quality is not just about prevention of problems, as a recent J.D. Power Survey (2003) announced:

Quality as defined by few defects is becoming the price of entry for automotive marketers rather than a competitive advantage.

It would not be an exaggeration to say that there has been a revolution in thinking and practice around the theme of quality. Firms recognize its potential as a source of competitive advantage; as one commentator in the aerospace industry pointed out, 'achieving six sigma (a measure of very-high-quality performance) is worth several points on Wall St – that's why we are going for it!' The following captures the mood with quality in the new millennium (*Financial Times*, 15 July 2002):

> When (the new CEO) took the top job at 3M in early 2001, one of his first moves was to launch a Six Sigma quality initiative across the group ... 3M has selected 500 up-and-coming managers to work on quality improvement projects full time for 2 years. It is providing a week of Six Sigma training for each of its 28,000 salaried employees. ... 'This is about addressing the DNA of the company. It is a 10- to 15-year commitment' [said the CEO].

Some spectacular results have been gained from adhering to high levels of quality (*Financial Times*, 15 July 2002):

> In 1996 ... Welch declared Six Sigma quality to be his next group-wide initiative for GE. By the end of the decade he was declaring it a spectacular success: his 1999 letter to shareholders attributed 'Dollars 2bn in benefits' to the Six Sigma programme. ... GE is also going out of its way to introduce its business partners to Six Sigma. Last year, the giant aero-engines and appliances group carried out 10,000 joint quality improvement projects with customers. Among those involved was Xerox, the company once heralded as America's quality champion.

Quality has moved from being something about which firms have much choice – it is now a competitive imperative. In general, customers make their purchase decisions based on price and a set of non-price factors, such as design, variety, speed of response and customization. Quality sits amongst these non-price factors and we can chart its evolution over the past 30 years from being a non-essential, to being a desirable feature, to being a necessary qualification to enter some markets.

But what of services, where much of what is involved is intangible? In many cases, quality is even more important. First, because service contains many tangible components and no one values poorly cooked or served food or bedrooms that are not cleaned properly. But perceptions of service go beyond this to the overall experience – and the likelihood of returning. For example, it has been estimated that the potential value of securing a customer for life (through good service) for a purchase as trivial as a home delivery pizza is of the order of $12 000! (Bentley, 1999).

For the operations manager, quality is of critical importance. Quality – as we shall see – is not the province of a specialist but the responsibility of everyone. It pervades all aspects of an organization's operations, and the development and maintenance of quality consciousness has become one of the key roles that strategic operations managers have to play.

What is quality?

Before we explore how operations managers can influence the quality performance, it will be useful to reflect for a moment on what we mean by the word 'quality'. The dictionary says it is '... *the degree of excellence which a thing possesses* ...', while John Ruskin, the nineteenth-century painter and art critic, makes a valuable additional point: '... *quality is never an accident, it is always a result of intelligent effort*'. Pirsig (1974) suggests that quality is not a physical attribute, nor a mental concept, but something embodying both: '... *even though quality cannot be defined, you know what it is*'. Garvin (1992, p. 126) states:

> Quality is an unusually slippery concept, easy to visualize and yet exasperatingly difficult to define.

Juran (1974) spoke of quality as 'fitness for use'. But the question is: for whose use? From this point of view, a better definition – certainly in terms of how markets perceive quality – is offered by Feigenbaum (1983, p. 7), who asserted that quality is:

> ... the total composite product and service characteristics ... through which the product or service in use will meet the expectations of the customer.

Feigenbaum (1983, p. 11) adds further insight to our understanding of the definition of quality when he ties it to quality control:

> ... control must start with identification of customer quality requirements and end only when the product has been placed in the hands of a customer who remains satisfied.

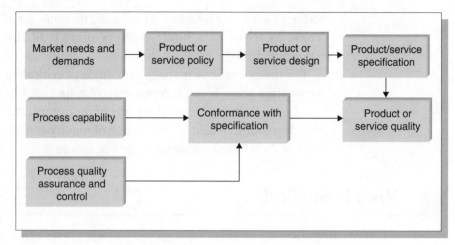

Figure 8.1
Quality in the design
process.

This user-oriented approach is helpful in focusing attention on the customer rather than the producer, but it can be argued that it needs some modification. In particular, as Garvin (1988) points out, it does not deal with two key problems:

- how to aggregate what may be widely varying individual perceptions of quality to provide something meaningful at the level of the market;
- how to identify the key product attributes that connote quality.

An alternative set of definitions emerge from considering the producer's side: these are concerned with establishing standards and measuring against them (Juran and Gryna, 1980). The *quality of design* represents the intentional quality that designers wish to see produced in order to meet their interpretations of the customer's needs. It is a multi-attribute definition, but has the advantages of permitting measurement against each of these attributes to assess whether or not the intentional quality level has been achieved.

Associated with this is the *quality of conformance*, which represents the degree to which the product when made conforms to the original design specifications. The extent to which this can be achieved will depend in turn on the various elements of manufacturing – people, processes, equipment, incoming raw materials quality, etc. This equates to Crosby's idea of quality as 'conformance to requirements' (Crosby, 1979). The quality process can be seen in Figure 8.1. Essentially, the market needs are translated into product strategy, which in turn feeds through to the R&D – and other key functions involved in design – in order to provide a suitable product and associated specification. It is against this that quality can be measured in terms of conformance to that specification.

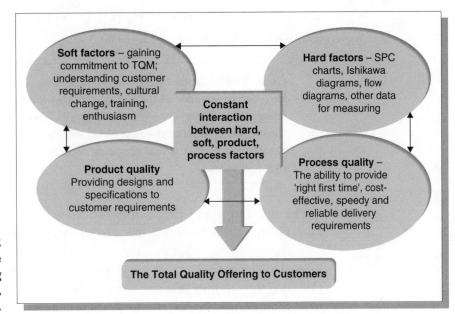

On the process side, quality will be affected by two things: the overall capability of the process (to hold tolerances, etc.) and the way in which quality is controlled within the process. The degree to which conformance to specification can be achieved will depend on these two factors.

Quality is complex but is dependent upon four, interlinking components – the hard side, the soft side, process quality and product quality – and these need to be linked and dynamically interfacing, as shown in Figure 8.2.

Strategic quality

There are two key reasons why quality has become strategic. The first is due to the *number* – and *capabilities* – of new entrants into many markets and industries. The second major factor is that, as a result of this fierce competition, customers now have far greater amounts of choice. For example, the major reason why quality became such a major issue for the 'Big Three' US car manufacturers in the 1980s was that it became abundantly clear that the Japanese plants' capabilities were vastly superior to their American competitors (Womack *et al.*, 1990). As Tom Peters (1995) succinctly stated, reflecting on the situation of the US auto industry at the beginning of the 1980s: 'Our cars were trash!'

Business Week (8 August 1994, p. 54) commented on the strategic importance of quality:

Detroit, for instance, finally caught the quality wave in the 1980s and it's hard not to shudder at the thought of how the Big Three would be faring today if they were still turning out Chevy Citations instead of Saturns. And much of the rest of US industry would be locked out of the game in today's global economy without the quality strides of the past few years.

The number – and capabilities – of new entrants into markets has raised competition between new and existing players, all of whom have to compete to 'world-class' standards. This intense competition has helped to redefine the term *world class*, when applied to quality. Kanter (1996) rightly argues that the term *world class* has less to do with being *better* than competitors – the term merely denotes the ability to compete *at all* in global competition. It may well be necessary to speak of 'world-class' quality capability as an order qualifier (Hill, 1995), in order to compete in markets. This has had enormous benefits for customers but has placed even higher standards on manufacturing capabilities. Production/operations have to be able to respond to changes with great speed to meet the mix, range and volume of customer requirements. The challenge for firms, though, is that although they may know that these capabilities need to be in place, they fail to understand *how* to put them in place. This chapter provides some of the keys to achieving this.

Looking back ...

We have seen in previous chapters how the transition from craft to mass production through to the modern era has had profound influence on operations management. This is clearly evident in quality. In the earliest days of manufacturing, quality was essentially built into the work of the craftsman. For example, the notion of 'taking pride in work' was a central pillar of the medieval guild system, whereby concern for quality was trained into the hearts and minds of apprentices onwards. The Industrial Revolution destroyed much of this one-to-one identification with the product and led to a loss of the craft ethic to be gradually replaced by the factory system. Although quality was important, especially in the pioneering applications of new technologies evident in the bridges, machinery and other products of that period, it was often in competition with the demands of high productivity for satisfying massively expanding demand.

In the latter part of the nineteenth century, the focus of attention in manufacturing shifted to the USA, where the ideas of Taylor and Ford were of particular importance. In Taylor's model of the effective factory, quality was one of eight key functions identified as of critical importance for shop foremen to manage (Taylor, 1911), while Radford's influential book, *The Control of Quality in Manufacturing*, placed further emphasis on the task of inspection as a separate function (Radford, 1922).

In services at this time, quality remained strongly associated with the traditional values: a high-quality solicitor or bank would be one that exhibited a haughtiness and aplomb, rather than measurably excellent service. A 'quality' school would be one to which well-known people sent their sons or daughters, rather than one in which the excellence of education could be assessed. This reflected the immaturity of markets (e.g. their inability to demand or complain), as well as some deeply entrenched vested interests (e.g. the superiority of some public schools). Lastly, the concept of 'professions' and the reflection in deference meant that service providers could get away with poor quality, simply telling the customer that failure was attributable to factors that could not be explained to the layman.

Taylor's model became the blueprint not only for the mass production factories of the 1920s and 1930s, but also for many other types of business. Typically, emphasis was placed on inspection as the main control mechanism for quality, supporting a process of gradual refinement in product and process design that aimed to eliminate variation and error. The essential character remained one in which the majority of people were not involved; the task of managing quality fell to a handful of specialists.

In 1931, in perhaps the most significant development, Walter Shewhart wrote a book based on his experience in the Bell Telephone Laboratories entitled *The Economic Control of Manufactured Products*. This study of methods for monitoring and measuring quality marked the emergence of the concept of *statistical quality control* as a sophisticated replacement for the simple inspection procedures of the 1920s (Shewhart, 1931). The development reinforced the idea of quality needing specialists (able to understand and use statistical methods) to manage it, further separating it from the labourer, the machinist and even the foreman.

Of particular interest was the work of a group of quality experts, including William Edwards Deming (1986) and Joseph Juran (who worked for a while with Bell Labs in the quality assurance department set up by Shewhart), who were involved in wartime training and who helped establish the American Society for Quality Control. Within this forum, many of the key ideas underpinning quality management today were first articulated, but their impact was limited and little understanding of quality control principles extended beyond the immediate vicinity of the shopfloor.

In 1951, Juran published his *Quality Control Handbook*, in which he highlighted not only the principles of quality control, but also the potential economic benefits of a more thorough approach to preventing defects and managing quality on a company-wide basis (Juran, 1951). He suggested that failure costs were often avoidable, and the economic pay-off from preventive measures to reduce or eliminate failures could be between $500 and $1000 per operator – what he referred to as the 'gold in the mine'. A few years later, Armand Feigenbaum extended these ideas into the concept of 'total quality control', in which he drew attention to the fact that quality was not determined simply in manufacturing, but began in the design of the product and extended throughout the entire factory (Feigenbaum, 1956). As he put it:

... the first principle to recognize is that quality is everybody's job.

Strangely, these ideas were not taken up with any enthusiasm in the West – but they did find a ready audience in post-war Japan, which was facing the twin problems of catching up with Western practice and rebuilding its shattered industrial base. Much of the reason for the relative lack of interest amongst Western firms can be traced back to economic factors. For most firms, the 1950s were a boom period – the era of 'you've never had it so good'. One consequence of this relatively easy market environment was that the stringencies of the war years were relaxed and there was a general slowdown in effort in both productivity growth and quality improvement practices.

In the 1960s, the concept of 'quality assurance' began to be promoted by the defence industry in response to pressure from the NATO defence ministries for some guarantees of quality and reliability. This grew out of work on 'reliability engineering' in the USA, which led to a number of military specifications establishing the requirements for reliability programmes in manufacturing organizations. (Some indication of the size of the problem can be gauged from the fact that, in 1950, only 30 per cent of the US Navy's electronics devices were working properly at any given time.) Such approaches were based on extensive application of statistical techniques to problems like that of predicting the reliability and performance of equipment over time. This link with the defence sector (and latterly, by association, with the aerospace industry) led to the formalizing of quality standards for products, including components and materials, supplied by subcontractors for military customers. In the USA and the UK, the so-called 'military specifications' and 'defence standards' gave rise to the practice of formal assessment of suppliers, for purposes of accreditation as acceptable sources.

Quality assurance (QA) is the name given to the set of systems (embodying rules and procedures) that are used by a firm to assure the manufacture of quality products. Although clearly a sound idea in principle, by 1969 it had become enshrined in an increasingly bureaucratic set of rules and procedures that suppliers needed to go through to obtain certification by defence agencies. Consequently, in the firms themselves, QA became an increasingly dogmatic, bureaucratic and specialized function – a book of rules rather than a live principle.

The combination of QA and the supplier assessment initiatives described above gave rise to the concept of supplier quality assurance (SQA). In order to ensure compliance with increasingly rigorous standards, certification and checking of suppliers began to take place, where the onus was placed upon suppliers to provide evidence of their ability to maintain quality in products and processes. Such vendor appraisal was often tied to the award of important contracts, and possession of certification could also be used as a marketing tool to secure new business because it provided an indication of the status of a quality supplier.

In keeping with the general tenor of quality management to date, however, SQA maintained the idea that quality was something 'outside' the process – as if it were the result of inspection (this time, with the customer wearing the 'white coat').

By the mid to late 1970s, there were many of these SQA schemes in operation, all complex and often different for each major customer. As a result, suppliers faced a major task in trying to ensure compliance and certification. Such congestion led to the need for some form of central register of approved schemes and some common agreement on the rules of good QA practice. There are now a number of national and international standards which relate to the whole area of quality assurance and require the establishment and codification of complete quality assurance systems, and achievement of certification (e.g. ISO 9000) has become a prerequisite for participation in many global markets. A summary of developments in quality is illustrated in Figure 8.3.

Emphasis	Major themes	Dates	Key figures
Inspection	Craft production	Prior to 1900s	
	Inspection	1900s	
	Standardized parts and gauging	1900s	
	Control charts and acceptance sampling	1920s	Walter Shewhart Harold Dodge Harry Romig
Statistical process control	Theory of SPC	1931	Walter Shewhart
	US experts visit Japan	1940s	W. Edwards Deming Joseph Juran Arnold Feigenbaum
Quality assurance	Cost of quality	1950s	Joseph Juran Arnold Feigenbaum
	Total quality control		
	Quality control circles in Japan	1950s	Kaoru Ishikawa Taiichi Ohno
	Reliability engineering	1960s	
	Zero defects		
Total quality management	Robust design	1960s	Genichi Taguchi
	Quality function deployment	1970s	
	Design for manufacture/assembly	1980s	
	TQM in West	1980s–present	

Figure 8.3
Major developments in quality (based on Nicholas, 1998, p. 20).

The Eastern promise – a new approach to quality

There is no doubt that such procedural approaches made a contribution to improving quality levels in the West. However, they still represented a traditional view which saw quality as the province of specialists and primarily controlled through inspection at all stages. Something very different had been happening in the Far East. During the 1960s, and particularly the 1970s, it became clear that Japanese firms had not only managed to shake off their image of offering poor quality products, but had actually managed to obtain significant competitive advantage through their improved performance in this field. In fact, their improved performance was the result of a long learning process, which began in the aftermath of World War II.

In 1948, the Japanese Union of Scientists and Engineers (itself only formed 2 years earlier) formed a quality control research group, and invited Deming to give a series of seminars. These were extremely influential, especially in introducing some of the statistical approaches, but also in encouraging a systematic approach to problem solving. So successful was his visit that the Deming Prize for quality was initiated in 1951 in his honour. Pride in quality became a key norm in the post-war development of Japanese industry and state support was also present in the form of the Industrial Standardization Law in 1949, which came out of Ministry for International Trade and Industry (MITI) attempts to improve the range of products being made and sold.

The early 1950s saw the growing trend towards SQC being applied across the organization, backed up by formal procedures and standardization. It is important to note that this trend was led by engineers and middle managers, and was not necessarily seen as a key strategic development by senior management at the time. The concept of company-wide quality control really emerged during the late 1950s as new mechanisms were developed and as the tools of statistical quality control were applied systematically across the piece. Once again, ideas that had originally developed in the West were influential here. Joseph Juran visited in 1954 and laid considerable emphasis on the responsibility that management had for quality planning and other organizational issues concerned with quality, while Armand Feigenbaum came 2 years later with his message about company-wide quality control, taking his cue from Juran.

One lesson emerging from this experience was the need to involve those in the production process much more, to teach them *why* as well as *what* they had to do to guarantee quality. A key feature of this is the idea that operators are much more than simply interchangeable resources as they are represented in the Taylor/Ford model. As Kaoru Ishikawa, son of one of the founders of the Japanese quality movement, said (Ishikawa, 1985):

> ... if Japanese workers ... were obliged to work under the Taylor system, without encouragement of voluntary will and creative initiative, they would lose much of their interest in work itself ... and do their work in a perfunctory manner.

In many ways this is an obvious point – after all, the likely consequences of treating people as 'cogs in a machine' include:

- uninterested operators;
- increased defects in products;
- drop in labour efficiency;
- no quality consciousness (why bother?);

- increased absenteeism;
- increased labour turnover.

Re-learning the quality lesson in the West

Growing awareness (and in many cases impact on market shares) of the Japanese total quality model led to a renewed focus of interest and effort in the quality area and the beginnings of adoption of Japanese practices in the West. For example, Garvin (1988) reports that the Martin Corporation managed to supply a defect-free Pershing missile 1 month ahead of schedule in 1961, a remarkable achievement at a time when extensive inspection and testing was the norm and defects were accepted as almost inevitable by final customers. Of particular significance was the fact that this had been achieved by focusing all employees on the common goal of 'zero defects'. As the company management reflected (Halpin, in Garvin, 1988):

> ... the reason behind the lack of perfection was simply that perfection had not been expected.

This led them, and others, to experiment with ways of building worker involvement in programmes that were designed to promote higher quality consciousness and the desire to do things 'right first time'. The first Western quality circle was established in Lockheed in 1975 and others quickly followed. Firms quickly began to realize that there was no instant plug-in means of providing better quality – and many early QCs failed after early success. Gradually firms recognized the need for more of a company-wide approach, which included operator involvement and a total system approach to quality management.

New tools helped this process, particularly the idea of statistical process control (SPC), which had been developed in the 1940s but which became easier to implement in total systems that stressed operator involvement. SPC, which was applied extensively in the early 1980s, not only improved the control of quality but, importantly, changed the location of responsibility. It brought control of the quality back to the point of manufacture, rather than placing it at the end of the process. Such approaches call for operator involvement, for top management commitment, for quality to be seen as a concept being applied to much more than just the product, and for the extension of problem-solving techniques beyond the quality area – in short, to company-wide quality control or *total quality* management.

Quality today

The picture today is very different to the mass production approach to quality. Quality has been re-integrated into the mainstream of operations thinking, and concern for the development and maintenance of high standards runs throughout business. It is seen as a national imperative, something which affects international competitiveness and is too important to be left to chance. (An indication of this can be seen in the number of government-backed programmes that have promoted the adoption of quality standards, such as the ISO 9000 series, which provide a measure of the overall quality of processes.)

Importantly, we have also moved on from the view that quality is the province (and problem) of a small group of specialists. These days, quality is everyone's problem – and everyone can make a contribution to its development and maintenance. As we shall see, the notion of employee involvement in problem finding and solving is beginning to be recognized as a significant – and low-cost – source of competitive advantage.

It will be useful to look at some of the key components of today's quality practice – at what is involved in building and maintaining quality in creating and delivering products and services of consistently high quality. Much is made of the term 'total quality management', but there is a risk that the term itself becomes meaningless. In essence, little has changed from the principles discovered (or perhaps rediscovered) in post-war Japan and later in the West; quality still comes from an approach that emphasizes everyone's involvement, from a view that integrates quality thinking and action into all operations, and from the pursuit of excellence. The target should always be an uncompromising 'zero defects'; though every step towards this will be useful, it is also important to reflect that 'best is the enemy of better'.

In putting this philosophy into action, three areas are of interest – the *process* whereby quality is built into what we do, the *tools and techniques* which enable that to happen, and the *involvement and commitment* of everyone towards continuous improvement.

ISO 9000

ISO 9000 is an internationally recognized standard of quality that many firms strive for in order to demonstrate that quality standards and processes are in place. ISO 9000 and TQM are not one and the same thing. More pointedly, we should bear in mind that many firms that have ISO 9000 go out of business and so it is not a guarantee of business success. The interest in the ISO series standard is pervasive in many countries and ISO 9000 certification is used extensively by companies in the European Community. For example, firms that manufacture products for the health, safety or environmental sectors often cannot be considered as suppliers without having ISO 9000 in place. But this says more about how companies are desperate to be seen to have standards in place, and to display some sort of badge, than it says about world-class capabilities in quality. Some firms will use ISO 9000 as part of other, wider systems. There are valid reasons for pursuing ISO 9000:

1   As mentioned earlier, it is often a necessary part of the 'entrance criteria' in order to compete in particular industries.
2   ISO 9000 can be a good starting point when trying to reach other, more demanding awards, such as the criteria for the Malcolm Baldridge National Quality Award.
3   ISO 9000 can offer a framework for showing customers how products are tested, employees are trained, documentation is assured and defects are corrected.
4   It can provide good discipline in education, registration and gap analysis, registrar selection, action plans, internal audits and registrar audits. Documentation by itself can be an important element provided that it does not become too bureaucratic – and therein lies the big problem with ISO 9000 and other quality standards. It can lead to voluminous amounts of unnecessary documentation.
5   It can become a key ingredient in the 'hard' side of quality – measurement. The problem is, though, it is easy to be obsessive about, and to concentrate on, measuring the wrong things – and to measure in great, and unnecessary, detail. The ability to demonstrate that such systems are in place does not mean that customer satisfaction has been achieved. ISO 9000 almost assumes that *customers needs are known and being satisfied,* and that is a large and often unjustified assumption. Some firms will achieve ISO certification and then sit back, believing that the pursuit of quality is now over – this is the fatal flaw in any firm when it comes to quality.

Thus, ISO 9000 has created both benefits and problems for firms intent on pursuing quality. It can be useful – vital even – in some industries. But it is not enough and it certainly cannot be seen as synonymous with TQM.

The quality process

At its heart, quality is the result of a sequence of activities embodied in a process within the business. The advantage of looking at it in this way is that it becomes possible to map the process and monitor and measure the outputs – and to use this information to identify where and how the process itself can be improved. This kind of thinking is central to the original statistical approaches developed in the early part of the century, but it can be applied on a broader scale to explore all the areas where quality is introduced, and to the influences on the process.

At the simplest level, we can consider a machine making a part; we know the desired output specification and can use this to compare what actually comes out of the process with what is supposed to. If there is a difference, we know there is a problem affecting quality – and we can then apply tools and techniques to finding and rectifying the problem and eventually preventing its recurrence. This approach can be used on a single machine, on a series of machines, on the intangible processes that schedule those machines, on the various linked activities upstream and downstream of the machines, and so on. We can even look at the quality management process itself and how that might be improved.

Taking a process approach is a powerful start to improving quality and has the advantage of being generic – as long as we can define the process and specify inputs, outputs and relevant measures, we can apply this approach. The argument then runs that if we can guarantee the process is OK then it follows that the quality coming out of that process will be OK. This kind of thinking underpins the many national and international standards around total quality management – such as ISO 9000. In this, firms are required to define and document each process they employ and to show how quality assurance and improvement are built into it. If they do so, then they have the framework for ensuring high and improving quality. (Of course, it is possible to write elegant descriptions of processes and suitable procedures for monitoring and measurement that have nothing to do with the way things work in practice – but in principle such process-based standards are a powerful tool.)

Benchmarking in quality

An extension of the process idea is the use of benchmarking to compare performance on quality indicators – for example, defective parts per million – and the practices which different firms use to achieve such performance. This approach – which was originally developed in the Xerox Corporation – provides a powerful learning and development aid to quality improvement. Regular benchmarking can provide both the stimulus for improvement (because of the performance gap that has to be closed) and new ideas about things to try in terms of organizational tools, mechanisms and practices.

Further development of these ideas of assessment and improvement comes in the form of integrated frameworks, which provide definitions of 'ideal' quality organizations against which firms can benchmark themselves. Such models are sometimes associated with a prize – for example, the Deming prize in Japan – but their real value lies in offering a well-publicized target for which firms can aim in their quality improvement activities. In the USA, the Malcolm Baldridge Award provides such a framework, whilst in Europe the model originally developed by the European Foundation for Quality Management (EFQM) is finding increasing application. Importantly, these models not only look at processes within the firm, but increasingly at its interactions with the wider community; equally they are not simply concerned with aspects of product quality but also consider issues such as the quality of working life within the firm.

Figure 8.4 reproduces the model used in the EFQM approach, and shows the concern for both performance (essentially the 'results' measures) and practices which create that performance (the 'enablers' measures). Such models are used by firms for self-assessment or for feedback and guidance offered by a team of trained external and independent assessors.

It is important to remember that benchmarking is limited to the immediate and tactical level of management. When used at the strategic level, benchmarking may prevent the organization from 'thinking

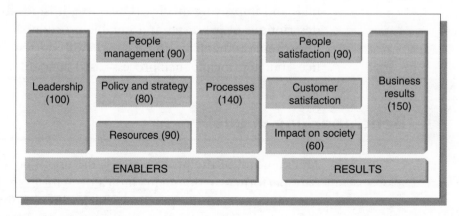

Figure 8.4
The EFQM model.

big' or 'outside the box'. To be best at meeting current expectations may mean one does not see the potential for competing by exceeding or changing expectations – thereby making competitors' competences redundant (see Chapter 4). This is what severely hampered the North American motor industry until its shock in the 1980s. Complacent benchmarking between the 'Big Three' led to their mutual loss of international competitiveness – a process that Abernathy and Utterback (1978) famously called a 'roadblock to innovation'.

Operationally, this might be captured in the rather effete term 'customer delight'. A train passenger is unlikely to be delighted by the train departing and arriving on time (the sort of thing that is benchmarked) because this is what is expected. The passenger might be delighted, however, to find a complimentary newspaper or cup of coffee is included in the service.

Customer satisfaction versus customer loyalty (SERVQUAL)

Clearly, a key element of ensuring quality is to measure customers' responses to the product or service they have received. Understanding this provides strategic feedback as to the likely future success of the firm. At first, it might seem simple to establish if customers are pleased or dissatisfied with their purchase – just ask them. With regards to products that have tangible characteristics, it is possible to ask customers about these and their degree of satisfaction with them. In services, it has been less straightforward. However, Parasuraman *et al.* (1985) have developed the SERVQUAL model based on measuring the difference between customer's expectation of a service and their perceptions of the actual experience. This has led them to identify five key characteristics which they claim apply across all services: tangibles, reliability, responsiveness, assurance and empathy. Despite its general applicability, this approach is modified to reflect the specific characteristics of different service industries and can only be used with other forms of quality measurement techniques. The SERVQUAL model is shown in Figure 8.5.

Parasuraman *et al.* (1985) identified five gaps that can lead to service quality failures:

1 Not understanding the needs of the customers.
2 Being unable to translate the needs of the customer into a service design that can address them.

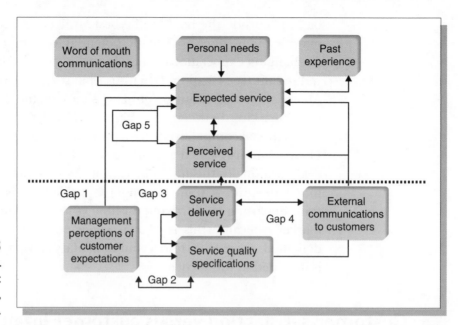

Figure 8.5
The SERVQUAL
model (*source*:
Parasuraman *et al.*,
1985).

3 Being unable to translate the design into service expectations or standards that can be implemented.
4 Being unable to deliver the services in line with specifications.
5 Creating expectations that cannot be met (gap between customers' expectations and actual delivery).

The task that the organization has, therefore, is in ensuring that these gaps are closed in order for the 'promise' of the offer to be on a par with the actual delivery. The various gaps are common, and an amusing example is given in the following anecdotal perception of management consultants.

SERVQUAL – an example

A reader sends the following story. A shepherd is tending his flock when a Jeep screeches to a halt beside him. The driver hops out and says: 'If I tell you how many sheep you've got, will you give me one?' The shepherd looks him up and down. 'OK,' he shrugs. The stranger takes out his laptop, plugs it into his mobile phone and, after a little work involving NASA websites and satellite readings, says: 'The answer is 931.' The shepherd nods. 'Choose your sheep,' he says. The stranger bundles the animal into his Jeep. 'Now,' says the shepherd. 'If I tell you what job you do, can I have it back?' Sure, the stranger replies. 'You're a management consultant,' the shepherd says. 'How did you know?' the astonished stranger asks. 'Easy,' the shepherd says. 'First, you charged me a fortune. Second, you told me something I already knew. And third, you know nothing about my business. Now please give me back my dog.'

Source: Financial Times, A flair for stating the obvious, 29 January 2003.

Although the SERVQUAL model has been one of the most used research instruments in the operations field throughout the world, it is not without some controversy. The single biggest issue is asking customers about their expectations and the difficulty of operationalizing this (Parasuraman, 1995).

Unfortunately, customer satisfaction measurement is more complex than simply asking questions. Completely satisfied customers may never repurchase because customer loyalty derives not solely from satisfaction, but two other factors – the relative importance of the purchase to the customer and the ease of switching. From a strategic perspective it is customer loyalty that should be sought, not just satisfaction. Satisfied customers may purchase a competitor's product or service because the purchase is not significant to them and hence they do not mind which brand they use. Likewise, satisfied customers purchase a competitor's product or service when they cannot perceive any difference between them – in effect, the product is a so-called 'commodity'. Firms therefore need to ensure that their product or service either is, or appears to be, a significant purchase and that their brand has features that no other brand has. From an operations perspective, making the product special, and the brand differentiated, derives from innovation (discussed in Chapter 4). The role of marketing is to ensure that this reality is also perceived by the customer.

Case: The roadside restaurant chain

Understanding customers is the key to making good products and delivering fine service. In the 1980s there were two major chains of roadside restaurants and the CEO of one of them decided to conduct market research into why motorists stopped at one of his restaurants rather than his competitors. The CEO was very experienced in this industry. Indeed, 20 years earlier he had travelled to the United States to investigate the roadside dining concept and on his return had set up the very first operations of this kind.

Despite his experience, he had never conducted market research. Demand was such that units had been opened and traded successfully without such data. But given the increasing competition, he decided the time was now right for more detailed information about his customers and their preferences.

Naturally enough, the first question the researchers asked was: 'Why have you stopped at this roadside restaurant?' The CEO was rather surprised to find that the principal reason given by 55 per cent of respondents was to use the washroom facilities. As he himself said: 'I had been in the industry for twenty years. I thought I was in the restaurant business, but it turned out I was in the toilet business.' As a result of this, the operations strategy of the chain was changed. Up to that point washrooms had deliberately been placed at the back of the operation so that customers had to walk through the restaurant to get to them. The theory was that they would feel guilty just doing this, so would stay to buy something. After the market research, the chain decided that in all its new build units from that moment on, they would put the facilities near the front entrance – making it easier for people to use. Their theory was that this would make more people stop – and once stopped, they would purchase something anyway. Moreover, the washrooms were built bigger and equipped with higher quality fittings. And along with this, a procedure was introduced to check cleanliness more frequently than before.

Quality management – tools and techniques

Although we are dealing with strategic issues in quality, it is important to be aware that quality tools and techniques can play an important part in strategic quality. There are numerous texts that deal with the tools of quality (see, for example, Oakland, 1994). There are 'seven basic tools' of quality management:

1 Pareto analysis – this recognizes that it is often the case that 80 per cent of failures are due to 20 per cent of problems, and therefore tries to find those 20 per cent and solve them first.
2 Histograms – used to represent this information in visual form.
3 Cause and effect diagrams (fishbone charts or Ishikawa diagrams) – used to identify the effect and work backwards, through symptoms to the root cause of the problem.
4 Stratification – identifying different levels of problems and symptoms using statistical techniques applied to each layer.
5 Check sheets – structured lists or frameworks of likely causes which can be worked through systematically. When new issues are found, they are added to the list.
6 Scatter diagrams – used to plot variables against each other and help identify where there is a correlation or other pattern.
7 Control charts – use SPC information to start the analytical process off, asking *why* these errors occur at this time.

Once a basic understanding of the problem and its contributing problems has been built up, other techniques for problem solving can be introduced. Since the search is on for as many different ways as possible of dealing with the problem, techniques that support creative problem solving are especially helpful here. Brainstorming and other related techniques are often used. There are also many new and powerful tools associated with more advanced forms of approach linked to the wider questions of quality management – sometimes referred to as the 'seven advanced tools' of quality management. These include affinity diagrams, relations diagrams, matrix diagrams, tree diagrams, arrow diagrams, matrix data analysis and process decision progress charts. All of these take a system-wide perspective and provide ways of relating different elements in the quality process. A full description of these tools can be found in Shiba *et al.* (1993).

Six Sigma

One of the recent 'management revolutions' being widely applied is 'Six Sigma'. Although apparently a new concept this is, in fact, an approach built on well-founded total quality principles, applied within a disciplined company-wide framework. Pioneered by GE in the USA, Six Sigma takes its name from a statistical term that measures how far a given process deviates from perfection. The central idea behind Six Sigma is that if you can measure how many 'defects' you have in a process, you can systematically figure out how to eliminate them and get as close to 'zero defects' as possible. To achieve Six Sigma quality, a process must produce no more than 3.4 defects per million opportunities. An 'opportunity' is defined as a chance for non-conformance, or not meeting the required specifications.

GE began moving towards a focus on quality in the late 1980s. A major employee involvement programme called 'Work-Out' established an approach that 'opened our culture to ideas from everyone, everywhere, decimated the bureaucracy and made boundary-less behaviour a reflexive, natural part of our culture, thereby creating the learning environment that led to Six Sigma. Now, Six Sigma, in turn, is embedding quality thinking – process thinking – across every level and in every operation of our Company around the globe' (GE website, http://www.ge.com/sixsigma/).

At its core, Six Sigma revolves around a few key concepts:

- *Critical to quality* – attributes most important to the customer.
- *Defect* – failing to deliver what the customer wants.
- *Process capability* – what your process can deliver.
- *Variation* – what the customer sees and feels.
- *Stable operations* – ensuring consistent, predictable processes to improve what the customer sees and feels.
- *Design for Six Sigma* – designing to meet customer needs and process capability.

Perhaps one of the key contributions to its success has been the highly disciplined approach taken to implementation and ongoing measurement. Taking a framework from the martial arts, Six Sigma involves a rigorous training and development process in which capability is measured in terms of grades, from beginner through to black belt.

A number of discussion forums have been set up where detailed information on tools, techniques and case experiences can be found – see, for example, www.isixsigma.com or the American Society for Quality (www.sixsigmaforum.com/).

Beyond tools to 'total' quality management

So far we have looked at the process aspects of quality and some of the tools that can enable its effective management. We now need to add the third essential ingredient – the active involvement of people in the process of quality control and improvement.

It is widely recognized that at the core of Japanese quality success has been the idea of *company-wide quality control* (CWQC) – a theme originally articulated by Feigenbaum (1956). The basis of this concept is to be able to design, produce and sell goods and services that satisfy the customer's requirements – and this takes us back to our initial definitions of quality. But CWQC recognizes that there are many dimensions to this, such as:

- customer service;
- quality of management;

Table 8.1

Stages of development in quality and related activities

Stage of development	Activities
Inspection	Salvaging, sorting, grading and corrective actions
Quality control	Quality manuals, product testing, basic quality planning, including statistics
Quality assurance	Third-party approvals, advanced planning, systems audits, SPC
Company-wide QC	Quality measured in all areas of the firm and employee involvement in continuous improvement
TQM	Company-wide QC principles applied across the whole system and in proactive fashion, emphasizing elements like continuous improvement; involvement of suppliers and customers; employee involvement and teamwork

Developed from Brown (1996).

- quality of company;
- quality of labour;
- quality of materials, techniques, equipment, etc.

Thus, quality becomes *total quality*, pervading everything both within the organization (all departments and functions) as well as the firm's supply network. The development from inspection under the mass production era, which we saw earlier, to TQM, reveals the increasing strategic importance of quality. The scope of each stage of development in quality is shown in Table 8.1.

TQM embraces the following points:

1 *Top management commitment.* In terms of 'setting an example' in their commitment to quality, particularly in terms of their willingness to invest in training and other important features of TQM.

2 *Continuous improvement.* Deming, Juran, Crosby and other quality 'gurus' may have slight differences in their actual approaches to quality. What becomes a common denominator, though, both for the 'quality gurus' and for firms involved in quality, is that quality is a 'moving target' and therefore a firm must have a strategic commitment to always improve performance (we discuss this in more depth within this chapter).

3 *All aspects of the business.* The quality drive relates to all personnel within the firm and also outside – all aspects of the supply chain.

4 *Long-term commitment.* TQM is not 'quick fix' but, ideally, an everlasting approach to managing quality. As each stage developed – from inspection to TQM – the preceding stage was included as part of the next stage. TQM therefore *includes* company-wide quality control rather than ignoring it.

A key factor in translating senior commitment to quality into 'front-line' operations comes from group-based activities, which provide a focus for much of the powerful continuous improvement effort characteristic of TQM. Originally termed quality circles, they represent a key link between the mechanics of quality tools and techniques and the behavioural components that make a living, developing quality system.

Quality circles

The origins of this approach lay in Japanese work in a number of different contexts; despite this variety there is considerable convergence around what makes for an effective quality circle (QC) and the core elements are simple. It involves a small group (five to ten people) who gather regularly in the firm's time to examine problems and discuss solutions to quality problems. They are usually drawn from the same area of the factory and participate voluntarily in the circle. The circle is usually chaired by a foreman or deputy and uses SQC methods and problem-solving aids as the basis of their problem-solving activity. An important feature, often neglected in considering QCs, is that there is an element of personal development involved, through formal training but also through having the opportunity to exercise individual creativity in contributing to improvements in the area in which participants work.

The basic activity cycle of a QC goes from selection of a problem through analysis, solution generation, presentations to management and implementation by management. Once the problem is analysed and the root problem identified, ways of dealing with it can be identified. The valuable techniques here include brainstorming (in its many variants) and goal orientation. However, it is important that the structure and operation of the group support suggestions from anyone (irrespective of levels in the organization, functional or craft skills background, etc.) and allow for high levels of creativity – even if some of the ideas appear wild and impractical at the time. The principles of brainstorming, especially regarding expert facilitation and enforcement of a 'no criticism' rule during idea generation sessions, are important.

The circle does not have to confine itself to current problems – it can also involve itself in forecasting. Here, the possible future problems resulting from each stage can be anticipated and explored, perhaps employing failure mode effects analysis (see above). Finally, the group presents the solution to management, who are expected to implement it. A key success factor in QCs' survival and effectiveness is the willingness of management to be seen to be committed to the principles of TQM and to act on suggestions for improvement.

Small group activity of this kind is a powerful way of moving quality forward, but it is not the only vehicle for involvement. Many variants have emerged, ranging from large group/task force approaches to individual problem-solving approaches, and there is a need to match the selection of methods to the particular culture and operations of the firm. Another important aspect is the extent to which such groups are 'in line' as opposed to 'off line' (as the early QCs were); evidence suggests that strategic quality improvement only takes place when it becomes part of the day-to-day operations of the business.

Continuous improvement (CI)

The underlying principle of continuous improvement is philosophically clear – and well expressed in the Japanese phrase 'best is the enemy of better'. Rather than assuming a single big hit change will deal with the elimination of waste and the causes of defects, CI posits a long-term systematic attack on the problem. A metaphor for this is the gradual wearing down of stone through the continuous dripping of water on to it from above – it doesn't happen overnight but the cumulative effect is as effective as a powerful drill. In the context of quality management, CI has come to mean not only this process of continuous attack on problems, but also the involvement of as many people as possible in the process. It could, perhaps, be more accurately called 'high involvement innovation', since it is about getting the majority of people in an organization to contribute, at least at the level of regular incremental innovation.

There is, of course, no reason why people cannot participate in this process. After all, they are all equipped with sophisticated problem-finding and -solving capabilities – a point well expressed by one manager, who commented 'the beauty of it is that with every pair of hands you get a free brain!' Nor is there now a difficulty of lack of evidence – organized systems for engaging such commitment are commonplace now and have in fact been around in documented form since the nineteenth century (Bessant, 2003).

But making CI happen is easier said than done. Early attempts to emulate Japanese success in the West often led to disillusionment – firms set up problem-solving teams and invested heavily in training all their staff in the relevant tools and techniques, only to find their programmes had run out of steam some 6 months later. These days, it has become clear that introducing and embedding the new behaviour patterns that make up CI is something that takes time and effort – and there is no magic bullet that will achieve this overnight.

The CI journey

In today's turbulent business environments, everyone is looking for continuous improvements in the products and services that they offer and the ways in which they produce them. Whether these come through the occasional 'big bang' breakthrough innovation or through the more typical incremental improvements and adjustments, constant change is essential, not just to remain competitive but often for the survival of the business itself.

Work in the CIRCA programme[1] in the UK has been concerned with trying to understand the geography of this journey, and with trying to make up some basic maps that organizations can use to position themselves and guide their next steps. It has also been concerned with collecting and identifying useful resources that can be used to overcome the different kinds of obstacles that get in the way of moving down the CI road.

A roadmap for the journey

As far as the roadmap is concerned, the research has developed a model composed of five levels or stages of evolution of CI. Each of these takes time to move through, and there is no guarantee that organizations will progress to the next level. Moving on means having to find ways of overcoming the particular obstacles associated with different stages.

The first stage – level 1 – is what we might call 'unconscious CI'. There is little, if any, CI activity going on, and when it does happen it is

---

[1] CIRCA = Continuous Improvement Research for Competitive Advantage, a 5-year industry-based research programme based at the University of Brighton, and supported by the Department of Trade and Industry and the Engineering and Physical Sciences Research Council. Over 100 organizations have been involved in experience-sharing research aimed at improving understanding and practice of CI.

essentially random in nature and occasional in frequency. People do help to solve problems from time to time – for example, they will pull together to iron out problems with a new system or working proced- ure, or getting the bugs out of a new product. But there is no formal attempt to mobilize or build on this activity, and many organizations may actively restrict the opportunities for it to take place. The normal state is one in which CI is not looked for, not recognized, not sup- ported – and often, not even noticed. Not surprisingly, there is little impact associated with this kind of change.

Level 2, on the other hand, represents an organization's first serious attempts to mobilize CI. It involves setting up a formal process for finding and solving problems in a structured and systematic way – and training and encouraging people to use it. Supporting this will be some form of reward/recognition arrangement to motivate and encourage con- tinued participation. Ideas will be managed through some form of system for processing and progressing as many as possible and handling those that cannot be implemented. Underpinning the whole set-up will be an infrastructure of appropriate mechanisms (teams, task forces or whatever), facilitators and some form of steering group to enable CI to take place and to monitor and adjust its operation over time. None of this can happen without top management support and commitment of resources to back that up.

Level 2 is all about establishing the habit of CI within at least part of the organization. It certainly contributes improvements but these may lack focus and are often concentrated at a local level, having minimal impact on more strategic concerns of the organization. The danger in such CI is that, once having established the habit of CI, it may lack any clear target and begin to fall away. In order to maintain progress there is a need to move to the next level of CI – concerned with strategic focus and systematic improvement.

Level 3 involves coupling the CI habit to the strategic goals of the organization such that all the various local level improvement activities of teams and individuals can be aligned. In order to do this, two key behaviours need to be added to the basic suite – those of strategy deploy- ment and of monitoring and measuring. Strategy (or policy) deploy- ment involves communicating the overall strategy of the organization and breaking it down into manageable objectives towards which CI activities in different areas can be targeted. Linked to this is the need to learn to monitor and measure the performance of a process and use this to drive the continuous improvement cycle.

Level 3 activity represents the point at which CI makes a significant impact on the bottom line – for example, in reducing throughput times, scrap rates, excess inventory, etc. It is particularly effective in conjunction with efforts to achieve external measurable standards (such as ISO 9000), where the disciplines of monitoring and measurement provide drivers for eliminating variation and tracking down root cause problems. The majority of 'success stories' in CI can be found at this level – but it is not the end of the journey.

One of the limits of level 3 CI is that the direction of activity is still largely set by management and within prescribed limits. Activities may take place at different levels, from individuals through small groups to cross-functional teams, but they are still largely responsive and steered externally. The move to level 4 introduces a new element – that of 'empowerment' of individuals and groups to experiment and innovate on their own initiative.

Clearly, this is not a step to be taken lightly, and there are many situations where it would be inappropriate – for example, where established procedures are safety critical. But the principle of 'internally directed' CI as opposed to externally steered activity is important, since it allows for the open-ended learning behaviour that we normally associate with professional research scientists and engineers. It requires a high degree of understanding of, and commitment to, the overall strategic objectives, together with training to a high level to enable effective experimentation. It is at this point that the kinds of 'fast learning' organizations described in some 'state-of-the-art' innovative company case studies can be found – places where everyone is a researcher and where knowledge is widely shared and used.

Level 5 is a notional end-point for the journey – a condition where everyone is fully involved in experimenting and improving things, in sharing knowledge and in creating the complete learning organization. No such organization exists in our experience, but it represents the ideal towards which CI development can be directed. Table 8.2 illustrates the key elements in each stage.

Learning continuous improvement

Moving along this journey is not a matter of time serving or even of resources – though without resources it is unlikely that things will get any further than a car without petrol can be expected to. But the essence of progress along the CI road is *learning* – acquiring, practising and repeating behaviours until they become ingrained as 'the way we do things round here' – the culture of the organization.

The basic behaviour patterns or routines that have to be learned are outlined in Table 8.3.

Table 8.2

Stages in the evolution of continuous improvement capability

Stage of development	Typical characteristics
(1) 'Natural'/background CI	Problem solving random No formal efforts or structure Occasional bursts punctuated by inactivity and non-participation Dominant mode of problem solving is by specialists Short-term benefits No strategic impact
(2) Structured CI	Formal attempts to create and sustain CI Use of a formal problem-solving process Use of participation Training in basic CI tools Structured idea management system Recognition system Often parallel system to operations
(3) Goal-oriented CI	All of the above, plus formal deployment of strategic goals Monitoring and measurement of CI against these goals In-line system
(4) Proactive/empowered CI	All of the above, plus responsibility for mechanisms, timing, etc., devolved to problem-solving unit Internally directed rather than externally directed CI High levels of experimentation
(5) Full CI capability – the learning organization	CI as the dominant way of life Automatic capture and sharing of learning Everyone actively involved in innovation process Incremental and radical innovation

Learning these behaviours begins with moving to a new level and then involves extensive broadening out and modifying within the level. There are plenty of problems to solve and bugs to iron out – but eventually there comes a point where a move to the next level is required. At this point, the organization needs to take a step back and reconfigure its approach to CI – and doing this involves learning of a different kind.

In both cases, learning is not only about practising behaviours – it is also about finding ways of overcoming blockages at particular points. But learning isn't easy – and many organizations don't learn at all. Others get blocked at particular points and never move on from there – which goes a long way to explaining why so many CI programmes, despite early enthusiasm and commitment, eventually peter out.

Table 8.3

Behavioural patterns in continuous improvement

Ability	Constituent behaviours
'Getting the CI habit' – developing the ability to generate sustained involvement in CI	■ People make use of some formal problem-finding and -solving cycle ■ People use appropriate simple tools and techniques to support CI ■ People begin to use simple measurement to shape the improvement process ■ People (as individuals and/or groups) initiate and carry through CI activities – they participate in the process ■ Ideas are responded to in a clearly defined and timely fashion – either implemented or otherwise dealt with ■ Managers support the CI process through allocation of time, money, space and other resources ■ Managers recognize in formal (but not necessarily financial) ways the contribution of employees to CI ■ Managers lead by example, becoming actively involved in design and implementation of CI ■ Managers support experiment by not punishing mistakes but by encouraging learning from them
'Focusing CI' – generating and sustaining the ability to link CI activities to the strategic goals of the company	■ Individuals and groups use the organization's strategic goals and objectives to focus and prioritize improvements ■ Everyone understands (i.e. is able to explain) what the company's or department's strategy, goals and objectives are ■ Individuals and groups (e.g. departments, CI teams) assess their proposed changes (before embarking on initial investigation and before implementing a solution) against departmental or company objectives to ensure they are consistent with them ■ Individuals and groups monitor/measure the results of their improvement activity and the impact it has on strategic or departmental objectives ■ CI activities are an integral part of the individual or group's work, not a parallel activity
'Spreading the word' – generating the ability to move CI activity across organizational boundaries	■ People co-operate across internal divisions (e.g. cross-functional groups) in CI as well as working in their own areas ■ People understand and share an holistic view (process understanding and ownership) ■ People are oriented towards internal and external customers in their CI activity ■ Specific CI projects with outside agencies – customers, suppliers, etc. – are taking place ■ Relevant CI activities involve representatives from different organizational levels

Table 8.3 *(contd)*

'Continuous improvement of continuous improvement' – generating the ability to strategically manage the development of CI	■ The CI system is continually monitored and developed; a designated individual or group monitors the CI system and measures the incidence (i.e. frequency and location) of CI activity and the results of CI activity ■ There is a cyclical planning process whereby the CI system is regularly reviewed and, if necessary, amended (single-loop learning) ■ There is periodic review of the CI system in relation to the organization as a whole, which may lead to a major regeneration (double-loop learning) ■ Senior management make available sufficient resources (time, money, personnel) to support the ongoing development of the CI system ■ Ongoing assessment ensures that the organization's structure and infrastructure and the CI system consistently support and reinforce each other ■ The individual/group responsible for designing the CI system design it to fit within the current structure and infrastructure ■ Individuals with responsibility for particular company processes/systems hold ongoing reviews to assess whether these processes/systems and the CI system remain compatible ■ People with responsibility for the CI system ensure that when a major organizational change is planned its potential impact on the CI system is assessed and adjustments are made as necessary
'Walking the talk' – generating the ability to articulate and demonstrate CI values	■ The 'management style' reflects commitment to CI values ■ When something goes wrong the natural reaction of people at all levels is to look for reasons why, etc. rather than to blame individual(s) ■ People at all levels demonstrate a shared belief in the value of small steps and that everyone can contribute, by themselves being actively involved in making and recognizing incremental improvements
'The learning organization' – generating the ability to learn through CI activity	■ Everyone learns from their experiences, both positive and negative ■ Individuals seek out opportunities for learning/personal development (e.g. actively experiment, set their own learning objectives) ■ Individuals and groups at all levels share (make available) their learning from *all* work experiences ■ The organization articulates and consolidates (captures and shares) the learning of individuals and groups ■ Managers accept and, where necessary, act on all the learning that takes place ■ People and teams ensure that their learning is captured by making use of the mechanisms provided for doing so ■ Designated individual(s) use organizational mechanisms to deploy the learning that is captured across the organization

Table 8.4
Enablers for continuous improvement

Behaviour/routines	Blockage	Enablers
Getting the CI habit	No formal process for finding and solving problems	PDCA or similar structured model plus training on real problems
	Ideas are not responded to	Simple idea management system, based on rapid response
	Lack of skills in problem solving	Training in simple CI tools – brainstorming, fishbone techniques, etc.
	Lack of motivation	Recognition system
	No structure for CI	Simple vehicles, based on groups
	Lack of group process skills	Facilitator training
Focusing CI	No strategic impact of CI	Focus problem solving on strategic targets/policy deployment
	No measurement of benefits	Process monitoring and measurement
Spreading the word	Lack of co-operation across divisions	Cross-functional CI teams
	Lack of process orientation	Process modelling tools and training
Walking the talk	Conflict between espoused and practised values	Articulation and review
The learning organization	No capture of learning	Post-project reviews
		Storyboard techniques
		Encapsulation in procedures
Continuous improvement of continuous improvement	Lack of direction	Formal CI steering group and strategic framework
	Running out of steam	Regular CI review and relaunch

Roadblocks and obstacles – and ways round them

Our research suggests that there are several helpful enabling resources for overcoming blocks to learning at different stages in the CI journey. Some examples are given in Table 8.4.

In the driving seat – managing the journey to CI

Creating a continuous improvement culture is not something that can be done overnight. Nor is it something that can be created by order. 'Culture' is essentially something that people 'buy into' and create for themselves as the accepted set of behaviour patterns which define 'the way we do things around here'. It takes time to establish, and it needs reinforcing with artefacts – structures, procedures, symbols, etc. – which help give it form. Doing this is particularly hard with CI because it involves not just learning and reinforcing new behaviours, but also a fair measure of 'unlearning' of old ones.

It is possible to make progress along the CI journey – as an increasing number of organizations have discovered to their advantage. The main requirement is to recognize the need to drive the vehicle along the road – there is no 'automatic pilot' but instead a need for consciously steering the process in strategic fashion.

Such a strategic approach needs a map – and some sense of where we are and where we are trying to get to next. This chapter has outlined a simple roadmap which organizations can use to help orientate them-selves and plan for the next steps along the journey. Such positioning can be helped by external or self-assessment to provide a more accur-ate picture of the current position and what needs to be done next; the CIRCA project has developed one such tool that is currently being tested in a number of organizations. Other frameworks are also avail-able – for example, the various quality awards or the software develop-ment model.

Moving down the road involves identifying obstacles and deploying suitable enablers to help deal with them. There are no standard solu-tions to dealing with these – each organization needs to work out its own particular variant. Evidence from practice suggests that the obs-tacles encountered at different stages are broadly similar and can be anticipated. More importantly, there are many robust enabling resources that can be adapted and developed to help deal with these.

Continuous reconfiguration

Perhaps one final point should be made in considering implementation. There is extensive evidence that TQM often falters or even disappears after the initial 'honeymoon' period after its implementation. This can be for many reasons, but it highlights the problem of maintaining momentum. Work by UK researchers on this question suggested that there are many different approaches to TQM and at least three com-mon entry points can be identified. The first is what they term 'vision-led TQM' and is characterized by a vision-led process usually starting at the top of the organization. This has powerful impact in terms of ener-gizing the rest of the organization, and is usually accompanied by sig-nificant input of resources for training and implementation. Its major weakness is that the vision may not be sufficient to sustain interest and there may not be sufficient structural underpinning to embed TQM in the organization's culture – 'the way we do things around here'. It also tends to be highly dependent on a senior manager as champion and when he or she moves on the initiative may falter.

A second approach is what is termed 'planned TQ', in which there is a formal planned and structured approach to implementation. This kind of initiative often originates with those responsible for quality standards, etc., and can be most closely linked to the kind of efforts made in seeking to obtain ISO 9000 or similar approvals. These approaches have the strength of structure and measurement, but may lack the overall motivation to involve and retain people in the quest for quality improvement.

Third is the approach termed 'training TQM', which tends to emerge from the human resources concerns of the business. Recognition that people can offer much more than just involvement as pairs of hands has led to a reappraisal of roles and mechanisms, and a concern with developing individual skills and competence. This kind of approach typifies much of the effort made to create 'learning organizations' and is empowering at the individual level. Its main weakness in respect of TQM is that it creates involvement but may lack the strategic direction and vision, and the structure and measurement frameworks, necessary to engage long-term systematic improvement.

Each of these components has much to offer, and most existing TQM programmes can be grouped under one or other of them. Ideally, long-term sustainable TQM depends on elements of all three, and the ability to switch between different modes in a continuous development cycle. This last approach – which essentially involves continuous monitoring and change of the change programme itself – is called 'transformational TQM'.

From the above, it is clear that, in the main, success in implementing a quality improvement programme depends upon the extent to which it is seen as a *total* activity, running company-wide and involving everyone in ownership of the quality problem and responsibility for solving it. Unfortunately, it lends itself to extensive partial innovation of the substitution variety, using more advanced techniques or tools to support local functions only, or using them in an isolated way, rather than as part of a company-wide package of change. In particular, the challenge to changing the culture of the organization is often shirked – not just because of the considerable effort that this involves, but also because of the perceived threats to the status quo.

In the end, the organization and management of quality requires a new kind of organization, one which communicates and owns the problem in integrated form. This model is similar to the one we saw earlier for supporting advanced and integrated IT applications, involving similar patterns of networking, of decentralization of responsibility within an integrated framework, where people own the problem and share in solving it. Rather than emphasizing structures, processes and a culture that is geared to doing the same thing, day after day, the new organization needs to find ways of becoming a 'learning organization' able to adapt and develop in a cycle of continuous improvement.

Problems with TQM and the emergence of business process re-engineering

In spite of the compelling evidence for firms to adopt and remain committed to quality, it remains clear that it is difficult to sustain. This is brought out in the following (McAbe and Wilkison, 1998):

> The 1990s have not been good to TQM: A survey of 500 executives in US manufacturing and service firms indicated that 'only one-third believe that TQM made them more competitive' ... a survey of 100 British firms that had implemented quality programs found that only one-fifth believed that their programs had 'a significant impact' ... an American Electronics Association survey revealed that use of TQM by member firms dropped from 86 per cent in 1988 to 73 per cent in 1991 and that 63 per cent of the firms reported that TQM failed to reduce defects by 10 per cent or more, even though they had been in operation for almost 2½ years on average. ... McKinsey & Company found that two-thirds of the TQM programs it examined had simply ground to a halt because they failed to produce expected results. At the same time, widely acclaimed TQM programs began to stumble:
>
> Florida Power and Light, winner of Japan's prestigious Deming Prize for Quality Management, slashed its quality department staff from 85 employees to three after group chairman James L. Broadbent found that many employees feared that the 'quality improvement process had become a tyrannical bureaucracy'. ... And the Wallace Company, a Malcolm Baldridge National Quality Award winner, filed for Chapter 11 bankruptcy protection.

At the beginning of the 1990s, business process re-engineering (BPR) emerged as a threat to quality. BPR is not meant to be the same as, or a replacement for, TQM. Although both TQM and BPR are strategic in scope, BPR has more fundamental consequences in terms of immediate – and sometimes radical – outcomes. There is some confusion about BPR, so let's revisit the definition of BPR from Hammer and Champy

(1993), who coined the term *business process engineering*. They defined business process re-engineering (BPR) as:

... the fundamental rethinking and radical redesign of business processes to achieve dramatic improvements in critical, contemporary measures of performance such as cost, quality, service and speed.
[p. 32]

These are important issues and the words are dramatic: *fundamental rethinking*; *radical redesign*; *dramatic improvements*. As we saw earlier, many firms have failed with TQM, and BPR took over from TQM as the most popular topic in the business press from early 1993 onwards (De Cock and Hipkin, 1997). Bearing in mind that the first major article on BPR appeared in 1990, probably no other single managerial innovation has acquired quite so much attention in such a short period as BPR. For example, in a 1993 survey of 224 North American senior business executives, BPR was listed as *the* most important management issue, and 72 per cent of those surveyed had committed to BPR in their organization (Conti and Warner, 1994). A large survey published in 1997 (Gemini Consulting, 1997) found that 782 companies would remain committed to, and would continue to invest in, BPR initiatives in spite of the negative reactions against BPR that had begun to appear in the business press. In fact, 70 per cent of the companies that had already undergone re-engineering fully expected to maintain or add still further to their present re-engineering budgets. However, only 47 per cent of the respondents reported revenue growth and only 37 per cent succeeded in increasing their market share.

BPR attempts to concentrate the firm on what it does best. In that sense, it has links with the profoundly important notions of focus, core competencies and resource-based approaches to strategy. However, the problem can be that, in the name of right-sizing, the brain of the firm – the essential expertise and know-how upon which core competencies must depend – can undergo a *corporate lobotomy*. *The Economist* picked out some of the dangers with this when it stated:

In the end, even the re-engineers are re-engineered. At a recent conference held by Arthur D. Little, a consultancy, representatives from 20 of America's most successful companies all agreed that re-engineering, which has been tried by two-thirds of America's biggest companies and most of Europe's, needs a little re-engineering of its own. ... As well as destroying morale, this approach leads to 'corporate anorexia', with firms too thin to take advantage of economic upturns.

Can TQM and BPR be combined? Some think so (Lee and Asllani, 1997, p. 5):

In today's challenging economic climate, many organizations have come to realize that improved quality is an essential entry ingredient for successful global competition. Total quality management (TQM) is based on a broad organizational commitment to make continuous quality enhancements in products and services for customers over a long term. Business process re-engineering (BPR) allows for radical changes in organizational processes intended to make quantum leaps in performance by taking advantage of the advances in the information and telecommunication technology. While they seem to be two completely opposite approaches, TQM and BPR can well be combined into the 'endless quality improvement' concept.

However, it is mighty difficult for firms who, having promised empowerment and involvement from the workforce in TQM, then cut out large numbers within the firm in the name of re-engineering and expect wonderful commitment from the workforce.

Looking forward ...

From the above discussion it is clear that even the most advanced firms still have a long way to go on their journey towards TQM. For this reason, much of the future direction is likely to involve work towards integrating TQM into the daily life of the firm rather than seeing it as a special initiative or a fashion. There are also some specific areas in which we can see new challenges emerging for thinking about quality and how it can be built into strategic operations work.

One area is clearly in the kind of environment that is non-repetitive in nature. Much of the theory of quality comes from work with processes that are by their nature reproduced many times – for example, the operations in a mass production factory. There is a sizeable and growing part of economic activity that is not dealing with this kind of work, but rather with one-off transactions or short-run work. Examples include most construction work, engineering prototypes, custom design and delivery of services, etc. Here the challenge is one of capturing learning rapidly and transferring it to new environments through generic procedures and principles. Many professionals work on this kind of approach, but there has been little work on routinizing it such that it can underpin quality improvement in project-type businesses.

A second area for further development lies in the field of non-production environments. Most of the attention in TQM has been in the direct manufacturing area or in services at the point of delivery – e.g. in customer care programmes. But many indirect activities support these – for example, R&D, finance, order processing, etc., and the challenge is to take TQM principles into these environments. This will mean adapting tools, mechanisms and structures, and looking for ways to motivate and involve different groups. For example, the R&D challenge is partly one of engaging the interest and commitment of professionals who often believe that they already practise TQM and have no need to join in more formal approaches. The future is also likely to see much more emphasis on building quality in from the design of products and services.

Finally, a major area for development lies in the concept of inter-organizational TQM. There is growing recognition of the need to think not just of operations within a business, but in terms of the overall value stream. Improving performance of a system such as this can employ the principles of TQM, but new tools and techniques need to be developed to help deal with some of the issues involved in developing the new relationships needed to underpin such work.

If the original driver for quality in the early 1980s was increased levels of competition, the key question has to be: is competition greater now than before? The answer is undoubtedly 'yes' and for this reason alone it is clear that organizations need to be very serious about quality in the modern business world. Quality is not a fad or a fashion, nor has it been replaced by BPR or other alternatives. The best organizations are those that remain committed to quality and strive for continuous improvement in their operations in order to meet or exceed customer expectations.

Case: Marvellous motors

This Japanese firm is a major conglomerate with key interests in aerospace and motor vehicles. Eighty per cent of sales now come from the automotive business and this is the prime source of growth for the company. However, the high value of the yen has hit exports hard, to the point that the company made a loss in 1990. They have responded to this crisis by systematic deployment of continuous targeted improvement, with three core themes:

1 development of new, attractive products;
2 maintaining productivity levels;
3 reconstruction of the company from within.

The long-term programme includes simultaneous attack on quality improvement, cost reduction employee motivation and increased education and training, and the specific 'stretch' targets are:

- zero defects;
- zero accidents;
- zero breakdown;
- 20 per cent increase in labour productivity.

The pillars on which these are to be achieved are:

- *jishu hozen* – voluntary operator inspection and maintenance;
- *kaizen teian* – individual improvement activities;
- education and training;
- planned maintenance;
- development management;
- quality maintenance activities, including ISO 9000;
- tool/mould/die maintenance management aimed at zero defects and breakdowns.

They began by setting up separate task forces to deal with each area, and developed a formal structure aimed at promoting TQM; in particular, they emphasized 'total productive maintenance' (TPM), which targeted quality improvements around machine reliability and availability. The results undoubtedly helped in their recovery from losses by the end of 1995; examples of gains include a reduction in breakdowns per month across their major manufacturing site of 96 per cent (from over 5000 in 1992 to 194 in 1996).

As with other Japanese companies, the 3-year mid-term plan is the key mechanism for focusing and refocusing attention in continuous improvement. In this case, the recent plans have involved three main themes over the past decade:

1 TQM aimed at increasing productivity and quality.
2 TPS (Toyota Production System) aimed at waste reduction.
3 TPM aimed at obtaining high machine efficiency and availability, and at increasing production rates through more reliable plants.

Visualization of this is important; the dominant image is one of 'equipment and operator upgrading'. There are storyboards and display boards throughout the factory, including a master chart, which is a giant Gantt chart tracking progress to date and plans for the future. Each work group meets daily and this take place around their own storyboard.

The implementation of TPM includes a number of components:

- daily review and improvement cycle – i.e. high frequency of small innovations;
- small and regular inputs of training – 'one-point lesson system';
- motivation events;
- individual *kaizen teian* (small and simple to implement) activities;
- small group *kaizen* (successors to quality circles);
- five-S activities to ensure workplace cleanliness and order;
- preventive maintenance analysis;
- design for maintenance;
- 'zero orientation' – no tolerance for waste, defects, stoppages, etc., as the target;
- step-by-step approach;
- voluntary participation and high commitment.

The implementation of TPM involves a 5-year programme spanning two mid-term planning periods. Part 1 ran from 1992 to 1995 and was designed to introduce the basic TPM mechanisms; activities included awareness and training and practice to embed the behavioural routines. Part 2 – the current phase – involves aiming for the Japanese Production Management Association's Special Award for TPM. Significantly, the company is using very clear behaviour modelling approaches – articulating the desired behaviours and systematically reinforcing them to the point where they become routines.

Policy deployment is the link between these broad objectives and the specific improvement activities at shop floor level. For each of the eight pillars of TPM there are specific targets that can be decomposed into improvement projects. For example, 'maintain your machine by yourself', 'increase efficiency of machine to the limit' or 'reduce start-up times'. These vague signposts are quantified and analysed in terms of how they can be achieved and the problems that would have to be solved to make that happen – using simple tools such as five whys and fishbone charts. Diagnosis is top down in terms of setting the actual numerical targets or the extent to which operators can maintain their own machines; a team of specialist engineers carries this out.

As with other plants there is a step-by-step process for increasing capability in TPM, and this is linked to training inputs. For example:

Step 1   clean up your machine
Step 2   learn to detect different sensitive points
Step 3   develop a procedure for lubrication and cleaning work
Step 4   total inspection and check of different key points
Step 5   autonomous inspection
Step 6   adjustment and ordering
Step 7   execution of this in self-management (unsupervised) mode

The company places strong emphasis on mechanisms for embedding these behaviours in the culture so that they become the way things are done and taught to others. An important aspect of Part 2 – the current mid-term plan – is to find mechanisms for doing this. These include extensive use of training and development – for example, each employee receives 10 hours initial training in TPM and then 3 hours/month additional training on the job. They are also allocated 30 minutes per day to carry out their individual maintenance and to learn and improve this.

In addition to this operator development and individual improvement there are also CI projects in particular areas on which groups work in team mode – for example, projects on sputterless welding or cleaning engine coolant, which involve consistent attack on problem areas over a period of weeks or months. Activities of this kind have led to, for example, major set-up time reductions; the Komatsu 1000-tonne presses take less than 10 minutes to change and are changed four or five times per shift. Projects of this kind tend to take around 3 months.

There are some thirty-odd groups working – ten to fifteen in trim, twelve in body and assembly, and six to eight in the press shop. Group leaders spend half their time with the groups, facilitating, training, etc., and the remainder acting as a floating resource to cover sickness, holidays, etc.

The evolution of *kaizen* has been through early team activities going back 20 or more years. Individual *kaizen teian* ideas did not come through at first, so a campaign was launched with the theme of 'what makes your job easier?'; prior to that the focus was outside the individual operator's own job area. The evolution of suggestions can be seen in data collected by the Japanese Human Relations Management Association, which suggest that on the site there is now 100 per cent participation of the 'eligible employees' (around 85 per cent of the total workforce). Of their suggestions, around 88 per cent are implemented, giving a 1995–6 saving of around Y3.2bn.

At present they are receiving around twenty suggestions per employee per month. One of the difficulties raised by the generation of some 40 000 suggestions per month is how to process them; this is primarily the responsibility of the group leader. Many of the ideas are minor changes to standard operating procedures and foremen/team leaders are authorized to make these. Ideas are judged against four levels as below:

Level	Reward	Volume
1 – high level, considerable potential benefits and judged by senior management team	150 000Y upwards	only 4–5 per year
2 – again reviewed by senior team	medium – 10 000Y plus	20/year
3 – basic, handled by team leader	300Y	
4 – minor, recognized to encourage continuous improvement activity	50Y	

The importance of recognizing and rewarding the low-level simple ideas was expressed by one manager: 'If we don't encourage fertile soil at the bottom, we'll never get the high grade ideas later.' Motivation is also secured by strong top-level commitment. When the TPM programme was launched, the first stage built on five-S principles and involved cleaning up machinery and plant. The plant director held a site briefing explaining his concern and the ideas behind TPM, and then led the setting up of a 'section chief's model line', which was a line cleaned up and improved by all the senior managers as a demonstration. Symbolically, the plant director was the first to pick up a broom and begin the process. The line was followed by an 'assistant chief's model line', again to reinforce the commitment top down.

Summary

- Quality has moved from being an 'optional extra', something you could have if you were prepared to pay for it – to an essential feature of the products and services that we consume. International competitiveness depends not only on price factors but also on non-price factors, and quality is the first and most essential of these. So a crucial challenge for the strategic operations manager is to ensure that the design of such products and services – and the management of the operations that go into their creation and delivery – ensures quality. The framework for doing this involves a combination of strategy, tools, procedures, structures and employee involvement, and is conveniently grouped under the heading of 'total quality management'. In this chapter we have tried to trace the development of this approach and describe its key components.
- In many ways, the biggest challenge in TQM is not in the components but in their implementation. Evidence shows that although companies recognize the quality imperative, they are not always able to respond – or if they do they have difficulties in sustaining such performance for the long haul. Building total quality operations and sustaining them in the long term so that they become part of the organization's culture – 'the way we do things around here' – is still the biggest challenge, and one to which strategic operations managers can make a major contribution.

Key questions

1. 'Quality is free!' proclaimed the title of Philip Crosby's book in the 1970s. In what ways can investments in developing quality management in the business pay for themselves and make a difference to the overall bottom line of the company?

2. 'Total' quality management involves an integrated approach, combining tools, strategy, structure and involvement. What are the key components in a successful programme and how can strategic operations managers establish and sustain TQM in organizations?

3. What do you think are the main barriers to effective implementation of TQM – and how might they be overcome?

4. Why does quality matter to a business?

5. Quality management used to be a specialist function carried out by a specialist manager. Why has it become a mainstream task and a key part of the strategic operations manager's job? How can strategic operations managers contribute to creating businesses capable of competing on quality?

References and further reading

Abernathy, W. and Utterback, J. (1978) Patterns of industrial innovation. *Technology Review*, **80**(7), 40–47.

Bentley, J. (1999) Fit for the future. *CIPS Annual Conference*, Egham, UK. Chartered Institute of Purchasing and Supply.

Bessant, J. (2003) *High Involvement Innovation*. Chichester: John Wiley.

Boer, H., Berger, A., Chapman, R. and Gertsen, F. (1999) *CI Changes: From Suggestion Box to the Learning Organisation*. Aldershot: Ashgate.

Brown, S. (1996) *Strategic Manufacturing for Competitive Advantage*. Hemel Hempstead: Prentice Hall.

Brown, S. (2000) *Manufacturing the Future – Strategic Resonance for Resonant Manufacturing*. London: Financial Times/Pearson Books.

Business Week, 8 August 1994.

Conti, R.F. and Warner, M. (1994) Taylorism, teams and technology in 'reengineering' work-organization. *New Technology, Work, and Employment*, **9**.

Crosby, P. (1979) *Quality is Free*. New York: McGraw-Hill.

De Cock, C. and Hipkin, I. (1997) TQM and BPR: beyond the beyond myth. *Journal of Management Studies*, **34**(5).

Deming, W.E. (1986) *Out of the Crisis*. Cambridge, MA: MIT Press.

Feigenbaum, A. (1956) Total quality control. *Harvard Business Review*, November, 56.

Feigenbaum, A. (1983) *Total Quality Control*, 3rd Edition. New York: McGraw-Hill.

Financial Times, When quality is not quite enough: programmes such as Six Sigma and TQM are in vain unless top executives address their own shortcomings, 15 July 2002.

Financial Times, A flair for stating the obvious, 29 January 2003.

Garvin, D. (1988) *Managing Quality*. New York: Free Press.

Garvin, D. (1992) *Operations Strategy, Text and Cases*. Englewood Cliffs, NJ: Prentice Hall.

Gemini Consulting (1997) A report in the *Journal of Business Strategy*, May–June, **18**(3).

Hammer, M. and Champy, J. (1993) *Reengineering the Corporation*. New York: Harper Business.

Hill, T. (1995) *Manufacturing Strategy*. Macmillan.

Imai, K. (1987) *Kaizen*. New York: Random House.

Imai, M. (1997) *Gemba Kaizen*. New York: McGraw-Hill.

Ishikawa, K. (1985) *What is Total Quality Control?* Englewood Cliffs, NJ: Prentice Hall.

J.D. Power Survey (2003).

Juran, J. (1951) *Quality Control Handbook*. New York: McGraw-Hill.

Juran, J. (1974) *Quality Control Handbook*, 3rd Edition. New York: McGraw-Hill.

Juran, J. (1985) *Juran on Leadership for Quality*. New York: Free Press.

Juran, J. and Gryna, F. (1980) *Quality Planning and Analysis*. New York: McGraw-Hill.

Kanter, R. (1996) *World Class*. New York: Simon & Schuster.

Lee, S. and Asllani, A. (1997) TQM and BPR: symbiosis and a new approach for integration. *Management Decision*, May–June, **35**(5–6).

Lillrank, P. and Kano, N. (1990) *Continuous Improvement; Quality Control Circles in Japanese Industry*. Ann Arbor: University of Michigan Press.

McAbe, D. and Wilkison, A. (1998) The rise and the fall of TQM: the vision, meaning and operation of change. *Industrial Relations Journal*, March, **29**(1).

Nicholas, J. (1998) *Competitive Manufacturing Management*. Irwin: McGraw-Hill.

Oakland, J. (1994) *Total Quality Management*. Oxford: Butterworth-Heinemann.

Parasuraman, A. (1995) Measuring and Monitoring Service Quality. In Glynn, W.J. and Barnes, J.G. (eds.) (1995) *Understanding Services Management*. Wiley: New York, pp 143–177

Parasuraman, A., Zeithaml, V.A. and Berry, L.L. (1985) A conceptual model of service quality and its implications for future research. *Journal of Marketing*, **49**, Fall, 41–50.

Peters, T. (1990) *Tom Peters – Business Evangelist*. BBC TV.

Peters, T. (1995) Quote taken from Tom Peters in conversation. *The Money Programme*, BBC TV, 29 October.

Pirsig, R. (1974) *Zen and the Art of Motorcycle Maintenance*. New York: Bantam.

Radford, G. (1922) *The Control of Quality in Manufacturing*. New York: Ronald Press.

Schroeder, M. and Robinson, A. (1993) Training, continuous improvement and human relations: the US TWI programs and Japanese management style. *California Management Review*, **35**(2).

Shewhart, W. (1931) *Economic Control of Manufactured Product*. New York: Van Nostrand Rheinhold.

Shiba, S. and Graham, A. *et al.* (1993) *A New American TQM; Four Practical Revolutions in Management*. Portland, OR: Productivity Press.

Taylor, F. (1947) *The Principles of Scientific Management*. London: Harper & Row (first published in 1911).

Womack, J., Jones, D. and Roos, D. (1990) *The Machine that Changed the World*. New York: Rawson Associates.

CHAPTER 9

Human resources and strategic operations management

Introduction

We saw in Chapter 1 that one of the major responsibilities for operations managers is in managing people. This is because human resources can be a source of advantage for firms. The latest process technology can be bought and accumulated, but human skills are more complex. In any event, as we saw in Chapter 3 on process technology, an important ingredient in successfully managing technology is in having appropriate skills levels in place.

The purpose of this chapter is for the reader to:

- understand the strategic importance of human resource management in world-class operations;
- appreciate the problems that firms have in managing human resource management in fast, volatile markets;
- understand the changes to human resources over time within operations management;
- recognize the need for ongoing development, training and learning within organizations.

The vital importance of human resources is indicated in a telling quote from the Managing Director of British Chrome and Steel who, in 1998, stated:

> There is no other source of competitive advantage! Others can copy our investment, technology and scale – but NOT the quality of our people ...

Tampoe (1994) argues that 'the basis of competitive advantage is moving from capital, natural resources to human capital' and Grindley (1991) endorses this sentiment:

> The skills base is one of the firm's main assets. It is hard for competitors to imitate ... this calls for an attitude to encourage learning and to reward efforts which add to the firm's knowledge. Skills go out of date and need constant replenishment. In the long term what is most important may not be the particular skills, but the ability to keep learning new ones.

Human resources can be closely linked with the firm's core competences. Hamel and Prahalad (1994) describe core competences as 'a bundle of skills and technologies rather than a single discrete skill or technology'. Although we cannot limit core competences to human resources only, it is clear that human resource management must form at least part of the organization's core competence because 'skills' are grounded in human capabilities. Human resource management must be a key core competence for any world-class manufacturing firm. New ideas for innovation, new products, continuous improvement and so on, come from harnessing this creativity from humans, not via machines or 'technology'.

But managing human resources as part of strategic operations management is difficult for many firms. Although, as we saw in Chapter 6, human resources will account for a small proportion of direct costs (typically less than 10 per cent in high-volume manufacturing), human resources will often be the first target in cost-cutting initiatives. The reason for this is that such reductions are easily identifiable and quantifiable. But such an approach is hardly strategic. There are major negative repercussions in firms that downsize radically. First, many firms attempt to be lean but end up becoming anorexic in the process. Second, the 'brain of the firm', which is focused on human resources, can suffer from what might be called a *corporate lobotomy* – i.e. the firm forgets how to do things. Third, getting rid of staff is easy but dealing with the survivors is immensely difficult. For example, we saw in Chapter 8 how vital continuous improvement initiatives can be. It is remarkably difficult to motivate people in continuous improvement initiatives when staff are leaving and surviving personnel are in fear of their jobs.

The fact is that people matter. This apparently obvious statement underpins one of the key lessons that strategic operations management has learned in the last part of the twentieth century. From a position in which people were seen simply as factors of production, as 'hands' to work in factories and offices, we have moved to a recognition of the enormous potential contribution which human resources can offer. Whether in systematic and widespread problem solving (such as helped the Japanese manufacturing miracle), in the flexibility of teamworking or in the emerging role of 'knowledge workers', the distinctive capabilities of human beings are now being recognized. In the 'resource-based' view of strategy, organizations are encouraged to identify and build upon their core competencies; what is now clear is that a major (but still often under-utilized) resource is the people involved in the organization – the 'human resources'. There is already compelling evidence about the benefits of strategic human resource management, seeing people as part of the solution rather than as the problem. In work on US companies, Pfeffer (1998) notes the strong correlation between proactive people management practices and the performance of firms in a variety of sectors. Such 'competitive advantage through people' is also to be found elsewhere; in the UK, a series of studies on 'high-performance workplaces' and on the contribution of advanced human resource practices to improved competitiveness provide clear evidence of the link (Guest *et al.*, 2000; CIPD, 2001; DTI, 2003).

All of this raises a challenge for strategic operations management. Whilst there is undoubted potential in the staff of any organization, unlocking it – for example, in systematic high involvement in problem solving around the quality question – is not easy. Fashions abound – for teamworking, for empowerment, for knowledge and learning workers – but implementing these themes requires fundamental changes in the way people think and behave within the organization. Obtaining commitment and 'buy-in' to new ways of working requires a skilful combination of leadership, communication and motivation, coupled with appropriate designs for new work organization. Simple recipes are not enough – for example, 'empowerment' sounds good, but allowing people freedom to decide what they do and how they do it may be somewhat dangerous when applied in the context of complex systems or safety-critical operations. 'Teamworking' requires more than just throwing a group of individuals together; effective teams are the result of careful selection, training and experience. 'Employee involvement' in problem solving (sometimes called *kaizen* or continuous improvement) requires a supporting and enabling system, and a long-term commitment to establishing this as the 'way we do things around here'.

In the past, looking after people-related issues was the province of specialists – in personnel and industrial relations – working on basic issues of recruitment, reward, working conditions, etc. But it is becoming a critical concern for operations management. The emerging model sees, on the one hand, a much higher profile for the developmental side of human resource management – for example, the need to train and equip people to make a contribution to the operational competencies of the organization – and on the other an integration of this role into that of line or work-group management. Human resources matter much more than they ever did and they are moving centre stage. So one of the key skills in strategic operations management is going to be learning how to motivate and direct such resources.

Why bother with people?

If you had been asked to predict the stocks that would do best in the USA over the last quarter of the twentieth century, it is unlikely that you would have chosen a small regional airline, a small publisher, an unknown retailer, a poultry farmer or a video rental business. Yet each of these outperformed the rest of the stock market, including some of the most glamorous and high-technology stocks (Pfeffer, 1994). This is a significant achievement in itself, but it takes on even more importance when set against the performance of the rest of the sectors in which these firms operate. They are not niche markets but highly competitive and overcrowded sectors – with the result that many firms within them have gone bankrupt and all face serious challenges. To perform well under these conditions takes a particular kind of competitive advantage – one that is highly firm-specific and difficult to imitate. In resource-based strategy theory, such firms have a 'distinctive' capability or competence (Kay, 1993).

In these firms, it was not the possession of specific assets or market share or scale economy or advanced technology that accounted for success. They achieved (and attribute) their growth through the ways in which they managed to organize and work with their people to produce competitive advantage. This is evident in both manufacturing and service sectors.

A good example is the case of Southwest Airlines – the role model for the many low-cost airlines now coming to dominate the air travel market. This firm did not have specially designed aircraft but used industry-standard equipment. They did not have access to major international reservation systems, and for many years they were unable to fly in and out of their primary regional airport – Dallas-Fort Worth – and for a long time had to make do with smaller local airports. Their chosen market segment was not in a small niche but in the mainstream business of trying to sell a commodity product – low-price, no-frills air travel. Yet Southwest achieved significantly better productivity than the industry average (79 employees vs. 131 average per aircraft in 1991), more passengers/ employee (2318 vs. 848) and more seat miles/employee (1 891 082 vs. 1 339 995). One of its most significant achievements was to slash the turnaround time at airports, getting its planes back in the air faster than others. In 1992, 80 per cent of its flights were turned around in only 15 minutes against the industry average of 45; even now the best the industry can manage is around 30 minutes. All of this is not at a cost to service quality; SWA is one of the only airlines to have achieved the industry's 'triple' crown (fewest lost bags, fewest passenger complaints, best on-time performance in the same month). No other airline has managed the 'triple', yet SWA has done it nine times! (Pfeffer and Veiga, 1999).

This is not an isolated example; many other studies point to the same important message. For example, research on the global automobile industry in the 1980s showed that there were very significant performance differences between the best plants in the world (almost entirely Japanese operated at that time) and the rest. The gaps were not trivial (Womack *et al.*, 1990):

> … our findings were eye-opening. The Japanese plants require one-half the effort of the American luxury-car plants, half the effort of the best European plant, a quarter of the effort of the average European plant, and one-sixth the effort of the worst European luxury-car producer. At the same time, the Japanese plant greatly exceeds the quality level of all plants except one in Europe – and this European plant required four times the effort of the Japanese plant to assemble a comparable product …

Not surprisingly, this triggered a search for explanations of this huge difference, and companies began looking to see if scale of operations, or specialized automation equipment or government subsidy might be behind it. What they found was that there were few differences in areas like automation – indeed, in many cases non-Japanese plants had higher levels of automation and use of robots. But there *were* major differences in the way work was organized and in the approach taken to human resources.

A comprehensive study of UK experience (Richardson and Thompson, 1999) carried out for the Chartered Institute of Personnel and Development collected evidence to support the contention that in the twenty-first century (CIPD, 2001):

> Tayloristic task management gives way to knowledge management; the latter seeking to be cost-efficient by developing an organization's people assets, unlike the former which views labour as a cost to be minimized.

They observe that although the task of convincing sceptical managers and shareholders remains difficult (Caulkin, 2001):

> ... more than 30 studies carried out in the UK and US since the early 1990s leave no room to doubt that there is a correlation between people management and business performance, that the relationship is positive, and that it is cumulative: the more and the more effective the practices, the better the result ...

Other relevant work includes:

- A study carried out by the Institute of Work Psychology at Sheffield University, which found that in a sample of manufacturing businesses, 18 per cent of variations in productivity and 19 per cent in profitability could be attributed to people management practices (Patterson *et al.*, 1997). They concluded that people management was a better predictor of company performance than strategy, technology or research and development.
- Analysis of the national UK Workplace Employee Relations Survey by Guest *et al.* (2000) found a link between the use of more human resource practices and a range of positive outcomes, including greater employee involvement, satisfaction and commitment, productivity and better financial performance. Another study (Stern and Sommerblad, 1999) concluded that:

> Practices that encourage workers to think and interact to improve the production process are strongly linked to increase productivity.

Similar findings have also been reported by Blimes *et al.* (1997) and by Wood and de Menezes (1998).

■ In the UK a major study of high-performance (scoring in the upper quartile on various financial and business measures) organizations drew similar conclusions (DTI, 1997). Size, technology and other variables were not particularly significant but 'partnerships with people' were. As one manager in the study (Chief Executive, Leyland Trucks, 738 employees, 1998) expressed it:

Our operating costs are reducing year on year due to improved efficiencies. We have seen a 35% reduction in costs within 2½ years by improving quality. There are an average of 21 ideas per employee today compared to nil in 1990. Our people have accomplished this.

■ According to research on firms in the UK that have acquired the 'Investors in People' award, there is evidence of a correlation with higher business performance. Such businesses have a higher rate of return on capital (ROCE), higher turnover/ sales per employee and have higher profits per employee, as shown in Table 9.1.

Perhaps it is particularly at the level of the case study that we can see some of the strong arguments in favour of high involvement innovation. The direct benefits that come from people making suggestions are of course significant, particularly when taken in aggregate. But we

Table 9.1

Performance table of Investors in People companies versus others

	Average company	Investors company	Gain (%)
ROCE	9.21%	16.27%	77
Turnover/sales per employee	£64 912	£86 625	33
Profit per employee	£1815	£3198	76

Source: Hambledon Group (2001), cited on DTI website (www.dti.gov.uk).

Human resource management and operations at 3M

3M as an example of an innovative culture based on people:

As our business grows, it becomes increasingly necessary to delegate responsibility and to encourage men and women to exercise their initiative. This requires considerable tolerance. Those men and women, to whom we delegate authority and responsibility, if they are good people, are going to want to do their jobs in their own way.

Mistakes will be made. But if a person is essentially right, the mistakes he or she makes are not as serious in the long run as the mistakes management will make if it undertakes to tell those in authority exactly how they must do their jobs.

These comments are from William McKnight, who was CEO of 3M from 1949 but who joined the company as a book-keeper in 1907. He is widely credited with having articulated some of the key principles on which the company culture is based and which has led to such an effective track record in innovation. It is often cited as an example of successful and consistent innovation, drawing on what is clearly a highly innovative culture. 3M has around 50 000 products in its range and yet is so confident of its ability to innovate that it sets the stretching target of deriving half of its sales from products it develops and introduces during the last 3 years. Not only are they able to keep this ambitious flywheel of innovation turning, but they do so with a mixture of product improvements and breakthrough radical new product concepts.

Significantly, 3M do not attribute their success to a single organizational 'lever'. Although they are famous for their '15 per cent' rule in which people are encouraged to explore and play with ideas that may not be directly relevant to their main job, this space for innovation is only one element of a complex culture. Other components include policies to allow people to progress their ideas if they feel a personal commitment and are prepared to champion them – this is enabled through a rising series of funding options from simple 'seed' money through to more extensive resources made available if the Board can be convinced by the ideas and the enthusiasm of the proposer. There is a deliberate attempt to create a sense of company history based on valuing as heroes and heroines those people who challenged the system – and a deliberate policy of encouraging 'bootlegging' behaviour – progressing projects which do not necessarily have official sanction but which people pursue often in highly innovative and improvisational mode.

The complex set of behaviours that the firm has discovered works and their subsequent embodiment in a set of reinforcing processes, structures and mechanisms make it difficult for others to imitate the 3M approach – it is not simply a matter of copying, but rather of learning and configuring to suit particular circumstances.

For a detailed discussion of how 3M has built an innovative culture, see Mitchell (1991), Kanter (1997) and Gundling (2000).

need to add to this the longer-term improvements in morale and motivation that can emerge from increasing participation in innovation. A flavour of the case level experience can be seen in the following examples.

In a detailed study of seven leading firms in the fast-moving consumer goods (FMCG) sector, Westbrook and Barwise reported a wide range of benefits, including:

- waste reduction of £500 k in year 1, for a one-off expense of £100 k;

- a recurrent problem costing over 25 k/year of lost time, rework and scrapped materials eliminated by establishing and correcting root cause;
- 70 per cent reduction in scrap year on year;
- 50 per cent reduction in set-up times, in another case 60–90 per cent;
- uptime increased on previous year by 50 per cent through CI project recommendations;
- £56 k/year overfilling problems eliminated;
- reduction in raw material and component stocks over 20 per cent in 18 months;
- reduced labour cost per unit of output from 53 to 43 pence;
- raised service levels (order fill) from 73 to 91 per cent;
- raised factory quality rating from 87.6 to 89.6 per cent.

The US financial services group Capital One saw major growth between 1999 and 2002, equivalent to 430 per cent, and built a large customer base of around 44 million people. Its growth rate (30 per cent in turnover 2000–2001) made it one of the most admired and innovative companies in its sector. But, as Wall (2002) points out:

> Innovation at Capital One cannot be traced to a single department or set of activities. It's not a unique R&D function, there is no internal think-tank. Innovation is not localized but systemic. It's the lifeblood of this organization and drives its remarkable growth. ... It comes through people who are passionate enough to pursue an idea they believe in, even if doing so means extending well beyond their primary responsibilities.

Chevron Texaco is another example of a high growth company which incorporates – in this case in its formal mission – a commitment to high involvement innovation. It views its 53 000 employees worldwide as (Abraham and Pickett, 2002):

> ... fertile and largely untapped resources for new business ideas. ... Texaco believed that nearly everyone in the company had ideas about different products the company could offer or ways it could run its business. It felt it had thousands of oil and gas experts inside its walls and wanted them to focus on creating and sharing innovative ideas ...

In implementing high involvement of employees in innovation in a large South African mining company, suggestions made by employees led to (De Jager *et al.*, 2004):

- improvements in operating income at one dolomite mine of 23 per cent despite deteriorating market conditions;
- increase in truck fleet availability at a large coal mine of 7 per cent (since these are 180-ton trucks the improvement in coal hauled is considerable);
- increase in truck utilization of 6 per cent on another iron ore mine.

Kaplinsky (1994a,b) reports on a series of applications of 'Japanese' manufacturing techniques (including the extensive use of *kaizen* in a variety of developing country factories in Brazil, India, Zimbabwe, Dominican Republic and Mexico). In each case there is clear evidence of the potential benefits that emerge where high involvement approaches are adopted – although the book stresses the difficulties of creating the conditions under which this can take place.

Gallagher and Austin (1997) report on a series of detailed case studies of manufacturing and service sector organizations that have made progress towards implementing some form of high involvement innovation. The cases highlight the point that although the sectors involved differ widely – insurance, aerospace, electronics, pharmaceuticals, etc. – the basic challenge of securing high involvement remains broadly similar.

Another source of support for the high involvement approach can be drawn from the increasing number of studies of employee involvement programmes themselves. Studies of this kind concentrate on reports describing structures that are put in place to enable employee involvement and the number of suggestions or ideas that are offered by members of the workforce. For example, a recent survey by ideasUK (based on 79 responses from their membership of around 200 firms) indicated a total of 93 285 ideas received during 2000–2001. Not every idea is implemented, but from the survey and from previous data it appears that around 25 per cent are – and the savings that emerged as a direct consequence were reported as being £88 million for the period. This pattern has been stable over many years and indicates the type of direct benefit obtained. In addition, firms in the survey reported other valuable outcomes from the process of employee involvement.[1]

---

[1] Source: Personal communication with ideasUK. For more information, see their website (http://www.ideasuk.com/).

From all of these – and many other examples (Clark, 1993; Huselid, 1995; Blimes *et al.*, 1997) – the evidence is clear. Competitive advantage is coming not through scale of operations, or special market position or the deployment of major new technologies, but rather from what these organizations do with their people. Teamworking, employee involvement, decentralization of many decisions, training, flexibility, all of these become meshed into a pattern of behaving – 'the way we do things around here' – which we call the company culture. Although 'soft' and intangible, the evidence is clear that possessing such a culture is as powerful a strategic resource as a major patent or an advantageous location. But such cultures don't emerge by accident – they must be built and maintained.

Looking back ...

Attempts to utilize this approach in a formal way, trying to engender performance improvement through active participation of the workforce, can be traced back to the eighteenth century, when the eighth shogun Yoshimune Tokugawa introduced the suggestion box in Japan (Schroeder and Robinson, 1991). In 1871, Denny's shipyard in Dumbarton, Scotland, employed a programme of incentives to encourage suggestions about productivity-improving techniques; they sought to draw out *any change by which work is rendered either superior in quality or more economical in cost*. In 1894, the National Cash Register company made considerable efforts to mobilize the 'hundred-headed brain' that their staff represented, whilst the Lincoln Electric Company started implementing an 'incentive management system' in 1915. NCR's ideas, especially around suggestion schemes, found their way back to Japan, where the textile firm of Kanebuchi Boseki introduced them in 1905.

One of the difficult questions to answer when considering the evolution of operations management is how the potential contribution of people has become marginalized. Clearly, this is not the product of a conspiracy on the part of operations managers, but rather an unfortunate by-product of centuries of trying to make operations more efficient and effective. To understand what has happened, we need to take a brief look at the history of operations management.

Managing agricultural production was the dominant challenge for all countries until comparatively recently. And whilst the forms of management were often less than enlightened (including a sizeable element of slavery), there was a clear relationship between what people did and what they produced. The vast majority of work was as direct labour rather than involved in indirect activity, and the challenges faced were relatively simple tasks. Where specialized skills were needed – craftsmen working as wheelwrights, blacksmiths, masons, carpenters, etc. – there was the Guild system to regulate and professionalize. Here, strong emphasis was placed on a learning process, from apprenticeship, through journeyman to master craftsman, and this process established clear standards of performance and what might be termed 'professional' values. Again, there was a close link between what a craftsman produced and the man himself, and a strong sense of pride in quality.

The Industrial Revolution changed all of this. The gradual drift towards the cities and the increasing use of machinery led to a rethink of how operations were managed. Its origins can be traced back to Adam Smith and his famous observations of the pin-making process, which marked the emergence of the concept of the division of labour. By breaking up the task into smaller, specialized tasks performed by a skilled worker or special machine, productivity could be maximized. During the next 100 years or so, considerable emphasis was placed on trying to extend this further, by splitting tasks up and then mechanizing the resulting smaller tasks wherever possible, to eliminate variation and enhance overall managerial control.

The resulting model saw people increasingly involved as only one of several 'factors of production' – and in a rapidly mechanizing world, often in a marginal 'machine-minding' role. At the same time, the need to co-ordinate different operations in the emerging factories led to a rise in indirect activity and a separation between doing and thinking/deciding. This process accelerated with the increasing demand for manufactured goods throughout the nineteenth century, and much work was done to devise ways of producing high volumes in reproducible quality and at low prices.

This 'American system' stressed the notion of the 'mechanization of work'. As Jaikumar (1988) puts it:

… whereas the English system saw in work the combination of skill in machinists and versatility in machines, the American system introduced to mechanisms the modern scientific principles of reductionism and reproducibility. It examined the processes involved in the manufacture of a product, broke them up into sequences of simple operations, and mechanized the simple operations by constraining the motions of a cutting tool with jigs and fixtures. Verification of performance through the use of simple gauges insured reproducibility. Each operation could now be studied and optimized.

That the convergent blueprint for this kind of manufacturing has come to be known as 'Fordism' reflects the enormous influence of Henry Ford in the way in which he (and his gifted team of engineers) developed and systematized such approaches. His model for the manufacture of cars was based on a number of innovations which reduced the need for skilled labour, mechanized much of the assembly process, integrated preparation and manufacturing operations for both components and finished product, and systematized the entire process. As Tidd (1989) points out, the basic elements of the Ford system were largely already in existence; the key was in *synthesizing* them into a new system. (Even the idea of flow production lines for motor cars was first used in the Olds Motor Works in 1902, while Leland's Cadillac design of 1906 won an award for the innovation of using interchangeable, standardized parts.) The challenge of high-volume, low-cost production of the Model T led Ford engineers to extend the application of these ideas to new extremes – involving heavy investment in highly specialized machine tools and handling systems, and extending the division and separation of labour to provide workers whose main tasks were feeding the machines. The dramatic impact of this pattern on productivity can be seen in the case of the first assembly line, installed in 1913 for flywheel assembly, where the assembly time fell from 20 man minutes to five. By 1914, three lines were being used in the chassis department to reduce assembly time from around 12 hours to less than 2.

This approach extended beyond the actual assembly operations to embrace raw material supply (such as steelmaking) and transport and distribution. At its height, a factory operating on this principle was able to turn out high volumes (8000 cars/day) with short lead times – for example, as a consequence of the smooth flow that could be achieved it took only 81 hours to produce a finished car from raw iron ore, and this included 48 hours for the raw materials to be transported from the mine to the factory! (Tidd, 1989). In the heyday of the integrated plants such as at River Rouge, productivity, quality, inventory and other measures of manufacturing performance were at levels that would still be the envy even of the best organized Japanese plants today.

Some of the key features of this blueprint for manufacturing, typified in the car plants of Henry Ford, but applied to many other industries throughout the 1930s and beyond, are outlined below:

- Standardization of products and components, of manufacturing process equipment, of tasks in the manufacturing process, and of control over the process.

- Time and work study, to identify the optimum conditions for carrying out a particular operation and job analysis, to break up the task into small, highly controllable and reproducible steps.
- Specialization of functions and tasks within all areas of operation. Once job analysis and work-study information was available, it became possible to decide which activities were central to a particular task and to train an operator to perform those smoothly and efficiently. Those activities which detracted from this smooth performance were separated out and became, in turn, the task of another worker. So, for example, in a machine shop the activities of obtaining materials and tools, or maintenance of machines, or of progressing the part to the next stage in manufacture, or quality control and inspection, were all outside the core task of actually operating the machine to cut metal. Thus, there was considerable narrowing and routinization of individual tasks and an extension of the division of labour. One other consequence was that training for such narrow tasks became simple and reproducible, and thus new workers could quickly be brought on stream and slotted into new areas as and when needed.
- Uniform output rates and systemization of the entire manufacturing process. The best example of this is probably the assembly line for motor cars, where the speed of the line determined all activity.
- Payment and incentive schemes based on results – on output, productivity, etc.
- Elimination of worker discretion and passing of control to specialists.
- Concentration of control of work into the hands of management within a bureaucratic hierarchy with extensive reliance on rules and procedures – doing things by the book.

Alternative routes

There were, of course, competing models which saw a different role for people in the operations of industrial and service businesses. Even in the early days of mass production, other work was going on to try and understand how people could work more productively in an industrial rather than a craft environment.

Criticism is often levelled at the scientific management school (represented by figures like Frederick Taylor and Frank and Lilian Gilbreth) for helping to institutionalize standardized working practices modelled around a single 'best' way to carry out a task. But this is to mask the significant role that their systematic approach took to encourage and implement worker suggestions. It was Frank Gilbreth, for example, who is credited with having first used the slogan 'work smarter, not harder' – a phrase which has since come to underpin the philosophy of continuous improvement innovation. As Taylor (1912, cited in Boer *et al.*, 1999) wrote:

> You must have standards. We get some of our greatest improvements from the workmen in that way. The workmen, instead of holding back, are eager to make suggestions. When one is adopted it is named after the man who suggested it, and he is given a premium for having developed a new standard. So, in that way, we get the finest kind of team work, we have true co-operation, and our method ... leads on always to something better than has been known before.

In particular, a whole series of experiments at the Hawthorne plant of the Western Electric Company led to the emergence of what has come to be termed the 'human relations' school of management – an approach which tries to re-integrate people into work processes rather than marginalizing them (Lewin, 1947; Morgan, 1986).

Another significant development was the recognition of the value of teamworking in improving both productivity and flexibility. Work in the UK, for example, looked at the problems of mechanization and automation in the coal industry. The aim was to improve productivity through the use of a new process for cutting coal, but early experience with the machinery was disappointing. Researchers from the Tavistock Institute highlighted the fact that the new system and equipment broke up what had been productive teams under the old system – and by working on both the social and technical systems simultaneously they produced a model for effective teamworking with new technology. Such 'socio-technical systems design' provided a strong influence on the development of capital intensive industries like petrochemicals and for experiments in the car industry (for example, at Volvo's Kalmar plant in the 1960s – Miller and Rice, 1967).

Mass production begins to unwind

It was not until the 1970s that the cracks began to appear in this view – essentially reflecting the problems of such systems in meeting the changing demands of fragmenting markets and shifting patterns of demand. In particular, meeting the growing demand for high perform-ance in non-price factor areas – quality, flexibility, variety, speed – became increasingly difficult with systems geared around assumptions of stable, unlimited demand and a market in which price was the key competitive factor. The position was exacerbated by the growth in global competi-tion – it became increasingly clear that those enterprises that did not adapt to offer price and non-price advantages would be overtaken by those who did. The demise of much UK manufacturing, for example, can be attributed to a failure to keep up with Japanese competition based on superior quality and delivery performance.

The inherent inflexibility in the 'mass production' approach was reflected particularly in the ways in which people were involved only as replaceable cogs in a large machine-like organization. As Piore and Sabel (1982) stated:

> Mass production offered those industries in which it was developed and applied enormous gains in productivity – gains that increased in step with the growth of these industries. Progress along these technological trajectories brought higher profits, higher wages, lower consumer prices and a whole range of new products. But these gains had a price. Mass production required large investments in highly specialized equipment and narrowly trained workers. In the language of manufacturing, these resources were 'dedicated'; suited to the manufacture of a particular product – often, in fact, to make just one model. Mass production was therefore profitable only with markets that were large enough to absorb an enormous output of a single, standardized commodity, and stable enough to keep the resources involved in the production of the commodity continuously employed.

The influence of 'lean' thinking

Early attempts to emulate the Japanese experience often failed. For example, the widespread adoption of quality circles in the late 1970s often led to short-term gains and then gradual disillusionment and abandonment of the schemes later (Dale and Hayward, 1984; Lillrank and Kano, 1990). In large measure this can be attributed to a mistaken belief in there being a single transferable solution to the problem of quality which Western firms had to try and acquire. The reality was, of course, that the 'Japanese' model involved a completely different philosophy of organizing and managing production.

This became increasingly clear as Western firms began to explore other dimensions of Japanese practice – for example, their approach to production scheduling, to inventory control, to flow, to maintenance and to flexibility (Suzaki, 1988; Schonberger, 1982). The emergent model was one in which people were treated as a key part of the solution to the problems of production – and as a problem-finding and -solving resource for dealing with new ones. In order to mobilize this potential it was necessary to invest in training, and the more widely this was done, the more flexibly people could be used across a manufacturing facility. Having trained staff with the capability of finding and solving problems, it made sense to pass the responsibility for much of the operational decision making to them, so workers became involved in quality, in maintenance, in production scheduling and smoothing, etc. And in order to maximize the flexibility associated with devolution of decision making, new forms of work organization, especially based around teamworking, made sense.

It is important to recognize that there is nothing peculiarly Japanese in any of these concepts – rather, they simply represent a re-integration of tasks and responsibilities which had been systematically fragmented and separated off by the traditions of the factory system in the nineteenth century and Ford/Taylor-style mass production in the twentieth. None the less, the gap that had opened up was significant, and was highlighted in particular by a series of studies of the world automobile industry in the late 1980s. This work looked systematically at both the performance of car assembly plants right across the world and also the practices that led to particular levels of performance. It became clear that Japanese operated plants were significantly better performers across a range of dimensions – and that the difference could only be explained by recognizing that a fundamentally different philosophy of manufacturing was in operation. Efforts to identify the source of these significant advantages revealed that the major differences lay not in higher levels of capital investment or more modern equipment, but in the ways in which production was organized and managed.

The authors christened this 'lean production' – implying an approach that focused on the elimination of waste of all kinds – physical (as in poor-quality components or processes), space, movement, etc. And one of the biggest areas of waste was in the human resource potential, which was not being used in most Western operations. Schroder and Robinson present figures for suggestions made by ordinary shopfloor workers in major Japanese companies, both in terms of the volume and the number implemented; typically, the number of ideas offered runs into many millions per year! (Schroeder and Robinson, 1993). If we add to this the information that many firms – such as Toyota – have been doing since the 1960s, we can see that a great deal of creative problem-solving capability has been mobilized. Whilst critics often argue that this data simply reflects tiny changes and improvements, the counter argument is that even if each suggestion is tiny, millions per year over a sustained 20- or 30-year period add up to significant benefit. To underline the point further, studies of the auto industry in 1989 suggested that the average rate for Japanese plants worked out at around one suggestion per worker per week. The US data indicated a rate of around half a suggestion, per worker, per year!

Putting people back into operations management

This extended look at history highlights several key points. First, that things change – no model is appropriate for every circumstance. The craft system would not have been sufficient to cope with the explosive demands of expanding markets in the twentieth century – something like mass production had to emerge. In similar fashion, mass production is no longer an appropriate model for the twenty-first century (although we must be careful not to throw the baby out with the bathwater – there are many features that are still very relevant under certain contingencies).

Second, people are a key part of the puzzle – they are resources that can be mobilized in different ways. With hindsight it is easy to be critical of the Ford/Taylor models – but we should also remember that they represented very effective solutions for their time. To get the kind of productivity which Ford's early plants achieved from unskilled and often illiterate workers, and to do so at consistent levels of quality, suggests that many ideas from that period had relevance. But the weakness in the model probably lay in its marginalizing of those characteristics of human beings which make them so useful in uncertain conditions – creativity, problem solving, flexibility in teamworking, etc. In an environment characterized by uncertainty we need to find models of organizing that maximize the opportunities to deploy these characteristics.

Third, we need to recognize that we are not dealing with particular country solutions. Much is often made of the Japanese miracle – but although the conditions for the emergence of a new model were present in post-war Japan, the underlying principles are of much wider relevance. Just as mass production evolved in the factories of the USA but then diffused widely, so those of lean (and beyond) began life in Japan but have come to dominate the operations management agenda across the world.

Finally, we need to be aware of sectoral issues. Much of the preceding discussion has been about manufacturing – because this is where the changes first took place and where we can see most clearly the relationship between people and the tasks they do. But the same pattern has been going on in the service sector – for example, McDonald's very sophisticated model for fast-food production and service replicates across 185 000 outlets, a model with which Henry Ford would feel quite comfortable. (It is also important to note that whilst Japanese manufacturing has been held up as a role model for much of the last quarter century, the service sector in that country remains far less developed and has a serious productivity problem.)

Current 'good practice' in strategic human resource management

Pfeffer (1998) and Pfeffer and Veiga (1999) report on a study of high-performance work practices of 968 US firms representing all major industries. The study found that a one standard deviation increase in the use of such practices was associated with a 7.05 per cent decrease in staff turnover and, on a per-employee basis, a $27 044 increase in sales/employee, an $18 641 increase in stock market valuation and a $3814 increase in profits (Huselid, 1995). Similar data comes from a German study, which found 'a strong link between investing in employees and stock market performance' (Blimes *et al.*, 1997), and from UK studies, which demonstrate a high degree of correlation between new human resource practices and performance (DTI, 1994, 2003; Guest *et al.*, 2000; CIPD, 2001).

It is important to note two points in such studies. First, they are not saying that a single practice will change things overnight. Rather, success comes through a systematic and integrated approach carried through over a sustained period of time. Changing the way an organization behaves is a matter of consistent reinforcement and the establishment of a different set of values.

The second point is that we can see a high degree of convergence in different studies around the key dimensions of high-performance human resource management. For example, Pfeffer (1994) lists seven key practices of successful organizations, whilst the UK 'Competitiveness through partnerships with people' study highlights five key areas for change. We can group the key factors into a simple model (Figure 9.1), which provides an overview of the challenges for strategic operations management in this field.

Under each of these headings are a number of factors: Table 9.2 lists the key elements. In the following section we discuss them in a little more detail.

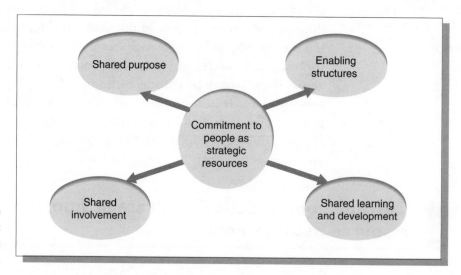

Figure 9.1
Human resource
issues in strategic
operations
management.

Table 9.2

Key elements in human resource management in strategic operations

Area	Key elements
Commitment to people as strategic resources	Employment security Choosing the right people Valuing and rewarding them Wage compression Symbolic egalitarianism
Shared purpose	Strategic leadership Shared planning processes Policy deployment Information sharing Employee ownership
Enabling structures	Appropriate organization design Job and work organization design Devolved decision making Supportive communications
Shared learning and development	Commitment to training and development Embedding a learning cycle Measurement Continuous improvement culture
Shared involvement	Teamworking Cross-boundary working Participation and involvement mechanisms Stakeholder focus and involvement

Commitment to people as strategic resources

There is no 'magic ingredient' in the recipe for developing high-performance organizations of this kind – but there is a need to work on some basic principles. At the heart of such organizations lies a belief in the importance and potential contribution that employees can make. From this a series of practices follow which reinforce the message and enable sometimes 'extraordinary efforts from ordinary people' (Joynson, 1994). One of the basic human needs is for security, and in an uncertain world providing some measure of employment security is a powerful way of signalling the value placed on human resources. Of course, this is not something that can be guaranteed and there is a risk of 'feather-bedding' employees – but providing some form of contract that shares the risks and the benefits is strongly correlated with success. For example, one of the most successful US firms is Lincoln Electric, who operate on this basis (cited in Pfeffer, 1994):

> ... Our guarantee of employment states that no employee with 3 years or more of service will be laid off for lack of work ... this policy does not protect any employee who fails to perform his or her job properly, it does emphasize that management is responsible for maintaining a level of business that will keep every employee working productively. The institution of guaranteed employment sprang from our belief that fear is an ineffective motivator ... relief from anxiety frees people to do their best work ...

The converse of this is also true; if people feel their efforts are likely to have a negative impact on their employment security, they will not make them. So introducing programmes which engage employees in improvement activities that raise productivity will only work if there is some form of reassurance that these employees are not improving themselves out of a job!

Much depends on ensuring that the right people are involved in the first place, and there is a clear trend towards more selective and careful recruitment practices within organizations. For example, Southwest Airlines received nearly 100 000 job applications in 1993; 16 000 were interviewed and only 2700 people were actually employed (Pfeffer and Veiga, 1999). Given the flexibility and creativity required and the increasing emphasis on teamworking in the emerging operations environment, a broad range of social skills become an important part of the skills mix that firms are seeking.

Reward systems are another area in which significant change is taking place. The traditional view concentrated on simple reward systems, often linking wages to output in systems like piece-work. But our understanding of what motivates people, and our need for performance across a broad range of factors like quality, flexibility and speed, has led to the emergence of new approaches. New arrangements include payment for acquiring skills, for effective teamworking and for participation in problem finding and solving; perhaps more important is the recognition that non-financial rewards are an important part of the package (Luthans and Stajkovic, 1999).

There is also some evidence that paying high wages is associated with improved performance (Pfeffer, 1994, 1998). But of greater significance is the reduction of wage and status differentials; eliminating symbols that imply there are more or less valued people in the organization is a critical step in building a new culture. For example, the presence of separate and hierarchically arranged facilities like office space, canteens, car parking, etc. sends out powerful messages about valuing some people more than others. By contrast, shared facilities, company uniforms and other symbols help reduce this sense of status difference.

In the end, the task is one of building a shared set of values which bind people in the organization together and enable them to participate in its development. As one manager put it in a UK study (DTI, 1997):

... we never use the word empowerment! You can't empower people – you can only create the climate and structure in which they will take responsibility ...

Shared purpose

Successful organizations do not happen by accident – they have a clear and thought-out sense of direction, and can mobilize support for their strategic goals. Whilst charismatic leaders can and do make a difference, it is not sufficient to rely upon this phenomenon. Instead, high-performance organizations need ways of building a sense of shared purpose.

This can be accomplished in a number of ways, not least through participation in the planning process itself. A growing number of firms make use of workshops and other mechanisms to gain input and discussion of strategic issues, whilst many others take pains to ensure the ideas are communicated throughout the organization – for example, via team briefings, newsletters, videos, etc. Others make use of the appraisal process to provide a mechanism for involvement in strategic planning and particularly for aligning the goals of the individual to those of the organization.

A key issue here is what is sometimes called 'policy deployment' – essentially a process of connecting the high-level strategic goals of the business with specific tasks and targets with which individuals and groups can engage. This requires two key enablers – the creation of a clear and coherent strategy for the business and the deployment of it through a cascade process that builds understanding and ownership of the goals and sub-goals.

This is a characteristic feature of many Japanese '*kaizen*' systems and may help explain why there is such a strong 'track record' of strategic gains through continuous improvement (CI) (Bessant, 2003). In such plants overall business strategy is broken down into focused 3-year mid-term plans (MTPs); typically, the plan is given a slogan or motto to help identify it. This forms the basis of banners and other illustrations, but its real effect is to provide a backdrop against which efforts over the next 3 years can be focused. The MTP is specified not just in vague terms but with specific and measurable objectives – often described as pillars. These are, in turn, decomposed into manageable projects that have clear targets and measurable achievement milestones, and it is to these that CI is systematically applied (Bessant and Francis, 1999). Policy deployment of this kind requires suitable tools and techniques, and examples include hoshin planning, how-why charts, 'bowling charts' and briefing groups (Shiba *et al.*, 1993).

One way in which shared purpose can be developed is through involving employees as key stake- or share-holders. In the five high-performance firms that Pfeffer mentions, more than 4 per cent of the stock is owned by employees, whilst in Japan there is a clear link between ESOPs (employee share ownership programmes) and reduced labour turnover. By the same token, reward systems that emphasize some element of gain sharing – bonus schemes linked to stretching strategic targets that reflect high levels of active involvement – provide powerful mechanisms for ensuring commitment to common purpose.

Linked to this is the need for shared understanding about what is happening and where the organization is going. Information sharing and effective communication systems that operate in two-way mode are critical to building shared purpose. As one manager put it (John Mackey, CEO of Whole Foods Markets, cited in Pfeffer and Veiga, 1999):

> ... if you're trying to create a high trust organization ... an organization where people are all-for-one and one-for-all, you can't have secrets!

The case of Springfield ReManufacturing Company in the USA provides a powerful illustration of this; when faced with a cancelled order from General Motors, which represented around 40 per cent of their business, the senior management chose to let everyone know exactly what was going on. The response to the crisis was a series of employee-led initiatives which raised productivity and has subsequently allowed major expansion of the business. Open-book management of this kind has become central to their development and growth – and has helped them move from a position in 1986 where the 119 employees faced being laid off to one where they now employ over 700. Similar stories of turnaround through high commitment can be found in Sirkin and Stalk (1990), who looked at a large paper-maker in the US, and Semler (1993), who explains his approach to revitalizing a number of white goods plants in Brazil.

Enabling structures – the limits to chaos

Central to this is the idea of structure – and here it is important to be clear that the prescription is not simply flat and loose. Whilst there are significant limitations to the kind of hierarchical design that characterized organizations in Henry Ford's day, simply substituting a new 'one size fits all' model may be the wrong thing to do. What we have learned over decades of research on organizational structures is that the choice is contingent on factors like size, technology, the environment the firm works in – and what it is trying to do (strategy). There are some cases where it makes a great deal of sense to devolve decision making to the shopfloor self-managed team looking after a self-contained cell – for example, in a highly uncertain customer-focused business where each order is a special project. But that model may not be the best idea where we are trying to co-ordinate the activities of many different people in the production of a complex product or assembly. For example, empowering people working on the drug manufacture and packing lines in a pharmaceutical business to use their own judgement and come up with their own solutions may not be the safest or most reliable way to run things.

In general, organizational structures are influenced by the nature of tasks to be performed within the organization. In essence, the less programmed and more uncertain the tasks, the greater the need for flexibility around the structuring of relationships (Preece, 1995). For example, activities like production, order processing, purchasing, etc. are characterized by decision making that is subject to little variation.

(Indeed, in some cases these decisions can be automated through employing particular decision rules embodied in computer systems, etc.) But others require judgement and insight and vary considerably from day to day – and these include those decisions associated with innovation. Activities of this kind are unlikely to lend themselves to routine, structured and formalized relationships, but instead require flexibility and extensive interaction.

Valuable insights into this issue came originally from the work done in the late 1950s by researchers Burns and Stalker (1961), who outlined the characteristics of what they termed 'organic' and 'mechanistic' organizations. Organic forms are suited to conditions of rapid change, whilst mechanistic forms are appropriate to stable conditions. The relevance of this model can be seen in an increasing number of cases where organizations have restructured to become less mechanistic. For example, firms like General Electric in the USA underwent a painful but ultimately successful transformation, moving away from a rigid and mechanistic structure to a looser and decentralized form (Moody, 1995), whilst in the 1980s ABB, the Swiss–Swedish engineering group, developed a particular approach to their global business based on operating as a federation of small businesses, each of which retains much of the organic character of small firms (Barnevik, in Champy and Nohria, 1996). Other examples of radical changes in structure include the Brazilian white goods firm Semco and the Danish hearing aid company Oertikon (Kaplinsky *et al.*, 1995; Semler, 1993).

Another important strand in thinking about organization design is the relationship between different external environments and organizational form. Once again, the evidence suggests that the higher the uncertainty and complexity in the environment, the greater the need for flexible structures and processes to deal with it (Smith, 1992). In part, this explains why some fast-growing sectors – for example, electronics or biotechnology – are often associated with more organic organizational forms, whereas mature industries often involve more mechanistic arrangements.

An important contribution to our understanding of organizational design came in studies originated by Joan Woodward (1965), associated with the nature of the industrial processes being carried out. These studies suggested that organizational structures varied between industries; those with a relatively high degree of discretion (such as small batch manufacturing) tended to have more decentralized and organic forms, whereas in those involving mass production more hierarchical and heavily structured forms prevailed. Significantly, the process industries, although also capital intensive, allowed a higher level of discretion.

Many other factors have an influence on the structuring of organizations – these include size, age and company strategy (Child, 1980; Johnson and Scholes, 1999). What became a long-running debate on what determined organization structure began to resolve itself into a 'contingency' model in the 1970s. The basic idea here is that there is no single 'best' structure, but that successful organizations tend to be those which develop the most suitable 'fit' between structure and operating contingencies (Mintzberg, 1979). So if we were trying to replicate the operations of a company like McDonald's, so that it offered the same products and standards of service in thousands of locations around the world, it would make sense to structure it in a mechanistic and highly controlled form. But if we were trying to develop new drugs or respond to a rapidly changing 'fashion' market, we would need a more flexible and loose structure.

Stretching learning and development

One lesson which emerges consistently when looking at high-performance organizations is their commitment to training and development. If a firm is to make the best use of new equipment or to produce products and services with novelty in design, quality or performance, then it needs to recognize that this depends to a large extent on the knowledge and skills of those involved.

Training and development has two contributions to make. First, of course, it equips people with the necessary skills and capabilities for understanding and operating equipment or processes. But it also has considerable potential as a motivator – people value the experience of acquiring new skills and abilities, and also feel valued as part of the organization. For example, a survey of employee involvement in continuous improvement in the UK found that the opportunity for personal development was ranked higher than financial motivators as a reward mechanism (Caffyn *et al.*, 1996). Similarly, if we want people to take on more responsibility and demonstrate more initiative – so-called 'empowerment' exercises – then training and development provide an important aid to the process. And if we are concerned with harnessing creativity and encouraging experiment, then we need to recognize that this depends on people having the necessary skills and confidence to deploy them (IPD, 1995).

Change management – the planned and effective introduction of new systems, structures or procedures – is one of the big challenges in contemporary organizations, and it is likely to become even more so in an environment where organizations need to re-invent themselves on a continuous basis. When major innovations are introduced, people often resist the change for a variety of reasons, not all of which are rational or clearly articulated (Smith and Tranfield, 1990). Research suggests that a key element of this anxiety is the sense that the innovation will require abilities or skills which the individual does not possess, or pose challenges which are not fully understood. So training and development – not only in the narrow sense of 'know-how', but also a component of education around the strategic rationale for the change (the 'know-why') – can provide a powerful lubricant for oiling the wheels of such innovation programmes (Walton, 1986; Bessant and Buckingham, 1993).

A final but key point concerns the use of training and development activities to develop the habit of learning. Any 'learning organization' will require the continual discovery and sharing of new knowledge – in other words, a continuing and shared learning process (Garvin, 1993; Leonard-Barton, 1992). Putting this in place requires that employees understand *how* to learn, and an increasing number of organizations have recognized that this is not an automatic process. Consequently, they have designed and implemented training programmes designed less to equip employees with skills than to engender the habit of learning. Examples include firms offering access to courses in foreign languages, hobby-skills and other activities unrelated to work, but with the twin aims of motivating staff and getting them back into the habit of learning.

Getting the learning habit

Successful firms invest in training of various kinds – to give staff an understanding of the targets towards which continuous improvement (CI) should be focused, to develop the skills of problem solving and learning, and to equip them with the necessary skills and familiarity with key tools and techniques. Some also stress the importance of developing the habit of learning by encouraging employees to take on training of any kind – foreign languages, construction skills, anything to get them into the swing of acquiring and using new skills.

Examples of particular training inputs amongst some UK organizations include:

- A major manufacturer of auto components reports saving £850 000 per year from its extensive continuous improvement (CI) activities. In building its process improvement teams it provided 3 days of training for each team member, to establish the basic process and concepts of CI; its LIFE (little improvements from everyone) programme is now carrying out similar training inputs, and so far some 500 staff have been involved.

- An engine manufacturer has around 60 per cent of its staff actively involved in CI across some 530 projects, has provided a minimum of 3 days training for every one of its employees, which provides the basic platform for CI understanding and establishes the process in people's minds. Additional inputs – for example, for those with the responsibility for facilitating CI – are also made, and there are periodic updates in such training. Its initial investment in training during the 18-month start-up period was of the order of 16 000 person days.

- A major UK power generator has an overall training budget of £1 m and each employee receives a minimum of 10 days training; this is equivalent to £1400/employee. In addition, they give every employee £100 worth of training, which can be in anything – from gardening or sewing to work-related topics. The aim is to encourage a learning culture in which more work-specific inputs can take root. Similar programmes are in operation at Ford (where demand for training far exceeded expectations) and at Baxi, where employees can study a wide range of courses at local colleges with the company paying the fees and providing some time release.
- Unipart has become one of the most successful companies in the European automotive components sector. A key element in its continuing drive for reduced costs and improved performance is the mobilization of high levels of creativity across its workforce, and this is in turn enabled by a strong commitment to education and training. In order to facilitate this, the company set up 'Unipart U' (short for university) as a place where all employees could access learning opportunities across a wide range of work- and non-work-related activities.

Shared involvement

Although there is scope for individual activity, one of the main advantages in working in organizations is to benefit from the team effect, whereby the benefits of working together outweigh those of the same number of people working alone. But simply throwing a group of people together does not make a team; the whole can only become greater than the sum of its parts if careful attention is paid to design and operation, and to training the skills for effective teamworking.

Teams have become a fashionable concept as organizations recognize the value in the flexibility and problem-solving capability that they can offer. Research has consistently shown that teams are both more fluent (the number of ideas they generate) and more flexible (the number of different ideas they generate) than individuals in problem-solving tasks, and this attribute makes them a very suitable vehicle for dealing with the uncertainties of the current environment. At the same time, the psychological pressure to conform means that teams become a powerful way of articulating and reinforcing patterns of behaviour – a culture – within an organization. Building effective routines for organizational activities can often be best achieved through the development and support of team norms.

Much research has been carried out to try and understand how teams work and how they might be developed. Two conclusions emerge strongly. First, as with the design of organizations, the design and working of a team depends on what it is trying to do and the context in which it works. Second, high-performance teams for whatever purpose do not emerge by accident – they have to be built and sustained (Francis and

Young, 1988). They result from a combination of selection and invest-ment in team building, allied to clear guidance on their roles and tasks, and a concentration on managing group process as well as task aspects (Thamhain and Wilemon, 1987). For example, work by researchers in the USA on a variety of engineering companies aimed at identifying key drivers and barriers to effective performance found that effective team building is a critical determinant of project success. Bixby (1987) drew similar conclusions in work with organizations associated with the Ashridge Management College teamworking programme; this model for 'superteams' includes components of building and managing the internal team, and also its interfaces with the rest of the organization. Key elements include:

- clearly defined tasks and objectives;
- effective team leadership;
- good balance of team roles and match to individual behavioural style;
- effective conflict resolution mechanisms within the group;
- continuing liaison with external organization.

Extensive work on 'group dynamics' in the 1950s and 1960s found that there is a pattern to the way in which teams emerge. Teams typically go through four stages of development, popularly known as 'forming, storming, norming and performing'. In practice, they are put together and then go through phases of resolving internal differences and con-flicts around leadership, objectives, etc. Emerging from this process is a commitment to shared values and norms governing the way the team will work, and it is only after this stage that teams can move on to effective performance of their task.

Obviously, a key influence on team performance will be the mix of people involved – in terms of personality type and behavioural style. There has to be good matching between the role requirements of the group and the behavioural preferences of the individuals involved. Again, this has been the subject of extensive work, and one of the most useful models derives from the research carried out by Meredith Belbin (1984). In this model of team behaviour, he classifies people into a number of preferred role types – for example, 'the plant' (someone who is a source of new ideas), 'the resource investigator', 'the shaper' and the 'completer/finisher'. Research has shown that the most effective teams are those with diversity in background, ability and behavioural style. In one noted experiment, highly talented but similar people in what he terms 'Apollo' teams consistently performed less well than mixed, average groups (Belbin, 1984).

Team building is not the only aspect affecting performance. Other influential factors include:

- team size;
- team structure;
- team process – the way in which meetings are organized and decisions taken;
- team leadership;
- team environment/organizational context.

Holti *et al.* (1995) provide a useful summary of the key factors involved in developing teamworking. Although there is considerable current emphasis on teamworking, we should remember that teams are not always the answer. In particular, there are dangers in putting nominal teams together where unresolved conflicts, personality clashes, lack of effective group processes and other factors can diminish their effectiveness.

An important point to remember is that different kinds of teams are required for different situations. Tranfield *et al.* (1998) found several different 'archetypes' where the team structure and dynamics needed to be different to cope with different kinds of context, ranging from repetitive manufacturing operations through to highly uncertain and unpredictable task environments. Increasingly, their role as enablers of knowledge generation, sharing and diffusion is also being recognized (Sapsed *et al.*, 2002).

Teams are increasingly being seen as a mechanism for bridging boundaries within the organization – and indeed, in dealing with inter-organizational issues. Cross-functional teams can bring together the different knowledge sets needed for tasks like product development or process improvement – but they also represent a forum where often deep-rooted differences in perspectives can be resolved. However, as we indicated above, building such teams is a major strategic task – they will not happen by accident, and they will require additional efforts to ensure that the implicit conflicts of values and beliefs are resolved effectively.

Teams also provide a powerful enabling mechanism for achieving the kind of decentralized and agile operating structure that many organizations aspire to. As a substitute for hierarchical control, self-managed teams working within a defined area of autonomy can be very effective. For example, Honeywell's defence avionics factory reports a dramatic improvement in on-time delivery – from below 40 per cent in the 1980s to 99 per cent in 1996 – due to the implementation of self-managing teams. In the Netherlands, one of the most successful bus companies is Vancom Zuid-Limburg, which has improved both price and non-price performance and has high customer satisfaction ratings. Again, they attribute this to the use of self-managing teams and to the reduction in overhead costs that results. In their system, one manager supervises over 40 drivers, where the average for the sector is a ratio of 1:8. Drivers are also encouraged to participate in problem finding and solving in areas like maintenance, customer service and planning (Van Beusekom, 1996).

Learning

The last area is in many ways the most significant for the future. One of the fundamental flaws in the Ford/Taylor model was the assumption that it represented the 'one best way' – that it was possible to design something which represented the 'perfect' manufacturing system. It was undoubtedly effective in terms of productivity (rises of 300 per cent in the first year of operation vs. craft production, for example) and in its impact on costs (when competitors entered, Ford was able to drop and continue to drop his prices to remain competitive). It was also attractive as an employment option – despite the hard conditions and the high labour turnover, people flocked to work in his plants because of the high wages being paid. The problem for Ford was that the world doesn't remain static and if you have invested heavily in 'one best way', then it is a costly business to change.

Arguably, Ford's plants represented the most efficient response to the market environment of its time. But that environment changed rapidly during the 1920s, so that what had begun as a winning formula for manufacturing began gradually to represent a major obstacle to change. Production of the Model T began in 1909 and for 15 years or so it was the market leader. As Abernathy points out, despite falling margins the company managed to exploit its blueprint for factory technology and organization to ensure continuing profits. But by the mid-1920s, growing competition (particularly from General Motors, with its strategy of product differentiation) was shifting away from trying to offer the customer low-cost personal transportation and towards other design features – such as the closed body – and Ford was increasingly forced to add features to the Model T. Eventually, it was clear that a new model was needed and production of the Model T stopped in 1927.

Changing over to the new Model A was a massive undertaking and involved crippling investments of time and money – since the blueprint for the highly integrated and productive Ford factories was only designed to make one model well. During the year it took to change over, Ford lost \$200 m and was forced to lay off thousands of workers – 60 000 in Detroit alone; 15 000 machine tools were scrapped and a further 25 000 had to be rebuilt, and even though the Model A eventually became competitive, Ford lost its market leadership to General Motors.

These days we face a much more uncertain environment, where the only certainty is change itself. So the response cannot be 'one best way' because even if it were possible to find it, tomorrow's conditions would put it out of date. Instead, we have to look towards organizations that are adaptive and experimental – in other words, organizations that learn.

Of course, organizations don't learn, it is the people within them who do; what we need to look for are those behaviour patterns that the organization develops to enable the learning process, and in particular on the ways in which individual and shared learning can be mobilized. For example, Garvin (1993) suggests the following mechanisms as important:

- training and development of staff;
- development of a formal learning process based on a problem-solving cycle;
- monitoring and measurement;
- documentation;
- experiment;
- display;
- challenge existing practices;
- use of different perspectives;
- reflection – learning from the past.

Garvin (1993, p. 80) provides further insight about a would-be learning organization:

> A learning organization is an organization skilled at creating, acquiring, and transferring knowledge, and at modifying its behavior to reflect new knowledge and insights.

He continues by saying that learning organizations are adept at five activities:

1 Problem solving.
2 Experimentation with new approaches.
3 Learning from their own experience and past history.
4 Learning from others.
5 Efficiently (and speedily) transferring this knowledge throughout the organization.

Learning gained from both the firm's own experience and learning from others demand that organizations make time to reflect on this learning in order to reinforce and confirm what has been learned. Learning in all of the ways cited above is a feature of world-class manufacturing firms. These firms learn quickly and effectively; these outstanding firms also learn quickly from mistakes and failures, and then utilize the intellectual capability from their trained workforces to rectify the situation. Such learning then manifests itself in competitive areas such as lower cost, enhanced delivery speed and reliability, higher levels of process quality, and speedier new product development. But the alarming thing is that, in the quick-fix management culture, not enough firms take time to learn, as Garvin (1993) observes:

> ... few companies ... have established processes that require their managers to periodically think about the past and learn ... [p. 85]. ... There must be time for reflection and analysis, to think about strategic plans. ... Only if top management explicitly frees up employees' time for the purpose does learning occur with any frequency. [p. 91]

Learning is an invaluable ingredient: it includes forgetting bad practice as well as embracing new ideas. Learning undoubtedly impacts upon key areas in manufacturing processes. It would seem, therefore, very sensible for firms to set aside time for learning rather than having an ongoing pursuit of being busy – often in the wrong things.

Looking forward

If the twentieth century marked the shift from labour intensity to capital intensity, with people and manual work being gradually substituted by mechanization and automation, the transition to the twenty-first is proving to be equally dramatic. Many commentators argue that the emerging era is one in which the key to competitiveness will be knowledge. Simply possessing assets or technology or access to raw materials or cheap labour is no longer sufficient – in a global business economy, these advantages can be matched (Teece, 1998).

The key will be knowledge – and particularly the firm-specific knowledge that an organization can accumulate and protect. This may be in the form of codified knowledge – in patents or copyrighted materials – but much is likely to be in the form of knowledge embedded in the minds and behaviour patterns of the people working in the organization (Tidd *et al.*, 1997). The potential of such resources is considerable – from the tacit knowledge possessed by research scientists and engineers through to the day-to-day, hands-on knowledge about how to get the best out of processes and machinery that shopfloor employees possess (Nonaka, 1991). Capturing and sharing such knowledge – and creating new knowledge through experimentation and experience – is perhaps the key task in developing competitive edge in organizations. As we saw earlier, the ability to mobilize the problem-finding and -solving capacity of the workforce has played a major role in creating Japanese capability as a manufacturing nation and this model is increasingly recognized as relevant (Hayes and Wheelwright, 1984; Senge, 1990a,b; Bessant, 1998).

But there is another pattern that is also of critical importance – the shift from manufacturing into services. Over the past centuries we have seen an inexorable drift from agricultural employment into manufacturing and, during the twentieth century, from manufacturing employment into services. Although the proportions vary by country and by level of industrialization, overall there is a clear and continuing trend towards the growth of the service sector, both in terms of economic activity and as the primary source of employment.

With the rise in the service economy comes a greater reliance on human resources to deliver, especially at the critical customer interface. Even where services can be automated – for example, in banking and insurance operations – the need for some form of human interaction is still a key factor in determining competitiveness. Consumer reluctance to work only with automated systems, and the need for a human problem-solving capability for the non-standard and exceptional issues that arise, means that there will continue to be a role for people, even in these service businesses. In many others it is the perceived quality of service – expressed through interactions with customers as well as 'back-office' efficient processes – which makes the competitive difference.

So, once again, the key resource that operations managers will need to work with is the human one – particularly in terms of its flexibility, problem-solving and creative capabilities. Operations can and will be significantly improved through the use of technology to automate and streamline processes for creation and delivery of products and services. But dealing with the exceptions and managing the customer interfaces will continue to depend on human resources, and their success will be linked to the level of training and capability of those people.

If strategic HRM is going to play such a significant role in the future, how will it be handled and what needs to be done? In parallel with the developments outlined in this chapter, we have seen the task of enabling the involvement of people changing. In the Ford/Taylor model, the issue was one of hiring, firing and managing contractual and other employment issues on a formal maintenance basis. The response was to create a specialist function of personnel management with capabilities in industrial relations, employment law and contracts, payment systems, etc.

With the growing recognition of the potential contribution of human resources came a need to think about the development of people as assets – much as equipment needs retooling. Thus, the role shifted from employment to development, with an increase in the scope of training and the use of more creative forms of motivation (including non-financial methods) and appraisal systems linked to career development. Recognition of the need for changing the shape and operation of the organization to enable people to contribute more meant that organizational development also came into the picture. The resulting – present-day – model of HRM is thus much more developmental in nature, addressing the individual and the organization in a long-term fashion (Clark, 1993). Even the name of the major professional body in the UK has changed to reflect this – from the Institute of Personnel Management to the Institute of Personnel and Development.

The next step in the process is likely to see an increasing shift of responsibility for this broad set of HRM activities to operations managers. As we have argued throughout this chapter, strategic development and deployment of this set of resources may be the most important task facing operations management in the future, and whilst professional expertise can provide valuable help in design and implementation of relevant structures and processes, the responsibility for HRM will be integrated into the day-to-day and future planning role of strategic operations management.

What do strategic operations managers need to look for in the future? Essentially, their role will increasingly be to facilitate and co-ordinate the activities of a highly involved and committed workforce – and this will depend on constructing and maintaining the kind of conditions outlined in this chapter. The challenge is to enable more self-direction and autonomy within clear and bounded limits – the laboratory for learning rather than the factory or office. Agility comes through being able to respond and be proactive, but above all from fast learning. In an environment where we do not know what is coming, only that the challenges themselves will be new and need new responses, enabling this agility will be key.

Case: Human resources to strategic operations at XYZ Systems

At first sight, XYZ Systems does not appear to be anyone's idea of a 'world-class' manufacturing outfit. Set in a small town in the Midlands with a predominantly agricultural industry, XYZ employs around 30 people, producing gauges and other measuring devices for the forecourts of filling stations. Their products are used to monitor and measure levels and other parameters in the big fuel tanks underneath the stations, and on the tankers that deliver to them. Despite their small size (although they are part of a larger but decentralized group), XYZ have managed to command around 80 per cent of the European market. Their processes are competitive against even large manufacturers, their delivery and service level the envy of the industry. They have a fistful of awards for their quality and yet manage to do this across a wide range of products, some dating back 30 years, which still need service and repair. They use technologies from complex electronics and remote sensing right down to basics – they still make a wooden measuring stick, for example.

Their success can be gauged from profitability figures, but also from the many awards that they receive and continue to receive as one of the best factories in the UK.

Yet if you go through the doors of XYZ, you would have to look hard for the physical evidence of how they achieved this enviable position. This is not a highly automated business – it would not be appropriate. Nor is it laid out in modern facilities; instead, they have clearly made much of their existing environment and organized it and themselves to best effect.

Where does the difference lie? Fundamentally, in the approach taken with the workforce. This is an organization where training matters – investment is well above the average and everyone receives x hours per year, not only in their own particular skills area, but across a wide range of tasks and skills. One consequence of this is that the workforce is very flexible; having been trained to carry out most of the operations, they can quickly move to where they are most needed. The payment system encourages such co-operation and teamworking, with its simple structure and emphasis on payment for skill, quality and teamworking. The strategic targets are clear and simple, and are discussed with everyone before being broken down into a series of small, manageable improvement projects in a process of policy deployment. All around the works there are copies of the 'bowling chart', which sets out simply – like a tenpin bowling scoresheet – the tasks to be worked on as improvement projects and how they could contribute to the overall strategic aims of the business. And if they achieve or exceed those strategic targets, then everyone gains thorough a profit-sharing and employee ownership scheme.

Being a small firm there is little in the way of hierarchy, but the sense of teamworking is heightened by active leadership and encouragement to discuss and explore issues together, and it doesn't hurt that the Operations Director practises a form of MBWA – management by walking about!

Perhaps the real secret lies in the way in which people feel enabled to find and solve problems, often experimenting with different solutions and frequently failing – but at least learning and sharing that information for others to build on. Walking round the factory it is clear that this place isn't standing still. Whilst major investment in new machines is not an everyday thing, little improvement projects – *kaizens* as they call them – are everywhere. More significant is the fact that the Operations Director is often surprised by what he finds people doing – it is clear that he has not got a detailed idea of which projects people are working on and what they are doing. But if you ask him if this worries him the answer is clear – and challenging. 'No, it doesn't bother me that I don't know in detail what's going on. They all know the strategy, they all have a clear idea of what we have to do (via the "bowling charts"). They've all been trained, they know how to run improvement projects and they work as a team. And I trust them …'

Summary

- This chapter has reviewed the ways in which strategic development and deployment of human resources can make a significant impact on an organization's performance. In crude terms, we have moved a long way from the position at the beginning of the twentieth century, where people were seen as part of the problem, something to be eliminated or at worst kept on the sidelines because they were a source of unwanted variation in the operation of carefully designed manufacturing systems. Today's view is very different, seeing the contribution of people's flexibility and problem-solving capability as critical resources in dealing with a world characterized by uncertainty – and in which business systems and organizations have to change on a continuing basis. And it is likely that the future will bring increasing emphasis on the ability of organizations to learn, to remember and to deploy their collective knowledge more effectively – again, a process that depends critically on the people within them.

■ Putting people at the centre of the stage rather than on the sidelines requires new approaches to their organization and management, and the chapter has tried to highlight the key areas in which such management needs to take place. These are big challenges for the strategic operations manager – not only does he or she have to create and implement new structures and procedures to enable and support more active participation in the development and improvement of the business, they also have to play a key role in the process of helping the organization 'unlearn' some of the beliefs and accompanying practices that pushed people to the side of the stage.

Key questions

1   It is commonplace to hear managers and chairmen of companies say that 'people are our biggest asset' – but often this is nothing more than words. In what ways can people make a difference to the way a business operates – and how can this potential be realized?

2   How and why has human resource management moved from a simple concern with recruitment and reward to a more strategic role in the business? In what ways is people management becoming a central concern for strategic operations managers – and in what ways can they enable human resources to make a strategically important contribution to the business?

3   In the 1980s there was great enthusiasm for the 'lights out' factory – a totally automated operation in which almost no people would be required. Why do you think this idea has fallen from favour, and why are advanced organizations in many sectors now seeing people as a key resource in their businesses?

4   'The beauty of it is that with every pair of hands you get a free brain!' This quote from a manager highlights the potential of employee involvement, but the fact remains that most organizations still do not manage to engage their workforce on a systematic and sustained basis. What are the main barriers to doing so – and how would you, as a strategic operations manager, try and increase active employee involvement in continuous improvement of the business?

5   Many pictures of the future stress themes like 'the learning organization' or 'the knowledge-based business'. Such visions are likely to depend on human resources, and achieving them poses challenges for how such resources are recruited, developed and managed.

How can strategic operations managers contribute to the design and operation of such organizations?

References and further reading

Abraham, D. and Pickett, S. (2002) Refining the innovation process at Texaco. *Perspectives on Business Innovation* (online), www.cbi.cgey.com(8).

Belbin, M. (1984) *Management Teams – Why They Succeed or Fail.* London: Heinemann.

Bessant, J. (1997) *Report on Kaizen Mission.* Brighton: University of Brighton.

Bessant, J. (1998) Learning and continuous improvement. In: Tidd, J. (ed.), *Measuring Strategic Competencies: Technological, Market and Organisational Indicators of Innovation.* London: Imperial College Press.

Bessant, J. (2003) *High Involvement Innovation.* Chichester: John Wiley.

Bessant, J. and Buckingham, J. (1993) Organisational learning for effective use of CAPM. *British Journal of Management,* **4**(4), 219–234.

Bessant, J. and Francis, D. (1999) Developing strategic continuous improvement capability. *International Journal of Operations and Production Management,* **19**(11).

Bixby, K. (1987) *Superteams.* London: Fontana.

Blimes, L., Wetzker, K. and Xhonneux, P. (1997) *Value in Human Resources.* London: Financial Times.

Boer, H., Berger, A., Chapman, R. and Gertsen, F. (1999) *CI Changes: From Suggestion Box to the Learning Organisation.* Aldershot: Ashgate.

Burns, T. and Stalker, G. (1961) *The Management of Innovation.* London: Tavistock.

Caffyn, S., Bessant, J. and Silano, M. (1996) Continuous improvement in the UK. *Works Management,* July.

Caulkin, S. (2001) *Performance Through People.* London: Chartered Institute of Personnel and Development.

Champy, J. and Nohria, N. (eds) (1996) *Fast Forward.* Cambridge, MA: Harvard Business School Press.

Child, J. (1980) *Organisations.* London: Harper & Row.

CIPD (2001) *Raising UK Productivity: Why People Management Matters.* London: Chartered Institute of Personnel and Development.

Clark, J. (ed.) (1993) *Human Resource Management and Technical Change.* London: Sage.

Dale, B. and Hayward, S. (1984) *A Study of Quality Circle Failures.* UMIST.

De Jager, B., Minnie, C., De Jager, C., Welgemoed, M., Bessant, J. and Francis, D. (2004) Enabling continuous improvement – an implementation case study. *International Journal of Manufacturing Technology Management.*

DTI (1994) *Innovation – Your Move.* Department of Trade and Industry.

DTI (1997) *Competitiveness Through Partnerships with People.* London: Department of Trade and Industry.

DTI (2003) *Competing in the Global Economy: The Innovation Challenge.* London: Department of Trade and Industry.

Francis, D. and Young, D. (1988) *Top Team Building.* Aldershot: Gower.

Gallagher, M. and Austin, S. (1997) *Continuous Improvement Casebook.* London: Kogan Page.

Garvin, D. (1993) Building a learning organisation. *Harvard Business Review,* July–August, 78–91.

Grindley, P. (1991) Turning technology into competitive advantage. *Business Strategy Review,* Spring, 35–47.

Guest, D., Michie, J., Sheehan, M. and Conway, N. (2000) *Employment Relations, HRM and Business Performance: An Analysis of the 1998 Workplace Employee Relations Survey.* London: CIPD.

Gundling, E. (2000) *The 3M Way to Innovation: Balancing People and Profit.* New York: Kodansha International.

Hamel, G. and Prahalad, C. (1994) *Competing for the Future.* Cambridge, MA: Harvard Business School Press.

Hayes, R. and Wheelwright, S. (1984) *Restoring Our Competitive Edge.* New York: Wiley.

Hayes, R., Wheelwright, S. and Clark, K. (1988) *Dynamic Manufacturing: Creating the Learning Organisation.* New York: Free Press.

Holti, R., Neumann, J. and Standing, H. (1995) *Change Everything at Once: The Tavistock Institute's Guide to Developing Teamwork in Manufacturing.* London: Management Books 2000.

Huselid, M. (1995) The impact of human resource management practices on turnover, productivity and corporate financial performance. *Academy of Management Journal,* **38**, 647.

IPD (1995) *People Make the Difference.* Institute of Personnel and Development.

Jaikumar, R. (1988) *From Filing and Fitting to Flexible Manufacturing.* Cambridge, MA: Harvard Business School Press.

Johnson, G. and Scholes, K. (1999) *Exploring Corporate Strategy,* 5th Edition. Hemel Hempstead: Prentice Hall.

Joynson, S. (1994) *Sid's Heroes: Uplifting Business Performance and the Human Spirit.* London: BBC Books.

Kanter, R. (ed.) (1997) *Innovation: Breakthrough Thinking at 3M, DuPont, GE, Pfizer and Rubbermaid.* New York: Harper Business.

Kaplinsky, R. (1994a) *The Challenge of Easternisation.* London: Frank Cass.

Kaplinsky, R. (1994b) *Easternization: The Spread of Japanese Management Techniques to Developing Countries.* London: Frank Cass.

Kaplinsky, R., den Hertog, F. and Coriat, B. (1995) *Europe's Next Step.* London: Frank Cass.

Kay, J. (1993) *Foundations of Corporate Success: How Business Strategies Add Value.* Oxford: Oxford University Press.

Leonard-Barton, D. (1992) The organisation as learning laboratory. *Sloan Management Review*, **34**(1), 23–38.

Lewin, K. (1947) Frontiers in group dynamics: concept, method and reality in the social sciences. *Human Relations*, **1**(1), 5–41.

Lewis, K. and Lytton, S. (1994) *How to Transform Your Company and Enjoy it.* London: Management Books 2000.

Lillrank, P. and Kano, N. (1990) *Continuous Improvement; Quality Control Circles in Japanese Industry.* Ann Arbor: University of Michigan Press.

Luthans, F. and Stajkovic, A. (1999) Reinforce for performance: The need to go beyond pay and even rewards. *Academy of Management Executive*, **13**(2), 49–57.

Miller, E. and Rice, A. (1967) *Systems of Organisation.* London: Tavistock.

Mintzberg, H. (1979) *The Structuring of Organisations.* Englewood Cliffs, NJ: Prentice Hall.

Mitchell, R. (1991) How 3M keeps the new products coming. In: Henry, J. and Walker, D. (eds), *Managing Innovation.* London: Sage.

Moody, F. (1995) *I Sing the Body Electronic.* London: Hodder & Stoughton.

Morgan, G. (1986) *Images of Organisation.* London: Sage.

Nonaka, I. (1991) The knowledge creating company. *Harvard Business Review*, November–December, 96–104.

Patterson, M., West, M., Lawthom, R. and Nickell, S. (1997) *The Impact of People Management Practices on Business Performance.* London: CIPD.

Pfeffer, J. (1994) *Competitive Advantage Through People.* Cambridge, MA: Harvard Business School Press.

Pfeffer, J. (1998) *The Human Equation: Building Profits by Putting People First.* Cambridge, MA: Harvard Business School Press.

Pfeffer, J. and Veiga, J. (1999) Putting people first for organizational success. *Academy of Management Executive*, **13**(2), 37–48.

Piore, M. and Sabel, C. (1982) *The Second Industrial Divide.* New York: Basic Books.

Preece, D. (1995) In: Bessant, J. and Preece, D. (eds), *Organisations and Technical Change*, Routledge Series in the Management of Technology. London: Routledge/International Thompson.

Richardson, R. and Thompson, M. (1999) *The Impact of People Management Practices on Business Performance: A Literature Review*. London: CIPD.

Sapsed, J., Bessant, J., Partington, D., Tranfield, D. and Young, M. (2002) Teamworking and knowledge management; a review of converging themes. *International Journal of Management Review*, **4**(1).

Schonberger, R. (1982) *Japanese Manufacturing Techniques; Nine Hidden Lessons in Simplicity*. New York: Free Press.

Schroeder, D. and Robinson, A. (1991) America's most successful export to Japan – continuous improvement programmes. *Sloan Management Review*, **32**(3), 67–81.

Schroeder, M. and Robinson, A. (1993) Training, continuous improvement and human relations: the US TWI programs and Japanese management style. *California Management Review*, **35**(2).

Semler, R. (1993) *Maverick*. London: Century Books.

Senge, P. (1990a) *The Fifth Discipline*. New York: Doubleday.

Senge, P. (1990b) The leader's new work: building learning organisations. *Sloan Management Review*, **32**(1), 7–23.

Shiba, S., Graham, A. and Walden, D. (1993) *A New American TQM; Four Practical Revolutions in Management*. Portland, OR: Productivity Press.

Sirkin, H. and Stalk, G. (1990) Fix the process, not the problem. *Harvard Business Review*, July–August, 26–33.

Smith, S. (1992) Factory 2000: organization design for the factory of the future. *International Studies of Management and Organisation*, **22**(4), 61–68.

Smith, S. and Tranfield, D. (1990) *Managing Change*. Kempston: IFS Publications.

Suzaki, K. (1988) *The New Manufacturing Challenge*. New York: Free Press.

Stern, E. and Sommerblad, E. (1999) *Workplace Learning, Culture and Performance*. London: CIPD.

Tampoe, M. (1994) Exploiting the core competences of your organization. *Long Range Planning*, **27**(4), 66–77.

Taylor, F. (1912) *Scientific Management*. Hanover, NH: Dartmouth College.

Teece, D. (1998) Capturing value from knowledge assets: the new economy, markets for know-how, and intangible assets. *California Management Review*, **40**(3), 55–79.

Thamhain, H. and Wilemon, D. (1987) Building high performing engineering project teams. *IEEE Transactions on Engineering Management*, **EM-34**(3), 130–137.

Tidd, J. (1989) *Flexible Automation*. London: Frances Pinter.

Tidd, J., Bessant, J. and Pavitt, K. (1997) *Managing Innovation: Integrating Technological, Organizational and Market Change*. Chichester: John Wiley.

Tranfield, D. *et al.* (1998) Teamworked organisational engineering: getting the most out of teamworking. *Management Decision*, **36**(6).

Van Beusekom, M. (1996) *Participation Pays! Cases of Successful Companies with Employee Participation*. Netherlands Participation Institute: The Hague.

Wall, J. (2002) Innovation based sustainability at Capital One Financial. *Perspectives on Business Innovation*. Internet: www.cbi.cgey.com(8).

Walton, R.E. (1986) *Human Resource Practices for Implementing AMT: Report of the Committee on Effective Implementation of AMT*. Washington, DC: National Research Council.

Womack, J., Jones, D. and Roos, D. (1990) *The Machine that Changed the World*. New York: Rawson Associates.

Wood, S. and de Menezes, L. (1998) High commitment management in the UK: evidence from the Workplace Industrial Relations Survey and Employers' Manpower and Skills Practices Survey. *Human Relations*, **51**, 485–517.

Woodward, J. (1965) *Industrial Organisation: Theory and Practice*. Oxford: Oxford University Press.

CHAPTER 10

The future for operations management

Introduction

In this book, we have developed a strategic understanding of operations management by considering how manufacturing and service operations have developed over the last 100 years. During this time there has been a marked transition, exemplified by the *Fortune* 500, which lists the top 500 US-based companies. When it was first compiled, all of these firms were manufacturing based. As the US economy shifted towards a service base, with service firms growing in size and economic significance, a separate listing called the Service 500 was developed. Over time, some companies moved from the *Fortune* 500 to the Service 500, as their stream of revenue from their services outstripped their income from the sale of manufactured goods. By the 1990s, the distinction between manufacturing and service companies was so slight that the two lists were combined. Moreover, most, if not all, of these firms are now global in scope, with operations on a worldwide basis. It is this notion of a modern, global, integrated product/service firm that has been the focus of previous chapters' discussions on contemporary operations management practice.

A key feature in this, of course, will be the extent to which the Internet empowers companies and consumers. Already it is possible for Internet users to exchange goods using 'e-credits', which perform the same function as money but have no value except on the Internet. It has contributed significantly to the notion of Lester Thurow's vision of a global village, in which 'neighbours' can trade or barter with each other, just as they used to before the world became so complex. As Thurow says: 'For the first time in human history, anything can be made anywhere and sold anywhere.' Davis and Meyer (1999) predicted the emergence of powerful consumer groups, made up of very large numbers of like-minded people. They suggested a notional 'Value 500' of such groups, which will be the consumer equivalent of, and rival to, the *Fortune* 500. This has still to happen, but seems to fit with the ways in which global markets are developing. The ability of consumer groups to mobilize their collective will has always been important, with some groups having notable successes, such as those concerned with US automobile safety, led by Ralph Nader, the Campaign for Real Ale (CAMRA) in the UK, and current popular concern in Europe with respect to genetically modified foods. Such mobilization has previously been difficult due to the relative isolation of each consumer. The Internet overcomes this isolation and enables each consumer to, first of all, identify like-minded souls and then to communicate with them extremely quickly and on a very large scale.

The immense impact of global terrorism that occurred in the first 4 years of the twenty-first century also holds special challenges for operations management – especially in the assumptions that may be made about geographical locations and logistics. The costs of security (for example, in air freight) are great but they must be borne by producers who are also facing intense price-driven competition.

The future challenges for operations management

So, what are the future challenges for operations management? What lies ahead for managers concerned with the value creation processes discussed in this book? In this final chapter, we focus on three of the central challenges: we cannot foretell the future, of course, but we hope we can set the scene. The three challenges are: managing global growth, understanding and gaining competitive advantage from e-commerce, and achieving environmental soundness in operations. We shall examine each of these in turn.

The challenge of global growth

As newly industrializing countries seek to achieve widespread improvements in quality of life and political stability, so their industries simultaneously present new consumer markets and new sources of products and services to the world. In such countries, labour costs are low, development grants are available to tempt inwards investors, and local markets are homogeneous and tolerant.

These were the conditions within which mass production was born at the end of the nineteenth century. Now, widespread communications mean that consumers in newly developing countries are aware of the array of products and services from which their counterparts in the West may choose, and want some of the same for themselves. While it may be true, at the end of the twentieth century, that three-quarters of the people in the world had never used a telephone, influences such as television and American feature films are effective stimulants for demand in new consumer markets. More significantly, the growth of mobile phone technology has become common place throughout the world.

Within this context, while many of the challenges relate to international (or global) marketing, it is clear that operations strategy is of pivotal importance. The windows of opportunity for commercial exploitation that appear as developing countries emerge as potential manufacturing bases may be brief. Developing countries must export to earn foreign capital, but will inevitably import goods as well. Once goods produced for Western markets are available in developing countries, the nascent consumers there will begin to demand Western levels of quality. This may seem obvious but the implications for operations management are immense.

Under mass production principles, the typical practice in setting up a manufacturing plant in a developing country would be a compromise – based upon low expectations of competence in workforces and local management. The local government's motivation for allowing in a foreign investor would be jobs (and thus prosperity) and a chance to export – at least to elsewhere in its region. For the investor, however, the primary motivation would be sell goods in the host country – and perhaps in those surrounding it: the expectation would be that products made in the new plant would not be acceptable for import to the home country of the investor. The opportunity for its firms to hit the affluent export markets of the West (where the real money lay) would thus be very limited for the host country. In this practice, products or component parts that were considered good enough for export would typically be separated out from a batch – leaving those of inferior quality to be sold to the local market. Now, as soon as the local market has experienced (albeit vicariously) export quality, and has the income to allow it, such consumers may be expected not to accept second best.

The wish of the developing country's government to achieve export income is, of course, very much in tune with foreign investors' wishes to play global games with their capacity – reducing the need to transport goods around the world. The strategy in some manufacturing industries is now to produce for local requirements in each region and then cross-ship products from one region to another to create niche (smaller quantity) markets. Thus, for example, when Honda began to produce the Accord in the USA in the mid-1980s, it developed a popular two-door coupé model for local tastes, and found that it could ship it to Japan as a niche vehicle there (in left-hand drive – the 'wrong' side for Japan, but very fashionable in Tokyo). In this way, Honda was treating the USA as a developing country but naturally exploiting the developed manufacturing ability that existed there (although it had fallen behind world-class levels by the 1980s). The coupé was also sold in Europe (and the USA) and, later in the 1990s, Honda used the replacement model to introduce its V6 engine to the Accord range in Europe (i.e. in small numbers, as a niche product).

While playing a global game with capacity has been a central part of corporate strategy since the days of Henry Ford, actually exploiting global positions and developing economies in the present day requires redefined excellence in operating strategy. In the expansion of mass production in the early part of the twentieth century, American firms showed Europeans (and subsequently others) how to apply Taylorism and Fordism, both for local consumption and for regional exports. The same happened with the Japanese in the 1970s and 1980s, as lean production was rolled into North America and Europe.

Some of the rationale for global manufacturing relates more to financial and marketing matters than operations – and there are cases where, despite excellence in manufacturing, firms have met failure. For example, the well-respected firm Hewlett Packard moved production of its disk drives from the USA to Malaysia in the early 1990s, in order to benefit from low taxation in the developing country. In fact, the market for these products collapsed shortly afterwards and HP made losses in the Malaysian operation. Had the production facility been in the USA, HP could have set these losses against its profits there. Having moved to Malaysia, however, this was not possible. HP was thus unable to reduce its tax burden in the USA and was faced with operating losses in Malaysia – the worst of both worlds. The lesson is that, no matter how good the manufacturing is, globalizing business may not always be the best path.

This has developed further into the partial or even complete exit from manufacturing of many product-related firms (including HP). Instead of producing laptop computers, for example, most of the main brands have moved to outsourced production – thereby avoiding some of the difficulties of global networking, by leaving them to the specialist firms that have grown up to address them. This is a trend that may be expected to continue – at least until international agreements on such things as environmental impacts (and thus costs) of large-scale logistics, and perhaps the intolerable risks of terrorism, are established and addressed.

Globalization and service operations

It can be argued that the internationalization of manufacturing has been one of the key drivers of service firm internationalization. Airlines, hotels and banks have expanded into countries in order to serve their globalizing customers, especially business travellers, who visit and work outside their home country. Thus, the average split between domestic and foreign business in the hotel industry is 50:50 worldwide. Some of the early growth in international hotel development was linked directly to the airlines' desire to have suitable accommodation available for their passengers. For instance, TWA developed the Inter-Continental chain and Air France the Meridien brand. Increasingly, service firm international expansion is fuelled by scale economies that can be leveraged from strong brands, loyal customers and centralized facilities, especially reservations and distribution systems.

Inward investment is both capital intensive and risky. The political, financial, economic and social circumstances in a country may vary widely. Hence, service firms have developed alternative strategies for creating brand presence without a high degree of financial investment. The two most common alternatives are franchising and management contracting. These two alternative business formats both involve collaboration between the international service firm and a local investor. In the case of a franchise, the franchisee typically builds or leases the local infrastructure, such as the restaurant, hotel or retail outlet, and agrees to run the business in conformance with the precise system developed by the franchisor. McDonald's, Holiday Inn and the retail division of Benetton are examples of highly successful global service firms that have adopted this approach. A management contract, on the other hand, involves the local developer appointing an international firm, such as Hyatt Hotels, to manage and operate their business on their behalf.

It is clear that internationalization for service firms is of itself a challenge. The geographic distance between operating units, the differences in the environmental context, local market and labour conditions all create an operations challenge with regards to successful, consistent performance, especially if the service is strongly branded. However, the lack of direct control over the business through the adoption of these alternative business formats creates an additional challenge. There are three main forms of control: centralizing, which means that all decisions are taken by senior managers, usually at corporate head-quarters; bureaucratic, which involves highly detailed policies and procedures limiting subordinate discretion; and socialization, which is largely through the adoption and dissemination of a shared organizational culture, especially amongst operational managers.

In the past, firms tended to attempt to exert a very strong control over their service offering so that the customer experience was as identical as possible wherever the customer was in the world. Service firms that owned and operated their own units were typically centralized, and those that franchised or contracted their expertise were highly bureaucratic. Increasingly, however, service firms are tending to adopt the slogan 'think global, act local', recognizing that even their international travellers welcome some adaptation of the provision to reflect the destination or region in which the operation is located. As a result, there has been a reduction in centralization and bureaucracy and an increase in socialization control over operational units. For instance, hotel management contractors typically move their managers from one hotel to another every 2 years, despite hotel owners' expressed preference to retain managers for longer. The firm believes that keeping managers on the move supports and reinforces the firm's organizational culture.

There is some evidence emerging to suggest that hybrid firms, those that own and manage their own operations *and* franchise them, have so-called 'plural processes' (Bradach, 1998) that help them outperform firms that rely solely on one business format. Such processes include:

- modelling – franchise operators model themselves on company-run units, thereby encouraging the adoption of system-wide standards;
- ratcheting – the juxtaposition of company-owned and franchised units encourages benchmarking across the two, thereby creating a climate of friendly competition, with each trying to outperform the other;
- local learning – the franchisee's closeness to their market enables the firm to learn quickly about local market conditions;
- market pressure – corporate staff services developed to support operations are exposed to market conditions when franchisees can opt out of utilizing these services;

■ mutual learning – hybrid firms have a more diverse source of new ideas and alternative range of screening processes than those available to firms operating within one business format.

The role of operations in corporate expansion

The spirit of business in the twenty-first century reveals that there is no 'one best way' to follow in managing operations. There is also a range of approaches available to the operations strategist – those concepts we have discussed earlier. As corporations expand, they find the manufacturing management techniques and the process of knowledge exchange are such that new plants in developing countries can be expected to work at world-class levels almost immediately.

In describing how some expanding firms address this phenomenon, observers in the West have captured the strategic approach under the rather unfortunate sobriquet of 'the China box'. The name of China (i.e. the country) appears because that is where this concept has most resonance until now, but it could be any developing country. It is important for this discussion because it illustrates very clearly the changing nature of the challenges that operations strategy must address. It works as follows:

Let us say an American firm wishes to set up a manufacturing facility in a developing Asian country. It already has world-class manufacturing facilities in California but it needs to exploit the growth of the domestic market in the developing country, simultaneously providing a base for exporting to other Asian countries (and, possibly, Europe and North America).

Traditionally, this firm would have shipped old production tooling (dedicated machinery, fixtures, factory equipment, etc.) and old working practices to the developing country, seconded managers from its US plants, recruited a local workforce to assemble kits of components sent from suppliers in the USA, and expected the local quality to be poor. This last factor would provide a very useful political argument (i.e. when dealing with the local government's industrial policy makers) for not buying local components – since the quality would be inferior and the products made could not subsequently be exported. (Ironically, in practice, these arguments often included the claim that the production costs were too high to warrant selling the components or products on the export market: an anomaly in light of the primary reason for manufacturing in the country – inexpensive labour.)

The order of events in the old way of doing things, therefore, was: negotiate development grants, build factory, recruit staff, import parts, export the good products, sell others locally. The plant would start to assemble products to sell locally and the consumers in the developing country, who were used to this and accepted this poor quality, would buy them. Politically, this was not good news for anybody: the local production would be considered token at best and the workforce treated poorly. In the 1980s, the term 'screwdriver plants' was used to describe such facilities – the operatives did nothing but screw together imported parts. Since labour costs were low, the local operation did not add much value and thus did little for the country's gross domestic product. In addition, of course, the local operatives and managers did not learn very much about international standards of operation – a situation which would suit the investing firm well but not please the host country.

By the time our American firm starts to plan its new plant, however, the developing country has begun to seek to increase its added value and will require the American firm to purchase components locally – to increase its 'local content'. No foreign investor is going to do this voluntarily, and the government may have to implement an 'import substitution' policy – banning the import of selected items it wants to have made locally. Even in the absence of such a severe measure, the nature of local content is political rather than economic: extending the manufacturing base to the suppliers means increasing the number of jobs (a proxy for votes!). Also, the degree of learning and skills development within the local workforce is much higher if the proportion of manufacturing done locally is higher. For these and other reasons, the host country's government may be expected to push for a high local content. Leaving aside the political manoeuvring in negotiations between foreign investors and governments, this would mean the investing firm must consider local supply sources rather than simply importing kits.

Just as service firm infrastructure has always had to conform to international standards of performance, so manufacturing investment also has to be world-class. The nature of foreign investment for production facilities, an essential part of corporate growth, has changed from one of assembly to one of more extensive manufacture and supply management. This can no longer be based on the principle of transferring old tooling and working practices, however, as the final products simply won't work if they are made from poor components. In our case, the practices in the Asian plant will begin to reflect world standards. (When the Japanese did this in North America and Europe with lean production in the 1980s, the term 'transplant' was born; the Japanese, not surprisingly, never liked it!)

operations managers have to take on board these additional, major competitive requirements, there are also other vitally important social/environmental pressures that need to be managed, as we have outlined in this chapter. In the future, the pressure put on production/operations managers will be greater than ever. A key issue for operations managers in trying to manage the future is that operations strategy must be in place to enable the firm to deal with such changes. Undoubtedly, having strategic operations in place will decide the fate of firms in both manufacturing and services settings, and combinations of both.

References and further reading

BBC (2000) Gap and Nike: no sweat? *Panorama*, 15 October.

Bradach, J.L. (1998) *Franchise Organisations*. Cambridge, MA: Harvard Business School Press.

Brookings Institution (2002) *Corporate Social Responsibility: Partners for Progress*.

Business Week, 28 October 2002.

Business Week, 22 September 2003.

CEP (1998) *Research Report: Social Accountability 8000*. New York: Council on Economic Priorities.

Davis, S. and Meyer, C. (1999) *Blur: The Speed of Change in the Connected Economy*. New York: Capstone.

Drumwright, M. (1994) Socially responsible organisational buying: environmental concern as a non-economic buying criterion. *Journal of Marketing*, **58**.

The Economist, 20 June 1998, **347**(8073), p. S8(3).

ENDS 232 (1994) Public concern for the environment rides the recession.

Financial Times, 19 September 1997.

Fortune, 11 May 1998, **137**(9), p. 59.

Harland, C.M., Lamming, R.C. and Cousins, P.D. (1999) Developing the concept of supply strategy. *International Journal of Operations and Production Management*, **19**(7).

Harvard Business Review (2003) *HBR on Corporate Responsibility*. Harvard Business Review Paperbacks.

Hopkins, M. (2003) *The Planetary Bargain: Corporate Social Responsibility Matters*. London: Earth scan.

Industry Week, 16 November 1998.

Industry Week, June 2003, **252**(6), pp. 22–27.

Lamming, R.C., Faruk, A.C. and Cousins, P.D. (1999) Environmental soundness: a pragmatic alternative to expectations of sustainable development in business strategy. *Business Strategy and the Environment*, **8**(3), 177–188.

Larson, E.R. and Cox, B. (1998) Social Accountability 8000: measuring workplace conditions worldwide. *Quality Digest*, February, 26–29.

Shi, Y. and Gregory, M.J. (1994) International manufacturing strategy: structuring worldwide manufacturing networks. *Working Papers in Manufacturing*, No. 11, Cambridge University.

Standard and Poor's Industry Survey, 3 June 1999.

WCED (World Commission on Environment and Development) (1987) *Our Common Future.* Oxford: Oxford University Press.

Womack, J., Jones, D. and Roos, D. (1990) *The Machine that Changed the World.* New York: Rawson Associates.

Index